ENVIRONMENTAL ANALYSIS

FOR LAND USE
AND SITE PLANNING

ENVIRONMENTAL ANALYSIS

FOR LAND USE AND SITE PLANNING

WILLIAM M. MARSH

Department of Physical Geography, The University of Michigan—Flint

McGraw-Hill Book Company

New York St. Louis San Francisco Auckland Bogotá
Düsseldorf Johannesburg London Madrid Mexico
Montreal New Delhi Panama Paris São Paulo
Singapore Sydney Tokyo Toronto

Library of Congress Cataloging in Publication Data

Marsh, William M
     Environmental analysis: for land use and site
planning.
     Includes index.
     1.   Land use—Environmental aspects—United States.
2.   Environmental impact analysis.   I.   Title.
HC110.E5M37   33.7'0973   77-7028
ISBN 0-07-040490-9

1234567890   HDHD   7654321098

The editors for this book were Jeremy Robinson and Patricia A. Allen, the designer was Richard A. Roth, and the production supervisor was Frank P. Bellantoni. It was set in Univers 55 by University Graphics, Inc.

Printed and bound by Halliday Lithograph Corporation.

The preparation of this book was funded partially by a grant (No. GI-30027) to the Environmental Research Institute of Michigan from the National Science Foundation, RANN Program.

CONTENTS

CONTRIBUTORS

Richard N. L. Andrews Associate Professor of Regional Planning, School of Natural Resources, The University of Michigan, Ann Arbor, Michigan (CHAPTERS 7 and 9.3)

G. Dale Bishop Planning Consultant, Thousand Island Area Residents Association, Lansdowne, Ontario (CHAPTER 1)

M. Leonard Bryan Senior Scientist, Jet Propulsion Laboratory, California Institute of Technology, Pasadena, California (formerly of the Environmental Research Institute of Michigan) (CHAPTER 6)

Jeff Dozier Assistant Professor Geography, University of California, Santa Barbara, Santa Barbara, California (CHAPTER 5)

John M. Grossa Assistant Professor of Geography, Central Michigan University, Mt. Pleasant, Michigan (CHAPTER 4)

John M. Koerner Environmental Liaison, De Leuw—Cather/Parsons and Assoc., Washington, D.C. (CHAPTER 4)

Peter Van Dusen Associate Professor of Physical Geography, The University of Michigan—Flint, Flint, Michigan (CHAPTER 5)

John D. Vitek Assistant Professor of Physical Geography, The University of Michigan—Flint, Flint, Michigan (CHAPTER 9.1)

Katharine P. Warner Associate Professor of Urban Planning, School of Architecture and Urban Planning, The University of Michigan, Ann Arbor, Michigan (CHAPTER 8)

C. T. Wezernak Environmental Consultant, Boca Raton, Florida (formerly of the Environmental Research Institute of Michigan) (CHAPTER 9.2)

PREFACE

The time is upon us when scientists, planners, and designers must focus their combined knowledge and talents on the problems of land use and environment. Indeed, so knotty are the demands of today's problems that no one field can afford to tackle them single-handedly. The solution seems to lie not so much in requiring broader training for each of us—though that would be helpful—but in more effective teamwork and communication among planners, scientists, and designers. This book is an attempt to draw science a little closer to the planner.

Environmental Analysis is in many ways an outgrowth of the aspirations, frustrations, failures, and small successes of a project team which several years ago set about to explore the application of remote-sensing systems in public planning. The project was ambitious, a bit naïve, but in retrospect, a necessary undertaking at the time. From the project evolved the realization that despite the exciting possibilities posed by new data-generating and -processing technologies, the practicing planner must still rely heavily on "desk-top" techniques for the generation of environmental information. We have attempted to present not only a core set of such techniques, but guidelines and methods for the application of environmental information as well.

We gratefully acknowledge the assistance of many persons associated with the development of this book. R. Keith Raney of the Environmental Research Institute of Michigan and Larry Tombaugh of the National Science Foundation provided the administrative framework necessary to design and write the volume. G. Dale Bishop helped conceptualize the main themes, Peter Van Dusen styled the graphics, and Gary Claypool assisted in publication arrangements. Mary Clodfelter, Jackie Brayan, and Venita Bishop patiently typed and compiled the manuscript. Lively discussions were provided by all.

William M. Marsh

Many of the problems that society confronts are of such inordinate complexity that it takes the greatest dedication and zeal to assemble the necessary data, analyze and prescribe. Happily there are other problems, where a very small perception can produce astonishing results. If one accepts the simple proposition that nature is the arena of life and that a modicum of knowledge of her processes is indispensable for survival and rather more for existence, health and delight, it is amazing how many apparently difficult problems present ready resolution.

Ian McHarg
Design with Nature (1969)

LANDSAT I Image
Southern tip of Lake Huron,
March 27, 1973

INTRODUCTION | *William M. Marsh*

INCREASED CONCERN WITH the environment in virtually every sector of society has produced a surge in the demand for environmental information. Preparation of environmental impact statements as required by the U.S. Environmental Protection Agency, for example, requires careful assessment of the feasibility of a proposed land use in the context of the natural environment. This demands reliable information on slope, soils, vegetation, and drainage which is usually not readily available in a communicable information form. Nevertheless, the *sources* of such information are available to virtually everyone. These sources represent processed environmental data, namely topographic contour maps, aerial photographs, soil maps, hydrographic maps, drainage data, and remotely sensed imagery.

In the United States nearly 1.5 million acres of agricultural land are annually converted to other uses. These uses are mainly residential and affiliated activities which together make up the burgeoning urban fringe. Much of the energy of planning is devoted to the copious and complex problems of land use and environment within this fringe and at its interface with agricultural and natural lands. It is this landscape which provides the conceptual setting for this volume.

In *Design with Nature,* Ian McHarg developed a number of excellent principles for land-use planning in the context of the natural environment. Though illustrated with many case studies, *Design with Nature* is fundamentally conceptual in focus and, while setting goals for land use planning, offers little guidance as to how the information base is built in support of these goals. This book, on the other hand, is directly concerned with how environmental information can be generated by planners for use in environmental inventory and analysis and in the assessment of land use proposals vis-à-vis the physical environment.

Much of the environmental information currently produced by major public agencies is generated by means of aerial photograph interpretation. With the development of more technologically advanced remote-sensing systems in the past few decades, however, our environmental detection capabilities have been extended well beyond that of black-and-white aerial photography. Today planners, engineers, and scientists generally agree that these new systems hold good potential as sources of information on land and water environments. Efforts at the application of remote sensing to planning, however, have admittedly been somewhat disappointing. Most have been heuristic and experimental in nature and few have effectively found a place in the milieu of the operational planning agencies.

This book is partially a product of a project which attempted to evaluate the utility of remotely sensed data and information in the context of the tasks, problems, and general operations of a county metropolitan planning agency. In the course of the project, we identified several general trends in the use of environmental information in planning, and these form the basis for much of this book:

1. Public sources of environmental information are decidedly underutilized in most planning agencies. Excellent aerial photographs, topographic contour maps, soil maps, drainage maps, and associated information abound in the files of essentially every planning office. Nevertheless, extensive reviews of documents produced by planners show that these sources could be far more effectively utilized as the basis for environmental and physiographic information.

2. To be most useful, any source of information or data must be integrated with information from other sources. This is mainly due to the eclectic nature of most planning problems, which demands a wide array of information types.

3. For land use planning as a whole, remote sensing, including aerial photography, has greatest potential as a source of environmental and physiographic information, that is, drainage, vegetation, land use, and so on. In its current state, remote sensing is marginal as a generator of useful socioeconomic data, particularly in urbanized areas.

Trained as social scientists, many planners presently seek the skills necessary to transform processed environmental data into information. Within this context, the main purpose of this book is to illustrate, with a set of rudimentary techniques, a methodology for the generation of environmental information from ready sources of processed data or information. In addition, governmental sources of data and information are identified, and application methods are also discussed.

To use data and information sources to produce reliable, timely, and appropriate environmental information for land use planning, two kinds of knowledge are necessary: that of (1) the essential processes of landscape formation and (2) the nature of planning processes involved in the problem or task at hand. The land use opportunities and constraints posed by a steep, forested slope, for instance, can be critically evaluated only when it is appreciated that the slope is itself the product of many ongoing geophysical processes and at the same time the residence of other processes such as plant growth and animal life. Recommendations regarding the use of the slope must be founded on the scientific principles of hillslope formation and the dynamics of the slope environment, else they may lack the substance that is often necessary in the decision-making arena.

Equally important in the development of information on the slope is the consideration of the nature of the assigned task and the planning processes that are involved or should be employed. For example, who is the audience and how much time and money are available for the study? This governs how much information should or can be produced, the form in which it should be represented, and the formats that could be used to display it.

It is in the spirit of questions such as those above that the topics of this book have been selected. The first five chapters deal with the techniques of terrain analysis, including area measurement and sampling, slope and soil mapping, vegetation interpretation, and flood analysis. Chapter 6 surveys sources of data and information available from governmental agencies, and Chapters 7, 8, and 9 examine the use of environmental information in planning, including the types of tasks and problems for which it is produced and the methods that can be employed to communicate it.

Though they may find sections useful, this book is *not* directed at natural scientists. Rather, it is aimed at practicing land use planners, planning students, architects, landscape architects, land developers, and public officials who find themselves faced with environmental considerations in land planning and management. Virtually all techniques, as well as the information and data sources treated in the following pages, are also treated in the literature from the fields of ecology, forestry, civil engineering, geography, geology, planning, and remote sensing. These sources are widely scattered, however, and it is only rarely that they are specifically oriented to the task of land use planning and environmental assessment. This effort is an attempt to synthesize and refocus the various techniques and information of a number of fields in a single volume.

It is assumed throughout this book that the reader has access to public sources of environmental information such as topographic contour maps and black-and-white aerial photographs. Most information-generation techniques discussed herein demand no systematic fieldwork, though field reconnaissance is advisable in many cases. Both the text and the accompanying illustrations are designed to maximize communication effectiveness. Though much emphasis is placed on graphic, simple, quantitative and information synthesis techniques, a conscious effort is made to avoid specialized terminology, mathematical techniques, and abstract graphics. In addition, chapters are designed to encourage reference to a particular technique without requiring extensive reading.

CHAPTER **1**

SPATIAL ORGANIZATION

G. Dale Bishop and William M. Marsh

INTRODUCTION

THE PROCESS OF urbanization can be characterized as one of social conflict over use of the physical environment. As urban populations grow, they promote inevitable expansion of suburban territory. On the suburban fringe, the very combination of natural amenities that sustains a productive rural landscape is also a forceful enticement for residential development. The result is usually a serious struggle, albeit usually a lopsided one, between development and agriculture. The dramatic increase in population mobility over the past several decades has produced a similar confrontation in coastal and wilderness lands. Functioning in their natural state as the primary habitats for diverse plants and animals, these areas have come under increased pressure to serve both recreational and residential needs. In addition, a generally increased awareness of, and concern for, the fragility of the natural environment has served to highlight land use conflicts that were barely acknowledged only a decade ago.

The potential conflict over use of the land is not solely confined to those areas situated on the leading edges of urban areas, however. In the core of metropolitan centers, deliberations over proposals for the reuse of land currently occupied by outmoded structures are often underscored by altercations between proponents of the intense development and proponents of medium or low-density renewal schemes. As one response to the competitive demands on the limited available space both within the urban area and on its periphery, we have turned to land use planning. In the face of potentially calamitous confrontations, planning has acquired the role of assessing impacts and alternatives with an ultimate responsibility for recommending solutions in the land use arena.

The assigned focus of land use planning, however, extends well beyond the simple resolution of impending conflict. Where the activity of planning has been accorded a degree of respectability within the political systems, the character of the proposed solutions has necessarily assumed more foresight than expediency. Society has come to expect planning assessments and proposals that will serve to avert conflict by providing a clear and unambiguous guide to private as well as public development. That expectation, and the associated institutional activity of formulating a methodology for conflict resolution; is an implicit acknowledgment of the fundamental purpose of land use planning; namely, the design, surveillance, and assessment of the physical environment to facilitate an optimum utilization of scarce resources. Recognition of this as the principal goal of planning helps set guidances as to which analytical techniques must be employed in problems of land-use planning.

The techniques of land use planning are primarily those of *spatial analysis.* Even as the planner's focus of inquiry is directed toward the environmental components of a site, the methods utilized to treat soils, topography, vegetation, and water center on a spatial analysis. Moreover, the notions of spatial organization and design encompass a tacit acknowledgment of a unique aspect of space itself. It can be identified, in a limited sense, as the tangible manifestation of physical space per se. Campaigns for the creation and maintenance of open space such as parks and greenbelts are an explicit recognition of space as a resource commodity. This places the concept of space in a relatively unique position in land use planning, for it must be viewed simultaneously as a primary property of all components in the landscape and as a principal resource in its own right.

PERSPECTIVES ON ENVIRONMENTAL SPACE

In order to assess the various components of space and their relationship to the tasks of environmental site analysis, a clarification of the terms *space* and *spatial organization* is necessary. As Chapin suggests, the latter term has generally come to be used in reference to the physical arrangement and relationships of the various components of the landscape, particularly in the context of their formation and transformation over time and space. A generalized definition of space, particularly as it must be treated in planning, is somewhat more difficult to discover, however.

If space is viewed in the least complex of its abstract formats, that of simple area and volume, then we need only be concerned with identifying two variables, distance and direction (Figure 1.1). Distance is a measure of the separation between any two or more points in the environment. Direction is a measure of the relative orientation from point to point. With the measurements of distance and direction in hand, it is only a matter of applying the standard formula of length times width to derive a quantitative expression of two-dimensional space or area. In similar fashion, the formula of length times width times height provides a definition of true, three-dimensional space, expressed in volumetric units. It may appear on first glance that the concept of direction is superfluous to this physical definition of space in terms of area or volume, particularly in the abstract. A closer examination, however, reveals that before the variables of length, width, or height can be assigned values, an explicit recognition of direction is necessary in order to determine which distances are relevant.

The brief review above provides a definition of one type of geometric space, called classical space, and it is this definition that supports most of the familiar spatial parameters used in land use planning. The examination of dispersion or clustering of elements in the landscape, while often abstractly expressed by statistical

Geometric Space

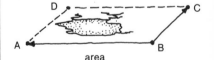

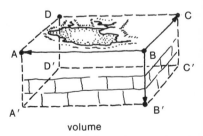

Figure 1.1. The principal properties of environmental space: points, lines, direction, area, and volume.

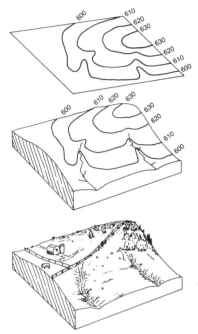

Figure 1.2. The topographic contour map is a representation of three-dimensional space in a two-dimensional format.

Topological Space

Dynamic Space

measurements such as regression analysis and factor analysis, is, in fact, a spatial inquiry based on the concepts of Euclidian geometry. Forms of cartography such as land-use and line maps are also types of spatial analysis carried out within this framework. However, topographic contour maps, though founded on principles of classical space, are a special example in that they call for perception of three-dimensional space by the interpreter.

Contour maps are designed to represent three-dimensional space on a two-dimensional surface. While most maps encountered by the planner are intended to convey distance and orientation, many are presented in a form that depicts the landscape, for the sake of clarity and convenience, as a flat plane. The land-use map and common road map are typical examples. Topographic maps differ inasmuch as contour lines represent a third dimension value, that of elevation, superimposed on the original two-dimensional interpretation of space. By reading from one contour line to the next, it is possible to determine the shape of the terrain. The key feature of note in the topographic map is its two-dimensional format. It is an intentional distortion of volumetric space that relies on the viewer's ability to perceive the information being conveyed and to transform it into a mental image of the actual terrain (Figure 1.2).

Another example of spatial distortion is found in the notion of topological space. Though based on a fundamental distance and directional spatial format, topological space relies for its coherence on a concept referred to by the geographer Nystuen (1963) as *connectiveness.* The idea of connectiveness is most succinctly expressed by the terms relative position, contiguity, or adjacency. The concept is intended to focus the analyst's attention on specific interrelationships that exist among the composite elements of a particular space. It is possible to express spatial organization in terms of connectiveness alone. The idea can be visualized by imagining a standard line map portraying true relationships of distance and direction which has been drawn on a rubber sheet and then stretched out of shape (Figure 1.3). While distance and direction will be altered radically, the relative order of each feature on the map remains nonvariant. That is, the lines connecting points A, B, and C in Figure 1.3 always connect those points irrespective of how one orients them. As an example of "functional distortion," the rubber map may seem, at first glance, to be somewhat farfetched. However, rapid transit route maps, indicating the proper sequence of stops, have essentially assumed this format as a means of allowing observers to quickly perceive limited but pertinent information about the complex spatial organization involved in a transportation network (Figure 1.4). This example of topological distortion serves to direct attention to another, and more significant variable, that must be considered in formulating a working definition of space for planning: human perception.

Human perception inherently distorts the properties of classical space. The senses of sight, hearing, touch, and smell normally affect rather radical alterations in the properties of true geometric space. People perceive space with a three-dimensional visual perspective afforded by the physiological nature of the eyes. Additionally, human eyes have the capacity to make rapid changes in focus, thus allowing for the near concomitant perception of different spa-

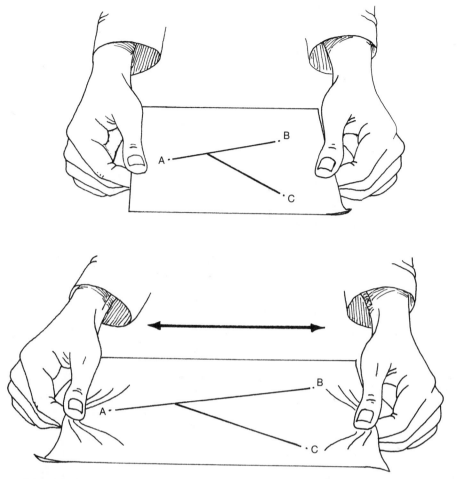

Figure 1.3. *Topologically, both these maps are the same, because the relative order, or connectiveness, between the three points is unchanged after stretching.* (Illustration by Peter Van Dusen)

tial frameworks. Unlike standard geometric space that remains static once defined, space acknowledged by humans is continually contracting or expanding with movement through the landscape. This produces the impression of *dynamic space,* with objects in the line of sight appearing to grow larger as they are approached or smaller as they fall into the distance. It can be argued that the complexities wrought by this notion of dynamic space might be alleviated if perceived space is examined in a stop-action manner based on parameters of classical space. It makes little more sense for the planner to do this, however, than it does for a film critic to evaluate the plot of a movie by examining the individual frames of the motion picture. It follows that spatial analysis in the context of land use planning must include a time dimension of long enough duration to characterize the varying dimensions of the human activities and natural processes under consideration. By its very definition, land use planning deals with the dynamic expression of space at the interface between processes and the landscape.

Sight is only one of the several senses that will affect the human perception of space. Acoustic space is defined by the intensity and frequency of sound and is a further example of dynamic distortion.

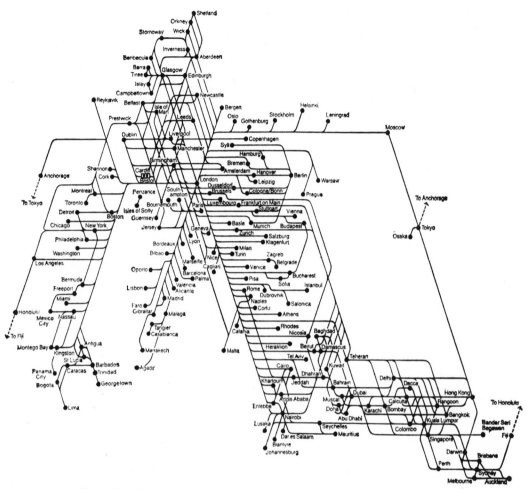

Figure 1.4. A good example of a topological map is provided by airway route maps; in this case, a British Airways route map of the world.

As features of the terrain either filter or amplify the noises that confront the ear, the space within which an observer consciously functions will diminish or grow. Traveling from behind the protection of a dense thicket to within earshot of an expressway provides for a rapid expansion of perceived space, even when the expressway cannot be seen. The senses of smell and touch can affect the working definition of space in a similar manner. It is perhaps of greatest importance, however, to recognize that the concept of dynamic spatial distortion is founded on a different set of principles than that of Euclidian geometry. Each of the human senses involves a *qualitative* assessment of space, in contrast to the strictly *quantitative* aspects of the classical measures.

Our mental image of functional space is influenced by variables other than those described as physiological senses, however. People operate within the context of an intricate set of sociocultural norms. Depending on the society, these norms not only define "rational behavior," but also influence the way in which we decipher and employ information received through the sensory processes. That is to say, functional space may differ radically from one group of persons to another, even though the external stimuli are identical. The recognition of this interplay between cultural filters and the physical environment is of critical importance if one is to achieve an understanding of functional space.

Attempts to characterize environmental space usually lead to the notion of boundaries. Boundaries are familiar features in every land use plan. Complex systems of legal boundaries often exert the major influence on the areal extent of land use and environmental planning projects. Too often, however, these legal delineators serve as the only spatial parameters that are employed. A detailed analysis of the spatial components of the landscape usually requires a more comprehensive recognition of the types and properties of boundaries than one limited to the boundaries of political jurisdictions. Points and lines are adequate to define space in most problems dealing with the differentiation of legal territory. However, the biophysical features of the environment rarely order themselves in such neat fashion, and their boundaries therefore often tend to be indistinct.

The form and extent of boundaries vary with the processes delimited. It is clear that a planning site with a single operation designation is also the common locus of many different functional spaces. A legal property description dictates a finite boundary line, while visual space is often demarcated by a broad transitional zone, in which no one point or line can be identified as the absolute limit. Additionally, this visual boundary will fluctuate depending upon the activity of the observer. The automobile rider will perceive the limits of the space differently than will the pedestrian. Boundaries also vary considerably in permeability, again, as related to function. The legal property line can be transgressed by natural processes such as runoff and wind but can prove to be a formidable barrier for sociocultural processes such as foot and vehicular travel. In a similar fashion, a narrow row of shrubbery can be a near impermeable boundary to sight while offering little impediment to sound. Finally, as the photographs in Figure 1.5 illustrate, boundaries may be drastically altered with seasonal changes in the plant cover. The heavy foliage of deciduous trees, so important a part of the bounds of summer yard and street space, for example, disappears in the winter, leaving the observer with an expanded visual setting. In short, boundaries can be as varied and complex as the spaces they delimit.

We may now return to the original question of a definition of space that is appropriate to the tasks of environmental analysis for land use planning. Throughout the foregoing section, we have attempted to illustrate that no single characteristic or class of characteristics conclusively describes space as it must be approached in problems of land use and environment. The measure of distance and direction are adequate in describing the quantitative dimensions of geometric space. However, as the mechanical spaces depicted on a land use map are massaged by natural processes and by various mediators of human perception, they assume additional and more complex dimensions. Each influencing factor prompts a unique areal interpretation of the planning site. The result is functionally distorted space. Embraced by different and often fluid boundaries, these functional spaces of perception and environmen-

Figure 1.5. Many types of boundaries change drastically from season to season. This is illustrated by the vegetation in these photographs, taken in January and June.

tal processes typically transgress the legal limits of the planning site. The site is thus the focal point of a dynamic composite of overlapping spaces, each contributing to the character and utility of the area.

The concept of connectiveness ultimately emerges as the theme to unify the various spatial images associated with a site. Expressed as contiguity, adjacency, or relative position, connectiveness provides a coherent linkage within and between different sets of spaces. By way of example, let us consider a problem involving the impact of runoff from small drainage basins on an inland lake or a reservoir. The quantity and quality of water available for runoff in a basin depend on factors such as drainage area, surface cover, and the intensity and type of land use. But how much of the runoff actually reaches the lake depends less on these factors than it does on the efficiency of the drainage system that links the basin to the lake. If the system is highly efficient, as in the case of a storm sewer, then the level of connectiveness is obviously high. The movement of runoff to lake is rapid, and little or no water is lost en route. In the language of hydrology, the "time of concentration" of the runoff is said to be very low. In contrast, if the drainage system allows only slow passage of runoff, which would be expected in the case of wetlands, for example, then the level of connectiveness is low. Although absolute distance between basin and lake has not changed, functional distance, defined on the basis of the amount and time response of run off into the lake, is considerably greater. By combining the linkage concept with the variables of water quality and total discharge, it is possible to compute the relative influence of small drainage basins in the lake watershed (Marsh and Borton, 1976). Expressed in the form of a number value, this provides a reliable basis for assessing impacts on the lake and for assigning planning and management priorities in the watershed (Figure 1.6).

The following section focuses on some of the basic types of information and techniques that are of value in isolating and measuring the spaces that influence the utility of a site. Inasmuch as a lot of the data available to planners are in map form, the first part deals with cartographic scales and the use of locational and grid systems. With these as points of reference, several methods are explored for calculating area from maps. Topographic contour maps and aerial photographs are examined as sources of three-dimensional spatial information. Sampling techniques are reviewed as a means of data generation when maps and aerial photographs prove inadequate.

MAP DISTANCE

Scale

Maps and aerial imagery are miniature replicas of the landscape. They constitute two of the most accessible sources of data for spatial analysis. The utility of the data conveyed in these formats is limited, however, by the user's ability to interpret the map or photograph and relate it to the actual physical environment. The principal key that must be employed in this process is the map

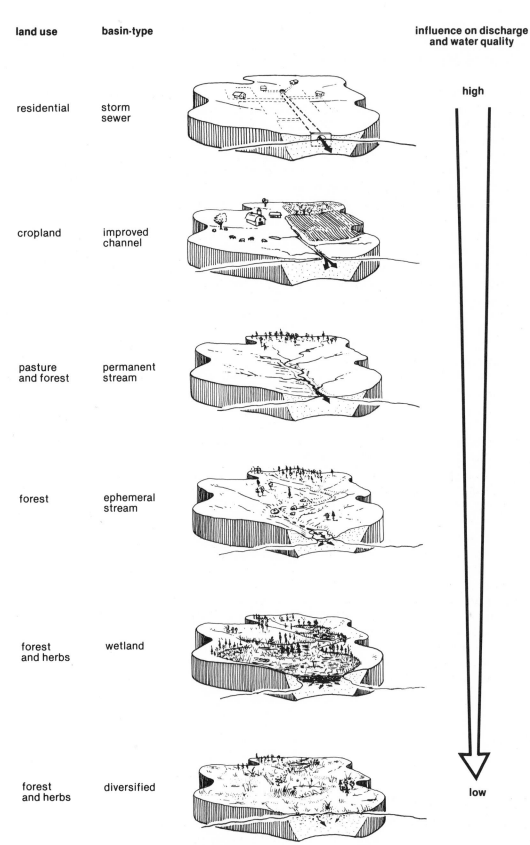

land use	basin-type		influence on discharge and water quality
residential	storm sewer		high
cropland	improved channel		
pasture and forest	permanent stream		
forest	ephemeral stream		
forest and herbs	wetland		
forest and herbs	diversified		low

Figure 1.6. Six types of small drainage basins, each with different development and drainage systems. The runoff that each contributes to the lake is regulated by the efficiency of the flow system, an example of the connectiveness concept (from Marsh and Borton, 1976).

scale. In both the cartographic and photographic formats, scale is defined as the relationship between distance on the map or photograph and the corresponding distance on the earth's surface. Maps of small areas are produced at a specific scale that is virtually constant over the entire surface of the document. However, scale may differ considerably between maps. Because much of the information available from both maps and imagery is scale dependent, it is necessary to be cognizant of the scale at which the data are presented.

Scale is generally indicated on a map in one of two ways, either graphically or arithmetically, and occasionally both are included as part of the map legend. Perhaps the simplest scale indicator employed is the graphic or bar scale. This consists of an actual line or bar which is calibrated to indicate a precise map distance and labeled to indicate the corresponding ground distance. Any linear measurement on the map can be compared directly to the bar scale to determine the actual ground distance. However, as can be seen from the examples, bar scales are generally restricted to the given system and even unit of measurement for which they have been calibrated. If the bar has been constructed to indicate miles on the surface of the map, a determination of distance in kilometers is not readily obtainable. The arithmetic type of scale representation does not suffer from this problem, however.

Commonly referred to as the representative fraction or simply RF, the arithmetic scale representation is in fact a ratio of units on the map to like units on the ground. Thus, an RF of 1:50,000 or 1/50,000 indicates that 1 unit on the map is equivalent to 50,000 of the same units on the earth's surface. Since the scale is expressed in terms of a ratio, the proportion between the two distances (map and ground) is constant. Thus, the representation fraction is applicable to all systems and all units of measurement simultaneously. Hence, 1:50,000 can be read as "1 map inch to 50,000 ground inches" or "1 map centimeter to 50,000 ground centimeters." Similarly, any other unit of measurement can be substituted, and the need for conversion factors between measurement systems is thus avoided.

Table 1.1 presents some of the most commonly used RF map scales. As may be apparent, the principal drawback of this particular type of scale representation is that convenient units of measurement on a map rarely lend themselves to a suitable representation of distance on the ground. As a result, it is often necessary to carry the calculations one step further and convert the right half of the ratio from a small unit within a measuring system to another larger unit. Thus, 1:63,360 is often converted to read "1 inch to 1 mile" (since there are 63,360 inches to the mile), and 1:100,000 is conveniently converted to read "1 centimeter to 1 kilometer." This form of the arithmetic scale is generally referred to as the verbal scale, as it is most commonly employed when orally relating the proportions of a map. Because both portions of the verbal scale (inches and miles or centimeters and kilometers, etc.) can be stated in recognizable units of measure for the majority of people, this method of indicating scale allows the direct and immediate recognition and transference of distances from the map to the ground and vice versa.

To facilitate the transformation from a representative fraction to a

Bar Scales

Representative Fraction

Verbal Scale

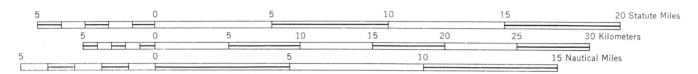

U.S. Geological Survey Topographic
1:250,000

County Land Use
1:87,000

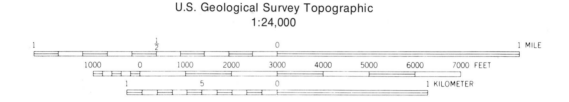

U.S. Geological Survey Topographic
1:24,000

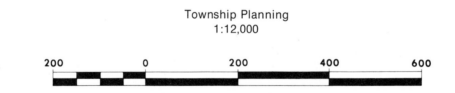

Township Planning
1:12,000

Conversion Factors

verbal scale, Table 1.2 presents a matrix of the conversion factors between various units of linear measurements. As noted above, a representative fraction is a ratio of like units, thus the right-hand or ground distance portion of the RF can be converted to a larger unit of measurement without altering the integrity of the ratio, if it is divided by the appropriate factor read from the table. The first step in making a transformation is to choose the two units of measurement that are to be included in the verbal scale. Some of the more common combinations are inch and feet, inch and miles, centimeter and meters, and finally centimeter and kilometers. As an example of the conversion procedure, let us suppose that we wish to restate the representative fraction 1:24,000 as a verbal scale relating map inches to ground feet. Since 1:24,000 can be read as "1 map inch to 24,000 ground inches," the problem is simply one of determining how many feet are represented by 24,000 inches. The divisor for converting the ground units is determined by reading, along the top of Table 1.2, the unit of measure to be represented by the left-hand (or map) portion of the verbal scale and then reading down the column to that factor listed opposite the unit of measure

TABLE 1.2 CONVERSION FACTORS FOR LINEAR UNITS

The conversion factor is the number in the table. Divide the conversion factor into the "from" unit to obtain the "to" unit. For example, 1 yard to feet $= \frac{1}{0.33} = 3.0$ feet.

To ↓ / From ←	Centimeter	Inch	Link	Foot	Vara (California)	Vara (Texas)	Yard	Meter	Rod, pole or perch	Chain	Furlong	Kilometer	Mile (statute)
Centimeter	1	0.3937	0.049710	0.032808	0.011930	0.011811	0.010936	0.01	0.001988				
Inch	2.54001	1	0.12626	0.08333	0.03030	0.03	0.02778	0.02540	0.00505	0.00126			
Link	20.1168	7.92	1	0.66	0.24	0.2376	0.22	0.20117	0.04	0.01	0.001		
Foot	30.4801	12	1.51515	1	0.36364	0.36	0.33333	0.30480	0.06061	0.01515	0.00152		
Vara (California)	83.8202	33	4.16667	2.75	1	0.99	0.91667	0.8382	0.16667	0.04167	0.00417		
Vara (Texas)	84.6668	33.333	4.20875	2.77778	1.01010	1	0.92583	0.84667	0.16835	0.04209	0.0042		
Yard	91.4402	36	4.54545	3	1.09091	1.08	1	0.9144	0.18182	0.04545	0.00455		
Meter	100	39.37	4.97096	3.28083	1.19303	1.1811	1.09361	1	0.19884	0.04971	0.00497	0.001	
Rod, pole, or perch	502.921	198	25	16.5	6	5.94	5.5	5.02921	1	0.25	0.025	0.00503	0.00313
Chain	1,828.80	792	100	66	24	23.76	22	20.1168	4	1	0.1	0.02012	0.0125
Furlong	20,116.8	7,920	1,000	660	240	237.6	220	201.168	40	10	1	0.20117	0.125
Kilometer	100,000	39,370	4,970.96	3,280.83	1,193.03	1,181.1	1,093.61	1,000	198.838	49.7096	4.97096	1	0.62137
Mile (statute)	160,935	63,360	8,000	5,280	1,920	1,900.8	1,760	1,609.35	320	80	8	1.60935	1

to be represented by the right-hand or ground portion. For the example above, if one reads down the "Inch" column, it is apparent that the conversion factor, listed opposite "Foot," is 12. Transformation of the right-hand portion into the new units of measure requires only that the original number of ground units stated in the RF be divided by the conversion factor. Thus,

$$\frac{\text{Ground portion of RF}}{\text{Conversion factor from Table 2}}$$

$$= \frac{24,000 \text{ inches}}{12 \text{ inches in 1 foot}} = 2,000 \text{ feet}$$

and the verbal scale is read as "1 inch to 2000 feet." While it is common to use the same system of measurement for both portions of the verbal scale, this is not a requirement. 1:24,000 can be converted from a scale of inches to meters by following the general procedure outlined above. In this instance, the conversion factor is determined to be 39.37 (from the "Inch" column opposite "Meter") and the verbal scale would be 1 inch to 609.6 meters, that is,

$$\frac{24,000 \text{ inches}}{39.37 \text{ inches in 1 meter}} = 609.6 \text{ meters}$$

As a timesaving device, Table 1.3 presents some useful conversions for most of the standard representative fractions that are employed in cartography and demonstrates the various ways in which the verbal scale can be presented. For example, across the bottom line of the table, the factors can be read as follows: the representative fraction 1:1,000,000 is equivalent to the verbal scale of 15.78 (ground) miles to 1 (map) inch *or* 0.063 (map) inches to 1 (ground) mile.

It should be noted that the graphic or bar scale has one major advantage over the mathematical representation. Should it be necessary to enlarge or reduce the map or the aerial photograph, a bar scale fixed into the document will remain true with the change in size of the map or photo. This, of course, is not the case with either the representative fraction or the verbal scales. As a result, it is

TABLE 1.3 CONVERSION FACTORS FOR REPRESENTATIVE FRACTIONS

Ratio scale	Feet per inch	Inches per 1000 feet	Inches per mile	Miles per inch	Meters per inch
1: 500	41.667	24.00	126.72	0.008	12.700
1: 600	50.00	20.00	105.60	0.009	15.240
1: 1,000	83.333	12.00	63.36	0.016	25.400
1: 1,200	100.00	10.00	52.80	0.019	30.480
1: 1,500	125.00	8.00	42.24	0.024	38.100
1: 2,000	166.667	6.00	31.68	0.032	50.800
1: 2,400	200.00	5.00	26.40	0.038	60.960
1: 2,500	208.333	4.80	25.344	0.039	63.500
1: 3,000	250.00	4.00	21.12	0.047	76.200
1: 3,600	300.00	3.333	17.60	0.057	91.440
1: 4,000	333.333	3.00	15.84	0.063	101.600
1: 4,800	400.00	2.50	13.20	0.076	121.920
1: 5,000	416.667	2.40	12.672	0.079	127.000
1: 6,000	500.00	2.00	10.56	0.095	152.400
1: 7,000	583.333	1.714	9.051	0.110	177.800
1: 7,200	600.00	1.667	8.80	0.114	182.880
1: 7,920	660.00	1.515	8.00	0.125	201.168
1: 8,000	666.667	1.500	7.92	0.126	203.200
1: 8,400	700.00	1.429	7.543	0.133	213.360
1: 9,000	750.00	1.333	7.041	0.142	228.600
1: 9,600	800.00	1.250	6.60	0.152	243.840
1: 10,000	833.333	1.200	6.336	0.158	254.000
1: 10,800	900.00	1.111	5.867	0.170	
1: 12,000	1,000.00	1.0	5.280	0.189	304.801
1: 13,200	1,100.00	0.909	4.800	0.208	335.281
1: 14,400	1,200.00	0.833	4.400	0.227	365.761
1: 15,000	1,250.00	0.80	4.224	0.237	381.001
1: 15,600	1,300.00	0.769	4.062	0.246	396.241
1: 15,840	1,320.00	0.758	4.00	0.250	402.337
1: 16,000	1,333.333	0.750	3.96	0.253	406.400
1: 16,800	1,400.00	0.714	3.771	0.265	426.721
1: 18,000	1,500.00	0.667	3.52	0.284	457.201
1: 19,200	1,600.00	0.625	3.30	0.303	487.681
1: 20,000	1,666.667	0.60	3.168	0.316	508.002
1: 20,400	1,700.00	0.588	3.106	0.322	518.161
1: 21,120	1,760.00	0.568	3.00	0.333	536.449
1: 21,600	1,800.00	0.556	2.933	0.341	548.641
1: 22,800	1,900.00	0.526	2.779	0.360	579.121
1: 24,000	2,000.00	0.50	2.640	0.379	609.601
1: 25,000	2,083.333	0.480	2.534	0.395	635.001
1: 31,680	2,640.00	0.379	2.000	0.500	804.674
1: 48,000	4,000.00	0.250	1.320	0.758	1,219.202
1: 62,500	5,208.333	0.192	1.014	0.986	1,587.503
1: 63,360	5,280.00	0.189	1.000	1.000	1.609.347
1: 96,000	8,000.00	0.125	0.660	1.515	2,438.405
1: 125,000	10,416.667	0.096	0.507	1.973	3,175.006
1: 126,720	10,560.00	0.095	0.500	2.00	3,218.694
1: 250,000	20,833.333	0.048	0.253	3.946	6,350.012
1: 253,440	21,120.00	0.047	0.250	4.00	6,437.389
1: 500,000	41,666.667	0.024	0.127	7.891	12,700.025
1: 1,000,000	83,333.333	0.012	0.063	15.783	25,400.050

(SOURCE: U.S. Department of Agriculture, *Agricultural Handbook,* 294, 1966.)

often advantageous, in those instances where only a representative fraction is presented, to convert the RF to a bar scale before changing the size of the original document.

The task of constructing a bar scale is a relatively simple one. As most graph scales are drawn to represent miles or kilometers, it is necessary to remember that 1 mile contains precisely 63,360 inches and 1 kilometer contains exactly 100,000 centimeters. The conversion is accomplished by first restating the RF as a verbal scale in which ground distance, rather than map distance, is treated as unity. This is done by choosing the unit of measurement that is to be represented by the graph scale, that is, miles *or* kilometers, and dividing the right-hand side, or the ground-units portion of the representative fraction, into either the number of inches in a mile or number of centimeters in a kilometer, whichever is appropriate. The answer is the number of inches (or centimeters) on the map that corresponds to 1 mile (or 1 kilometer) on the ground. That is,

$$\frac{63,360 \text{ inches in 1 mile}}{\text{Ground portion of the RD}} = \text{map inches to 1 mile}$$

and

$$\frac{100,000 \text{ centimeters in 1 kilometer}}{\text{Ground portion of the RF}}$$
$$= \text{map centimeters to 1 kilometer}$$

Thus, on a map constructed to the RF scale of 1:62,500, 1 mile is represented by

$$\frac{63,360}{62,500} = 1.014 \text{ inches on the map}$$

Similarly, a kilometer is represented by

$$\frac{100,000}{62,500} = 1.6 \text{ centimeters on the map}$$

Therefore, to construct a bar scale to indicate, say, a ground distance of 5 miles, it is only necessary to draw a line

$$5 \times 1.014 = 5.07 \text{ inches in length}$$

Following the same procedure, a bar scale drawn to represent a ground distance of 5 kilometers would be

$$5 \times 1.6 = 8 \text{ centimeters in length}$$

Most graph scales are drawn to represent a multiple of base units; for instance, kilometers or miles are divided into smaller segments. The subdivision of a bar graph into units of equal length can be problematic in map construction. This task can be carried out with the aid of a technique based on the geometric principle of similar triangles, as is demonstrated in Figure 1.7. This method will produce equal divisions on the bar scale, each demarcating the base unit of the scale. Figure 2 illustrates this technique for the 5-kilometer bar scale that was calculated in the 8-centimeter example, where the RF was 1:62,500. It should be noted that for many of the standard representative fractions, columns 1 and 3 of Table 1.2 provide the equivalent verbal scales in English and metric units, thus alleviating the necessity for much of the above calculation.

Aerial photographs can present one further problem. In most instances, the scale of the photograph is not given on the print itself. Though the RF is usually given with an order of aerial photo-

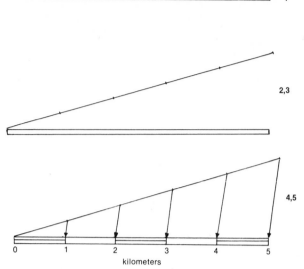

Figure 1.7. Bar-scale construction based on the principle of similar triangles. The steps should include:
  1. Construct a base line which is to be divided into the desired number of units to form the bar graph.
  2. From the left end of this line, construct a second line at an angle to the base line.
  3. Subdivide the second line into equal segments, the total number of which is equal to the desired number of units into which the bar graph will be divided. The size of the units is inconsequential.
  4. Draw a line connecting the right end of the subdivided line with the right end of the base line.
  5. From each segment on the subdivided line, construct a line to the base line which is parallel to the end line.

graphs, it may be necessary in some cases to calculate the ratio. If an accurate map is available of the area shown in the print, the scale of the aerial photograph can be determined by comparing map and photo distances between two identifiable points. Using the bar or representative fraction scale on the map, the exact ground distance between the two points can be determined. If 1.5 ground miles separate two points on the map and 2 inches separate the same points on the photo, the verbal scale of the photograph is 2 inches to 1.5 miles or 1 inch to 0.75 miles. If a suitable map is not available, the RF of an aerial photograph can be calculated based on one focal length of the camera and the altitude of the aircraft. With standard aerial photographs, the following formula may be employed:

$$RF = \frac{\text{focal length of the camera lens}}{\text{altitude of the aircraft at the time of photo}}$$

The focal length and the altitude must be expressed in the *same* units. Therefore, if the aerial camera lens has a focal length of 9 inches (23 centimeters) and the aircraft was 12,000 feet (3,657 meters) above the ground at the time the exposure was made, the calculations would be

$$RF = \frac{9 \text{ inches}}{(12,000 \times 12) \text{ inches}} \text{ or } \frac{9}{144,000}$$
$$= \frac{1}{16,000} \text{ or } 1:16,000$$

It must be cautioned, however, that this method of calculation assumes that the ground surface recorded on the photograph is a *flat plane.* In undulating terrain, the tops of the hills are naturally closer to the camera lens than are the floors of the valleys and are thus recorded in different scales. While normally inconsequential for photos taken from 50,000 feet (15.24 kilometers) or more, the problem is particularly acute where the altitude of the aircraft is low and the terrain very uneven. Over hilly terrain where the elevation varies up to 300 feet (91.5 meters), for example, the representative fractions calculated in the previous example would vary from 1:15,800 to 1:16,200 over the aerial photo, depending on the topography. It can be seen that this method of calculating the RF might best be referred to as a means of estimating the scale and should not be employed in those cases where the investigator is dealing with very low-altitude aerial photography of rough terrain. For more precise and somewhat more mathematically complex formulas designed to calculate the RF of aerial photos that do not lend themselves to the method described above, the reader is directed to books such as *Elements of Photogrammetry* by Paul R. Wolf.

One further note on scale is called for here. There is a commmon confusion among those who do not use maps regularly as to the meaning of the terms *large scale* and *small scale.* In part, this difficulty stems from the fact that the phrases combine the abstract meaning of scale as it is intuitively employed to compare the size of objects in the environment and the meaning of scale as it is applied to maps.

In the abstract, the term *scale* has come to represent a type of subjective measure that we use to define the relationship between ourselves and those objects around us. When we refer to something as large scale, the implication is not only that the object so described is big, but perhaps more importantly, that we expect visually clear detail. On the other hand, normal references to small scale elicit images of comparative petiteness in which detail is difficult to distinguish. It is the notion of size and clarity of detail that is the basis for the concept of scale when reference is made to large- and small-scale maps. A large-scale map is one in which even complex detail can be clearly represented, by virtue of the fact that it has been drawn at a scale that represents a comparatively few ground miles (or kilometers) to the map inch. Thus, a map drawn at 1 inch to the mile is at a *larger scale* than the map drawn at 1 inch to 10 miles. The confusion in terms is almost inevitable when we find ourselves having to reconcile the fact that 1:1,000,000 is somehow smaller than 1:1,000. The gross numbers are the source of the difficulty. Perhaps the simplest manner in which to remember the scale differences is to equate small and large with the size of the map that one would expect if the same territory were to be portrayed in each of the two scale categories. A small-scale map of Maine, for example, would be physically small and show comparatively little detail when compared to a large-scale map of the state or a portion of the state. While the differentiation is partially subjective, it is generally acknowledged that maps drawn in RFs ranging above 1:63,360—that is 1:100,000, 1:250,000, etc—are referred to as small scale while those constructed at 1:63,360 or less are referred to as large scale.

Large-Scale and Small-Scale Maps

LOCATION

Location is a second important consideration in the translation of map data into reliable information. Several standard location and grid systems are used for the ready identification of an area. The principal geographic grid consists of a rectilinear network of orthogonally intersecting lines. It consists of parallels and meridians which are designated in degrees, minutes, and seconds, all of which are described in most geography texts.

Of greater import to land-use planning is the locational scheme that is used throughout much of North America, the township and range system. Originally devised for the divison of the landscape in the old Northwest Territories of the United States, it has since been extended to the majority of the United States as well as to northern Ontario and the western provinces of Canada. This modified rectangular grid is based on a set of selected meridians, termed principal meridians, and parallels called base lines, which intersect at an initial point. Distances are measured in the four cardinal directions from the initial point, and locations are identified at 24-mile intervals along the base line and principal meridian. However, due to the earth's shape, meridians converge toward the poles, making it impossible to fit an exact square to the earth's surface. Consequently, the ideal planimetric grid that forms the basis of the township and range system is intentionally and necessarily distorted at certain points in order to conform to the earth's curvature. By establishing the east-west and north-south lines of the survey system on the basis of true direction rather than constant distance, an additional set of meridians, termed guide meridians, was produced which incorporated the convergence toward the poles. As a result, the squares produced by the township and range system are in fact broader along the southern boundary than they are along the north, as shown in Figure 1.8.

The Township and Range System

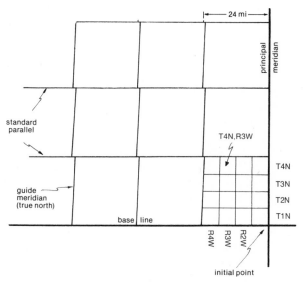

Figure 1.8. The township and range system of land survey. Note that the grid may be distorted to compensate for the curvature of the earth. Numbering of townships and ranges proceeds sequentially from the initial point.

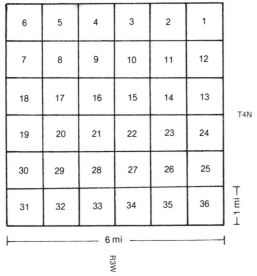

T4N

1 mi

6 mi

R3W

Figure 1.9. The number system for sections begins in the northeast corner of the township and proceeds westward, then eastward in the second tier, westward in the third tier, and so on.

Within each set of 24-mile-wide strips, 6-mile strips are defined. The strips oriented east-west are defined by the parallels and are termed townships, while those oriented north-south and bounded by the principal guide meridians are termed ranges. Each township and range strip is assigned a number to indicate its position vis-à-vis the initial point. Thus, each small square, generally referred to simply as a township and measuring 6 miles on a side, is easily identified by a notation such as T4N, R3W, read "township 4 north, range 3 west." This notation identifies the township that is formed by the convergence of the fourth township strip north of the base line and the third range strip west of the principal meridian (Figure 1.8).

Every township is subdivided into 36 segments, termed sections, each measuring 1 mile on a side. Each section within a township is given a number designation beginning with section 1 in the northeast corner and proceeding sequentially westward to section 6, then dropping down to the next tier and proceeding back to the east and so forth as indicated in Figure 1.9. The errors due to the convergence of the meridians toward the poles are accumulated along the eastern and northern column and row in each township. Thus, sections 1, 2, 3, 4, 5, 6, 7, 18, 19, 30, and 31 are often a fraction less than 640 acres (1 square mile) in area.

The township and range system was originally devised to aid land subdivisions for agricultural and settlement purposes. As a result, it was often necessary to further divide the sections. Figure 1.10 illustrates the types of standard subdivisions that can be made of a section. Descriptions of these subdivisions are from the smallest to the largest unit and are generally based on a set of halves. Parcel A is legally described as SW¼, SE¼, Sec. 3, read as "southwest quarter, southeast quarter, section 3." To complete the description, this designation would be followed by the township and range number as noted in Figure 1.8.

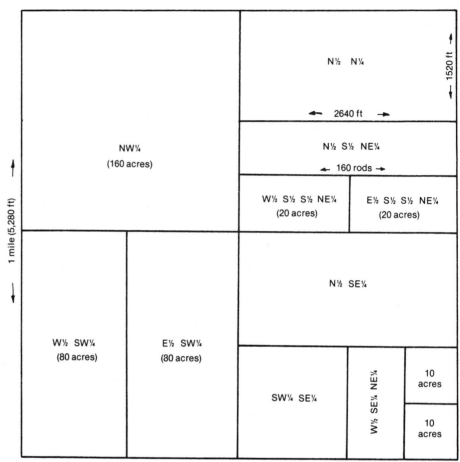

Figure 1.10. Common subdivisions of a standard survey section of 640 acres.

MEASUREMENT OF AREA

Following the locational description of a parcel, the planner is often faced with the task of describing various features within the parcel. An important part of this description is the area occupied by natural and artifical features. While the total area of a designated parcel, such as a development site, is usually provided by land-survey records, determination of the area covered by cultivated land, wetland, forest, and impervious surfaces, for example, are the responsibility of the planner. The importance of these determinations is underscored frequently in the examination of topography, soils, vegetation, and drainage in the following four chapters.

Rectangular Areas

If fortunate circumstance prevails, the area in question will coincide with the boundaries of the township and range system. In such a case, Figure 1.10 provides all the square measurement, in acres, necessary to determine the areal extent of the feature being examined. In addition, the lengths of the sides of the various subdivisions of a section are shown in feet, yards, chains, and rods (regardless of the scale at which they are presented) such that an application of the standard formula

Area = length × width

(where length and width are measured in like units) will produce an accurate ground-area measurement in any of these units. Recall, however, that some sections are fractional, and thus their area will not coincide with the values shown in Figure 1.10. The same basic formula holds true, of course, for any rectangular parcel, regardless of whether it is coterminous with the subdivision of a section. Calculation of the area of a rectangular parcel from a map or an aerial photograph necessitates first measuring the length and width on the original document and then converting these figures to actual ground distances. For example, if a rectangular plot measured 2.3 inches (7.3 centimeters) long by 1.2 inches (3.1 centimeters) wide on a map constructed to the scale of 1:62,500, the ground distance would be

Length = 2.3 × 0.986 = 2.27 miles (3.65 kilometers)

and

Width = 1.2 × 0.986 = 1.18 miles (1.9 kilometers)

where 0.986 is the conversion factor found in column 5 of Table 1.3 opposite 62,500. As we are dealing with a rectangle, the ground area is determined by multiplying adjacent sides as indicated above. Thus, the area of the example plot is determined to be

2.27 miles × 1.18 miles
                    = 2.68 square miles (6.93 square kilometers)

It should be noted that for those scales not included in Table 1.3, the conversion factor, which is in fact the ground portion of the verbal scale, can be computed by using the technique described earlier for converting an RF to a verbal scale. Unfortunately, many parcels that must be measured are not as geometrically simple as a rectangle. Several relatively accurate manual methods exist for calculating the area of irregularly shaped two-dimensional surfaces. It must be noted that the following techniques assume that the investigator is working with maps or aerial photographs which depict the land as a flat surface. The methods outlined in Figure 1.11 are applicable if the parcel being measured is bounded by any number of straight segments from which it can be subdivided into two or more geometrically regular subparcels. In these cases, the area of each subparcel can be determined and then summed with the other subparcels to provide the total area of the parcel.

Figure 1.11 illustrates the boundaries of two types of irregularly shaped parcels that might be encountered. The uppermost parcel (T) can be subdivided into squares and rectangles and the area calculated for each. The total ground area of the parcel is then equal to the sum of the areas of the individual portions. Thus,

Area of T = area of T_1 + area of T_2 + area of T_3

Should a parcel have the shape of a polygon, such as diagram B in Figure 1.11, it can be divided into triangles, the individual areas of which can be determined according to this formula:

Area of a triangle = $\dfrac{\text{height} \times \text{base length}}{2}$

Any side of a triangle can be identified and measured as the base. Height is the distance along a perpendicular line from the base to

Area of Irregular Shapes

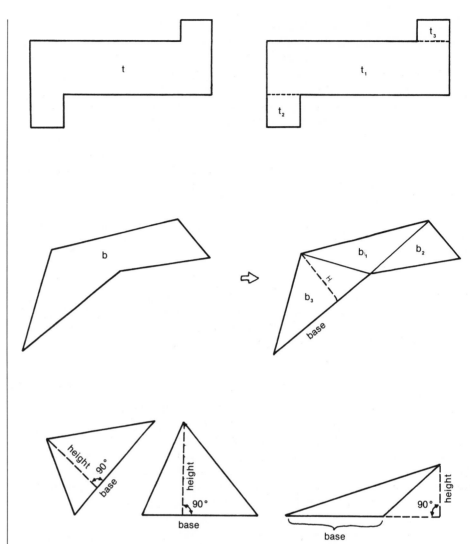

Figure 1.11. Methods for determining the area of irregularly shaped parcels.

the apex of the triangle, as illustrated in the bottom diagrams of Figure 1.11. Thus, if triangle B_2 has a base length equivalent to 1000 feet on the ground and a height of 500 ground feet, then the area of this subparcel is

$$\text{Area of } B_2 = \frac{500 \text{ feet} \times 1000 \text{ feet}}{2}$$
$$= 250{,}000 \text{ square feet (23,225 square meters)}$$

and the total area of larger parcel B would be

Area of B = area of triangle B_1 +
area of triangle B_2 +
area of triangle B_3

Many features are of such an irregular nature, however, that the techniques described above become excessively tedious.

Dot Grid Method

Another method for determining the area of irregularly shaped features, particularly those with curved boundaries, is with the use of a dot grid. This is a system of dots uniformly spaced in a grid pattern which has been constructed on a transparent overlay sheet. Each dot on the overlay is intended to represent a specified area, depending on the scale of the map or photograph and the density of the dot pattern. The dots in the grid in Figure 1.12 are spaced 0.2 inch (0.5 centimeters) apart; therefore, there are 5 dots to the inch (2 to the centimeter). If this grid is placed on a map with a scale of 1 inch to 500 feet, then the distance from one dot to the next is 100 feet (30.5 meters). To tabulate area, one needs only to interpret each dot as the center of a grid cell and then count the dots which lie within the area in question. Since each dot represents a cell 100 feet on a side, then each is equivalent to 10,000 square feet (929 square meters). Dots falling on the boundary are counted as one-half. The total number of dots falling within the area in question plus one-half of those falling on the boundary are multiplied by the area assigned to each dot to determine the total area.

The parcel shown in the aerial photograph represents a quarter section of land at a scale of 1 inch to 1100 feet (1 centimeter to 132 meters). Within the parcel is an irregularly shaped wooded area. To measure this area, the quarter section has been overlayed with a dot grid at a density of 10 dots to the inch. The ground distance between dots is 110 feet (33.5 meters) (10 dots to the inch), and each dot represents an area of 0.2778 acres. A count of the dots

Figure 1.12. A grid overlay designed for the computation of area. Each dot represents an area of 10,000 square feet. In computing the area of forest, for example, dots falling on the border would count one-half.

indicates that 195 lie within the woodlot and 40 lie on the boundary. Thus the wooded area is computed to be

$$[195 + (\frac{1}{2} \times 40)] \times 0.2778 = 59.73 \text{ acres}$$

Transect Method

Another very simple and rapid, although usually less accurate, means of determining area is the transect method. A series of equally spaced parallel lines are constructed across the features to be measured. The areas between the transect lines actually form a series of rectangles as is illustrated in Figure 1.13. The area of the inland lake in Figure 1.13 may be calculated by computing its area as a percentage of the larger rectangle that has been constructed around it. The calculation involves first measuring the distance from shore to shore along each transect line and then expresssing the sum of these distances as a percentage of the total length of all transects. For this problem, the total of the transect distances across the lake is 39.1 centimeters on the map. The total length of all transects from border to border is 142.5 centimeters; therefore the lake surface comprises 27.44 percent of the total transect lengths within the rectangle, that is,

$$\frac{39.1}{142.5} = 27.44 \text{ percent}$$

Given the scale of the map, the area of the framing rectangle can be determined, and this figure multiplied times the above percentage yields the area of the lake. In this case, the area of the rectangle is 44,024,900 square meters and that of the lake is 12,080,423 square meters. This figure, incidentally, represents less than a 2 percent difference from the true area of this inland lake.

It is noteworthy that the reliability of the transect method depends not only upon the accuracy of distance measurements, but

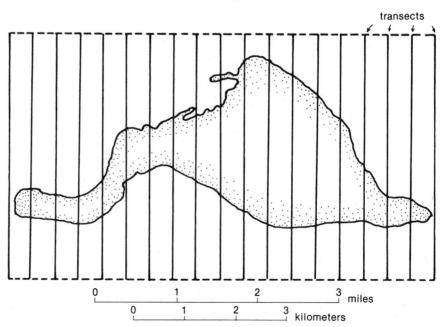

Figure 1.13. Computing area based on transects requires measuring the proportion of each transect that falls within the area of concern.

also on the number of transects and the scale of the map or the photograph. The smaller the scale and/or the fewer the transects, the less accurate will be the results.

The methods described above are simple, relatively fast, and require no specialized equipment. Measurements of area requiring a high degree of accuracy should be made with a mechanical device called a polar planimeter. Although relatively expensive, this piece of equipment is necessary if a high level of confidence is required in areal data. The area of a feature is determined by tracing clockwise around its boundaries with the planimeter pointer. The total area is read off the vernier scale, which is calibrated in square inches and square centimeters, and then converted to ground area according to the scale of the map or photograph. It must be cautioned again, however, that significant errors can occur if measurements are made from aerial photographs depicting terrain which is mountainous.

Finally, it is sometimes necessary or convenient to convert from one area unit of measure to another. To avoid the tedium of recalculation, Table 1.4 provides a matrix of square conversion factors for most units of square measure.

Polar Planimeter

Conversion of Square Measures

TABLE 1.4 CONVERSION OF SQUARE MEASURES

Divide conversion factor into "from" units to obtain "to" units.

To ↓ \ From ←	Square centimeter	Square inch	Square link	Square foot	Square vara (California)	Square vara (Texas)	Square yard	Square meter	Square rod, pole, or perch	Square chain	Rod	Acre	Hectare	Square kilometer	Square mile (statute)
Square centimeter	1	0.154999	0.002471	0.001076											
Square inch	6.45165	1	0.01594	0.00694											
Square link	404.686	62.7264	1	0.4356	0.0576	0.05645	0.0484	0.04047	0.0016						
Square foot	929.036	144	2.29568	1	0.13223	0.1296	0.11111	0.0929	0.00367						
Square vara (California)	7,025.83	1089	17.3611	7.5625	1	0.9801	0.84028	0.70258	0.02778	0.00174					
Square vara (Texas)	7,168.47	1111.11	17.7136	7.71605	1.0203	1	0.85734	0.71685	0.02834	0.00177					
Square yard	8,361.31	1296	20.6612	9	1.19008	1.1664	1	0.83613	0.03306	0.00207					
Square meter	10,000	1,549.80	24.7104	10.7639	1.42332	1.395	1.19599	1	0.03954	0.00247					
Square rod, pole, or perch			625	272.25	36	35.2836	30.25	25.2930	1	0.0625	0.025	0.00625			
Square chain			10,000	4,356	576	564.538	·484	404.687	16	1	0.4	0.1	0.04047		
Rod			25,000	10,890	1,440	1411.34	1,210	1011.72	40	2.5	1	0.25	0.10117	0.00101	
Acre			100,000	43,560	5,760	5,645.38	4,840	4046.87	160	10	4	1	0.40469	0.00405	0.00156
Hectare			247,104	107,638	14,233.2	13,950	11,959.8	10000	395.366	24.7104	9.88418	2.47104	1	0.01	0.003861
Square kilometer								1000,000.	3,9536.6	2,471.044	988.418	247.104	100	1	0.3861
Square mile (statute)									102,400	6,400	2,560	640	259	2.59	1

TOPOGRAPHIC CONTOUR MAPS

In most places the ground has a varied configuration, and we are fortunate to possess maps which portray this important aspect of the land. Topographic contour maps are composed of a series of lines that designate the elevation of the land above sea level. Each line, called a contour or contour line, represents a specified elevation. The difference in elevation values between adjacent contours is termed the contour interval. This figure indicates the elevation change from one contour to the next. The contour interval on the

Contours

Topography

largest-scale topographic maps produced by the U.S. Geological Survey is 10 feet (3 meters).

A considerable amount of information can be generated from topographic contour maps. From a visual scan of the pattern of contour lines, a notion can be gained about the topographic fabric of the land. For instance, if the contour lines are evenly spaced and curve gently across the map, then the terrain tends to be rolling. On the other hand, if the contours are irregularly spaced and follow jagged paths across the map, then the terrain is rough. In addition to topographic fabric, the contour map is a key source of surface-drainage information. Drainage divides, depressions, valleys, and drainage patterns can be readily identified, and this information can be valuable in environmental assessment and site planning and design (Figure 1.14). Chapter 3 provides further discussion of this topic.

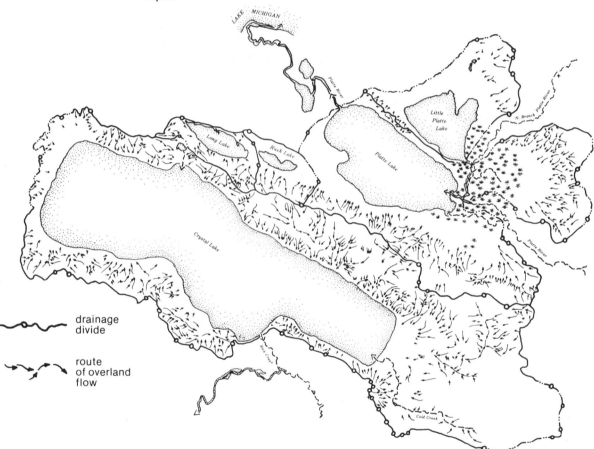

Figure 1.14. An example of the kinds of drainage features that can be interpreted from topographic contour maps (from Marsh and Borton, Michigan Inland Lakes and their Watersheds: An Atlas, 1974).

Slope

One of the most important types of information that can be generated from topographic contour maps is slope inclination. A visual approximation of slope steepness can be gained simply by noting the relative spacing of contours from one place to another. The closer the spacing, the steeper the slope. In most planning problems it is advisable, however, to measure slope inclination and express it numerically. This necessitates drawing two types of data from the map: (1) slope "run," which is the map distance from the top to the foot of the slope, and (2) slope "rise," which is the elevation differential from top to foot. Slope inclination may be expressed as a ratio, ("rise to run"), as a percent, or in degrees. These expressions are explained in Chapter 2.

The accuracy of slope measurements is very dependent on map scale and contour interval. For areawide problems, the U.S. Geological Survey maps are usually suitable; however, for detailed site-level problems, very large-scale maps with contour intervals in the range of 2 to 5 feet (0.6 to 1.5 meters) are often necessary. Such site maps must be prepared by private mapping firms and they are sometimes available from civil engineers, who use them mainly for drainage analysis.

Occasionally a planning problem may call for an estimate of the topographic area of a site. This area is measured along the topographic lay of the land and is distinguished from the geographic or map area described earlier which ignores variations in relief and assumes the land to be a horizontal plane. As the diagram in Figure 1.15 shows, topographic area can vary substantially from map area. And, of course, the hillier the terrain, the greater the variance.

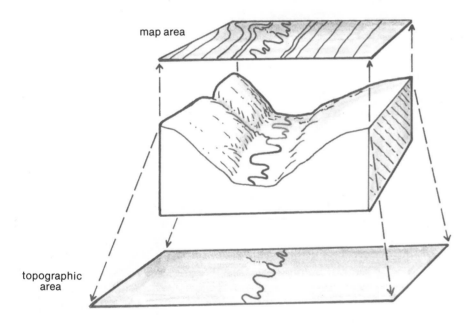

Figure 1.15. Maps (above) disregard slope in representing land area; therefore in rough terrain, topographic area (below) may be much greater. This can be an important consideration in projects concerning surface cover, for instance, reforestation, sodding, and cropping.

The technique for deriving an estimate of topographic area is based on the right triangle. In the example in Figure 1.16, line AC is used to calculate map area, whereas line AB is used to calculate topographic area. The length of both lines CD and BE is the same. Given a measurement of map area and the amount of slope rise per

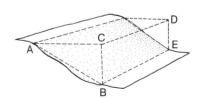

Figure 1.16. Topographic area represented by ABE, can be computed using slope data read from topographic contour maps.

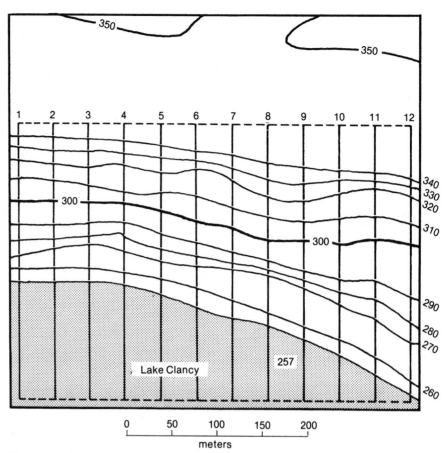

Figure 1.17. Data for computation of topographic area can be generated using the transect method. For each transect, run distance and rise height can be measured and expressed as a ratio. This ratio is keyed to a correction factor in Table 1.5 and, when multiplied times run distance, will yield the topographic length of the slope. This figure, along with many others like it, can then be used to compute topographic area.

TABLE 1.5 CONVERSION FACTORS FOR COMPUTING TOPOGRAPHIC DISTANCE ALONG A SLOPE

Rise to run ratio	Correction factor
0.10:1	1.0050
0.15:1	1.0112
0.20:1	1.0198
0.25:1	1.0308
0.30:1	1.0440
0.35:1	1.0595
0.40:1	1.0770
0.45:1	1.0966
0.50:1	1.1180
0.55:1	1.1413
0.60:1	1.1662
0.65:1	1.1927
0.70:1	1.2207
0.75:1	1.2500
0.80:1	1.2806
0.85:1	1.3124
0.90:1	1.3454
0.95:1	1.3793
1:1	1.4142

foot or meter of run (horizontal distance) from slope crest to foot, one can compute topographic area with a fair level of accuracy.

In Figure 1.17 a number of transects have been run across the slope in question. The slope extends from the shore of Lake Clancy to the 340-meter contour line. The distance along each transect between these two points represents the run, whereas the elevation difference between the lake at 257 meters and the 340-meter contour represents the rise. In the case of transect 1, the rise is 83 meters and the run is 157.5 meters. Expressed as a ratio, rise to run is equal to 0.53:1. We may now turn to Table 1.5 for the appropriate correction factor for this ratio. Using the closest ratio (0.55:1), a correction factor of 1.1413 is given. This factor is multiplied times the run distance to obtain the topographic distance along this transect:

157.5 × 1.1413 = 179.75 meters

This procedure can be repeated for each transect, and an average slope length calculated for the slope area. This figure multiplied times the width of the area yields topographic area.

STEREOPAIR AERIAL PHOTOGRAPHS

Topographic contour maps are not the only information source which provides a three-dimensional perspective of the environment. Vertical aerial photographs can also provide this perspective and in fact have an inherent advantage over maps in that they depict the landscape with a level of detail that cannot be attained with map symbolization. Although aerial photographs can be enlarged and interpreted individually, they are put to best use when combined in pairs and viewed stereoscopically. Chapter 4 illustrates an example of the utility of the three-dimensional image in vegetation interpretation.

The three-dimensional effect that can be gained from a pair of aerial photographs is an optical illusion. It is made possible because the aerial photographs are taken with an overlap of about 40 to 50 percent between successive prints (Figure 1.18). The stereographic view is afforded because each object in the landscape is photographed twice, with each shot taken from a slightly different angle.

Stereo Perspective

Figure 1.18. Aerial photographs arranged as they were taken, with an overlap of 50 to 60 percent.

When a pair of photographs showing the same object is examined through stereo glasses, the eyes combine the two perspectives, and a three-dimensional optical illusion is produced.

The stereo glasses manufactured for aerial photograph interpretation are neither exceptionally complex nor expensive. The cheaper models, which can be purchased for less than $5, are composed of two eyepieces (usually with 2X magnification) mounted in an adjustable plastic frame. The frame incorporates a collapsible wire stand that, when extended for the purpose of viewing, places the lenses at a distance of approximately 4 inches above the photopair. Some users will find that they require practice in order to achieve the impression of a third dimension, but with patience, the technique can usually be mastered in less than an hour.

A stereopair of aerial photographs can be constructed from any two overlapping frames which have been shot in succession. Construction requires that the principal or optical point of each photograph be located. This is accomplished by first locating the reference marks called fiducial marks, which appear along each side of the photograph (Figure 1.19).

Lines are then drawn connecting the marks on opposite sides of the print. In order to avoid damaging the photograph, this may be done on tracing paper firmly affixed over the photographs. The point of intersection, illustrated in Figure 1.19, is the principal point, generally referred to as PP. A pinhole can then be pricked at this

Construction of the Stereopair

Preparing the Photographs

Figure 1.19. A standard aerial photograph with lines drawn from the fiducial marks, the intersection of which is the principal center or principal point (PP).

intersection. The next task is to locate on each photo to be used in the stereo model the ground position that corresponds exactly to the ground position of the principal point of the other photograph in the pair. These points, one on either photograph, are referred to as the conjugate (or transferred) principal points (CPP), and should be carefully marked as demonstrated in Figure 1.20. The principal point (PP) of each photo should then be joined with a fine line to the conjugate principal point (CPP) on the same photograph. This line corresponds to the flight line of the aircraft, and the photo distance between the two points is known as the air base. The air base should be carefully measured and recorded, since it is used in the formulas outlined below for calculating the height of objects that can be seen in the stereopair.

With the PP and CPP marked on each photograph, it is now possible to arrange the pair for stereo viewing. The initial procedure is as follows:

1. Securely fix one of the photographs to a viewing surface, ensuring that the shadows from desk or room lighting fall toward the viewer.

2. Arrange the second photograph such that its CPP is approximately 2.2 inches from the corresponding PP on the first photograph. (If the arrangement is proper, the data printed in the corner of each photograph will read sequentially.) The second photo should then be securely fastened in position.

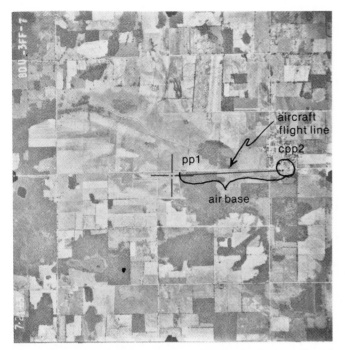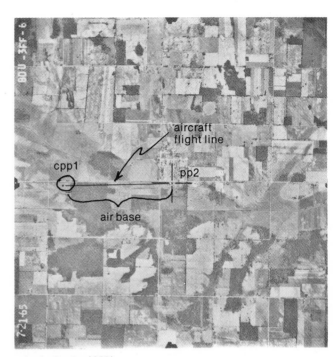

Figure 1.20. The distance between principal point (PP) 1 and conjugate principal point (CPP) 2 is the air base, and the line connecting the two represents the flight path of the aircraft.

3. Place the stereoscope on the photographs with its long axis parallel to the flight line and the lenses over corresponding photo images.

This procedure will produce a stereoscope model in which a three-dimensional perspective can be gained in the overlapping strip. By moving the stereoscope up and down the overlapped area, it is possible on standard 9- by 9-inch aerial photographs to view stereoscopically an area measuring 2.2 inches by 9 inches.

It should be noted that the successful assembly and viewing of a stereopair will depend on several points. First, it is extremely important that the photographs be aligned properly. This can be ensured by checking that the shadows of objects in both prints fall toward the viewer and that the flight lines recorded on each print form a straight line across the stereopair. Second, it is essential that the long axis of the stereoscope be kept parallel to the flight line. Finally, the lenses of the stereoscope should be adjusted to suit the interpupillary distance of the user's eyes. For most people the interpupillary distance is about 62 to 64 millimeters. Figure 1.21 is a stereopair that has been constructed from the photos used in Figure 1.20. The PP and CPP as well as the flight line have been marked on each. Viewed with a stereoscope, these photographs will produce a three-dimensional image of the landscape in the overlap area. It should be noted that the overlap illustrated is not the only area that can be viewed in stereo. By rearranging the photographs and combining them with accompanying photographs in the flight line, any site may be seen in stereo, so long as identical points are separated by approximately 2.2 inches and the integrity of the flight line is maintained.

Figure 1.21. The photograph from Figure 1.20 arranged in a stereopair. A three-dimensional image is possible along a strip about 2.2 inches wide where the photographs overlap.

The stereoscopic image of objects on the earth's surface is normally exaggerated in height or depth. At first, stereo exaggeration may seem somewhat misleading; however, after some practice, it usually becomes a highly useful aid in discerning slight variations in elevation.

HEIGHT DETERMINATION FROM STEREOPAIRS

Height Distortion

An estimate of the relative height of any object in the landscape can, of course, be made by simply comparing it with nearby objects in the stereoscopic scene. However, a reasonably accurate measurement of true height can also be made from the stereopair. This is accomplished by taking advantage of the inherent "perspective distortion" that results when three-dimensional objects are recorded on a two-dimensional photograph. Unlike a planimetric map, which depicts all features from a truly vertical view of the terrain, the aerial photograph depicts the landscape as it is "seen" through the lens of the camera from the belly of an aircraft. The result, as illustrated in Figure 1.22, is an apparent displacement between the tops and bottoms of three-dimensional objects such as tall buildings. This is evident in some of the recently published aerial views of New York City's skyscrapers. The effect is known as relief displacement. As the position of the aircraft changes from photo to photo, the vantage point on any object changes accord-

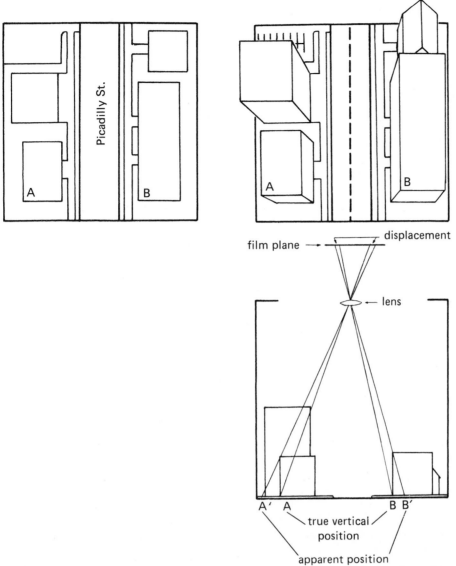

Figure 1.22. In the upper left diagram the area is portrayed in planimetric map form. The second diagram portrays the same area as seen through the lens of an aerial camera, and the lower diagram shows the geometry of the perspective distortion in side view. (Illustration by G. D. Bishop)

ingly, thereby producing an apparent displacement known as parallax. The true height of the object can be determined from a stereopair by measuring parallax.

If both the top and the base of an object can be seen in the stereoscopic model, a simple inexpensive device called a parallax wedge can be used to measure the change in displacement. The parallax wedge, as illustrated in Figure 1.23, is usually printed on transparent plastic. It consists of two adjacent lines of equal length, separated at the bottom of the wedge by a distance of 2.5 inches (6.35 centimeters) and converging until they are approximately 1.7 inches (4.3 centimeters) apart. The lines on either side of the wedge are graduated into 0.002-inch increments. Height determination is made by placing the wedge on a stereopair, such that the device is

Parallax Wedge

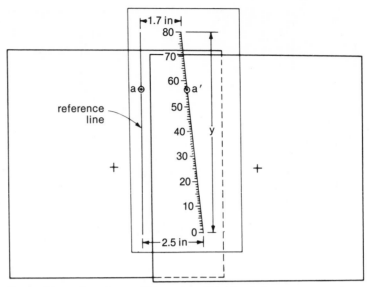

Figure 1.23. An illustration of a parallax wedge. This simple instrument can be used to measure the heights of objects that appear in stereopairs. (From Wolf, Elements of Photogrammetry, *1974.)*

perpendicular to the flight line, with the left line over the image of the feature on the left photo and the right line lying over the comparable image on the right photograph. While looking through the stereoscope, the position of the wedge is adjusted in order to achieve the illusion that a portion of the two lines have merged into a single sloping line (some practice is usually required to achieve this effect). The sloping line will appear to split again. The floating gradation that appears at the top of the object is noted. The difference between the readings taken at the base and the top of the object is the differential displacement due to height. The value of the differential displacement is then employed in a simple equation to determine the height of the object. Two other pieces of information, the average air base and the altitude from which the photographs were taken, must be obtained before the formula can be utilized, however.

As described previously, the average air base is the photo distance between the principal point (PP) and that conjugate principal point (CPP) which corresponds to the ground position of the principal point of the adjacent photograph. While an estimation of the CPP can be made by eye, it should be identified precisely with the use of stereo glasses. If the PP of each photo has been identified with a pin prick, it is possible while viewing the stereoscopic model to locate the CPP by moving a pinhead over the approximate positions on each photo where they are expected to be found. When the pinhead appears to fall into the hole that has been pricked for the PP of the adjacent photograph, the CPP has been located exactly and can be marked. The precise air base on each photo can then be measured. Since the speed of the aircraft is not necessarily constant, the average of the two measurements should be used as air base.

The flight altitude, if not readily available, can be calculated if the focal length of the camera lens and the RF scale of the photograph is known. It may be remembered from the previous discussion of scale that the RF of an aerial photograph is equal to the focal length of the camera lens divided by the altitude of the aircraft. Restating that relationship in a different manner, it can be seen that

Altitude = focal length of camera lens × RF

With the three pieces of necessary information in hand, the height of any feature can be determined. Object height is calculated by multiplying the altitude of the aircraft (in feet or meters) times the differential parallax (in inches or centimeters) and then dividing by the average air base (in inches or centimeters) *plus* the differential parallax (in inches or centimeters). That is,

$$\text{Height} = \frac{\text{altitude (ft or m)} \times \text{differential parallax (in or cm)}}{\text{average air base (in or cm)} + \text{differential parallax (in or cm)}}$$

Thus, if an object, measured with the parallax wedge, showed a differential displacement of 0.02 inch (0.5 centimeters) (i.e., the base was separated from the top by 10 gradients on the wedge) and it had been determined that the average air base of a stereopair was 3.1 inches and the flight altitude had been 10,000 feet, the height of the object would be

$$\text{Ho} = \frac{10,000 \times 0.02}{3.1 + 0.02} = \frac{200}{3.12}$$
$$= \text{approximately 64.1 ft (19.5 meters)}$$

It must be noted that while the height measurements made in this manner can be expected to be reasonably close, they are limited to the accuracy of variables used in the formula. The altitude given for any particular set of aerial photographs, for instance, is the average for the flight. The altitude of an individual photograph in the sequence may, of course, vary somewhat with variations in topography and flying conditions. In addition, a small error in the calculation of the average air base would influence the height calculation. In the previous example, an air base of 3.0 inches would have produced a height of 62.1 feet and an air base of 3.2 inches would have resulted in a calculated height of 66.2 feet. Finally, care must be taken to read the parallax wedge accurately. A practiced interpreter who is able to read wedge gradient differences of 0.002 inch (0.005 centimeter) can usually measure heights of within 10 feet (3 meters) on standard-sized photographs taken from altitudes of 10,000 to 15,000 feet (3000 to 4500 meters). To maximize accuracy in height measurements, particularly for those not accustomed to either stereo viewing or the parallax wedge, it is advisable to take several different parallax readings of an object, average the results, and double-check the measurements made of the air base on each photo.

AREAL SAMPLING

Though convenient and highly useful as sources of environmental information, maps and aerial photographs both suffer from serious limitations. Aside from problems of scale, any map is a distortion of reality, because it is constructed such that it emphasizes certain phenomena. The price of this specificity is the distortion or omission of those features in the landscape that are beyond the intent of the map. Aerial photographs suffer from a similar problem, for they too emphasize certain aspects of the environment. In addition to the altitude from which the photos are taken, both the camera lens and the film can have a marked effect upon the detail or resolution of the final image. In general, the smaller the ground feature, the more difficult it is to record accurately on film; therefore, image "selectivity" is based on object size rather than on some set of defined criteria as is the case with maps. Beyond these problems, however, both maps and photographs necessarily represent time-bound information. At the very best these sources provide a reasonably accurate representation of some specific subset of the landscape on, or as of, a particular date. The potential problems stemming from this constraint are clearly manifest.

The desirability, and perhaps more accurately the necessity of timely environmental information is obvious to even the casual observer of land use planning. It follows that maps and aerial photographs must occasionally be updated or supplemented with auxiliary information in order to undertake accurate spatial analysis. Short of a complete field inventory of a problem area or a particular feature of the environment, one can resort to the technique of sampling to gain the necessary information.

Sampling Techniques

Sampling is a systematic means of selective observation that enables the observer to estimate various attributes of an entire population or study area after having examined only a small portion of it. On face value, sampling is often very attractive because of the economies of time and money it appears to represent. Unfortunately, the proper application of most sampling techniques can become excessively complex for the occasional user. Hence, most sampling problems should be approached with caution and, if possible, with the assistance of a colleague experienced in sampling procedures. There are, however, several techniques which lend themselves to reasonably fast and reliable applications to physical features such as soils and vegetation, and we would like to touch on some of them here: (1) quadrat sampling, (2) stratified sampling, (3) transect sampling, (4) systematic sampling, and (5) windshield-survey sampling.

The first concern in sampling is that of carefully defining the features or the population to be examined. In the case of vegetation, for example, this is usually accomplished by a technique known as area sampling. Rather than defining the vegetation as a statistical population, this involves first delimiting the geographical area occupied by the vegetation under consideration. Once located, this area is outlined on a large-scale map, and the vegetation can then be sampled using either the quadrat method or the transect method.

Quadrat Sampling

Quadrats are usually small square plots, the dimensions of which vary with the type of vegetation, soil, or whatever is being examined. The first step in the quadrat method involves subdividing the entire area into grid squares. For small areas, each square may represent a single quadrat, whereas for large areas, some fraction of the square may represent a quadrat. The entire set of quadrats constitutes the "parent population" from which the sample can be drawn. As a means of reference to the location of any quadrat, the coordinates (rows and columns) of the grid should be labeled or the individual quadrats should be numbered.

In the case of vegetation, the size of the individual quadrat is an important consideration. While no absolute rules dictate quadrat size, a set of guidelines based on known relations between species and area has been defined by plant scientists. From these guidelines, we have produced Table 1.6 to assist in the selection of a quadrat size. Once the appropriate quadrat size has been selected and the study area divided, the vegetation density and/or frequency can be sampled in one of several ways.

Perhaps the most straightforward technique that can be employed to draw a sample is random sampling. As the name suggests, in this procedure sample quadrats are selected at random from the parent population. In order to draw the sample, the quadrats must be designated by a reference system as indicated above. A random-numbers table can then be employed to generate a series of coordinate pairs, each of which designates a quadrat to be included in the sample. How many samples are selected is the next obstacle.

Technically, the determination of the "proper" number of samples (called the sample size) can be one of the most difficult problems of any sample survey. Sample sizes necessary to produce highly reliable estimates to within 1 to 5 percent of the true population attributes are excessively complex to calculate and beyond the scope of this discussion. Fortunately, however, a reasonably simple method exists which will generally produce an estimate that is within 10 to 15 percent of the true values. Rather than determining beforehand what the sample size should be, the question is left open ended, and an answer is arrived at as data are tabulated in the field.

The procedure simply amounts to calculating a progressive mean. This requires first that a large number of potential sample quadrats be identified with the use of a random-numbers table and recorded in the order of their selection. Thirty to thirty-five percent of the total number of quadrats in the parent population is normally sufficient. With the list of potential sample quadrats and map in hand, the surveyor can then proceed to the field site. The sampling procedure is begun by examining the quadrats in the order in which they have been drawn, recording for each the number of trees contained within the quadrat and, if necessary, the species. After a series of five quadrats has been sampled, the mean of the total sample collected to date should be calculated and plotted. This process should be repeated at each five-quadrat interval. Initially the plot of the progressive mean, as indicated for a hypothetical sample in Figure 1.24, will oscillate wildly. However, as the number of quadrats increases, the variation should significantly diminish. When subsequent groups of five quadrats fail to appreciably affect the mean of the sample, the sampling procedure can be terminated. Any potential sample plots remaining on the original list can then be discarded. Since the problems of vegetation density and species frequency are technically separate inquiries, it may be necessary to gather different-sized samples for each if more than two species

TABLE 1.6 RECOMMENDED QUADRAT SIZE FOR SAMPLING DIFFERENT TYPES OF VEGETATION

Vegetation type	Quadrat size, m^2
Wetland/grassland (herbaceous)	1.0–2.0
Low shrubs	4.0–6.0
Brush	15.0–20.0
Woodland/forest	30.0–100.0

Drawing the Sample

Progressive Mean

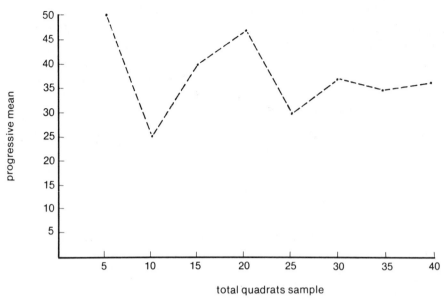

Figure 1.24. This graph illustrates the trend of a graph line representing the progressive mean. In the first 25 samples, the progressive mean varied widely, but after 30 it smoothed out, indicating that a sufficient number of samples had been reached.

types are being recorded. However, the sampling may be carried out simultaneously, using the same quadrats, if a progressive mean plot is maintained for each feature that is to be estimated.

Individual species or category frequency measures are normally expressed as a percentage of the total density of the vegetation cover. The sample means of each category or species can be quickly calculated, if the task has not been accomplished in the field. The frequency can then be expressed as a percent with the following formula:

$$\text{Frequency} = \frac{\text{mean density of the species or category}}{\text{mean density of all vegetation in the sample}} \times 100$$
$$= \text{percent}$$

The single greatest problem of the random-sample technique is that of bias in frequency analysis. If there is significant spatial clustering among the categories or if one of the categories appears to constitute less than 20 percent of the total population, the single random sample cannot be relied on to produce accurate results. In instances such as these, a second method of sampling, known as the stratified random sample, should be employed.

Stratified Sampling

Stratified sampling requires more prior knowledge of the study population than is the case with the simple random technique. The features to be surveyed must first be delimited on maps or aerial photographs and grouped into strata that have been defined according to some relevant characteristic or set of characteristics. In the case of frequency determination, this can be based on the pertinent vegetation types. Once the approximate locations of the strata are known, a random sample is taken *within each stratum* (Figure 1.25). The vegetation densities are initially calculated inde-

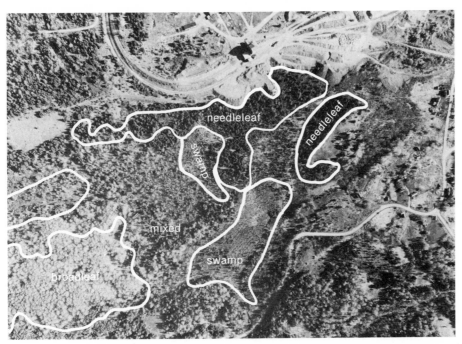

Figure 1.25. For sampling purposes, the vegetation in this area can be segregated in several strata. Each stratum defines the area within which the sample will be taken.

pendently for each stratum. The mean density of the entire plot can then be determined by summing the mean densities for each stratum and dividing by the number of strata within the survey site. Frequency determinations can be made in the same manner as described above.

While the random- and stratified random-sample techniques can be expected to produce reasonably reliable estimates when carefully employed, they both incorporate one major drawback—namely, matching the quadrats on the map with their actual locations in the field. In addition, the requirement that the quadrats must be sampled in the order in which they are drawn necessitates tedious backtracking and crisscrossing. Two alternate, though less accurate, means of sampling may also be used: the random transect method and the systematic sample.

The random transect sample is conducted in much the same manner as the random quadrat procedure. However, instead of defining a collection of quadrats, the study area is divided into a number of strips or transects. The width of the transects should be adjusted to the type of vegetation being examined. For most forests, however, a width of approximately 5 to 10 meters is usually adequate. The transects used in the sample should be randomly selected, and the progressive mean system can be employed to determine the appropriate sample size.

The fourth sampling procedure is the systematic method. Employed in both the vegetation and soils surveys, the systematic sample requires no previous knowledge of the population to be examined. A map of the area to be studied is simply overlaid with a grid and a sample is taken at each grid intersect. Where the focus of

Random Transect Sampling

Systematic Sampling

the study is vegetative analysis, quadrats can be used as the sample unit. The grid should be of sufficient dimensions to ensure a minimum of 20 percent areal coverage when all quadrats have been located. Since the size of the sample taken in this manner is predetermined by the grid design, the sample need not be collected in a specific order.

Windshield Survey

Sampling, as noted earlier, is simply a means of selective observation. The techniques outlined above provide a limited basis for surveying features such as vegetation and soils at the site scale. However, spatial analysis should not be limited to an assessment of resident site components. The planning site is also influenced by processes and features in the area surrounding the site. One method of locating and inventorying these features is to "sample" the adjacent territory by means of an automobile windshield survey. It is hardly necessary to point out the benefits of this technique, for example, ease of travel, low cost, and time efficiency. However, there are three common problems with this technique. The first is that of the encapsulating environment.

The inside of an automobile is itself a distinctly separate environment. The occupant is usually encapsulated in a vehicle that not only carries with it an artificial "climate" but also serves as a remarkably efficient acoustic barrier. Passengers, then, are necessarily external rather than integral observers of the surrounding terrain. The remoteness that results from this situation will invariably lead to distorted observations of the true characteristics and processes of the environment, unless a conscious effort is made to take counterbalancing measure. Two practices are helpful. Whenever possible, the windows of the automobile should be left down, and secondly, frequent stops should be made where the investigator can exit from the vehicle and experience the terrain at firsthand.

The second problem with the windshield technique is speed. Except for studies involving driver or passenger perception of highways, speed is usually a hindrance to observation. While it is difficult to eliminate this problem, it is fair to say that the more leisurely the pace of the survey, the more accurate will be the results.

The third problem with the windshield survey is that the environment bordering the road may not be representative of the environment of the larger area. This is often the case for several reasons: (1) road construction renders permanent change to vegetation, soils, and drainage; (2) in forested areas, the road provides an open corridor of light, resulting in heavy growth of shrubs and trees on the edge of the right-of-way; and (3) most roadways are "managed" environments where trees may have been planted and grass and weeds are periodically mowed.

SYNTHESIS AND DISPLAY OF SPATIAL INFORMATION

An important part of spatial analysis is the synthesis of data and information. Many techniques are available, ranging from computer processing to maps and diagrams, and most serve the dual function of an analytical tool and display format.

Sketch Mapping

Mapping undoubtedly has the greatest utility as synthesis technique and display tool for planning and environmental problems. In its least systematic form it may yield little more than a sketch map. Such maps have the advantage of showing all kinds of features, and the areal proximity between them; but require low inputs of time, money, and cartographic talent.

A more systematic technique for analysis and display of areal phenomena is choropleth mapping. A choropleth map can be used to show the extent of either a set of different features or different aspects of a single feature within a specified area. Like an international political map, they often have a quiltwork appearance and thus are sometimes referred to as color-patch maps. The features depicted may be quantitative expressions such as runoff coefficients or residential density; or qualitative expressions such as soil types and land use. Mapping must be done on a base map and it appears that U.S. Geological Survey topographic maps and enlarged aerial photographs can serve this purpose well. The U.S. Soil Conservation Service county soil maps, for instance, are constructed on aerial photographs (see Figure 3.3, Chapter 3).

Choropleth overlays have become one of the most popular synthesis and display techniques in environmental planning. The principal advantages of overlays are that they provide an excellent means of showing coincidental relations in the distributions of a number of features, and when used for display, they allow one to combine different sets of features by merely changing overlays. On the other hand, the overlay technique has some distinct disadvantages. Among them is the problem of representing quantitative data in the overlay format. Attempts to do so have often led to erroneous impressions about the meaning of boundaries and the various tones or colors that are formed.

The overlay technique generally attributed to Ian McHarg has found fairly wide usage in impact assessment and resource analysis. It is based on a ranking system for each feature that is mapped.

Choropleth Mapping

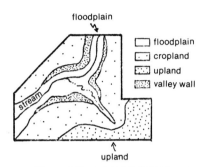

Choropleth map of land types.

Overlays

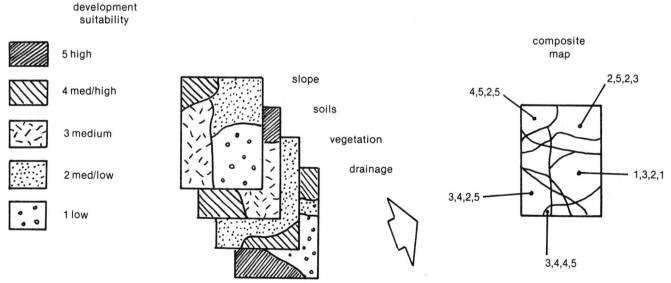

Figure 1.26. A schematic illustration of four overlays used to build a composite map on the suitability of the landscape for residential development. The feature mapped on each overlay is classified according to a five-part ranking system.

For example, if the problem involves the suitability of an area for residential development, the significant resources, such as soils, vegetation, drainage, and slope, are each broken into, say, a five-part ranking, ranging from highly suitable to unsuitable. When superimposed in an overlay, the composite map reveals areas with various development suitabilities (Figure 1.26).

Although this is a highly useful synthesis and display technique, two problems should be recognized. One relates to the definition of the ranking system for each feature, because any system must be at least partially arbitrary. The other relates to the number of combinations that are possible in the composite map. For example, 120 different combinations are possible in a composite overlay composed of 5 maps made up of 5 ranks (categories) each. This can result in copious intermediate categories that are especially difficult to evaluate; therefore it is generally advisable to group the categories into, say, high, intermediate, and low, or if appropriate, just critical areas with very high and very low values.

Isopleth Mapping   Isopleth maps (also called isarithmic, isobase, and isometric) are composed of a series of nonintersecting lines, each of which repre-

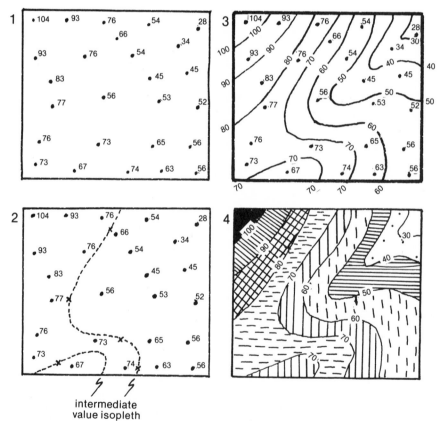

intermediate
value isopleth

Figure 1.27. The procedure for construction of an isopleth map:
  1. The data points are located on a base map, and an isopleth (contour) interval is selected based on the density, range, and variance of the data.
  2. The isopleth of intermediate value is plotted using a ruler to measure the proportional distances between pairs of values.
  3. Other isopleths are similarly plotted.
  4. Density shading may be applied between isopleths for display purposes.
(Adapted from Figures 11–14 in Maps and Diagrams by J. F. Monkhouse and H. R. Wilkinson, Methuen, London, 1963.)

sents a specific quantitative value. Topographic contour maps are probably the most familiar isopleth maps, but many other features are regularly mapped with this technique as well—for instance, population density, noise, and rainfall (see Figure 3.17, Chapter 3). The procedure for building an isopleth map is outlined in Figure 1.27.

Because isopleth maps portray a continous data surface, they are excellent for identifying spatial trends and calculating gradients such as topographic slope (see Figure 2.1 in Chapter 2). However, one should be cautioned about the reliability of values interpolated from an isopleth map, because this map represents a generalized statistical surface whose accuracy is limited by the original data base and the isopleth interval.

A wide array of graphs and diagrams are available for synthesizing and displaying spatial information. One of the most useful is the cross-profile or cross-sectional diagram (see Figure 3.29, Chapter 3). Data are plotted along a transect which is scaled for distance. The data may be quantitative—such as elevation, soil depth, and water-table elevation—or qualitative—such as soil type, predominant tree species, and land use. In any case, the chief advantage of this diagram is that it allows one to compare and contrast the distributions of many features and to display the spatial relations between them. As with the choropleth map, the cross-sectional diagram is readily adapted to the overlay technique.

The cross-sectional diagram has an important drawback in its vertical two-dimensional perspective, and one way of overcoming this is to use a three-dimensional or block diagram. By tipping the cross section a little, a map surface can be added to the diagram and some of the features can be extended from the cross section onto this surface. Because construction of a block diagram may require the use of special graphic techniques such as perspective and multiple vanishing points, they can be difficult to draft and, for some people, difficult to interpret. Nevertheless, they are certainly one of the most informative display tools available. A brief look at the next three chapters will provide several examples of block diagrams.

Graphs and Diagrams

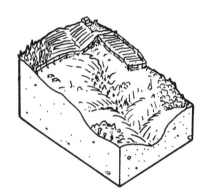

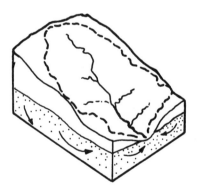

Block diagram

SUMMARY

This chapter has highlighted various methods for describing and analyzing individual spaces within the landscape. The emphasis has been on the use of manual techniques and conventional information sources for generating information on the location, area, and features of the planning site. In addition, four sampling methods as well as several synthesis and display techniques have been outlined. In the context of land use planning, spatial analysis is the task of assessing the collage of overlapping and extended spaces that affect and characterize any planning site. The key question, then, is one of how best to approach the task of integrated analysis. It is useful to remember that, while the site itself must ultimately emerge as the focus of any analysis, almost all planning sites are in fact artificial demarcations imposed upon the spatial arrangement of the landscape, both natural and human.

Bibliography

Avery, Eugene T.: *Interpretations of Aerial Photographs,* Burgess, Minneapolis, 1968. 324 pp. A standard text on aerial-photograph interpretation.

Berry, Brian J. L., and Frank E. Horton: *Urban Environmental Management: Planning for Pollution Control,* Prentice-Hall, Englewood Cliffs, N.J., 1974, p. 423.

Berry, Brian J. L., and Duane F. Marble (eds.): *Spatial Analysis,* Prentice-Hall, Englewood Cliffs, N.J., 1968. 512 pp. A collection of papers on problems and techniques in spatial analysis.

Eckbo, Garrett: *The Landscape We See,* McGraw-Hill, New York, 1969. 222 pp.

Lynch, Kevin: *Site Planning,* M.I.T., Cambridge, Mass., 1971. 384 pp. A well-established text on site-planning methods and principles.

McHarg, Ian L.: *Design with Nature,* Doubleday, Garden City, N.Y., 1969. 197 pp. Generally considered a classic statement on planning and environment; well-written, nicely presented.

Marsh, William M., and Thomas E. Borton: *Inland Lake Watershed Analysis: A Planning and Management Approach,* Environmental Protection Agency, Washington, D.C., 1976.

Nystuen, John D.: "Identification of Some Fundamental Spatial Concepts," *Papers of the Michigan Academy Science, Arts and Letters,* vol. 48, 1963, pp. 373–384. A definition of some of the basic concepts of spatial analysis.

Saarinen, Thomas F.: *Environmental Planning: Perception and Behavior,* Houghton Mifflin, Boston, 1976. An interesting treatment of environmental perception at seven different scales.

Smith, H. T. U.: *Aerial Photographs and Their Application,* Appleton-Century-Crofts, New York, 1943.

Wolf, Paul R.: *Elements of Photogrammetry,* McGraw-Hill, New York, 1974. 561 pp. A text and reference for scientists and engineers.

CHAPTER **2**

SLOPE AND TOPOGRAPHY | *William M. Marsh*

INTRODUCTION

LANDSCAPE IS AN assemblage of slopes. Slopes and slope processes are important considerations in land use planning both from the viewpoint of the environmental constraints they pose and the environmental impact related to their alteration. Slope problems generally fall into three categories:

1. *Grade (inclination)*—slopes that are too steep or too gentle for a particular land use and, therefore, must be changed by mechanical cut-and-fill processes.

2. *Erosion*—slopes with steep inclinations, light vegetative cover, and loose soil material and thus conducive to loss of soil by erosion.

3. *Failure*—slopes that are composed of weak, steeply inclined materials which have low bearing (weight-supporting) capacity and are prone to mass movements such as mudflows, slides, and creep.

It is difficult to generalize about the suitability of slope environments for land use. For example, hilly sites are poorly suited to low-cost, single-family residential development largely because of the current nature of the construction process and the irregular progress and quality of landscaping. During construction, sites are cleared of vegetation and topsoil, exposing the sloping land to erosion by runoff. Incomplete and low-quality landscaping by contractors and occupants may promote continued erosion for several years after construction. As a result, studies show that the sediment content of nearby streams and rivers can be greatly increased.

In sharp contrast to this is the suitability of hilly sites for high-cost, single-family residential development. In site design and construction, special consideration is given to the amenities of slope, vegetation, and soil. Houses are often constructed on an individual rather than en masse basis, and therefore, disturbance of slope is localized rather than geographically continuous. Landscaping closely follows construction and is usually complete with little or no soil left uncovered. Despite the hilliness of the site, comparatively little sediment is released to streams during construction, and much of the original slopes, soil, and preconstruction plant cover remain after construction and occupancy. Given information on the physical character of the site and the proposed land use, useful recommendations can be made on the suitability of residential construction techniques, in an effort to minimize deterioration of slopes and streams.

Certain slopes appear eminently well suited to particular land uses which, in fact, may severely impact the slope environment. Sanitary sewer trunk lines constructed in river floodplains are a case in point. Owing to their gradual, continuous gradients, floodplains present attractive sites for sewer trunk lines. However, in urbanized and agricultural areas, floodplains often represent the last vestiges of natural, forested landscape and as such are valuable as parklands and nature conservatories. Construction and maintenance of sewer lines may irreversibly impact the forest, soil, and drainage of the floodplain.

Artificial slopes are often especially problematic. In highway construction, for example, natural slopes are cut and steepened and new slopes are built along roadbeds. Since natural slopes represent an equilibrium condition between the forces tending to produce failure and erosion and those tending to maintain the slope, it is not uncommon that artificial slopes with changed inclination, drainage, and vegetation erode and fail despite efforts to stabilize them. Owing to the location of these slopes in areas of intensive human activity, failure not only poses a hazard to life but also represents dollar loss in damage to roads, fences, water lines, gas lines, and so on.

Land use planning and environmental impact assessment require, among other things, accurate slope information. Of the information sources readily available to the planner, topographic contour maps and aerial photographs provide the most extensive source of slope information. Most of eastern United States is covered by U.S. Geological Survey topographic contour maps at scales of 1 inch to 4 miles (1:250,000), 1 inch to 1 mile (1:62,500), and 1 inch to 0.38 mile (1:24,000) with contour intervals as small as 10 feet. Selected counties or metropolitan areas possess specially contracted large-scale topographic maps with contour intervals on the order of 5 feet. Most counties in the United States receive black-and-white aerial photographic coverage at scales near 1 inch to ⅓ mile once every five to eight years. Viewed stereoscopically, the exaggerated vertical dimension of these photographs accentuates slopes. Aerial photographs can provide useful information on problem slopes such as those undergoing active erosion. From contour maps, slope (or grade) may be determined and represented graphically or numerically. This, coupled with aerial photo interpretation, can provide information on slope erosional and stability potentials, drainage patterns, and the land use suitability of a particular site.

The following section illustrates some basic techniques for deriving slope information from contour maps and aerial photographs. Selected slope information helpful in land use planning and environmental impact assessment is also presented. The opening series of illustrations presents a hypothetical hilly site and demonstrates the techniques of topographic profiling and calculation of percent and degree of slope. This information, combined with the soil composition of the slope (from U.S. Department of Agriculture soil maps) and compared with the slope angles of repose, provides the basis for assessing the potential for slope failure. Slope, vegetation, and land use information derived from aerial photographs provide further bases for assessing erosion potential. Runoff, erosional and depositional processes, and the slope forms associated with each are illustrated. Finally, a sample slope classification scheme based on information derived from a topographic contour map and aerial photographs is presented.

MEASUREMENT OF SLOPE

Slope Profiling

The topographic contour map represents a record of processed elevation data. Graphical and quantitative slope information can be generated from a contour map with the aid of a set of simple

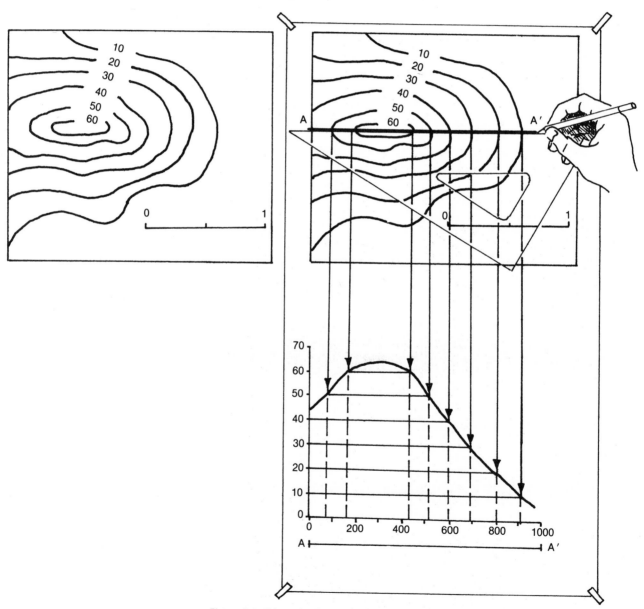

Figure 2.1. Diagrams illustrating the technique of slope profiling.

techniques. Construction of a slope profile involves plotting the elevation of contour lines on a two-dimensional graph. A line is drawn on the contour map across (up and down) the slope in question as shown in Figure 2.1. This line provides the base line A-A' for the graph. The points at which contour lines intersect the base line are marked and their elevations recorded. The vertical axis of the graph is scaled for elevation and constructed perpendicular to the base line. Points of elevation may now be plotted at the appropriate distances along the base line. For precise plotting, intersecting lines may be drawn from the corresponding values on the distance and elevation scales. Connecting the points, a line profile of the slope is produced as shown in the lower diagram in Figure 2.1.

True slope inclination may be numerically expressed as a percent or as degrees. Percent slope is calculated by dividing the total change in elevation along a slope by the ground distance covered by slope. These data can be read directly from the slope profile. The product, which is a decimal, multiplied times 100 yields the percent slope. The example calculated in Figure 2.2 is based on the slope profile constructed in Figure 2.1.

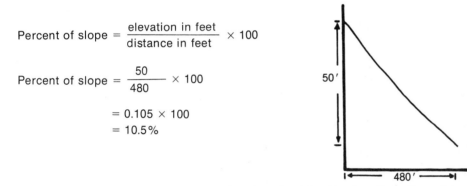

$$\text{Percent of slope} = \frac{\text{elevation in feet}}{\text{distance in feet}} \times 100$$

$$\text{Percent of slope} = \frac{50}{480} \times 100$$

$$= 0.105 \times 100$$

$$= 10.5\%$$

Figure 2.2. Computation of percent slope based on the right side of profile in Figure 2.1.

Slope inclination is usually expressed in degrees by civil engineers. A 100 percent slope represents an elevation to ground distance (or "rise to run") ratio of 1:1, which is equal to 45 degrees. The graph in Figure 2.3 gives the degree equivalent of percent slope. Note that the rate of change between percent and degrees is not arithmetically constant: for example, 50 percent is equal to 26.5 degrees, whereas 25 percent is equal to 14.1 degrees.

In determination of slope, it may be useful to bear in mind that visual-field estimates of inclination are notoriously inaccurate. As a rule, we usually estimate slopes to be much steeper than they really are, especially if one is standing on inclined ground. Even experienced mountaineers and skiers commonly overestimate slope by as much as 10 to 15 degrees.

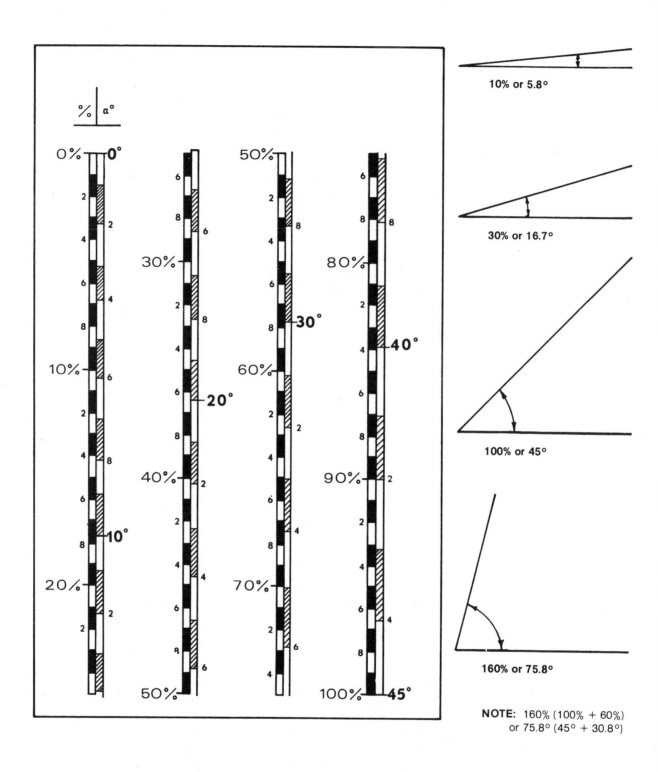

Figure 2.3. The degree equivalents for slope percentages.

Natural and Artificial Slopes

The contemporary landscape comprises both natural and artificial slopes. The illustrations in Figure 2.4 show some typical slopes, the gentlest of which is the longitudinal gradient of a river floodplain, less than 1 degree. Examples of steep slopes in nonmountainous settings are found along cuts and fills of expressways. Failure of these slopes due to seasonal saturation of the soil material and too weak vegetative cover is commonplace.

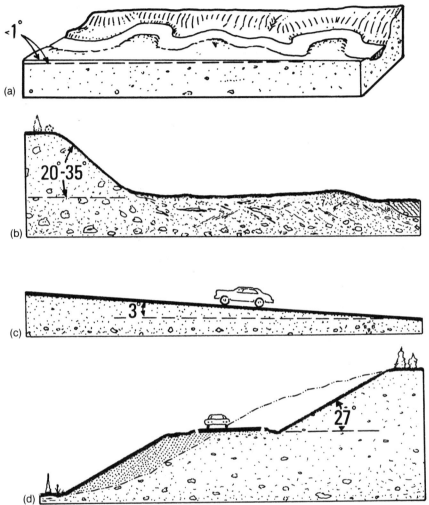

Figure 2.4. Some common natural and artificial slopes.

(a) Floodplain gradient: *Lateral erosion by meandering rivers results in the formation of floodplains. Therefore, the gradient of a floodplain is adjusted to that of the river. This diagram illustrates a typical downsteam gradient of a river floodplain. Representative of this is the Flint River in Genesee County, Michigan, where the gradient averages about 3 feet per mile. An example of a floodplain of a much larger river is the St. Lawrence between Montreal and Quebec City where the gradient is less than 1 foot per mile.*

(b) River valley cross profile: *The steepest slopes associated with river lowlands are usually the valley walls which delimit the edge of the floodplain. Valley-wall inclination is controlled by river erosion of the footslope, the composition of the wall, and its vegetative cover as well as human land use activities.*

(c) Expressway hill: *The maximum grade of an expressway as a rule does not exceed 3 degrees. The policy of restricting the grade to less than 6 feet (2m) per 100 feet (30m) necessitates extensive "cut and fill" in highway construction. The maximum inclination of expressway exit and entrance ramps, however, may be as much as three times greater than that of the expressway itself. This is in part a response to cost factors, because steep ramps require less bed fill and occupy less space than gentle ramps.*

(d) Highway cut and roadbed slopes: *Roadbed slope and cut slopes are often as great as 27 degrees. Seasonal saturation and weak vegetative covers commonly make these slopes susceptible to failure and severe erosion, especially during and immediately after construction. While gentler slopes would be preferable, land acquisition and cut-and-fill costs generally dictate construction of steep slopes.*

SLOPE FAILURE AND EROSION

"Angle of repose" refers to the maximum angle at which various soil and rock materials can be inclined before failure occurs such as landslide. The angle of repose for soil varies with texture (i.e., particle size), water content, and vegetative cover. For example, dry sand as in a sand dune can sustain an angle of repose around 33 degrees, but with a dense forest cover it may increase to as much as 45 degrees. The angle of repose can generally be estimated by combining soil, drainage, and vegetation information. Compared with the actual angle and conditions of a given slope, the potential for failure can then be assessed. The illustrations in Figure 2.5 give the angles of repose for some common slope materials. Failure of slopes at or near the angle of repose is usually caused by one or more of the following:

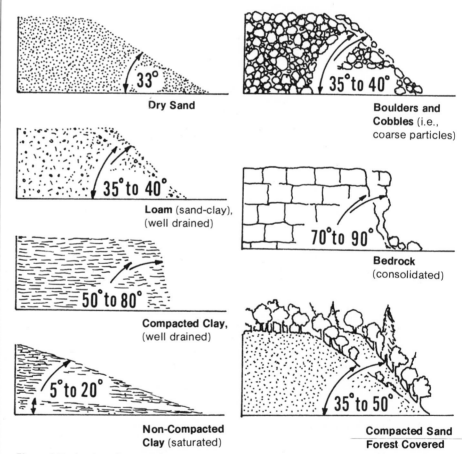

Figure 2.5. Angles of repose for some commonplace slope materials.

    1. *Undercutting* by waves, streams, or construction processes.
    2. *Increased groundwater* content as along the banks of a reservoir.
    3. *Devegetation,* particularly of forest cover.
    Failure of the example slope in Figure 2.6 is improbable unless its inclination, tree cover, or soil consistency are drastically altered.

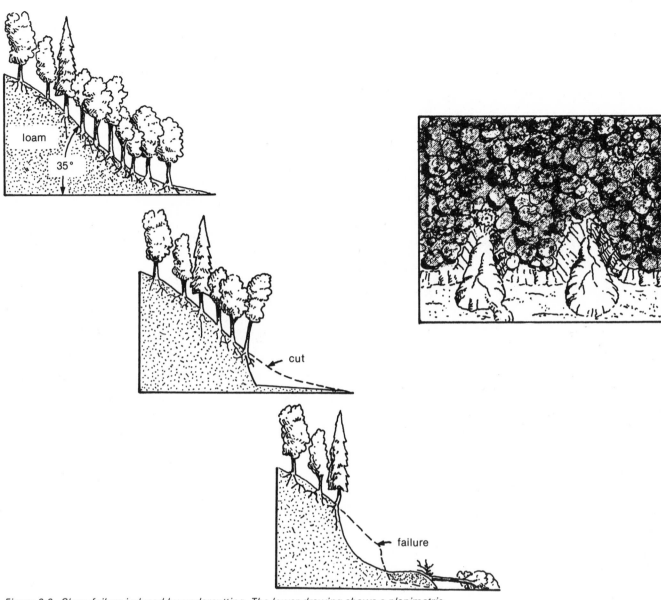

Figure 2.6. Slope failure induced by undercutting. The lower drawing shows a planimetric view of a slope failure.

Removal of the footslope by natural or human processes greatly decreases slope stability due to reduction of confining pressure (support strength) in the lower slope and soil-binding strength with the loss and decay of tree roots. Failure may not be spontaneous with undercutting. Rather, it is often associated with a seasonal increase in soil water content resulting in a more fluid soil consistency, or, in active mountainous regions, with earthquake tremors. Tremors may loosen and rotate particles, reducing their internal binding strength to the point of failure. The plane of failure is normally semicircular in shape, corresponding to the zone of least internal soil resistance to failure-producing forces. The forms produced by slope failure of this type are scallop-shaped scars and lobe-shaped deposits like those shown in the last diagram in Figure

Figure 2.7. A slope failure along a highway cut. Notice that the highway is completely covered by debris.

2.6. These features are observable on standard black-and-white aerial photographs, especially when viewed stereoscopically. Unvegetated slope cuts and failure scars are often distinguishable by their lighter, often whitish, tones and planimetric forms.

Examples of Slope Failure

A large slope failure which buried a section of highway is shown in Figure 2.7. Excavation of the footslope in construction of the highway was the main cause of failure. The increased inclination, coupled with seasonal and longer-term changes in soil consistency and internal binding strength, produced sudden failure after many years of apparent stability. The failure shown in Figure 2.8 resulted in several feet of soil displacement along a road cut. Damage to the fence and exposure of the subsoil are keys to identification of this type failure on aerial photographs.

Causes of Slope Erosion

Erosion by surface runoff is an ongoing process on virtually every slope. The rate of erosion is controlled by the velocity and the volume of runoff as well as by the resistance of the soil to the erosive power of moving water. These in turn are mainly regulated by vegetative cover and slope inclination. The steeper the slope and the lighter the vegetative cover, the greater the rate of erosion. The influence of vegetation is fourfold: (1) raindrop impact, a highly effective erosive process on barren soil, is mitigated by plant foliage; (2) percolation of water into the soil is increased by the presence of roots and organic litter, thereby decreasing the volume

Figure 2.8. The scar at the head of a failure along a highway. Such features are keys to identifying failures on aerial photographs.

of water available for surface runoff; (3) the friction posed to runoff by plant stems, foliage, and debris reduces the velocity of flow; and (4) the additional cohesiveness imparted to soil by plant roots increases greatly soil resistance to the erosive force of runoff.

Given uniform vegetative cover, the potential for slope erosion can initially be estimated on the basis of slope height and inclination. Generally, high slopes provide greater surface areas to collect rainfall and, as a result, yield a greater volume of runoff than do low slopes. It follows that on a single slope the volume of runoff increases progressively downslope as the size of the collection area increases. The velocity of runoff increases with slope inclination as shown in the upper diagram in Figure 2.9. Combining volume and velocity, it is evident that the low angles near the crest of a slope produce low-volume and low-velocity runoff resulting in relatively low rates of erosion. Midslope, normally the steepest segment, generates moderate volume but very high-velocity runoff and, as a result, is the most severely eroded part of the slope. The footslope,

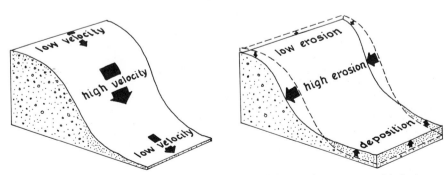
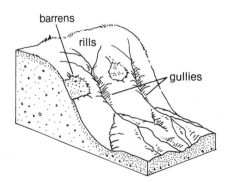

Figure 2.9. The relative velocity of slope runoff and the resultant geomorphic features.

Slope and Topography | **59**

crest slope

midslope

footslope

Figure 2.10. An example of crestslope, midslope and footslope features on an active slope.

despite the high volume of water, yields low-velocity runoff due to its gentle incline and is characterized by deposition rather than erosion. The resultant forms associated with each segment of an active slope are shown in the final illustration in Figure 2.9 and in the photograph in Figure 2.10.

Figure 2.11. This stereopair shows an active slope (enclosed area) where erosion has cut deep gullies into the slope face.

IDENTIFICATION OF ACTIVE SLOPES

Severe slope erosion is clearly evident on the aerial photopair in Figure 2.11 (enclosed area). Erosion by runoff has formed a deep network of gullies on this moderately steep slope. This same slope is shown on a large-scale topographic contour map in Figure 2.12 (enclosed area). Notice that it is actually *not* one of the steepest slopes in the area and that the erosion is *not* evident on this map. This illustrates the utility of aerial photographs in slope analysis. Combining the contour map and aerial photographic sources, the following information can be generated for slopes of this type. The information given for each category is based on the example slope in Figures 2.11 and 2.12.

1. Slope inclination	ranges from 15 to 25 percent (8.5 to 14.1 degrees)
2. Vegetative cover	herbs (grass and weeds), scattered shrubs, barren gullies
3. Distribution of gullies	relatively continuous but variable in density with largest gullies situated in the easternmost 200 feet (61 meters) of the slope
4. Surface area affected by gullying	245,000 square feet (22,760 square meters) (71 percent of slope area)
5. Points of sediment deposition	footslope and lakeshore
6. Locations of potential additional erosion	midslope and gully heads

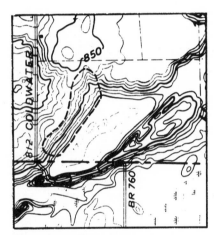

Figure 2.12. The active slope shown in Figure 2.11 as it appears on the U.S. Geological Survey topographic contour map. The erosional activity is not apparent on this map.

Much of the current emphasis in land-use planning focuses on agricultural and related wooded lands on the urban fringe. Due to the mechanized nature of modern agriculture, cropland is largely restricted to low-relief terrain. An example of such terrain is pictured in the photopair in Figure 2.13. Long slopes represented by features such as highways and farm fields are rarely more than 3 or 4 degrees inclination. Smaller slopes such as stream-valley walls, ditch banks, and road cuts are usually less than 10 feet (3 meters) high and of less than 15 to 20 degrees inclination. Although this information is obtainable from contour maps, information on the condition of slopes with respect to erosion, vegetative cover, and land use is most obtainable from aerial photographs. When viewed stereoscopically, it is evident from the photopair above that essentially no severe slope erosional problems exist in this area.

The landscape is drained by a myriad of natural and artificial channels. These are integrated into complex networks of rivers, streams, ditches, storm sewers, and field tiles. The physical, chemi-

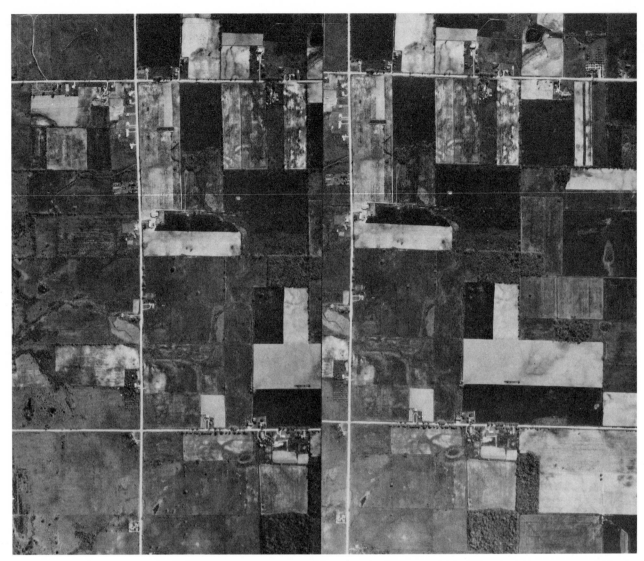

Figure 2.13. A typical Midwest rural landscape comprised of low, gentle slopes on which no severe erosion is evident.

cal, and biological condition of the water carried by these channels is directly and indirectly related to the conditions of the land and the use of the area drained.

Drainage Patterns

The drainage patterns of rivers and streams as well as some drainage ditches are generally depicted clearly on large-scale topographic contour maps. At the local scale, aerial photo interpretation can augment this information by identifying connections between field drainage and natural channels, for example. Careful stereoscopic observation will show that drainage from the field outlined in the photopair in Figure 2.14 crosses the road, passes through a wooded lowland, and empties into the lake on the right. In addition to the farm fields, a sand and gravel operation is also drained, thereby establishing the possibility of sedimentation in the wooded area and in the stream itself.

Slope and the Shape of Small Drainage Basins

Drainage patterns are often an indicator of slope and runoff conditions. The geographical shape of small drainage basins is

Figure 2.14. The drainage patterns such as the one in the enclosed field provide reliable information on the routes of runoff movement, likely points of sedimentation, and the locations of outfalls.

strongly influenced by slope inclination. Circular-shaped basins are often reflective of gentle slopes with relatively low rates of erosional downcutting by streams. As the slope is increased, downcutting increases and the basin becomes elongated (Figure 2.15). These basins are usually composed of fewer tributaries than are the gently sloping basins. This is due to the fact that the slower, meandering flow of the latter increases the frequency of stream mergers, termed ingrafting.

The processes responsible for most landforms are only infrequently observable in the landscape. Under humid climatic conditions, for instance, runoff in a gully may occur only twenty or thirty times a year. Casual observations and aerial photographs are not likely to record the processes in action. But since landforms themselves are recorded on contour maps and aerial photographs, the processes can be deduced from the forms (Figure 2.16).

From these sources, information is indeed available to the aware

Slope Processes and Forms

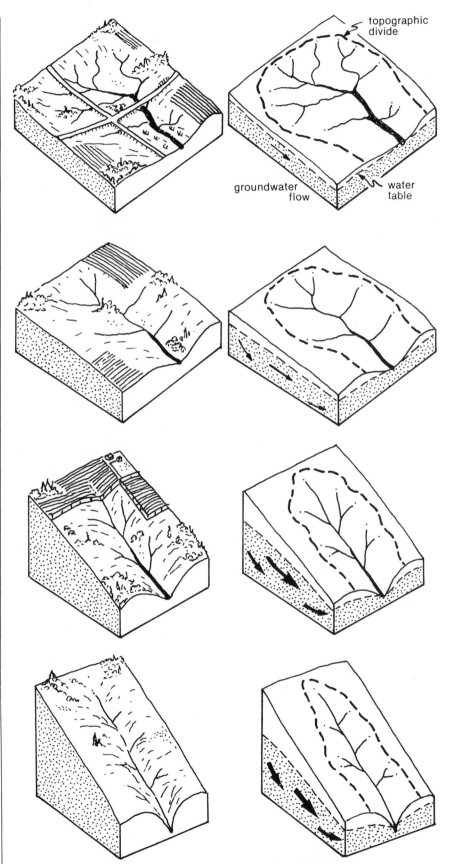

Figure 2.15. The shapes of small drainage basins can provide important clues on slope and runoff conditions. Elongated basins often indicate steep slopes and rapid runoff.

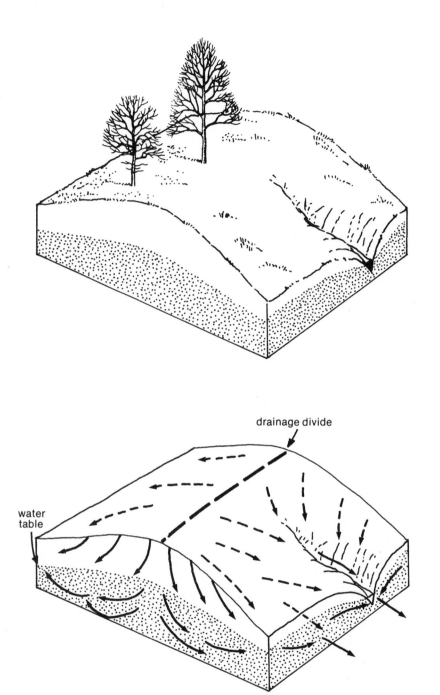

drainage divide

water
table

Figure 2.16. The lower illustration *is a schematic interpretation of runoff processes based on the slope forms in the site shown in the upper illustration. Information on surface and subsurface drainage directions, their relative velocities, and relative erosion potentialities may be interpreted, with proper qualification, from these forms.*

investigator. Slope profiles, angles, microforms such as gullies and rills, drainage patterns, and vegetative cover together provide information on the dynamics of the slope. Spatial changes in any of these variables influence slope processes and thus slope form.

Given topographic contour maps, aerial photographs, and a rudimentary description of soil (e.g., sandy loam, clay, or bedrock), a rational slope classification scheme may be devised for any area. The scheme should aim to describe the existing state of slopes as well as to identify potential slope problems given a proposed land use.

SLOPE CLASSIFICATION

No classification scheme is universally applicable. In terrain of exceptionally low relief such as the Central Valley of California or the Saginaw Valley of Michigan, only two slope classes may be appropriate for most land—namely, *flat* (less than 1 degree), on which water ponds and runs off slowly, and *sloping* (greater than 1 degree), on which runoff is fairly pronounced. For the hilly terrain shown in Figure 2.17(a), four slope inclination categories were found to be meaningful based on the following rationale:

Inclination Classes

1. *Very steep* (greater than 25 degrees)—if disturbed by construction processes or forest removal, widespread failure is highly probable.

2. *Steep* (15 to 25 degrees)—if plant cover is removed, slope is highly susceptible to erosion and gully formation.

3. *Moderate* (5 to 15 degrees)—will support residential and agri-

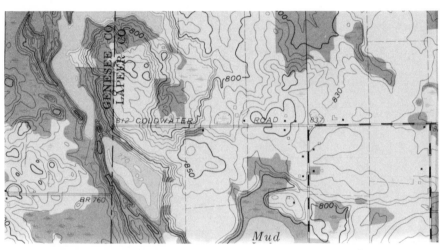

Figure 2.17(a). U.S. Geological Survey topographic quadrangle (excerpt).

Slope Inclination Categories

Very Steep (greater than 25°)
Steep (15-25°)
Moderate (5-15°)
Gentle (less than 5°)
Soil: loam

Figure 2.17(b). Slope inclination map.

cultural land uses; however, if misused, is definitely susceptible to serious erosion.

4. *Gentle* (less than 5 degrees)—for the terrain in question, slope will sustain the most intensive use with least management.

From the contour lines of the topographic map, the area was classified into these categories using the techniques described earlier in this chapter [Figure 2.17(b)]. To determine the condition of slopes, the area was next examined stereoscopically on aerial photographs [Figure 2.17(c)]. This yielded information on vegetative cover, drainage, erosion, and land use, which combined with the slope inclination map, provided the basis for a final classification useful for general land use planning purposes.

The final map establishes four slope types, each with different land use potential [Figure 2.17(d)]. In addition, natural waters presently impacted by sedimentation from slopes and those highly susceptible to sedimentation should slopes become activated are

Slope Conditions

Figure 2.17(c). Slope conditions.

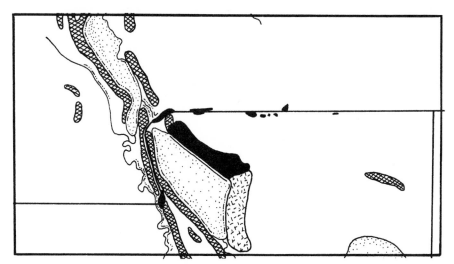

Figure 2.17(d). Slope classification map.

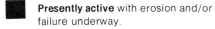 **Presently active** with erosion and/or failure underway.

Highly susceptible to failure and erosion should forest be removed.

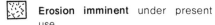 **Erosion imminent** under present use.

 **Least susceptible** to failure and erosion under agricultural, residential and related uses.

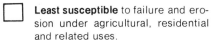 Natural waters presently influenced by sedimentation from eroded slopes.

Natural waters highly susceptible to sedimentation should nearby slopes be activated.

also identified. The large active slope represents abandoned farmland, apparently unmanaged for several decades: the small active slopes are associated with road cuts. Motorcycles have etched ruts into the "erosion imminent under present use" slope. Should this continue, it is likely that gullying will ensue. The very steep forested slopes, which reach angles as great as 40 degrees, are clearly highly susceptible to failure under a land use which would remove the forest cover. This, coupled with the natural amenity represented by such slopes on the urban fringe, makes any land use other than park or nature conservatory difficult to justify.

From the preceding map a variety of information may be extracted to aid in guiding land use and environmental planning of this area. Generalized according to development potential, the area can be divided into two sites. The corridor along the water features poses severe physical limitations as well as a propensity for serious damage from disturbance of the plant cover and soils. The remainder of the area is better suited for development, though not uniformly so throughout. Variations in drainage and soil composition, for instance, may provide the basis for further differentiation of site-development potential. The thread of this discussion is continued in the following chapter, "Soils and Drainage."

Bibliography

Chandler, R.J.: "The Inclination of Talus Terraces, and Other Slopes Composed of Granular Material," *The Journal of Geology,* vol. 81, 1973, pp. 1–14.

Eschman, Donald F., and Melvin G. Marcus: "The Geologic and Topographic Setting of Cities," in T. R. Detwyler and M. G. Marcus (eds.), *Urbanization and Environment,* Duxbury Press, Belmont, Calif., 1972, pp. 27–51.
Largely a discussion of the influence of landforms on the locations and the land use patterns of cities.

Flawn, Peter R.: *Environmental Geology: Conservation, Land Use Planning and Resource Management,* Random House, New York, 1970. 313 pp. An outline of geological phenomena that affect land use.

Poole, Donald H.: "The Development of Criteria for Recognizing and Identifying Slope Failure Forms as Depicted by Remote Sensor Forms." *Technical Report 12,* East Tennessee State University Remote Sensing Institution, Johnson City, Tenn., 1968, 59 pp.
Slope failure and erosional features are identifiable on aerial photography on the basis of pattern, color contrast and geometric form.

———: "An Evaluation of the Utility of Available Remote Sensor Returns for a Study of Slope Failure Phenomena." *Technical Report 14.* East Tenessee State University Remote Sensing Institution. Johnson City, Tenn., 1968. 36 pp.
Of available photographic imagery, Ecktachrome and Ektachrome infrared aerial photography at large scales (1:10,000 and 1:20,000) provide the best source of information on slope failure and erosion.

Sharpe, G. F. S.: *Landslides and Related Phenomena: A Study of Mass Movements of Soil and Rock.* Pageant Books, New Jersey, 1960. 137 pp.
A useful introduction to slope processes and related terminology.

Tank, Ronald W. (ed.): *Focus on Environmental Geology,* Oxford University Press, New York, 1973. 474 pp.
A collection of readings including slope failure, urban geology, and environmental impact related to geologic phenomena.

Wobber, Frank J.: "Photography of the Peru Earthquake: A Preliminary Analysis." *Photographic Applications,* vol. 6, 1971, pp. 20–29.
A brief examination of the utility of aerial photographs for preliminary assessment of the 1970 Peruvian earthquake damage: suggests use of aerial photography for relief planning purposes.

Wolman, M. Gordon.: "A Cycle of Sedimentation and Erosion in Urban River Channels." *Geografiska Annaler,* vol. 49A, 1967, pp. 385–395.

CHAPTER **3**

SOILS AND DRAINAGE | *William M. Marsh*

INTRODUCTION

SOIL IS TRANSITIONAL between the air, water, and life of the surface on one hand and the rock of the subsurface on the other. Accordingly, it is composed of gaseous, water, organic, and rock constituents. Variations in these constituents impart to soils a set of physical characteristics which influence and are influenced by surface phenomena, including land use. In the context of land use and environment, four aspects of soil should be highlighted:

1. *Bearing capacity*—the ability to support weight (overburden) such as buildings, roads, and vehicles.

2. *Erodibility and stability*—the susceptibility to erosion and failure in sloping terrain.

3. *Drainage*—the capacity to receive and transmit water.

4. *Resource value*—the economic worth, as for building material, road fill, and agriculture.

The influence of soil on land use is closely related to particle composition and water content. These are important determinants of drainage, bearing capacity, and resource value. Poorly drained, fine-grained (or clayey) soil poses the greatest limitation to most land uses. In contrast, coarse-grained soils, though often unattractive for crop agriculture, are most attractive to residential, transportation, and related land uses.

Perhaps no soil problem receives as much local public attention as drainage related to septic tanks. Clayey soils and soils with high water contents have low water-transmitting capacity. As a result, waste water does not readily pass from the septic-tank drain field into the soil. The soil drainage capacity can easily be exceeded, producing surface seepage of unsanitary water. Though less serious a problem today than in the past, septic systems are still prevalent on the suburban fringe, and despite governmental and health regulations throughout most of the United States and Canada, local streams and lakes are severely impacted by sewage-enriched runoff. Moreover, improper assessment of soil drainage by developers frequently raises legal battles which disrupt construction schedules, resulting not only in financial losses but also in environmental deterioration of the dormant construction sites.

The practice of mining soil for construction material, topsoil, or minerals obliterates the local soil environment and often alters the groundwater as well. Devoid of organic matter, the exposed subsoil of open pits is slowly and incompletely revegetated by natural means. Coupled with the steepened slopes and associated ground-water seepage, accelerated erosion accompanied by sedimentation of nearby lowlands and streams is often the result. Not infrequently these pits are used as refuse dumps or are fenced off and abandoned as is commonly the case with those which fill with groundwater. Rehabilitation of excavation sites requires vegetating and rebuilding the topsoil. In extreme cases such as the strip mines of Appalachia, this would involve tremendous costs as more than 20,000 miles of slope cuts have been formed over the years. On the urban fringe, however, pits and associated debris piles are localized and thus generally lend themselves to rehabilitation and reintegration with the landscape.

Bearing capacity can be a serious consideration in problems which involve loading the soil surface. Nearly all soils settle under the weight of surface structures, but in most cases the amount of subsidence is negligible with little influence on the structures themselves. In certain locales, however, soils of low-bearing capacity have presented some of the most critical land use problems. Usually clayey in composition, weakly consolidated and water saturated, these soils deform under the pressure of surface weight. Loss of water, compaction, and actual plastic movement reduce the volume of soil resulting in subsidence of the surface. Sections of modern Mexico City built on landfill and compressible volcanic clays have subsided to the point that former second stories of buildings are now ground-level first stories. In the Arctic of Canada, the United States and the U.S.S.R., human structures frequently have caused a weakening of the permafrost (due to increased conduction of heat into the ground), resulting in subsidence of the overlying saturated organic soil. The urbanized area of Houston, Texas, has subsided as a result of groundwater pumping for municipal water supplies. This case was due to the fact that groundwater is one of the weight-supporting components of soil, and its reduction can result in a volumetric decrease of soil. Less dramatic is the localized subsidence of organic soils under roads and highways in the Midwest.

Though traditionally the domain of the civil engineer, information on soil bearing capacity and drainage must also be part of the land use planner's decision-making scheme. "First-cut" decisions of highway-corridor location, for example, are often the responsibility of the planner. In areas of heterogeneous soils such as coastal lowlands, floodplains, and glaciated terrain, this involves recognition of the contrasts in land use potentials of organic and sandy soils as well as identification of marketable soils and of soils which support ecologically valuable environments.

Soils information may be derived from several sources. In areas of intensive agriculture, detailed surveys and analyses of soils have been undertaken by the U.S. Department of Agriculture (USDA). These are published in county soil survey reports. Though formerly oriented almost exclusively to agriculture, the soil information generated by the USDA now includes consideration of nonagricultural activities as well. Witness this excerpt from a 1973 USDA county soil survey report: "Community development, accompanied by the extension of public facilities, creates a need for information on soils. This information differs somewhat from that needed by farmers. . . ." This information includes data on bearing capacity, septic drainage capacity, as well as soil suitability for highway, reservoir, and waterway fill.

In areas of little or no agriculture, USDA soil information may be nonexistent or in a highly generated form. For land use planning, this necessitates generation of soil information from other sources—principally, geologic maps, aerial photographs, topographic contour maps, and drainage maps. From these sources soil environments can be identified, leading to definition of selected soil features such as drainage and organic content. Field sampling based on a simple hand test can provide textural (particle composition) data. In combination, geology, drainage, organic content, and texture can be used to establish a reasonably sound information base for assessing soil in the context of a proposed land use.

The following section examines existing soil classification schemes, soil texture, soil drainage, and selected soil problems related to land use. Additionally, several important engineering properties of soil and related processes are illustrated. The latter portion of the chapter suggests a scheme for identification of problem soils based on information drawn from topographic maps and aerial photographs. Since much of the soil information used in land use planning is gained from existing soil maps and reports, it is well to begin with a discussion of conventional soil classification schemes.

SOIL CLASSIFICATION

Texture

Of those in use today, it is the classification schemes based on texture, that is, particle size, that are generally most meaningful in land use planning. This is due to the fact that texture is an important determinant of soil drainage, erodibility, bearing capacity, and economic value. The USDA soil classification is based on three textural categories: sand, silt, and clay. Texture is determined by the average diameter of individual particles. According to the U.S. Department of Agriculture, these are the following:

Sand—2.0 to 0.05 millimeters diameter
Silt—0.05 to 0.002 millimeters diameter
Clay—smaller than 0.002 millimeters diameter

Soil composed of various admixtures of sand, silt, and clay are placed in intermediate categories such as sandy loam, loam, and silt loam. These designations are based on the percentage weight of a soil sample represented by sand, silt, and clay. Separation of the sample particles is accomplished by sieving the coarser soil particles through progressively smaller meshed screens and timing the rate of settling of the finer particles out of suspension in water. Table 3.1 gives the percentage of each size particle for the major textural categories recognized by the USDA.

In soil literature these classes are usually presented graphically in the form of a textural triangle (Figure 3.1). Each side of the triangle is scaled 0 to 100 percent for either sand, silt, or clay. The interior of the triangle is subdivided into the various textural classes, thereby

TABLE 3.1   THE PERCENTAGES OF SAND, SILT, AND CLAY IN THE MAJOR TEXTURAL CLASSES OF THE USDA (BASED ON INTERMEDIATE PERCENTAGES)

Soil class	Percent sand	Percent silt	Percent clay
Clay	20	20	60
Silty clay	5	45	55
Sandy clay	55	5	45
Clay loam	35	30	35
Sandy clay loam	60	15	25
Silty clay loam	10	55	35
Loam	40	40	20
Sandy loam	65	25	10
Silt loam	20	65	15
Silt	10	85	5
Loamy sand	80	15	5
Sand	90	5	5

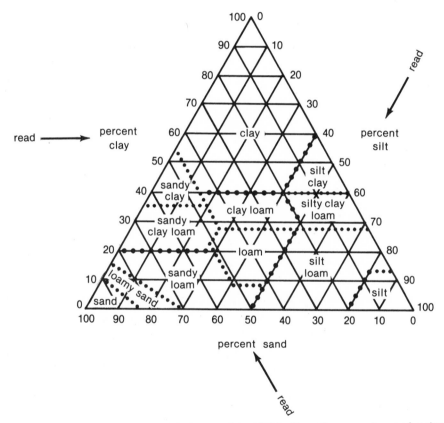

Figure 3.1. The standard textural triangle of the USDA. Given the percentages of various-sized particles in a soil sample, the appropriate textural class can be read from this graph.

facilitating ready classification of a soil given its particle composition by percent weight.

Even casual observations of soil usually reveal that in most locales particles larger than sand are present in the soil. Due to their unsuitability for cultivation, soils composed of chiefly pebbles, cobbles, or boulders are usually not included in the standard USDA

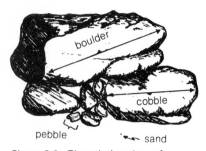

Figure 3.2. The relative sizes of boulders, cobbles, pebbles, and sand. At this scale, silt and clay are invisible.

textural classification (Figure 3.2). Nevertheless, coarse particle soils are especially important with respect to suburban and urban land use, because they greatly enhance soil drainage and bearing capacity. In sharp contrast to coarse-grained soils are soils composed mainly of organic matter. Usually designated as muck or peat, these soils form in areas of poor drainage and constitute one of the least-favorable soil types for suburban and urban land use. In addition to drainage problems, low bearing capacity renders organic soils virtually useless in support of buildings and other artificial overburden.

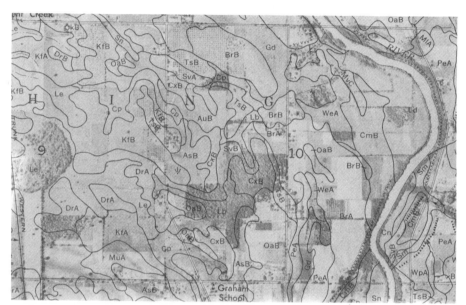

Figure 3.3. An excerpt from a USDA county soils map. In addition to showing the distribution of soils, these maps also show water features, roads, and steep slopes. Soils maps are currently printed on an aerial-photograph format.

Soil Conservation Service County Surveys

County soil surveys conducted by the Soil Conservation Service of the USDA are generally the most reliable extensive source of textural information (Figure 3.3). Classification is usually detailed and based on both field and laboratory analysis. Locally soils are given two designations: (1) a geographic name of a place representative of the soil type and (2) a textural classification. Hence, names such as "Boyer sandy loam," "Morley silt loam," and "Miami clay loam." Accompanying each soil type and soil series (a group of related soil types) is a written description which includes textural, drainage, color, slope, structural, key identification traits as well as pertinent agriculture information. Given careful scrutiny, these descriptions will yield valuable information for land use planning. In the soil description below, significant words and phrases have been italicized to illustrate this point.

Wasepi sandy loam, *0 to 2 percent slopes* (WeA)—This soil has the profile described as typical of the series. *It occupies sandy and gravelly benches* above rivers and streams and is slightly below the Boyer and Perrin soils. Slopes are dominantly less than 2 percent but are slightly steeper near drainageways.

The plow layer is a very dark grayish-brown *sandy loam.* The *depth to stratified sand and gravel is dominantly 24 to 42 inches* but is slightly greater in places. *This stratified material contains thin layers of silt loam or silty clay loam in some areas.*

Wetness and moderately low natural fertility are *the main limitations* to the use *of this soil for crops.* Runoff is slow, and shallow drainageways are needed in some areas. Tile or open-ditch drainage improves this soil for cultivated crops. Corn, small grains, and forage are the main crops grown. Capability unit IIIw-5 (4b).

Soil classification schemes developed by civil engineers can be very useful to the land use planner. Although readily available information based on these schemes is quite limited in geographical coverage, the USDA now includes an appreciable amount of it in county soil survey reports. The Unified Classification, which is widely used in civil engineering today, is based on general textural and performance criteria. It is especially useful first as a coarse-grained-soil information supplement to the USDA scheme and second as a fundamental information source on the performance traits of fine-grained soils.

The Unified Classification recognizes six basic soil types to which are given letter designations:

G—gravel and gravelly soils (basically pebble size, larger than 2 mm diameter)
S—sand and sandy soils
M—very fine sand and silt (inorganic)
C—clays (inorganic)
O—organic silts and clays
P_t—peat

The coarse-grained soils (S and S) are further classified according to uniformity of grain size and the presence of smaller materials such as clay and silt.

W—well graded (i.e., uniformly sized grains) and clean (absence of clays, silts, and organic debris)
C—well graded with clay fraction which binds soil together
P—poorly graded, fairly clean

Three fine-grained soils (M, C, and O) are further classified on the basis of two performance criteria: compressibility and plasticity.

L—low to medium compressibility and low plasticity
H—high compressibility and high plasticity

Compressibility is a measure of the capacity of soil under pressure (weight) to decrease in volume. Loosely packed soils with high water contents—for instance, organic soils—usually show high compressibility. Plasticity, on the other hand, indicates the capacity of a soil under differential stress to deform due to the internal slippage of particles. For example, saturated clayey soils situated on a steep slope may deform by slow flowage, or plastic, movement.

A general classification of soil can often be augmented by the use of a set of geological terminology pertaining to soil origins. Mineral composition and soil texture are largely derived from the parent material, that is, the geological stuff from which the soil formed.

Unified Classification

Classification Based on Soil Origins

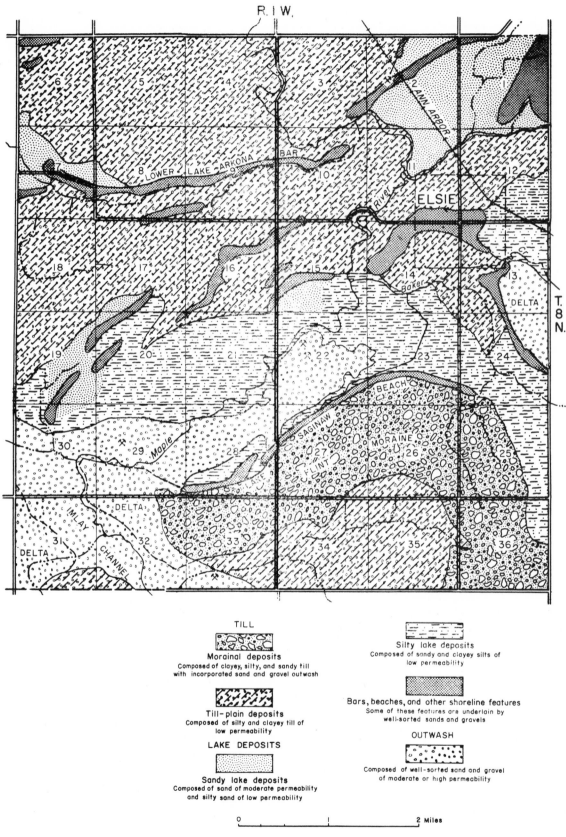

TILL

Morainal deposits
Composed of clayey, silty, and sandy till
with incorporated sand and gravel outwash

Till-plain deposits
Composed of silty and clayey till of
low permeability

LAKE DEPOSITS

Sandy lake deposits
Composed of sand of moderate permeability
and silty sand of low permeability

Silty lake deposits
Composed of sandy and clayey silts of
low permeability

Bars, beaches, and other shoreline features
Some of these features are underlain by
well-sorted sands and gravels

OUTWASH

Composed of well-sorted sand and gravel
of moderate or high permeability

0   1   2 Miles

Figure 3.4. An example of a surface geology map. Such maps are also titled "surficial deposits." (From Vanlier, 1965)

Parent material is decomposed by weathering processes forming chemically stable particle end products, principally silicate minerals in the form of sand, silt, and clay. Once formed, the particles may remain in place to form a residual soil or may be eroded, transported, and deposited by wind, water, or glaciers to form a transported soil. In areas of transported soils, which are often land use problem areas such as floodplains, coastal lowlands, and glaciated terrain, much can be learned about soil composition if the geomorphic processes which deposited the soil particles are known. "Surface geology" maps such as the one shown in Figure 3.4 provide information on the origin of surface materials. In glaciated areas such as the Midwest, deposits termed outwash, kame, and esker are sure indicators of sandy, gravelly soils deposited by glacial meltwater streams whereas deposits termed moraine and till plain are usually indicators of loamy soil composed of a mixture of clay, silt, sand, and larger particles.

Lacking maps on surface geology, firsthand interpretations of soil-forming processes leading to compositional information may be made with the aid of topographic maps, aerial photographs, and field observations. By way of example, in rugged terrain, marked changes in slope inclination usually correlate with (1) changes in the types of erosional-depositional processes or (2) changes in the intensity of a single process that operates over the entire slope. In each case, the result is a corresponding change in soil. Downslope from the bedrock cliff shown in Figure 3.5, the predominant processes and related soil composition would be as follows:

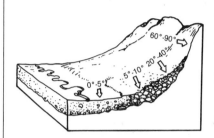

Figure 3.5. This diagram illustrates the changes in soil composition and thickness associated with various angles of a slope.

Slope segment (° angle)	Geomorphic processes	Soil texture	Geomorphic or geologic term
1. 60°–90°	weathering and mass movement (rock falls and slides)	none (solid bedrock)	escarpment, cuesta, scarp, or cliff
2. 20°–40°	rock deposition	cobble and boulder (rock rubble)	talus or scree
3. 5°–10°	runoff, rock deposition	cobble and boulder mixed with sand, silt, clay	footslope (or terrace if steplike in form)
4. 0°–5°	river deposition	sand, silt, clay with fraction larger particles	floodplain

On a vegetated hillslope, instead of a change in the type of slope process, there is likely to be a change in the intensity of a single process corresponding to changes in slope inclination. For instance, the erosive power of runoff increases with slope inclination and distance downhill. Therefore, on normal S-shaped slopes, erosion is most pronounced on the midslope or lower midslope. Here organic-rich topsoil is usually thin, whereas at the footslope,

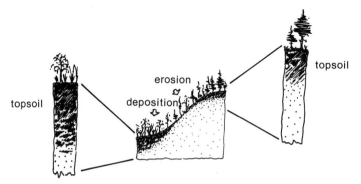

Figure. 3.6. Owing to the downslope changes in the erosive power of runoff, the topsoil layer is usually thickest near the footslope and thinnest near midslope.

topsoil is markedly thicker in part owing to deposition of organic material eroded from upslope (Figure 3.6).

Table 3.2 gives most of the conventional terms used to describe surface geology. To facilitate interpretation and description of soil, the principal process(es), the composition, and the drainage associated with each feature are also given.

TABLE 3.2 PROCESSES, COMPOSITION, AND DRAINAGE COMMONLY ASSOCIATED WITH GEOLOGICAL SURFACE FEATURES

Feature	Process	Composition	Drainage
Alluvial fan	stream deposition on mountain slope	sand, silt, clay with fraction pebbles and cobbles; markedly stratified and highly heterogeneous; all in the form of semiconical-shaped fan	variable; upper portions may be well drained, lower portions may be very poor owing to groundwater seepage
Alluvium	river channel and floodplain deposition	mainly sand, silt, clay with organic fractions locally; stratified and heterogeneous	typically very poor owing to high water table and periodic flooding
Arroyo (also gulch or wash)	stream depositions and erosion	silt, sand, and pebbles in bed and valley of stream in arid setting	poor; subject to seasonal and flash flooding
Barrier beach	deposition by waves and currents	sand and pebbles	good, but water table often within several feet of surface
Beach	shoreline wave action with secondary effects of wind	variable; typically sand and pebbles but may also be clayey and silty or bedrock and rock rubble	good if sandy, but water table usually within several feet of surface
Beach ridge	deposition by waves and wind	mainly sand but pebbles common in lower portion	excellent, especially in those with high elevation
Bog	standing water and organic deposition	organic (muck, peat) with fraction mineral clay	very poor

TABLE 3.2 PROCESSES, COMPOSITION, AND DRAINAGE COMMONLY ASSOCIATED WITH GEOLOGICAL SURFACE FEATURES (cont.)

Feature	Process	Composition	Drainage
Colluvium	integrated deposition from mass movement, runoff, streams	highly heterogeneous, may range from clay to boulders; stratified material mixed with undifferentiated material	highly variable, if situated near footslope, groundwater seepage may be present
Cuesta	complex of weathering and erosion of the outcropping end of bedrock formation	bedrock often with partial coverage of thin soil and talus footslope	good, but groundwater seepage common along footslope
Cusp or cuspate foreland	deposition by waves and currents	sand and pebbles	good, but water table often within several feet of surface
Delta	river deposition	usually clay, silt, and sand with local concentrations of organic material	very poor to poor
Drumlin	deposition and redistribution by glacial ice	clayey with admixture of coarser fractions as large as boulders; whale-shaped hilly form	good to poor
Escarpment (see cuesta)			
Esker	channel deposition by glacial meltwater stream	stratified sand and pebble mixture (gravelly) in the form of a sinuous ridge	excellent
Floodplain	river deposition	*see* alluvium	*see* alluvium
Ground moraine	deposition from glacial ice	often sand, silt, clay admixture, but may be highly variable ranging from compacted clays to sand, pebbles, cobbles, boulders; usually gently rolling	good to poor
Kame	deposition by glacial meltwater stream	mainly stratified sand and gravel in the form of a conical-shaped hill	excellent
Lake plain	wave and current action	clayey with local concentrations of beach and dune sand	poor to fair
Lake terrace	wave erosion and deposition	usually sand and pebbles but may be bedrock or clay and silt	excellent to good
Loess	wind deposition	silt, rather structureless	excellent and good
Marsh	standing water and organic deposition	organic (muck, peat) with fraction mineral clay	very poor

TABLE 3.2 PROCESSES, COMPOSITION, AND DRAINAGE COMMONLY ASSOCIATED WITH GEOLOGICAL SURFACE FEATURES (*cont.*)

Feature	Process	Composition	Drainage
Moraine	deposition from glacial ice	often sand, silt, clay mixture, but may be highly variable ranging from compacted clays to sand, pebbles, cobbles, boulders; usually in form of irregular hilly terrain	good to poor
Outwash plain	deposition over broad area by glacial meltwater streams	sandy	usually excellent, but high water table in some locales
River terrace	river erosion and deposition	variable; stratified clays, silts, sand	excellent to fair
Sand dune (barchans, seifs, parabolic, hairpin, transverse, or coastal)	wind deposition	pure sand	excellent
Scarp (*see* **cuesta**)			
Scree	mass movement (rock falls, rock slides)	cobbles and pebbles in form of 30°–40° slope	excellent
Spit	deposition by waves and currents	sand and pebbles	good, but water table often within several feet of surface
Swamp	standing water and organic deposition	organic (muck, peat) with fraction mineral clay	very poor
Talus	mass movement (rock falls, rock slides)	boulders in form of 30°–40° slope	excellent
Tidal flat	tidal inflow and outflow, wave and current action	sand, silt, or clay with local concentrations of organic material	very poor
Till	deposition from glacial ice	often sand, silt, clay admixture, but may be highly variable ranging from compacted clays to sand, pebbles, cobbles, boulders	good to poor
Till plain	deposition from glacial ice	often sand, silt, clay admixture, but may be highly variable ranging from compacted clays to sand, pebbles, cobbles, boulders; usually gently rolling	good to poor

Due to piecemeal geographical coverage of the United States by soil surveys and the need for information of site-scale detail, it is

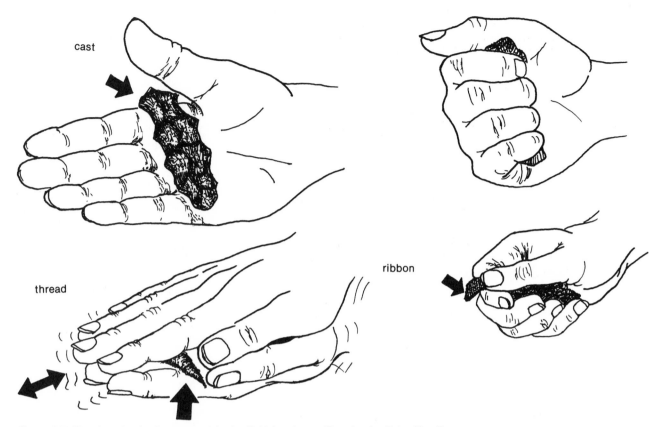

cast

thread

ribbon

Figure 3.7. The three basic shapes used in the field hand test. (Drawing by Peter Van Dusen and Gregory Jones)

often necessary for the planner to generate information on soil texture. The simplest technique currently in use is the field-soil hand test. This test is based on the performance of a hand-sized soil sample when molded into three basic shapes: (1) cast, (2) thread, and (3) ribbon (Figure 3.7). Clay-sized particles are highly cohesive and impart plasticity to a wetted soil sample. Therefore, as the clay content is increased, the capacity of the soil to be molded into more delicate shapes is increased. The opposite is true for sand which lacks cohesiveness. Thus, the performance of the hand-molded soil sample is a good indicator of the relative sand-clay content. With some practice, as many as five USDA soil textures can be identified with the aid of this technique.

Pure sand is incapable of retaining even bulky, crude shapes such as a hand cast. In contrast, clay can be molded into virtually any shape including a fine point and a thin ribbon. Table 3.3 gives the behavior traits of five standard soil types ranging from sandy loam to clay. For a more precise measure of the amount of clay in a soil, the "shaker" technique described below may be employed (Figure 3.8).

Soil samples for hand testing may be extracted with the aid of a shovel or a soil auger (drill). The depth and the spacing of sample points depends on the size of the area and the nature of the proposed use of the land under consideration. If the proposed use is residential with septic sewers, then the depth of sampling ought to be based on the depth of placement of the septic drain field.

Field Hand Test

TABLE 3.3 BEHAVIORAL CHARACTERISTICS OF THE BASIC SHAPES USED IN THE FIELD HAND TEST AND THE SOIL TYPE REPRESENTED BY EACH

Field test (shape)	Soil type				
	Sandy loam	Silty loam	Loam	Clay loam	Clay
Soil cast	Cast bears careful handling without breaking	Cohensionless silty loam bears careful handling without breaking. Better-graded silty loam casts may be handled freely without breaking	Cast may be handled freely without breaking	Cast bears much handling without breaking	Cast can be molded to various shapes without breaking
Soil thread	Thick, crumbly, easily broken	Thick, soft, easily broken	Can be pointed as fine as pencil lead that is easily broken	Strong thread can be rolled to a pinpoint	Strong, plastic thread that can be rolled to a pinpoint
Soil ribbon	Will not form ribbon	Will not form ribbon	Forms short, thick ribbon that breaks under its own weight	Forms thin ribbon that breaks under its own weight	Long, thin flexible ribbon that does not break under its own weight

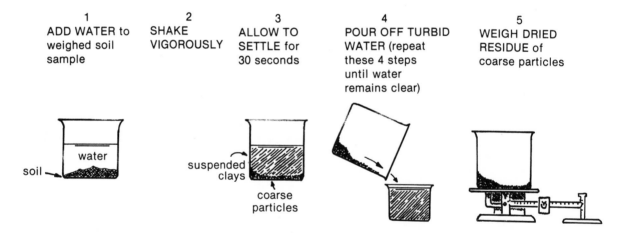

1. ADD WATER to weighed soil sample
2. SHAKE VIGOROUSLY
3. ALLOW TO SETTLE for 30 seconds
4. POUR OFF TURBID WATER (repeat these 4 steps until water remains clear)
5. WEIGH DRIED RESIDUE of coarse particles

6. WEIGHT OF CLAY = weight soil – weight coarse particles

7. PERCENTAGE OF CLAY = $\dfrac{\text{weight of clay}}{\text{weight of sample}} \times 100$

Figure 3.8. When dispersed into water, clay particles will remain suspended for an extended period of time. Therefore, separation of clays from silt, sand, and coarser particles can be accomplished by adding water to a small soil sample, shaking the mixture vigorously, and then pouring off the clay-enriched water. The residue of coarse particles can be dried, weighed, and subtracted from the original sample weight to determine the weight of clays. This figure divided by the weight of the original sample indicates the fraction that clay composed of the original soil sample.

SOIL DRAINAGE

Permeability

Permeability is a measure of the capacity of a soil to transmit water. It is mainly a function of soil texture but is also related to soil water content, vegetation, and interparticle chemical deposits. In general, the larger the soil particles, the larger and the more inter-connected the interparticle voids through which water can perco-late. It follows that high permeability is characteristic of sand whereas low permeability is characteristic of clay, especially com-pacted clay. Among the other variables influencing permeability, vegetation is most noteworthy because roots loosen the compact-ness of soil, forming points of entry and routes of movement for water. Measurement of permeability is based on the time taken for an inch of water to pass through a given quantity of soil. This is expressed as the rate of water transmission and may be stated in the form of a simple formula:

$$\text{Permeability (K)} = \frac{\text{water in inches}}{\text{time in minutes}}$$

Surface permeability, termed infiltration, regulates the amount of precipitation which is converted to surface runoff. For a given slope angle and length, comparative estimates of runoff from place to place can be made on the basis of soil texture and plant cover. Differences in the density and structure of the plant cover affect runoff in several ways. In forested areas precipitation is initially intercepted by the foliage. Once fully wetted, water begins to drop from the canopy and run down the branches to the trunk as stem flow. These processes result in (1) a reduction in the total amount of water which actually reaches the soil and (2) a reduction in the intensity of precipitation at the ground; that is, fall is extended over a longer time period. On the vegetated soil surface, runoff velocity is reduced due to the friction posed by stems and organic debris such as dead leaves, thereby allowing more time for water to enter

Runoff

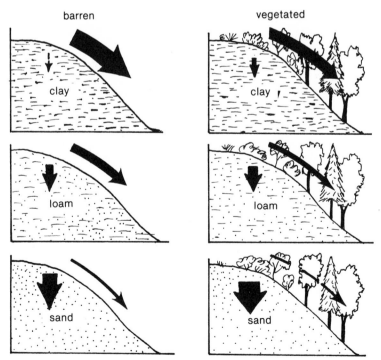

Figure 3.9. A set of schematic diagrams that attempts to show the relationship between runoff and soil texture and vegetative cover.

Runoff and Land Use

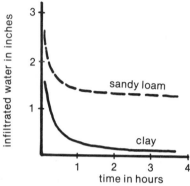

Figure 3.10. *This graph shows the marked difference in the infiltration capacities of a sandy soil and a clay soil. Under intensive rainfall, the clay may yield five to six times more runoff than the sandy soil.*

the soil. In sum, the net effect of the plant cover is to reduce the volume and intensity of runoff from that which could be expected on barren soil. The diagrams in Figure 3.9 are an attempt to portray schematically the influence of soil texture and plant cover on runoff. The relative intensities of runoff and infiltration are indicated by the sizes of the arrows.

The fact that clayey soils produce a significantly greater surface runoff from a given amount of rainfall or snowmelt than do sandy soils is often an important consideration in land use planning. Under residential land use, for example, clayey soils may require construction of more elaborate drainage systems than are necessary for sandy soils (Figure 3.10). Indeed, to prevent basement and surface flooding, it may be advisable to tile yards, maximize storm-sewer capacities and densities, as well as build drainage ditches. In addition, allowances must be made for the increased runoff produced by the impervious surface materials of developed areas. When residential areas become partially covered by concrete, asphalt, and roofs, total runoff may be increased as much as 100 to 200 percent (Figure 3.11).

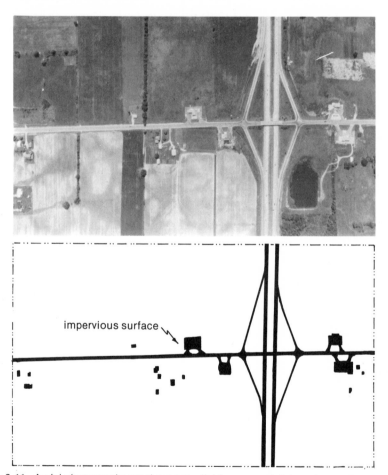

Figure 3.11. *Aerial photographs are the most reliable source of data on impervious surfaces. Hard-surface roads, parking lots, buildings, houses, and related features are easily discernible on standard black-and-white aerial photographs such as shown on the left. For actual areal determinations, the grid method described in Chapter 1 is adequate in most cases. For very large areas, estimates can be based on population density or on an areal sampling.*

Studies show that infiltration over large areas of inner cities is so low that virtually all precipitation is converted to runoff. Outward from the interior of an urbanized area, the percentage of impervious surface decreases, resulting in correspondingly lower average values of runoff. Measurements have demonstrated that the increased runoff due to the impervious land use surfaces in urban areas, together with related storm-sewer systems, has increased both the magnitude and frequency of stream flooding. Thus, the curious fact that stream discharge becomes "flashier" rather than more subdued as its drainage area becomes urbanized (Figure 3.12).

PHOTO BY W. M. MARSH

Figure 3.12. Storm-sewer outlet, Thames River, London, England. The sign offers warning to beach combers (lower left) of the possibility of massive storm-sewer discharge from urban runoff. The left bank of the Thames is just to the right of the photograph.

Although a detailed discussion of stream discharge and flooding is presented in Chapter 5, suffice it to point out here that urbanized streams respond more acutely to rainfall with quicker and higher rises. This is illustrated in the hydrograph in Figure 3.13 which plots the rise in discharge over hours time resulting from a given amount of rain *before* and *after* urbanization of the watershed. Most certainly, land use planning for urban floodplains is fundamentally more problematic than it is for rural floodplains.

Most land use planning sites present a variety of land covers with different infiltration and runoff rates. Determination of runoff for such sites, though inherently more tedious than for homogeneous sites, may be necessary in order to help establish use priorities, design constraints, and cost estimates. The relevance of information on runoff is demonstrable not only with respect to the land use plan but also with respect to the quality of natural waters, since most land uses markedly affect the physical and chemical character of runoff (Figure 3.14).

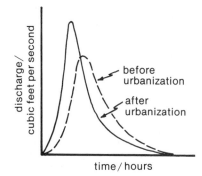

Figure 3.13. A stream hydrograph depicts the rise and fall of flow in response to a given amount of rainfall. The broken and solid graph lines represent the typical flow responses of a single stream to a given rainfall before and after urbanization of its drainage area (after Leopold, 1968).

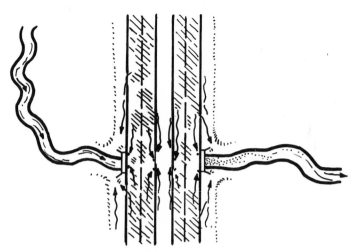

Figure 3.14. Measurements of stream turbidity made during light runoff (produced by 0.12 inches of rain over four hours) from a short section of highway over a small stream near Ann Arbor, Michigan, revealed that suspended sediment (turbidity) increased 250 percent from the upstream to the downstream side of the culvert. Observations indicate that runoff from city streets may increase stream turbidity near a storm-sewer terminus by more than 1000 percent.

Drainage Density

A distinction may be made between surface water and surface runoff. Runoff is flowing surface water generated by a rainfall. For purposes of land use planning, it is defined as discharge in some sort of channel. Discharge is a measure of the volume of water passing a point along a channel, say, a bridge or culvert, per unit of time and is usually expressed in cubic feet per second (cfs). Since channel flow is the most efficient means of water movement, the higher the density of channels on a site, the greater the runoff from a given rainfall. Sloping ground integrated by a dense network of channels, whether gullies, tiles, storm sewers, or stream channels,

High Channel
Density

Low Channel
Density

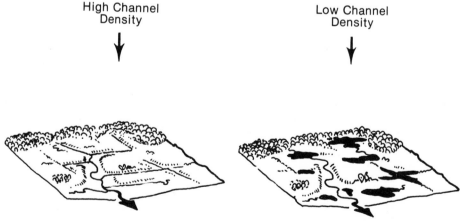

Figure 3.15. High drainage density tends to minimize local storage or ponding of water and, in turn, maximize the rate of runoff. In urbanized areas, natural channels are extended into the land in the form of storm sewers, ditches, tiles, and gutters, often resulting in drainage densities several times greater than under normal conditions. Information on natural drainage densities and patterns can usually be derived directly from large-scale topographic contour maps. Information on artificial drainage systems is usually available from several sources including county drain commissioners, county and state highway departments, health and sanitary departments, and the U.S. Army Corps of Engineers.

tends to maximize runoff discharge. In contrast, flat ground with a nonintegrated drainage net tends to minimize runoff. Such sites are characterized by slow runoff, often in the form of sheet flow, as well as large areas of standing water as shown in Figure 3.15.

If surface water leaves a site via a single channel and the area drained does not exceed 1 square mile, then a quantitative estimate of discharge can be made based on three variables:

  C = coefficient of runoff
  I = intensity of rainfall in inches per hour
  a = drainage area in acres

These are combined into the formula,

  Q = CIa

the product of which is peak discharge (Q) in cubic feet per second.[1] If the drainage area includes, for example, three surface covers each with a different C and a value, then the total discharge is equal to the sum of the products of the three sets of values:

  $Q = (C_i \cdot I \cdot a_i) + (C_w \cdot I \cdot a_w) + (C_p \cdot I \, a_p)$

The subscripts denote three example surface covers:

  i = impervious surface
  w = woodland
  p = pasture

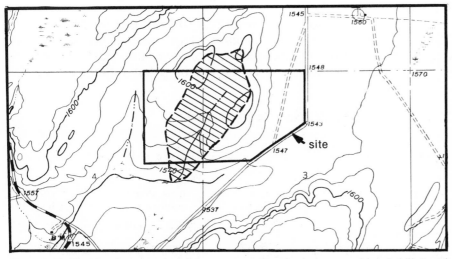

Figure 3.16. The site shown on the left is representative of a drainage problem in hilly terrain. The central section is drained by a stream whose drainage area, delineated by the broken line, extends beyond the site to the north. Determination of discharge for this section of the site must include the water contributed by the upper drainage area. Total discharge from this section represents peak channel flow in cubic feet per second at the point where the stream channel leaves the site, namely, the southern border. The remainder of the site is drained by several small channels each of which represents a separate discharge problem.

[1]Q is derived without converting *inches* per hour (I) and acres of area (a) to other units because it happens that true units, *inches-acres per hours,* are equivalent to *cubic feet per second.* Acre-feet of runoff per hour can be computed by converting rainfall intensity from inches to feet. To convert discharge (Q) to cubic meters, multiply cubic feet by the factor 0.02832.

Determination of Runoff Discharge: The Rational Method

Determination of drainage area can be made from aerial photographs or topographic maps. Several area measurement techniques may be employed, and these are discussed in Chapter 1, "Spatial Organization." In computing drainage area, care should be taken to determine whether the site lies within a single watershed. If not, the drainage divide must be located and the respective drainage areas computed (Figure 3.16). For sites situated in the lower part of a larger drainage area, additional runoff will be received from the upslope area, and this must be added to the discharge from the site itself. Again, definition of drainage area is predicated on the assumption that runoff leaves the site in one channel. If water leaves by more than one channel, the drainage areas of each must be defined and the runoff computed for each.

Coefficient of Runoff

The coefficient of runoff represents the fraction of rainfall which is not lost to infiltration. Expressed as a dimensionless number between 0 and 1.0, where 1.0 represents 100 percent runoff, this coefficient is based on field measurements of surface water available for runoff on various surface covers. The values in Table 3.4 are given by the American Society of Civil Engineers for standard land uses. For rural surfaces, the values in Table 3.5 can be used for estimating the coefficient of runoff.

For surfaces not listed in this table, it is often possible to estimate the coefficient. For example, formerly cultivated agricultural land now occupied by an irregular cover of weeds could be designated as intermediate between pasture and cultivated. If classed as rolling with clay loam soil, such a site would be given a coefficient of runoff of 0.48. Values for construction sites are generally equivalent to those of cultivated land.

Rainfall Intensity

Average hourly intensities of rainfall (I) for the United States and Canada amount to a small fraction of an inch of water and are incapable of producing strong runoff on even the most impervious surfaces. Rainfall intensities of 1 inch or greater have a low fre-

TABLE 3.4 COEFFICIENTS OF RUNOFF FOR DEVELOPED AREAS

Type of drainage area	Runoff coefficient, C	Type of drainage area	Runoff coefficient, C
Lawns:		Industrial:	
Sandy soil, flat, 2%	0.05–0.10	Light areas	0.50–0.80
Sandy soil, average, 2–7%	0.10–0.15	Heavy areas	0.60–0.90
Sandy soil, steep, 7%	0.15–0.20	Parks, cemeteries	0.10–0.25
Heavy soil, flat, 2%	0.13–0.17		
Heavy soil, average 2–7%	0.18–0.22	Playgrounds	0.20–0.35
Heavy soil, steep, 7%	0.25–0.35	Railroad-yard areas	0.20–0.40
Business:		Unimproved areas	0.10–0.30
Downtown areas	0.70–0.95		
Neighborhood areas	0.50–0.70	Streets:	
Residential:		Asphalt	0.70–0.95
Single-family areas	0.30–0.50	Concrete	0.80–0.95
Multiunits, detached	0.40–0.60	Brick	0.70–0.85
Multiunits, attached	0.60–0.75	Drives and walks	0.75–0.85
Suburban	0.25–0.40	Roofs	0.75–0.95
Apartment-dwelling areas	0.50–0.70		

SOURCE: The American Society of Civil Engineers.

TABLE 3.5 COEFFICIENTS OF RUNOFF FOR RURAL AREAS

Topography and vegetation	Open sandy loam	Clay and silt loam	Tight clay
Woodland			
Flat (0–5% slope)	0.10	0.30	0.40
Rolling (5–10% slope)	0.25	0.35	0.50
Hilly (10–30% slope)	0.30	0.50	0.60
Pasture			
Flat	0.10	0.30	0.40
Rolling	0.16	0.36	0.55
Hilly	0.22	0.42	0.60
Cultivated			
Flat	0.30	0.50	0.60
Rolling	0.40	0.60	0.70
Hilly	0.52	0.72	0.82

quency of occurrence, usually several years, and present the critical drainage problems. It is these infrequent rainstorms which bear careful consideration in evaluating runoff as a factor in land use planning. Rainfall intensity-frequency maps of the United States are available from the USDA or the office of any state climatologist

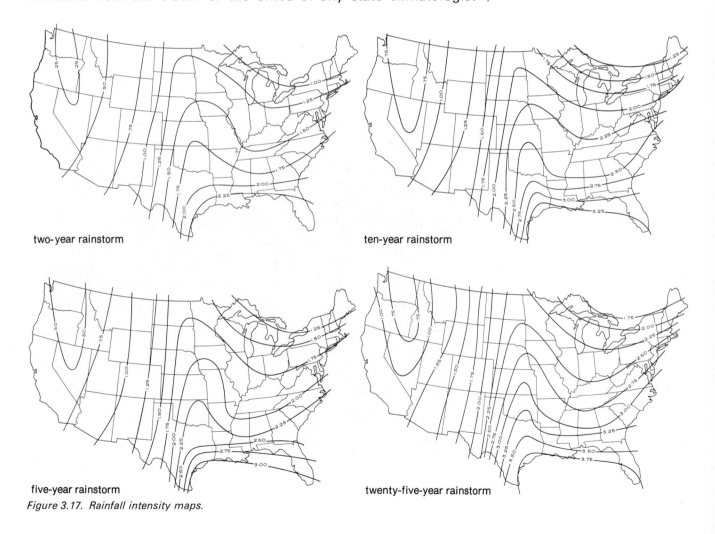

two-year rainstorm

ten-year rainstorm

five-year rainstorm

twenty-five-year rainstorm

Figure 3.17. Rainfall intensity maps.

(National Oceanic and Atmospheric Administration), and four are reproduced in Figure 3.17. They depict the maximum hourly rainfall intensity which can be expected in a two-year, five-year, ten-year, and twenty-five-year period.

SOIL EROSION

Land use planners are frequently faced with the problem of evaluating the feasibility of several sites for a proposed land use. Soil erosion may be a meaningful criterion to aid in evaluation, particularly in hilly terrain. The susceptibility of soil to erosion, termed erodibility, is controlled by vegetation, particle size, and cohesiveness as well as by slope geometry and the intensity and frequency of rainfall or wind. With more than 75 percent of the root mass of most plants concentrated in the upper foot of soil, vegetation is a vital soil stabilizer. Plant roots bind together aggregates of soil

PHOTO BY TOMMY G. BURDETTE

Figure 3.18. The loose sand in this photograph is protected from wind erosion by the grass cover. Despite the low density of stems, the grass presents a sufficiently rough frictional surface to lower wind speed beyond the threshold necessary for erosion. This carries important implications for management of dust and other debris which are blown from sanitary landfills into nearby developed areas.

particles, thereby increasing soil resistance to erosion by runoff or to displacement by mass movement. In addition, foliage and surface organic litter greatly mitigate the erosive (splash) power of raindrops, a most effective erosional process on barren soil. In brief, studies have repeatedly demonstrated that vegetation is the most important single factor controlling soil erosion on a given surface.

Wind Erosion

Soil erosion by wind is reduced to negligible levels by a plant cover of essentially any size. This is due to the fact that the effective frictional boundary of the wind is forced off the soil surface onto the body and foliage of the plant, leaving calm air next to the ground. Although not as prevalent as erosion problems related to runoff, in arid, semiarid, and coastal settings, wind erosion may be the predominant soil problem. In fact, active sand dunes may be problematic in coastal and desert environments. Of greater economic import, however, is wind erosion of cultivated fields, particularly silt and organic materials which are especially susceptible to movement by wind (Figure 3.18).

Erosion by Runoff

The influence of particle size and cohesiveness on soil erodibility to running water was demonstrated many years ago in an experiment conducted by the Swedish geoscientist Hjulstrom. He measured the water velocities at which the thresholds of erosion were reached for clay, silt, sand, and pebbles. The results, shown in Figure 3.19, revealed that sand yielded first, that is, eroded at the lowest velocity. In contrast, the threshold velocities for clay and pebbles were much higher in response to the cohesiveness of the former and the weight of the latter. Should a site be stripped of its plant cover, as is often the case during construction, this indicates that it is the sandy soils which would yield the most sediment to runoff.

Estimating Soil Erosion

Holding slope geometry and precipitation rates constant, a qualitative estimate of soil erodibility can be made on the basis of soil texture and plant cover. As a rule, unvegetated soil in the sand-silt-clay textural range is more susceptible to erosion than vegetated soil of the same texture. Unvegetated sandy loam soils tend to be highly erodible owing to (1) a capacity to produce fairly intensive runoff due to the clay content and (2) a low resistance to erosion due to a substantial sand content. Cobble- and boulder-sized particles are beyond the erosive competence of most runoff except that of large rivers. Compacted clay, especially if plant covered, is highly resistant to runoff.

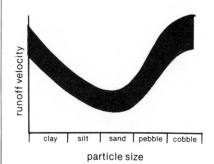

Figure 3.19. The relative threshold velocities for erosion by runoff of different-sized particles.

If vegetation and soil texture are held constant, relative estimates of erosion by runoff can be made on the basis of slope geometry. As was indicated in the previous chapter, long slopes collect much rainfall and produce a large volume of runoff. Steep slopes are characterized by higher rates of erosion than are short, gentle slopes. Table 3.6 gives the ratio of increase in sediment production as a function of slope steepness and length. This table is based largely on measurements made on farmland by soil scientists and agronomists, and since much of the development on the urban fringe involves former agricultural land, the data are reasonably applicable to site-scale land use planning. Utilization of this table necessitates slope measurements from topographic contour maps as described in the previous chapter, "Slope and Topography."

TABLE 3.6 SLOPE GEOMETRY FACTOR

Slope Length in Feet	Slope Steepness in Percent														
	4	6	8	10	12	14	16	18	20	25	30	35	40	45	50
50	.3	.5	.7	1.0	1.3	1.6	2.0	2.4	3.0	4.3	6.0	7.9	10.1	12.6	15.4
100	.4	.7	1.0	1.4	1.8	2.3	2.8	3.4	4.2	6.1	8.5	11.2	14.4	17.9	21.7
150	.5	.8	1.2	1.6	2.2	2.8	3.5	4.2	5.1	7.5	10.4	13.8	17.6	21.9	26.6
200	.6	.9	1.4	1.9	2.6	3.3	4.1	4.8	5.9	8.7	12.0	15.9	20.3	25.2	30.7
250	.7	1.0	1.6	2.2	2.9	3.7	4.5	5.4	6.6	9.7	13.4	17.8	22.7	28.2	34.4
300	.7	1.2	1.7	2.4	3.1	4.0	5.0	5.9	7.2	10.7	14.7	19.5	24.9	30.9	37.6
350	.8	1.2	1.8	2.6	3.4	4.3	5.4	6.4	7.8	11.5	15.9	21.0	26.9	33.4	40.6
400	.8	1.3	2.0	2.7	3.6	4.6	5.7	6.8	8.3	12.3	17.0	22.5	28.7	35.7	43.5
450	.9	1.4	2.1	2.9	3.8	4.9	6.1	7.2	8.9	13.1	18.0	23.8	30.5	37.9	46.1
500	.9	1.5	2.2	3.1	4.0	5.2	6.4	7.6	9.3	13.7	19.0	25.1	32.1	39.9	48.6
550	1.0	1.6	2.3	3.2	4.2	5.4	6.7	8.0	9.8	14.4	19.9	26.4	33.7	41.9	50.9
600	1.0	1.6	2.4	3.3	4.4	5.7	7.0	8.3	10.2	15.1	20.8	27.5	35.2	43.7	53.2
650	1.1	1.7	2.5	3.5	4.6	5.9	7.3	8.7	10.6	15.7	21.7	28.7	36.6	45.5	55.4
700	1.1	1.8	2.6	3.6	4.8	6.1	7.6	9.0	11.1	16.3	22.5	29.7	38.0	47.2	57.5
750	1.1	1.8	2.7	3.7	4.9	6.3	7.9	9.3	11.4	16.8	23.3	30.8	39.3	48.9	59.5
800	1.2	1.9	2.8	3.8	5.1	6.5	8.1	9.6	11.8	17.4	24.1	31.8	40.6	50.5	61.4
900	1.2	2.0	3.0	4.1	5.4	6.9	8.6	10.2	12.5	18.5	25.5	33.7	43.1	53.5	65.2
1000	1.3	2.1	3.1	4.3	5.7	7.3	9.1	10.8	13.2	19.5	26.9	35.5	45.4	56.4	68.7

As the preceding discussion begins to suggest, prediction of the *quantity* of soil loss per acre is very difficult, if not impossible, in most settings. However, if soil texture does not vary greatly from site to site, the slope geometry table can be used to generate a rank order of sites based on erosion potential. For instance, if the average slope lengths and percentages for three sites are (1) 55 feet and 10 percent, (2) 125 feet and 8 percent, and (3) 75 feet and 16 percent, the soil loss ratios are, respectively, (1) 1.0, (2) 1.1, and (3) 2.40. Clearly site 3 has the greatest potential for erosion, more than twice that of sites 1 and 2.

Since the intensity of runoff is strongly influenced by precipitation rates, a gross estimate of erosion can also be made on the basis of the rainfall- and frequency-intensity data compiled from the maps in Figure 3.17. As with most climatic data, this information is generalized and basically useful only at a regional scale. At a site scale, it is advisable to base determinations of erosion potential on slope geometry, plant cover, and soil texture. However, if it is necessary to assess erosion potentials of different areas within a region the size of most states, relative rainfall-erosion information may be useful. The map in Figure 3.20 shows the distribution of the average annual erosion index values for the eastern half of the United States. These values are an indication of the *relative* intensity of erosion which can be expected on *comparable sites* in the eastern half of the United States. That is to say, it indicates that for sites with comparable geometries, soils, and plant covers, twelve

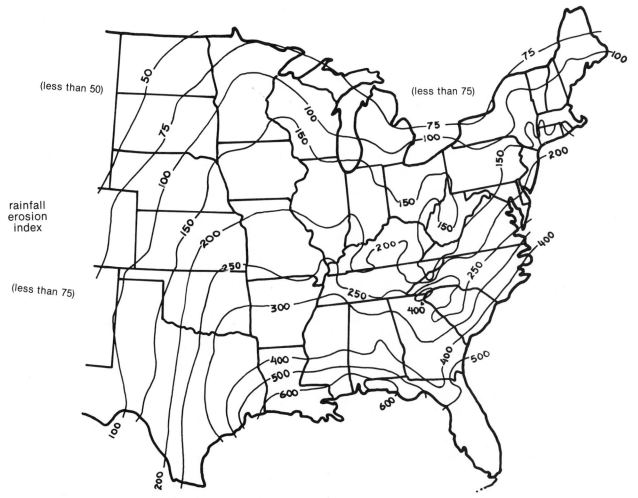

Figure 3.20. The rainfall erosion index for the eastern half of the United States. Virtually all values for the Western states are less than 50.

times more erosion could be expected in southern Louisiana than in central North Dakota. And likewise, two times more erosion could be expected in southern Alabama than in northern Alabama on comparable sites. The values depicted on the map are based on the erosive energy of total annual rainfall times the average annual maximum intensity of the thirty-minute rainfall for the location under consideration.

Finally, for the major agricultural states, it may be possible to integrate all four of the major soil erosion factors into a formula called the "universal soil loss equation." Despite its title, this equation has real utility only in states for which field tests have been conducted to measure the *erodibility* of the various soils. These tests are usually undertaken for each soil series of a state by the Soil Conservation Service (SCS). The universal soil loss equation combines the erodibility factor (K) with the factors of plant cover (C), rainfall erosion index (R), and slope geometry (S) (steepness and length) to provide an estimate of soil loss in tons per acre (A):

$$A = K \cdot R \cdot C \cdot S$$

The rainfall erosion value may be read from the map in Figure

Universal Soil Loss Equation

3.20 and slope geometry factor may be read as the soil loss ratio in Table 3.6. The plant-cover factor can be generalized into three categories:

	C value
Well-established grass (or comparable herb cover)	0.01 to 0.005
Weeds (irregular cover)	0.20 to 0.10
Unvegetated (disturbed)	1.0

The erodibility factor (K) for each soil series, if available for your state, can be obtained from the county or state Soil Conservation Service. It is given as a number between 0 and 1.0, where 1.0 represents those soils with the highest potential erodibility. In some cases two numbers are given for each series, one for undisturbed and one for disturbed soil. The latter is a soil which has been tilled or rearranged by construction processes.

The accuracy of erosion projections based on the universal soil loss equation can be maximized if the site is analyzed for variations in slope, plant cover, and soil. Analysis can be made from soils maps, topographic contour maps, and aerial photographs, as well as from onsite field inspection. This provides the rationale for delineating relatively homogeneous parcels within the site based on slope, soil, and plant cover factors. As a construction site in central Illinois, the area in Figure 3.21 could yield more than 2000 tons of sediment per year. This is based on a classification of the site into two parcels, denoted A and B. The northern parcel has an area of 2.8 acres, an average slope of 33 percent, an average slope length of 150 feet, and a soil erodibility factor of 0.23. These combine with a rainfall erosion factor of 175 and a plant-cover factor of 1.0 to produce an estimated annual soil loss of 1364 tons, or 487 tons per acre.

K (erodibility) = 0.23 (from SCS data)
R (rainfall erosion) = 175 (from rainfall erosion map)
C (plant cover) = 1.0 (barren construction site)
S (slope geometry) = 12.1 (from slope geometry table)

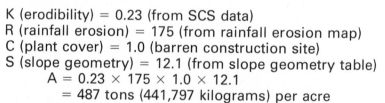

A = 0.23 × 175 × 1.0 × 12.1
  = 487 tons (441,797 kilograms) per acre

Parcel B has an area of 7 acres, an average slope length of 450 feet, an average slope of 7 percent, and a soil erodibility factor of 0.31. With rainfall erosion and plant-cover factors the same as parcel A, these 7 acres would produce a total of about 665 tons (603,274 kilograms) of sediment per year, or 95 tons (86,182 kilograms) per acre per year. The marked difference in estimated erosion on the two parcels is mainly due to the difference in slope angle. It is especially important to note that if both parcels were fully covered by ground plants, soil erosion would fall to about 15 tons (13,607 kilograms) per year.

EROSION, SEDIMENTATION, AND LAND USE

Recent studies in urbanized areas have demonstrated a rather striking relationship between land use on one hand and soil erosion

Computing Soil Erosion Loss

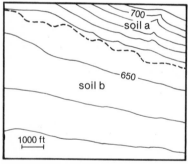

Figure 3.21. As a construction site in central Illinois, parcel A would annually yield as much as 487 tons of sediment per acre and parcel B as much as 95 tons per acre.

Urbanization and Soil Erosion

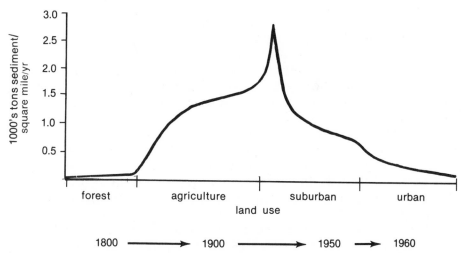

Figure 3.22. A diagram showing the changes in sediment released by erosion as related to land use (after Wolman, 1967).

and stream sedimentation on the other (Knott, 1973; Wolman and Schick, 1967). They show that changes from natural—say, forested—conditions to virtually any human use initiates a sharp rise in erosion and stream sedimentation. If one could trace the long-term sequence of land uses on a site subjected to urbanization, the record of erosion and sedimentation would likely resemble the graph in Figure 3.22. Measurements would initially show a strong increase related to land clearing and the inception of agriculture. A second increase would accompany the conversion of agricultural land to suburban residential uses. Finally, erosion and sedimentation would decline as suburbanization is completed.

Simply stated, those activities which bare the soil, especially during the peak runoff season, usually induce the greatest erosion and stream sedimentation. Loss of plant cover, its root network, and its humus layer maximize the potential for erosion in virtually any setting. The data in Table 3.7 are from a two-year sedimentation study of a small drainage basin in the San Francisco Bay area and are representative of yearly sediment yields from open space (vegetated land), urban (hard surface and lawns), construction (nonvegetated soil), and agricultural (seasonally vegetated and barren soil). If we substitute time for space and imagine a sequential change from open space to agricultural to construction to urban, one can envision the magnitude of change in soil erosion which accompanies the major phases of urbanization.

Sedimentation and soil erosion studies generally show that of the two high-yield land uses, construction sites are usually the most severely eroded. Movement of sediment from the site by runoff tends to be highly variable, depending on runoff intensity, soil texture, and nearness to stream channels. Much of the coarse material (sand and pebbles) is deposited in low spots in and around the site itself. That which reaches streams is often deposited in pools or farm ponds. In extreme cases, small streams may become choked with sediments rendering culverts and storm-sewer outlets inoperative. Clay and fine silt are carried farthest from the site. This is especially evident during periods of peak runoff as plumes of

TABLE 3.7 ANNUAL SEDIMENT YIELDS, COLMA CREEK BASIN, CALIFORNIA, FOR 1967 AND 1970

Land use	Average tons per square mile per year
Open space	382
Agricultural	25,400
Construction	32,750
Urban	938

SOURCE: Knott, 1973, Table 13; data from drainage area upstream from Colma Creek gauging station.

Erosion of Construction Sites

Identifying Stream Sedimentation Points

turbid water can often be seen emanating downstream from construction sites. Much of the clay may be carried far downstream into lakes, ponds, reservoirs, and harbors.

Assessment of the potential for stream sedimentation from a proposed construction site can be made from topographic maps and aerial photographs. Basic slope analysis coupled with determination of the nearness of the site of a stream, as suggested in the example at the end of the previous chapter, is sufficient to identify most potentially severe problems. Some cases, however, may require somewhat more detailed analysis, especially if the site is not situated directly on a permanently flowing stream. This may entail mapping the flow lines of runoff on a topographic map, as might be the case with the site delineated in Figure 3.23. If the flow lines are well defined and lead directly to a flowing stream, as in the northern sector of the site, then development of the site may produce a serious threat of stream sedimentation. On the other hand, if the routes of overland flow are not integrated or are closed (not through-flowing), then the chances of stream sedimentation are diminished. The west-central sector of the site in Figure 3.23 is a good example of a closed drainage pattern.

Finally, throughout most of the United States, there appear to be seasonal variations in the sediment yields from construction sites. Those which are active or left idle during the winter-spring season,

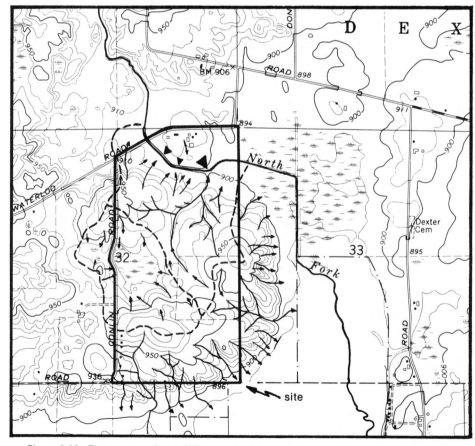

drainage pattern
formed by runoff

drainage divide

flowing stream

point of potentially
severe sedimentation

2000 ft

Figure 3.23. The pattern of runoff from a site based on topographic contours.

when soil moisture and runoff are highest, are most susceptible to severe erosion. In addition to suggesting site design features such as settling ponds and check dams, recommendations for construction schedules which minimize site exposure during the winter and spring may be helpful in averting high levels of stream sedimentation.

SUBSURFACE DRAINAGE AND GROUNDWATER

Below the soil surface infiltration, water moves outward and downward into the soil. Although the rate of percolation is mainly controlled by soil texture, the volume of water which can be received by the soil is controlled by soil porosity and the volume of soil above the water table. Porosity is the total void space between soil particles. The water table represents the upper surface of the groundwater, that is, the saturated subsoil zone. Above the water table only molecular water is permanently held in the soil, as is shown in Figure 3.24. This water usually occupies a small fraction of the total interparticle space, and, therefore, air may constitute as much as 20 percent of the soil volume. Percolating water temporarily fills these spaces on its way to the water table. If the total volume of these spaces, that is, porosity, is small and depth of soil above the water table is slight, then the volume of percolating water which can be held is also slight. If the rate and volume of water input to a

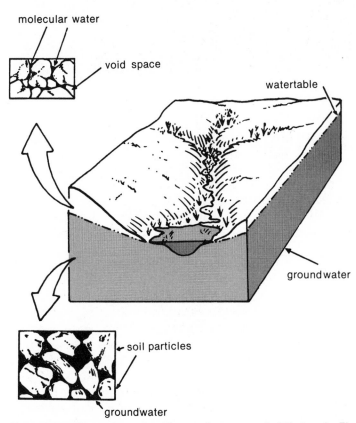

Figure 3.24. The configuration of groundwater zone in hilly terrain. The enlargements show molecular water and groundwater relative to the soil particles. (Illustration by W. M. Marsh)

Septic Drain Field Percolation Test

soil exceed its percolation capacity and gross porosity, then surface seepage may result.

Surface seepage conditions in septic drain fields may produce health hazards and pollution of natural waters. This can be avoided by testing the percolation capacity of the soil prior to building. This is a test of field permeability (as opposed to laboratory permeability tests) and usually involves the following steps:

1. Excavate a small pit about 2 by 2 by 2 foot (the exact dimensions may be dictated by state or local policy).

2. Fill the pit with water and allow to drain completely.

3. Refill with water, allow to drain, and determine the average time taken for the water to fall 1 inch, that is, the percolation rate (Figure 3.25).

Figure 3.25. A seepage zone in an expressway slope cut.

PHOTO BY W. M. MARSH AND G. D. BISHOP

TABLE 3.8 SOIL PERCOLATION RATES AND SIZE OF DISPOSAL AREAS

Percolation rate (average minutes for water to fall 1 inch)	Minimum disposal area (sq ft) required per bedroom
2 or less	85
3	100
4	115
5	125
10	165
15	190
30	250
45	300
60	300

Generally, if the percolation rate exceeds 60 minutes, the soil is unsuited for residential septic-tank facilities no matter how large the disposal field. At rates less than 60 minutes, a specified number of square feet of disposal field are required per bedroom (2 persons) per residence. An example table for a Michigan county is given in Table 3.8. Since it is not uncommon for water tables to fluctuate several feet from season to season, drain fields can become inoperative in the winter and spring due to high groundwater. After examination of the site, if this condition is suspected, several percolation tests in different seasons might be recommended.

Slope is also an important consideration in evaluating site suitability for septic drain fields. Since the passage of time is necessary for waste water to percolate from the drain tiles into the soil, it is advisable to lay the tiles at very gentle gradients to induce slow flow through them. Ideally, drains should be constructed on slopes with gradients less than 3 percent. Slopes up to 8 percent inclination may be used for drain fields; however, care must be taken to lay the tiles at gradients lower than the slope itself. Slopes steeper than 8 to 10 percent pose definite limitations for septic drain fields.

Slope and Septic Drain Fields

Use of such a slope can result in concentrated surface seepage near the lower end of the drain field.

SLOPE FAILURE RELATED TO GROUNDWATER

The water table generally follows the topographic configuration of the ground surface. It follows that on sloping terrain, groundwater is inclined in various directions. Along these inclines, called hydraulic gradients, groundwater moves at rates controlled by the steepness of the gradient and the permeability of the soil. A change in surface topography too abrupt to produce a corresponding change in groundwater elevation may result in interception of the water table by the surface as shown in the photograph in Figure 3.25. This condition will produce groundwater seepage at the surface. In sandy soils, permanent springs may actually form, whereas in clayey soils, with slower seepage rates, perennial surface dampness may develop.

Outflow of groundwater along a slope often leads to slope failure and erosion. This is related to three processes. First, the addition of water to clayey material produces a consistency change which reduces the resistance of the material to deformational forces, or shear stress. This is based on the fact that as water is added to clayey soil, it undergoes a sequence of phase changes; that is, its physical state changes from that of a solid to a plastic and finally to a liquid when fully saturated. The difference in moisture content between the beginning of the plastic phase and the beginning of the liquid phase is called the plastic limit. Depending on the type and the particle structure of the clays, the plastic limit varies considerably in soils. Since failure by flowage is most probable in the liquid state—because the resistance to shear stress is lowest—soils with low plastic limits, that is, those which become fluidlike with relatively small additions of water, are very unstable in slopes with groundwater seepage (Figure 3.26). Recall that the Unified soil classification scheme offers an indication of relative plasticity for fine-grained soils.

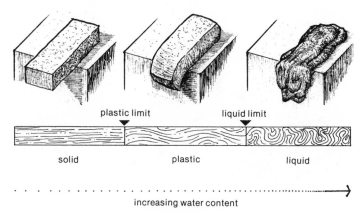

plastic limit   liquid limit

solid   plastic   liquid

increasing water content

Figure 3.26. These illustrations attempt to portray schematically the relationship between the water content and the behavior of clayey soil when placed under gravitational stress. As the water content is increased below, the strength of the soil to resist deformation is decreased (above). (Illustration by Gregory Jones)

Seepage

Pore Water Pressure

A second groundwater process inducing slope failure is pore water pressure. Under the pressure from the weight of the groundwater upslope, soil particles are driven apart, thereby reducing interparticle binding strength. Often working in combination with the plasticity factor, pore water pressure markedly reduces the capacity of soil to maintain a slope as is demonstrated in Figure 3.27. As the water table rises and steepens in the spring season or with the raising of a reservoir, slope stability may decline in response to increasing soil pore water pressure.

Sapping

The third slope process associated with groundwater is the erosion of fine particles by seepage outflow. Particles loosened by pore water pressure, for example, are readily transported by even the most miniscule flows. This process, known as sapping, and a similar process, called piping, which forms small tunnels along seepage lines, contribute to the weakening of slopes by removing supportive material. Points of concentrated sapping and piping often lead to gully formation, which, augmented by surface runoff, retreat at accelerated rates.

Parallel Slope Retreat

The processes of slope failure described above often menace developed areas for many years after construction. Under certain conditions, an activated slope can retreat a distance of many feet while maintaining a relatively constant angle, that is, without growing progressively lower. This phenomenon is known as parallel slope retreat and is dependent on three sequentially interrelated processes:

1. Undercutting of the footslope by sapping, piping, stream erosion, or mechanical excavation, resulting in loss of support strength in the lower slope.

2. Failure of the slope above the undercut.

3. Removal of the failure debris from the base of the slope by natural or mechanical means.

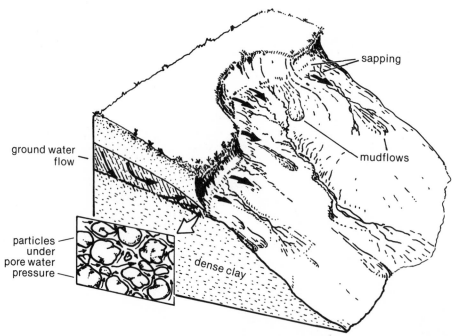

Figure 3.27. *Slope failure related to groundwater seepage and pore water pressure.* (Drawing by W. M. Marsh)

Once this debris is removed, the slope angle is brought up to its former inclination, and the sequence may repeat itself. Slopes with highly active footslopes and efficient debris removal processes have been known to retreat hundreds of feet in a period of several years.

In many cases, early recommendations in the site selection procedure may help to avoid problems of chronically active slopes. An estimate of the susceptibility of slopes to failure due to groundwater seepage is possible if several lines of evidence are examined. First, a survey of hillslopes for evidence of seepage zones is necessary. These features are often marked by a distinctive vegetative cover. In tree-covered areas, seepage zones are often distinguished by nonwoody, blade-leaf vegetation—for example, reeds and cattails—whereas in treeless areas, they are often distinguished by patches of trees or shrubs.

A second consideration is the soil type. If consolidated bedrock is the major constituent, a slope stands little chance of failure in spite of seepage. In contrast, clayey soils, if steepened and devegetated, may be instantly activated and remain so for years. Sandy soils tend to be somewhat intermediate between bedrock and clays. Although they do not liquefy with input of water, they do respond to pore water pressure, and under such conditions behave as a weak plastic, flowing short distances downslope.

The fastest slope retreat known to us is brought on by a process called spontaneous liquefaction. This occurs on slopes which comprise certain types of materials of marine origin which, under the force of ground shock such as an earthquake or even vibrations from construction activity, will instantaneously be transformed from a solid into a liquid state. In the stable phase, particles of silt and fine sand are arranged in a loose "house of cards" manner with clay and water occupying the interparticle spaces. Tremors may break this precarious structure and thereby affect the transformation to a liquid. Once initiated, an entire hillside can literally flow away in the course of several hours. The influence of slope failure caused by spontaneous liquefaction on land use and human life is usually catastrophic because the whole event occurs so suddenly that appropriate behavioral adjustments are usually impossible. Fortunately, liquefaction materials are limited to localized distribution; however, one should be aware of the possibility of their existence, especially in coastal regions.

A third consideration is the nature of the proposed land use. Along a playground or bathing beach, for example, slopes may be trampled by walkers who not only push soil downslope with each step but also weaken and destroy the plant cover on the slope face (Figure 3.28). In areas of residential, park, and institutional land uses, on the other hand, a conscious effort is often made to establish lawns on slopes. Grass sod is set down and then watered relentlessly to ensure its survival. If the slope is composed of low-permeability clayey soil, the water accumulates on the clay, saturating the overlying sod. With the reservoir of water above it, the upper part of the clay eventually becomes saturated itself and is transformed to a liquid state. This usually produces failure in the form of slumps, shallow slides, and mud flows. Unfortunately, people have a tendency to attribute the failure to insufficient root

Identification of Potentially Unstable Slopes

Spontaneous Liquefaction

PHOTO BY TOMMY G. BURDETTE

Figure 3.28. A slope kept active due to foot traffic.

strength in the sod and in response may apply even more water to the slope to promote faster root growth, but only promote more failure.

Land uses which require extensive slope cuts in the construction phase characteristically tend to be plagued by problems of slope stability. In order to create an adequate area of level ground, slopes are frequently truncated along expressways, parking lots, sports fields, and institutional sites, forming an oversteepened angle. Unless the slope is stabilized by structural means, it may become activated and produce debris deposits; gas lines, power lines, telephone lines, sewers, and water lines may be exposed and broken, and paved surfaces such as sidewalks and streets may subside, fracture, and ultimately deteriorate.

SUMMARY

In the previous chapter, we examined a slope classification scheme based on information derived from aerial photographs and topographic contour maps. Using the same information sources, a scheme may be designed to identify problem soils vis-à-vis land use and environmental planning interests. The particular problems soils pose to land use development fall into three general categories: (1) slope, (2) composition, and (3) drainage. Given an unde-

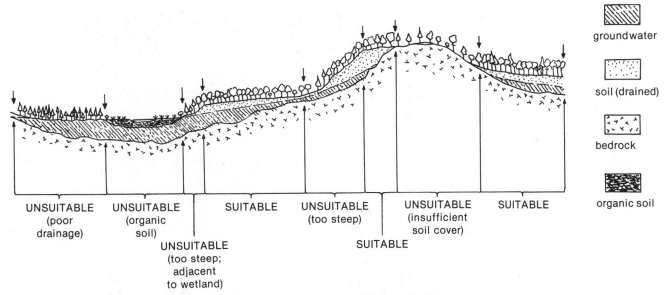

groundwater

soil (drained)

bedrock

organic soil

UNSUITABLE (poor drainage)

UNSUITABLE (organic soil)

UNSUITABLE (too steep; adjacent to wetland)

SUITABLE

UNSUITABLE (too steep)

SUITABLE

UNSUITABLE (insufficient soil cover)

SUITABLE

Figure 3.29. A schematic cross section along which the terrain is classified as suitable or unsuitable for development.

veloped and unincorporated area, sewage must be disposed of mainly by means of septic tanks and drain fields. This necessitates development on sites composed of well-drained soils of a minimum thickness of several feet and gently sloping or nearly flat surfaces. Houses, bridges, roads, and other structures require stable footings on noncompressible soils. This eliminates essentially all organic soils. And to minimize the impact of development on environment in terms of erosion, sedimentation, and runoff, steep slopes, especially near water features, should generally be avoided as development sites. In sum, we can identify a set of rudimentary criteria, most of which can be interpreted from aerial photographs and topographic maps, that can be used to delineate areas with serious limitations to residential and related land uses (Table 3.9). Figure 3.29 is a schematic cross section depicting suitable and unsuitable development sites. For each unsuitable site, the chief soil limitation or set of limitations is given in parenthesis.

For purposes of demonstration, let us examine a small area of diversified terrain in northern Michigan near the city of Marquette [Figure 3.30(a)]. The area offers a variety of soil conditions which is

Mapping Areas with Soil

TABLE 3.9   DEVELOPMENT SUITABILITY BASED ON DRAINAGE, SOIL, AND SLOPE

Development suitability	Soil property			
	Drainage	Composition	Thickness	Slope
Suitable	well drained (low water table)	nonorganic	greater than 3–4 ft	less than 8%
Unsuitable	poorly drained (high water table) within 1 ft or so of the surface	organic	less than 2–3 ft	more than 8%

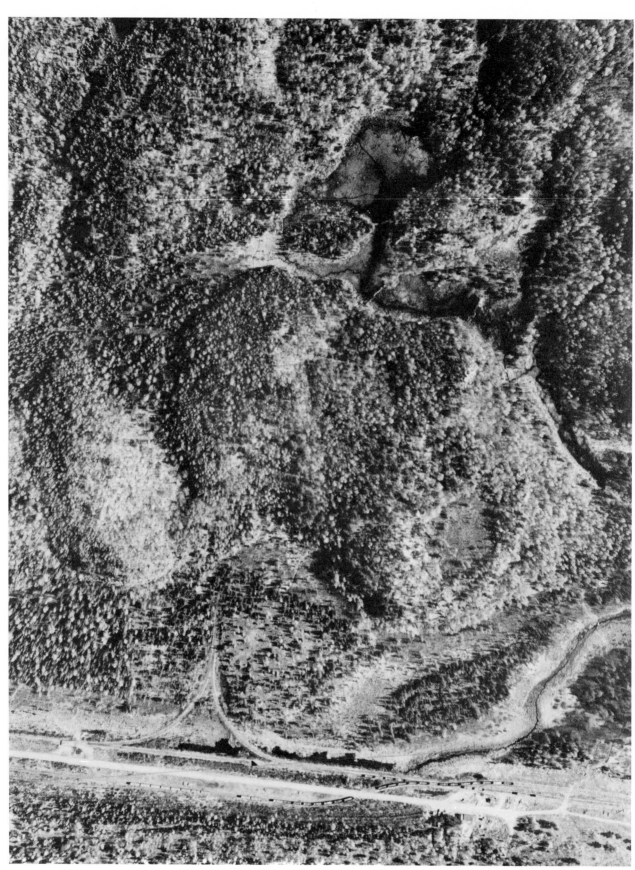

Figure 3.30(a). An aerial photograph of a diversified area of undeveloped terrain.

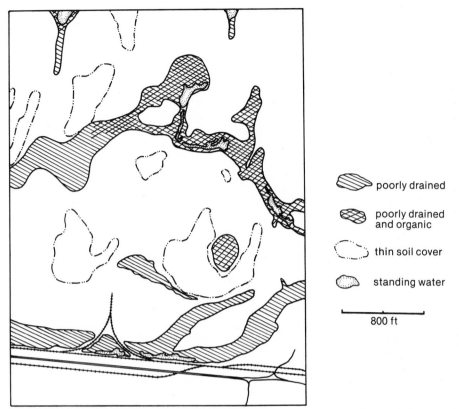

Figure 3.30(b). Classification of the terrain shown in Figure 3.30(a) according to drainage and soil.

poorly drained

poorly drained and organic

thin soil cover

standing water

800 ft

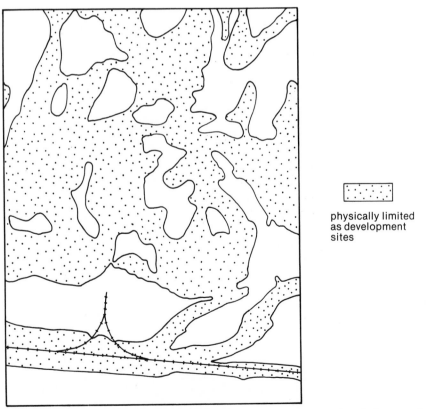

physically limited as development sites

Figure 3.30(c). Areas with physical limitations for development based on drainage, soils, and slope.

Item	Information Source	Description and Remarks
Slope Inclination	Contour Maps	
Soil Composition	SCS Maps, Topographic Maps, Field Sampling	
Soil Angle of Repose	Chapter 2, page 56	
Vegetative Cover	Aerial Photographs	
Condition of Slopes (e.g., gullied, seepage zones, trampled)	Aerial Photographs, Field Observations	
Proposed Land Use	Site Plan, Petition for Rezoning, etc.	
Site Preparation Processes; Site Conditions During Construction		
Environmental Problems Anticipated During and After Development		
Planning Recommendations		
Guidelines and Suggestions for Implementation		

Figure 3.31. A sample table for recording soil and slope information.

reflected in the vegetation patterns and these, in turn, facilitate differentiation of problem soils from soils suitable for development (see "Vegetation Indicators of Site Conditions," in Chapter 4). Careful stereoscopic examination of the area reveals several spots with light tree covers, where, based on visible exposure of bedrock, the soil cover is thin or absent. In addition, the absence of tree cover in low areas which evidence no previous logging operations, is a strong indication of poor drainage. Near ponds and streams in these locales, dead trees and low wetland vegetation suggest the presence of organic soils. Sites characterized by one or more of these soil conditions were mapped from the aerial photograph in Figure 3.30(a) and are shown in Figure 3.30(b).

From the topographic contour map of the area, slopes of an inclination greater than 8 percent were designated. Coupled with the information derived from the aerial photograph interpretation, a final map of sites with serious physical limitations for land development was constructed [Figure 3.30(c)]. The remaining land, less than half the total area, constitutes the land suitable for residential development based on soil conditions.

It is no news to the planning community that evaluation of development sites should be based on systematic analysis and presentation of information. Evaluation of environmental conditions, however, can prove difficult not only with respect to information generation but also with respect to documentation and dissemination of information. As the final item in this chapter, the table in Figure 3.31 is suggested as the sort of vehicle that may facilitate these processes for slope and soil information.

Bruce, J. P., and R. H. Clark: *Introduction to Hydrometeorology,* Pergamon Press, New York, 1966. 319 pp. A succinct treatment of many important topics in surface hydrology.

Frevert, R. K., G. O. Schwab, T. W. Edminster, and K. K. Barnes: *Soil and Water Conservation Engineering,* John Wiley, New York, 1955.

Gray, Donald H.: "Effects of Forest Clear-Cutting on the Stability of Natural Slopes," *Bulletin of the Association of Engineering Geologists,* 1970, vol. VII, nos. 1 and 2, pp. 45–66.

Hart, Earl W.: "Zoning for Surface Fault Hazards in California: The New Special Studies Zones Maps," *California Geology,* California Division of Mines and Geology, 1974, pp. 227–230.

Knott, J. M.: *Effects of Urbanization on Sedimentation and Floodflows in Colma Creek Basin, California,* U.S. Geological Survey Open-file Report, 1973. 54 pp. Report of a two-year study of stream sedimentation related to land use in a small San Francisco Bay area drainage basin.

Kraebel, C. J.: *Erosion Control on Mountain Roads,* U.S. Department of Agriculture Circular, no. 380, 1963, pp. 1–44.

Leopold, Luna B.: *Hydrology for Urban Land Planning—A Guidebook on the Hydrologic Effects of Urban Land Use,* U.S. Geological Survey Circular, no. 554, 1968. 18 pp. Mainly a review of findings on the influence of urbanization on surface hydrology.

Lynch, Kevin: *Site Planning,* MIT Press, Cambridge, Mass, 1973. 384 pp.

Marsh, William M., and John M. Koerner: "Role of Moss in Slope Formation," *Ecology,* vol. 53, no. 3, 1973, pp. 489–493. Illustration of the influence of moss in slope stabilization.

Rantz, S. E.: *Suggested Criteria for Hydrologic Design of Storm-Drainage Facilities in the San Francisco Bay Region, California,* U.S. Geological Survey Open-file Report, 1971. 69 pp. A discussion and test of methods for determining runoff.

Slosson, James E.: *Engineering Geology—Its Importance in Land Development,* Urban Land Institute Technical Bulletin 63, 1968. 20 pp.

Terzaghi, Karl: *Mechanisms of Landslides in Application of Geology to Engineering Practice,* Berkey Volume, Geological Society of America, 1951, pp. 83–123. Interesting examination of causes and settings of slope failures.

Vanlier, Kenneth E.: *Summary of Ground-Water Conditions in the Elsie Area, Michigan,* Michigan Conservation Department and U.S. Geological Survey Progress Report, no. 25, 1962. 35 pp.

Varnes, David J.: *Landslide Types and Processes in Landslides and Engineering Processes,* Highway Research Boards Special Publication 29, 1958, pp. 20–47. A nontechnical discussion of slope failure.

Wolman, M. Gordon, and Asher P. Schick: "Effects of Construction on Fluvial Sediment, Urban and Suburban Areas of Maryland," *Water Resources Research,* vol. 3, no. 2, 1967, pp. 451–464.

Yarnell, D. L.: *Rainfall Intensity-Frequency Data,* U.S. Department of Agriculture Miscellaneous Publication 204, 1935.

CHAPTER **4**

VEGETATION | *John M. Grossa,*
John M. Koerner,
and
William M. Marsh

PHOTO BY CHARLES SCHLINGER

INTRODUCTION

Classification Schemes

Vegetation conveys a wealth of information about environmental conditions. Until recently, though, little use appears to have been made of this information source in land use and environmental planning. Instead, vegetation has commonly been assessed solely in its capacity as the chief aesthetic component of most landscapes and as a potential conflicting-use arbitrator. Enactment of the National Environmental Protection Act of 1969 in the United States, however, has induced a significant change in the manner in which vegetation must be evaluated as a site component. The increasing sophistication demanded of environmental impact statements, requisite under this legislation, has dictated that vegetation be recognized in a much broader role than that of a visual amenity. As a functional element of the environment, the plant cover serves to stabilize slopes, retard erosion, conserve water quality and quantity, maintain local microclimates, filter the atmosphere, decrease noise, and provide habitat for wildlife. Viewed within this expanded context, vegetation can be utilized, not only as a primary determinant in gauging ecological sensitivity, but also as an indicator of environmental constraints that have influenced previous land use. Thus, the task of generating environmental information for land use planning must embrace a detailed analysis of vegetation, both as a development resource and an integral element of the natural or cultural landscape.

Plant classification schemes are often a source of much confusion and discouragement to the nonspecialist in plant sciences. Thus, it seems appropriate to identify the major classification schemes in use today and define those which are suitable for purposes of land use and environmental planning. The floristic (or the Linnaean) plant classification system is the scheme most widely used today among botanists, foresters, agronomists, ecologists, and other plant scientists. This is the scheme which uses Latin or Latinized words for plant names—for instance, *Pinus strobus* for white pine—and groups plants into classes, orders, families, genera, and species. The primary basis for classification is similarity of features like leaves, flowers, and reproductive processes. Strong similarities between two plants are taken as an indication of genetic affiliation, perhaps common parentage in the evolutionary pasts of the plants. With each level of classification from class to species, the degree of similarity increases. At the species level, member plants are so alike that they freely interbreed.

Several ecologically oriented schemes have been devised, though no one is currently predominant. These classifications are based on similarity of habitat and differ markedly from the floristic system inasmuch as strikingly dissimilar-looking plants and genetically unrelated plants often occupy the same habitat. One of these schemes is based on moisture and classifies plants into three major categories: (1) hydrophytes, which are water-loving plants, (2) xerophytes, which are drought-tolerant plants, and (3) mesophytes, which are intermediate.

A third set of classification schemes is based on the structure of the total assemblage of plants on a site. Closed forest, open forest, parkland, tundra, and grassland are examples of common structural classes. Although not specifically indicative of habitat, the structure or life-form of vegetation often reflects environmental conditions. For instance, natural grasslands usually indicate that moisture is insufficient to support trees, or in the case of alpine meadows, heat is insufficient to sustain trees.

TABLE 4.1

Level I (vegetative structure)		Level II (dominant plant types)	Level III (size and density)	Level IV (site and habitat or associated use)
Forest (trees with average height greater than 15 ft with at least 60% canopy cover)		e.g., oak, hickory, willow, cottonwood, elm, basswood, maple, beach, ash	tree size (diameter at breast height) density (number of average stems per acre) size range (difference between largest and smallest stems)	e.g., upland (i.e., well drained terrain), floodplain, slope face, woodlot, greenbelt, parkland, residential land
Woodland (trees with average height greater than 15 ft with 20–60% canopy cover)		e.g., pine, spruce, balsam fir, hemlock, douglas fir, cedar		
Orchard or Plantation (same as woodland or forest but with regular spacing)		e.g., apple, peach, cherry, spruce, pine	tree size; density	e.g., active farmland, abandoned farmland
Brush (trees and shrubs generally less than 15 ft high with high density of stems, but variable canopy cover)		e.g., sumac, willow, lilac, hawthorn, tag alder, pin cherry, scrub oak, juniper	density	e.g., vacant farmland, landfill, disturbed terrain (e.g., former construction site)
Fencerows (trees and shrubs of mixed forms along borders such as roads, fields, yards, playgrounds)		any trees or shrubs	tree size; density	e.g., active farmland, road right-of-way, yards, playgrounds
Wetland (generally low, dense plant covers in wet areas)		e.g., cattail, tag alder, cedar, cranberry, reeds	percent cover	e.g., floodplain, bog, tidal marsh, reservoir backwater, river delta
Grassland (herbs, with grasses dominant)		e.g., big blue stem bunch grass, dune grass	percent cover	e.g., prairie, tundra, pasture, vacant farmland
Field (tilled or recently tilled farmland)		e.g., corn, soybeans, wheat; also weeds	field size	e.g., sloping or flat, ditched and drained, muckland, irrigated

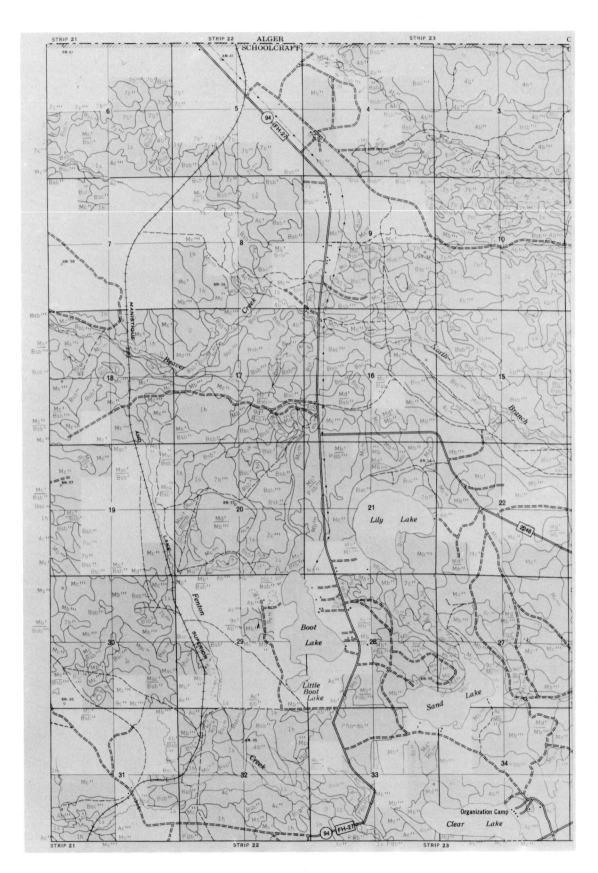

Figure 4.1. An example forest classification map from the U.S. Forest Service.

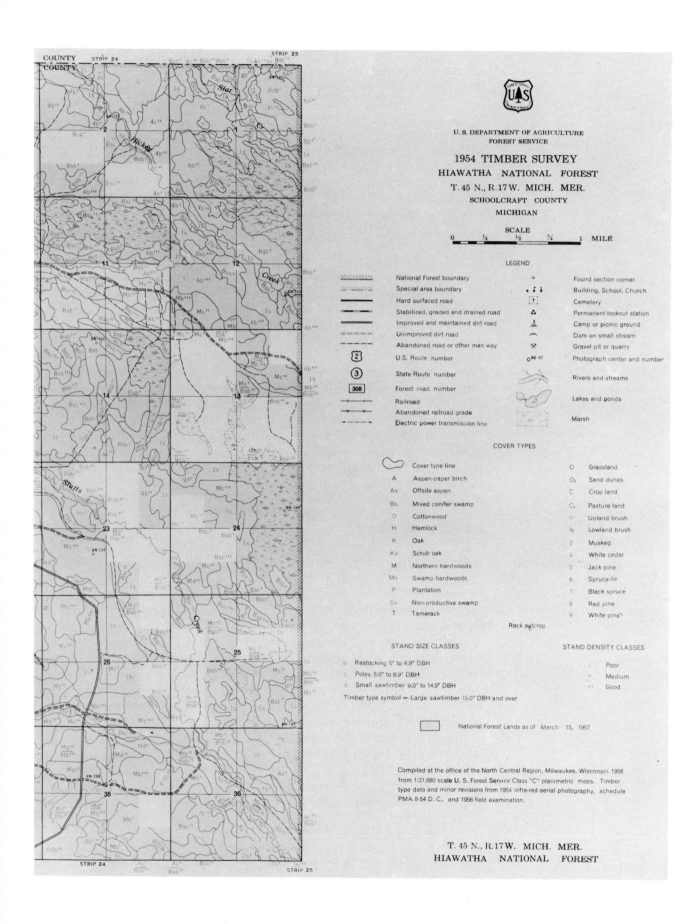

U. S. DEPARTMENT OF AGRICULTURE
FOREST SERVICE

1954 TIMBER SURVEY
HIAWATHA NATIONAL FOREST
T. 45 N., R. 17 W. MICH. MER.
SCHOOLCRAFT COUNTY
MICHIGAN

SCALE

0   ¼   ½   ¾   1   MILE

LEGEND

/////////	National Forest boundary	+	Found section corner
	Special area boundary	. ⚲ ⚲	Building, School, Church
	Hard surfaced road	⊡	Cemetery
	Stabilized, graded and drained road	△	Permanent lookout station
	Improved and maintained dirt road	⚐	Camp or picnic ground
	Unimproved dirt road	⌒	Dam on small stream
	Abandoned road or other man way	⚒	Gravel pit or quarry
②	U.S. Route number	○ ᴮᴳ⁻⁹⁷	Photograph center and number
③	State Route number		Rivers and streams
308	Forest road number		Lakes and ponds
	Railroad		
	Abandoned railroad grade		Marsh
	Electric power transmission line		

COVER TYPES

⬭	Cover type line	O	Grassland
A	Aspen-paper birch	O₁	Sand dunes
Ax	Offsite aspen	C	Crop land
Bs	Mixed conifer swamp	C₁	Pasture land
D	Cottonwood		Upland brush
H	Hemlock	ls	Lowland brush
K	Oak	2	Muskeg
Kx	Scrub oak	4	White cedar
M	Northern hardwoods	5	Jack pine
Ms	Swamp hardwoods	6	Spruce-fir
P	Plantation	7	Black spruce
Sx	Non-productive swamp	8	Red pine
T	Tamarack	9	White pine

Rock outcrop

STAND SIZE CLASSES

b   Restocking 0" to 4.9" DBH
c   Poles 5.0" to 8.9" DBH
d   Small sawtimber 9.0" to 14.9" DBH

Timber type symbol = Large sawtimber 15.0" DBH and over

STAND DENSITY CLASSES

'   Poor
''   Medium
'''   Good

National Forest Lands as of March 15, 1967

Compiled at the office of the North Central Region, Milwaukee, Wisconsin 1956 from 1:31,680 scale U. S. Forest Service Class "C" planimetric maps. Timber type data and minor revisions from 1954 infra-red aerial photography, schedule PMA 8-54 D. C., and 1956 field examination.

T. 45 N., R. 17 W. MICH. MER.
HIAWATHA NATIONAL FOREST

The structural scheme, augmented by the ecological and floristic schemes, appears to be a suitable reference framework for conveying plant-cover information for land use and environmental-planning purposes. In addition to identification of forest, shrub, or grassland structures, an indication of secondary structural features and salient floristic characteristics is usually valuable also. Table 4.1 provides an example of a four-level classification scheme. Level one is based on vegetative structure and includes height, percentage of area covered by canopy, and life-forms. Level two calls for identification of the dominant plants. This may involve only a single tree type in some areas, whereas in other areas it may involve as many as four or five types of plants. Level three calls for an indication of the density and the trunk sizes of trees and shrubs. This may be based on firsthand field measurements, though visual estimates may be adequate for most planning purposes. Level four is intended to provide information on the site in which the vegetation is found. Familiar terms such as *floodplain, upland, vacant farmland,* or *residential area* can be used to describe the physical setting. Greater specificity may be gained by indicating the habitats of certain plants within the site—for example, riverbank or slope face—or the use associated with the site—such as recreation or highway right-of-way. As a final note, it is necessary to add that the use of this classification scheme or a variant of it must be adjusted to the nature of the planning problem and the quality and abundance of available information sources. Level I may be more than adequate for township- and county-level planning, whereas all four levels may be barely adequate for site analysis in environmental impact statement preparation.

INFORMATION SOURCES

Vegetation Maps

Information on vegetation exists in a variety of forms. Modern large-scale U.S. Geological Survey topographic contour maps (discussed in Chapter 6) generally show major tree-covered areas, including orchards. In the arid to semiarid parts of the country, the maps show brush or chaparral vegetation. Topographic contour maps also indicate wetland areas; however, they give no evidence of the prevalence of standing water, swamp (tree forms) vegetation, or marsh (herb forms) vegetation. Similarly, the maps do not convey information on the nature of the vegetation. Dense, virgin forest, thinned conifer plantations, and mixed tree-scrub are all shown in the same fashion.

In some areas maps do exist which show forest composition and timber volumes, but nearly always these have been prepared for timber-production purposes. As such, the areas covered are generally reserved public lands or territory far removed from urban zones. Occasionally, however, U.S. Forest Service maps like the one shown in Figure 4.1 may be useful as an information source in environmental inventories. Other forest type maps have been prepared for selected large regions in states which have major areas of public forests; however, these maps tend to be very general and are often seriously outdated. They are, therefore, of limited value for detailed analysis of land use and environment.

Information on special or unique stands of vegetation including virgin woods, past plant cover, and occurrences of rare plant species or plants associated with historical sites, can often be obtained from local botanical societies and nature associations. These groups are active in nearly every city of the United States and Canada and represent a surprisingly valuable source of information on local plants. Personnel associated with arboretums and university herbaria can also lend valuable assistance in locating and identifying such vegetation and, as with most plant lovers, are usually eager to help those seeking information on the vegetative cover.

Local Sources

Aerial photographs and other remote-sensing imagery provide an excellent source of information on vegetation of all types. In fact, recent aerial imagery is virtually the only medium that can provide the basis for both qualitative and quantitative assessments of the vegetative cover. Standard black-and-white aerial photographs produced for the U.S. Department of Agriculture are available for most counties in the United States. A single photograph of this type can be used to differentiate between (1) tree and nontree vegetation

Black-and-White Aerial Photographs

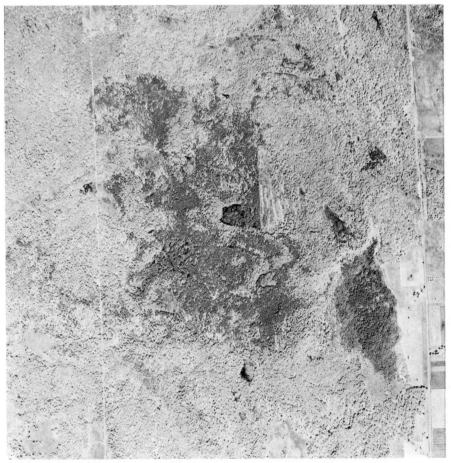

Figure 4.2. On standard black-and-white aerial photographs, it is generally difficult to distinguish between coniferous and deciduous trees, because the trees appear in similar tones of gray. But on black-and-white infrared photographs they are easily differentiated. This is apparent on this infrared photograph in which the dark-toned conifers contrast with the light-toned deciduous trees. (U.S. Forest Service photograph)

classes—including relative sizes, density, and areal extent—and (2) natural and cultivated vegetation, the latter identifiable on the basis of geometrically shaped tracts, rows, and relatively homogenous tone, texture, and size. Viewed in stereoscopic pairs, additional information such as tree height and vegetation type (e.g., broadleaf and coniferous) as well as plant habitat association can be generated.

On medium- and small-scale black-and-white aerial photographs it is generally difficult to distinguish coniferous tree species from most deciduous trees. In most instances there is very little apparent tonal variation between these vegetation types during the summer period, when the deciduous species have green leaves. Characteristic differences in shape and shadow which also may be useful bases for differentiation are generally not apparent at small and even medium scales. Fortunately, however, variation in reflected energy between coniferous and deciduous vegetation does exist in the infrared portion of the spectrum.

Black-and-White Infrared

Reflected infrared energy can be detected and recorded on specially prepared photographic film. The film, referred to as black-and-white infrared film, is sensitive to visible and infrared energy. Aerial photographs taken with this film will generally enable the interpreter to differentiate between deciduous and coniferous species (Figure 4.2). The deciduous trees which reflect more infrared energy than the coniferous trees will generally appear light in tone. The coniferous trees, reflecting less infrared energy, will appear darker (Figure 4.3).

Black-and-white infrared aerial photographs have been used

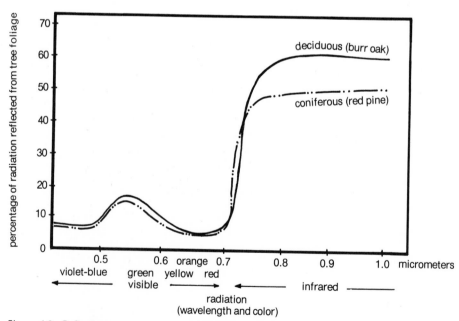

Figure 4.3. Reflectance curves representative of coniferous and deciduous trees. Note that the intensities of reflectance in the visible part of the spectrum (the radiation that black-and-white [or panchromatic] film is most sensitive to) are virtually the same. However, just beyond the visible, in the infrared part of the spectrum between 7.5 and 1.0 micrometers, there is a marked difference in radiation reflectance between conifer and broadleaf deciduous. Infrared film is sensitive to this difference and thus provides an effective means of distinguishing between these types of trees.

extensively by the U.S. Forest Service for over twenty years. Therefore, this type of photography is often available in areas having a mixed (deciduous and coniferous) forest cover. While black-and-white infrared film may be advantageous for certain aspects of vegetation analysis described above, it is probably less desirable than normal black-and-white aerial photography for most planning purposes. Image sharpness is usually reduced when infrared film is used. Light-tone objects such as unpaved forest roads and broad-leaf trees may blend together. Also, shadows are nearly opaque on infrared film, precluding the observation of objects in the shadowed areas.

Color Aerial Photographs

Color aerial photography is another medium that can prove to be of value in vegetation analysis. An outstanding characteristic of this mode of imagery is that it is easily interpreted. With modern aerial color films, colors generally appear on the photograph as they appear to the eye. This feature greatly facilitates the acquisition of environmental information. Therefore, vegetation analysis using color aerial photographs is made easier in some respects. The correct rendition of vegetation color afforded by aerial color films provides the planner with information about the status of many types of plants not as easily obtained on black-and-white photographs. For example, the relative vigor of herbaceous vegetation can be assessed readily on a color photograph. Senescing or dead herbaceous plants contrast sharply with the green hues of growing plants. Similar information about the status of deciduous trees can also be obtained based upon apparent color differences of the foliage. Color aerial photography of deciduous forest obtained during the autumn color changes can provide a relatively simple and picturesque means for species identification.

Areas covered by herbaceous vegetation are often difficult to distinguish from barren soil or rock on standard black-and-white aerial photography. On color film, however, vegetated and nonvegetated surfaces are readily distinguished.

Film and processing costs are higher for color aerial photography than for black-and-white. However, these factors become less significant when total costs are calculated, since aircraft operation is usually the most costly component of aerial surveys. It should be noted, however, that the overall cost of aerial photography need not be inordinately high. Using a light aircraft and a handheld camera, an investigator can take relatively inexpensive color slides of a study area. Although not highly accurate geometrically, slides such as these can provide a reasonably fast and efficient means of updating an information base established by more conventional methods.

Color Infrared Photographs

The use of color infrared aerial photography has become relatively widespread in recent years, and it is a most useful tool for vegetation analysis. When such photographs are acquired during the growing season, healthy vegetation generally appears bright red or magenta. The reason that growing vegetation appears in this false color is related to the fact that vegetation has relatively high infrared reflectance and relatively low reflectance in the visible portion of the spectrum as shown in the graph above. Reflected infrared energy which is invisible to our eyes, yet capable of sensitizing specially prepared photographic emulsions, is recorded and transformed into a visible format through the use of red or magenta dye. With this film, it is possible to distinguish between some vegetation types due to marked differences in infrared reflectance. For example, coniferous trees usually appear dark red while deciduous trees are bright red, since the needles of coniferous species reflect significantly less infrared energy than the leaves of deciduous species. The relative vigor or health of vegetation can also be ascertained, as diseased, damaged, or otherwise unhealthy or dying vegetation generally takes on a different shade or color on infrared film. In deciduous plants, this is often a lighter, whitish tone.

Color infrared photographs also permit differentiation between vegetation and bare soil or rock which is not always possible on black-and-white photographs (Figure 4.4). This feature is especially useful where vegetation is sparse or discontinuous, because the bright red color of the living plants on the infrared photo contrasts sharply with the nonvegetated surfaces.

Additional qualitative information can be generated from color

Figure 4.4. A black-and-white rendition of color infrared photograph which shows barren soil and other nonvegetated surface in the lighter tones. (Note: Color renditions of infrared photographs were not used in this book because of the high cost of color reproduction.) (Environmental Research Institute of Michigan photograph)

infrared photographs, including small drainage lines in fields, soil moisture conditions, and septic drain fields. The latter can often be identified on the basis of a dense and vigorous plant cover over the drain field. High concentrations of algae in water bodies often appear as pinkish blushes on color infrared photographs, providing one indicator of water quality.

Color infrared aerial photographs at a scale comparable to standard black-and-white photographs are not available on a regular basis from any federal government agencies. Nevertheless, color infrared photographs can be acquired with most standard 35-mm or 70-mm cameras, using Kodak Ektachrome Infrared film and a Wratten 12 lens filter (or other comparable yellow filter). Both the film and the filters can be purchased from many photographic shops. The Kodak Company and other color laboratories have the facilities to develop the film and print the photographs.

The first part of the following section describes the basic elements and techniques used in photo interpretation of vegetation. Although the focus is on black-and-white aerial photographs, a brief discussion of color infrared interpretation is also provided. The remainder of the chapter is devoted to a discussion of vegetation-site relations and the use of vegetation as an indicator of site conditions.

VEGETATION INTERPRETATION FROM BLACK-AND-WHITE AERIAL PHOTOGRAPHS

Tone and texture are two basic elements of interpretation used to classify vegetation on a black-and-white aerial photograph. Tone, the relative amount of light reflected by photographed objects, is fundamental to all the other recognition elements used in photo

Tone

PHOTOGRAPH BY TOMMY G. BURDETTE

Figure 4.5. Examples of the tonal variations found in black-and-white photographs.

interpretation. There must be an apparent difference in tone between objects in order to form a detectable image of those objects on the photograph. On black-and-white photographs variations in tone are, of course, depicted in shades of gray (Figure 4.5). The tones of photographed objects are not constant or uniform even when the same photographic system is used. The tones of deciduous trees and herbaceous vegetation vary significantly between seasons and even time of day, and water may appear in light or dark tones depending on the angle of the sun. Tonal variation may also be due to atmospheric conditions existing at the time of photography. On color photographs, variation in tone (hue and chroma) is the basis for differentiating coniferous and deciduous trees.

Texture

Texture, generally described in terms of smoothness, provides another useful guide for interpretation of vegetation on aerial photographs. The visual impression of texture results from the frequency of tonal changes which occurs when the individual plants (or plant structures) are too small to be clearly discerned. Planted vegetation will often appear to have a smoother texture than natural vegetation. Actively cultivated farmlands will generally have a finer, more uniform, texture than abandoned fields with their complex of herbaceous and shrub vegetation. Mature stands of deciduous trees will exhibit a relatively coarse, mottled texture, while dense stands of young second-growth trees will appear fine textured. Coniferous species with their narrow, conical crown often

Figure 4.6. A standard aerial photograph showing several different vegetation types, including trees, shrubs, and herbs.

appear more homogenous and smooth than most full-crowned deciduous species. As with tone, however, uniform stands of vegetation may vary in apparent texture due to variations in terrain or relative position of the camera. A stand of trees viewed vertically may appear to have a finer texture than similar trees viewed more obliquely, away from the center of the photograph.

Several vegetation types can readily be distinguished on the standard black-and-white photograph in Figure 4.6. Usually, it is a simple matter to differentiate between tree, shrub, and herbaceous vegetation. The rectangular field (A) in Figure 4.6 has a relatively homogenous tone and fine texture indicating a cover of herbaceous vegetation devoid of shrubs or trees. Shrubs are evident in an adjacent field (B) as the individual shrubs contrast sharply with the herbaceous cover. Individual trees can usually be differentiated from shrubs on the basis of crown size, shadow size, and shape. The full crowns of the mature deciduous trees along the road contrast with the relatively small crowns of shrubs found in adjacent fields (B).

Trees planted by people are often aligned or spaced in an apparent regular pattern. Fruit or nut orchards, tree plantations, and windbreaks are examples of such plantings. The orchard and the coniferous plantation (P) in the Figure 4.7 illustrate this regular pattern and differ markedly from the irregular heterogeneous shrub and tree assemblage (H). The presence of shrubs randomly interspersed throughout the orchard (O) and the lack of uniformity in

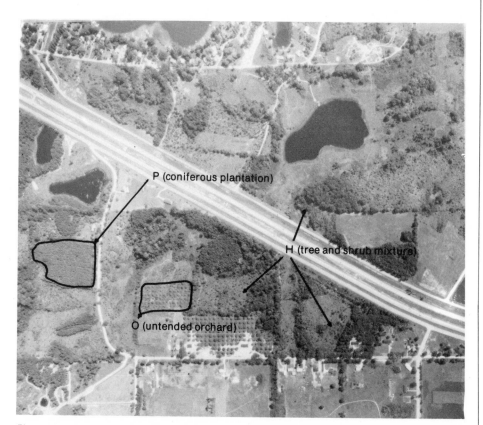

Figure 4.7. The relative uniformity of pattern and texture often indicate the type of vegetation.

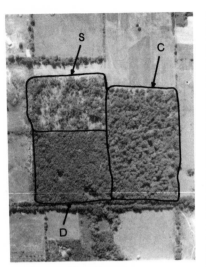

Figure 4.8. Closed canopy, selectively cut, and sparsely forested woodlots.

crown size and shape of the individual fruit trees are indications that this orchard has been untended for a number of years. Idle farmland and abandoned orchards are usually easily identified by the unkempt aspect of their vegetative covers.

Wild or remnant stands of trees are often found in rectilinear plots. However, these are most commonly an indirect result of the rectangular survey system used throughout much of the United States. Such natural woodlots can usually be distinguished from plantings because they lack the internal row patterns or alignment of planted vegetation. Woodlots which consist of mature trees of several species often have a coarse, mottled texture in which individual tree crowns may be distinguished. A similar texture may also occur as a result of selectively cutting portions of the woodlot. The mature deciduous woodlot (C) in the photograph in Figure 4.8 has been selectively cut. As a result, the crowns of the remaining trees have grown fuller and actually appear larger than trees of similar size growing in an adjacent stand (D), which has not been cut. Furthermore, the mottled texture is enhanced as a result of the shadows cast on the forest floor or understory.

Information regarding relative tree density can be obtained from a vertical black-and-white aerial photograph. Dense stands of trees, as in woodlot (D) in Figure 4.8, have complete crown closure with few if any indications of an understory or the ground itself. In selectively cut stands, on the other hand, the ground can usually be seen, which is apparent in woodlot (C). Sparse tree stands, exemplified by (S), lack continuous crown closure, and the ground is clearly visible throughout the area (Figure 4.9). Some herbaceous and shrub-size vegetation can be seen in these openings. Density infor-

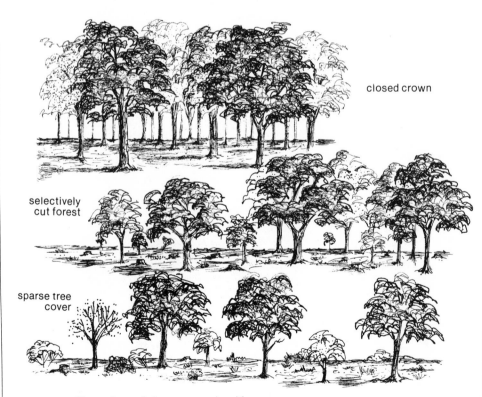

closed crown

selectively cut forest

sparse tree cover

Figure 4.9. Illustrations of three crown densities.

mation of this type is, of course, highly qualitative and somewhat subjective yet demands neither the aid of instruments nor a large amount of time to generate it.

Vegetation interpretation is made easier if a stereoscopic model can be arranged from adjacent vertical aerial photographs from the same flight line. In a stereoscopic image of the landscape, the dimension of height is added to the two-dimensional-plan view of a single aerial photograph. The relative height of vegetation can be ascertained quickly by comparing the apparent height of the vegetation in question with that of other objects such as barns, houses, or other stands of vegetation. While absolute heights cannot be determined in this fashion, comparisons that can be made on a relative basis will provide useful qualitative information regarding vegetation size. In Figure 4.10 the trees in the selectively cut woodlot (C) appear to be smaller than the trees in the other woodlot (D) when viewed on a single photograph. When these types of stands are inspected stereoscopically in the following photopair, it is apparent that both stands consist of trees nearly of the same height and size.

Absolute height of vegetation can be determined from a stereoscopic model, provided certain additional information is known. Precise measurements can be made with specially designed devices known as stereometers and parallax wedges. These instruments provide information which can, in turn, be substituted into

Figure 4.10. The textures of tree crowns in the aerial photograph above suggest that the trees in the small woodlot are larger than those in the large woodlot. However, when viewed stereoscopically, it is apparent that both woodlots are composed of trees of comparable height and size.

an equation, the product of which is the height of the object in question. Chapter 1 contains a discussion on their use.

The stereoscopic model facilitates vegetation analysis in other ways as well. Topographic features which may provide excellent clues to vegetation types associated with a particular site or locale yet difficult to see on a single photo can be readily observed stereoscopically. As discussed above, certain aspects or vegetation groups are usually found in particular sites or are associated with specific types of topographic features. Features such as the flood-plain walls can usually be observed when medium- and large-scale aerial photographs of stream valleys are viewed stereoscopically. These slopes mark the boundary between vegetation types associated with the floodplain and those found in upland areas. In addition, areas with moderate to high local relief such as the knob-and-kettle topography associated with some glacial landforms often exhibit a patchwork of vegetation types which is a function of site and slope. The stereopair provides a simple means for the qualitative assessment and differentiation of vegetation found in association with topographic lows, hilltops, or midslopes.

Two distinct woodland sites are shown on the stereopair in Figure 4.11. While it is *very* difficult to differentiate between vegetation assemblages even under stereoscopic study, some reasonable inferences can be made on site differences apparent on the stereopair. On the floodplain (F), hardwoods such as elm, ash, some aspen, and red maple are dominant, whereas the forest along the

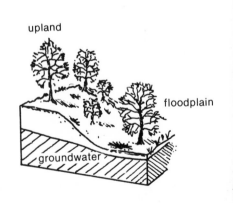

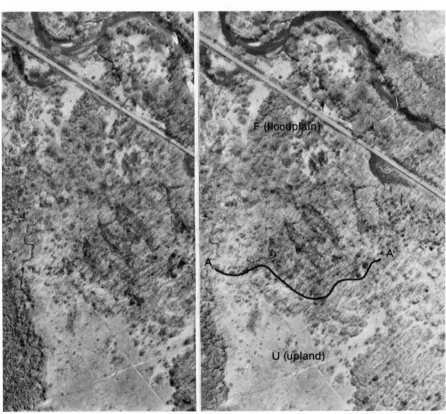

Figure 4.11. The marked change in site conditions from upland to floodplain, apparent only when viewed stereoscopically, can be an indicator of a corresponding change in tree types.

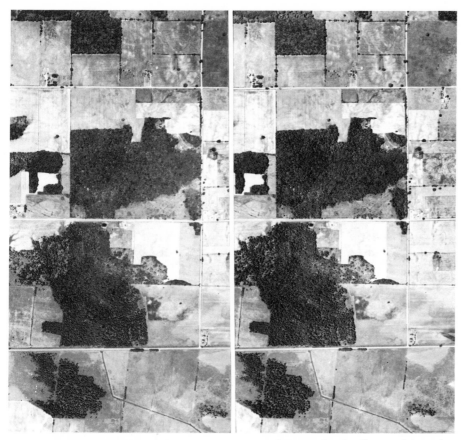
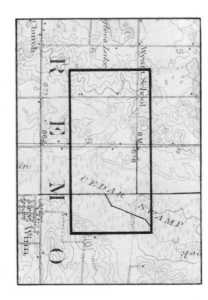

Figure 4.12. Subtle changes in topography and vegetation can often be discerned through aerial photograph interpretation. In this case, the forest composition changes from the lowland (shown on the map) to the adjacent ground which is only 50 feet or so higher.

floodplain wall and on the upland (U) consists of species such as beech, maple, and some oak. The abrupt change in site conditions from upland to floodplain, which is boldly portrayed in the stereoscopic scene, provides a basis for inferring a change in tree types. The change actually occurs at the base of the floodplain wall, marked by line A.

While the floodplain wall, in the example above, represents a sharp, distinctive boundary composed of a short yet steep slope separating upland from lowland sites, more gradual slopes often result in zones of transition between vegetation associations. Once again, stereoscopic study of the area will usually permit the viewer to discern even gentle slopes due to the characteristic exaggeration of relief. The forested area on the stereopair in Figure 4.12 gradually changes from a hardwood-deciduous forest association found on the fairly well-drained upland to a lowland association of white cedar, aspen, and birch found on the poorly drained soils. Even though the slope is very gradual, less than 30 vertical feet in approximately ½ mile, it is apparent on the relatively small-scale stereopair.

The vegetation assemblages associated with hilly terrain can also be influenced by the direction or orientation of the slope. South-facing slopes receive more intense sunlight and, therefore, are warmer than slopes with different orientations. The effect on plant types is, of course, a function of several variables including slope angle, soil type, and latitude. When viewed without the stereoscopic perspective, even moderate to steeply sloping terrain may not be apparent when cloaked by forest. Only when the illusion of the third dimension is perceived with the stereoscope do the patterns of hilltop and swale resolve and their attendant relations become evident. Through stereoscopic analysis the relative steepness of the slope can be assessed, which may provide additional information about the existing vegetation which could not be derived from a single photograph. A word of caution, however, is in order here, as slope characteristics are exaggerated considerably in the stereoscopic model. In order to avoid overestimating the steepness of local slopes or slope segments, a U.S. Geological Survey topographic map of the area should be used to determine the degree of slope and its precise orientation, as recommended in Chapter 2.

Rolling topography such as that shown in the stereopair in Figure 4.13 is only hinted by features such as the boggy swales at A and B and the pond at C when viewed monocularly. There is little evidence of the small but deeply incised stream (S) or the prominent vistas afforded by the hilltops (H) until viewed with the stereoscope. Again, vegetation changes can be inferred as site conditions change from the relatively dry, sandy hilltops and slopes to the wet soils of the swales and creek bottoms.

Color Infrared Aerial Photographs

The color infrared photograph in Figure 4.14 illustrates several advantages of this film for vegetation analysis. A coniferous planta-

Figure 4.13. In areas of hilly, diversified terrain, the relationship of vegetation to site conditions is especially apparent when aerial photographs are viewed stereoscopically.

Figure 4.14. A black-and-white rendition of a color infrared photograph showing a plantation of conifers in the upper left, forests of broadleaf deciduous trees, and open areas where herbs evidence low vigor. (Environmental Research Institute of Michigan photograph)

tion is easily differentiated from the adjacent deciduous forest on the basis of tone. As mentioned above, needleleaf-evergreen species have lower reflectance characteristics in the photographic infrared portion of the spectrum than the broadlead-deciduous species and, therefore, appear in a darker shade of red. Differentiation between these two general classes of trees can usually be accomplished more readily on color infrared photographs than on either black-and-white or color photographs. The relative vigor of vegetation can also be ascertained fairly accurately from color infrared energy, it appears bright red or magenta on the aerial photographs. When vegetation is under stress, is dying, or is dead, the infrared reflectance is usually reduced and the color rendition is different.

The infrared photographs in Figure 4.14, taken in late summer, illustrate this point well. The wild herbaceous vegetation in several upland fields has dried out during the summer months and appears as a grayish-green color on the original photograph. Though it is not apparent in the black-and-white rendition in Figure 4.14, it is clear on the original that growth of lawns, certain agricultural fields, and wild vegetation in the moist low-lying areas has maintained

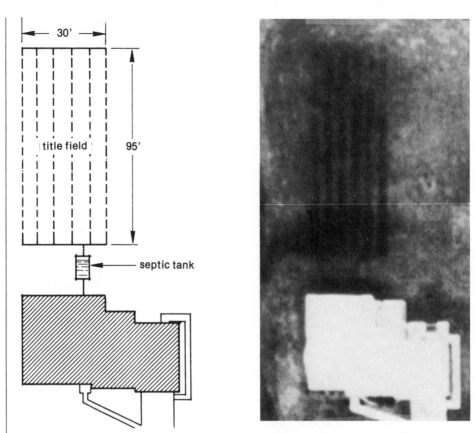

Figure 4.15. This is a black-and-white rendition of a portion of a color infrared photograph. It has been enlarged to highlight the differential vigor of grass in a residential lawn which is underlaid by a septic drain field. Note that vigor is greatest (dark tones) over the drain tiles, where grass evidently receives moisture and nutrients from tile seepage. The map on the left shows the actual pattern of the drain field tiles. (Environmental Research Institute of Michigan photograph)

relatively substantial vigor throughout the summer and appears in reddish shades.

The difference in relative vigor of the grass in the residential backyard in the infrared photograph in Figure 4.15 mirrors the tile field of the septic system. The growth is, of course, very vigorous above the drain tiles where seepage is confined as a result of relatively impervious clay soils.

VEGETATION INDICATORS OF SITE CONDITIONS

As the previous discussions have indicated, plants are not indiscriminately distributed in the environment. Beyond the normal vegetative relationship to climatic conditions, the general and often specific locations of local plant patterns are usually responses to geological, soil, slope-exposure, drainage, and previous land use conditions. These factors, and the related responses, are often complex and difficult to identify. Nevertheless, general relationships can often be discerned, and these in turn can be helpful in assessing a site. Acid-loving plant species in bog habitats, cattail marshes, and floodplain forests are common examples of site-related plant covers. In spite of the usefulness of vegetation as an indicator of environmental conditions, considerable care must be exercised in the interpretation.

Divergent plant species and vegetation associations do indicate different environmental conditions, but the same types can occur in variable environmental situations with just minor climatic variations. Tamarack trees, for example, prefer cold, deep swamps, but in the more northerly portions of their range, they occur on better-drained sites. Some plant species tolerate a wide variety of sites, even hostile ones, but in some situations, they may alter their form or structure. Many trees adopt shrub characteristics when growing under severe conditions. Accurate and detailed correlation between vegetation and site condition is, therefore, best prefaced on local experience and information.

Even with the difficulty of generalizing vegetation indicators of site, within a climatic region certain relationships are quite observable. In humid climates, the absence of tree cover, if not due to human activity, is usually an indication of soil, drainage, or environmental-disturbance conditions. Most trees will not grow where standing water covers the site through most of the growing season. Along shorelines, mountain and hill slopes, and road cuts, a survey of the tree cover may reveal locations where active erosion and sliding are occurring. Such locations, evident on the aerial photograph in Figure 4.16, are distinguishable as partially vegetated

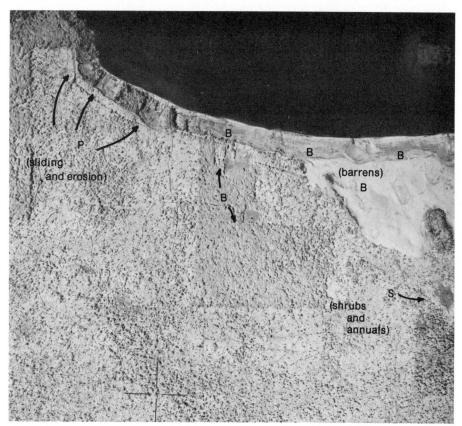

Figure 4.16. Vegetation or the absence of it can be good indicators of the geomorphic conditions of a site.

Figure 4.17. This aerial photograph illustrates some relationships between vegetation and drainage conditions.

swaths (P) or as barren patches (B) of exposed subsoil. In these same zones an isolated cover of young saplings, shrubs, or annuals (S) may evidence a similar recent environmental disturbance and indicate that such occurrences are likely in the area. This vegetation cover may also indicate recent fires or flash floods and, in mountainous regions, avalanches or late-lying snowbank zones. In all regions barren patches may be a response to exposed bedrock or bedrock with insufficient soil cover to sustain a tree cover.

Sites covered with standing water throughout the growing season, as is the case with the site in Figure 4.17, or those with permanently saturated soil are typically dominated by nonwoody plants with bladelike leaves such as cattails and reeds (C). Seasonally wet or more transitional sites are often characterized by these plants as well as by wetland trees such as alders, willows, cottonwoods, bald cypresses, and white cedars (W). Floodplains, coastal lowlands, lakeshores, and depressional areas such as kettle holes are common sites for these vegetation types. In coastal areas, variations in the tree and bladelike vegetation cover are generally indicative of the degree of salt- or freshwater saturation of the soil.

Wetland sites are commonly underlaid by organic soils. This is due to the slow rate of decomposition of saturated organic material and to the deposition of additional organic material by runoff from nearby higher ground. Even when organic soil sites are not saturated, they may nonetheless be too unstable for sustained tree growth. Trees may take root on these sites during drought years but suffer root rot or virtually cease growth when saturated conditions return. The unstable soil is often insufficient for their roots and, hence, they tend to topple over during windstorms.

Tree cover in active agricultural areas is often an indication of some limiting soil or topographic condition. Conversely, various vegetation types are often indicative of former agricultural or other land uses. Knowing that a site was previously suitable for cultivation or is underlaid by fill is helpful in determining its suitability for new uses. Thick hawthorns and noxious weeds reflect past intensive grazing and often sites with most topsoil eroded. The scrub-thorn woods of eastern Texas are largely a reflection of intensive grazing and control of fire. Sites covered by box elder, tree of heaven, and burdock are often areas of old fill or covered junk and rubble. Sites covered by a mixture of native and cultivated grasses, hawthorns, cherries, and oaks tend to reflect previously cultivated fields. The size of the trees provides evidence as to the time of abandonment.

Vegetation in semiarid to arid regions tends to concentrate where there is available moisture, and this localization intensifies as the climate becomes drier. Rills, stream valleys, springs, seepage zones, and even roadsides are zones of increased moisture availa-

Semiarid, Arid Climates

Figure 4.18. The heavy concentration of forests on north-facing slopes represents a response to favorable climatic conditions there compared to south-facing slopes.

bility and, therefore, of maximum plant cover. Lower mountain areas in these climates are cooler than the plains and receive additional precipitation, and drought-resistant trees such as pinyon pine, juniper, and scrub oak are often found there.

Particular situational aspects of these regions also concentrate plant cover or vegetation types. The cooler and more humid north-facing slopes support more and different types of trees than the warmer and drier south-facing slopes. In fact, as illustrated in Figure 4.18, south-facing slopes (S) may support no trees at all, yet the north slopes (N) may be heavily wooded. Commonly, Douglas fir and Engelmann spruce dominate north-facing slopes in the Rocky Mountains, while ponderosa pine and grasses cover southern slopes. In California, redwood trees tend to concentrate in the cooler and more humid locations, particularly where they are frequently reached by fog. Hogback ridges often support tree stands due to the aquiferous nature of the sandstone underlying the ridges, whereas the adjacent valleys may support only grasses or scattered trees due to the relatively impermeable shales which underly them (Figure 4.19). On plains and tablelands, trees often concentrate in depressions where they can acquire more moisture and receive protection from dessicating winds.

Table 4.2 is an attempt to relate broad vegetational categories to environmental situations or processes which would strongly influence the plant cover. In order to avoid the interpretation problems mentioned earlier, particularly across a wide range of climatic zones, the vegetation categories are based on structural or form characteristics rather than on floristic or species differences.

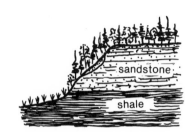

Figure 4.19. This diagram illustrates a typical vegetation change where the bedrock changes from sandstone to shale.

TABLE 4.2 STRUCTURAL VEGETATION INDICATORS OF GENERALIZED SITE CONDITIONS

Climatic region	Absence of plant cover	Sparse herb and shrub cover	Thick herb and shrub cover	Brush and small trees	Blade and reed plants	Highly localized tree cover
Humid (Eastern North America, Pacific Northwest, South)	bedrock at or very near surface active dunes recent human use, cultivation, etc. recent fire recent loss of water cover	bedrock near surface recent or sterile soils—dunes, fill recently disturbed (fallow, fire, flood) active slopes/erosion	recently logged or burned too wet for trees managed grazing organic soil old field regrowth	landslide/fire, flash-flood scars old field or woodlot regrowth shale/clay substrate organic soil moisture deficiency	organic soil standing water high groundwater table springs, seepage zones	wet depression, organic soil, steep slopes in agricultural areas flood-prone areas
Semiarid (High plains, S. California) **Arid** (Southwest, Great Basin)	caliche or salt pan (playa) at or very near surface desert pavement rock surface unstable ground such as dunes or rockslides too dry	localized water sources eolian erosion overgrazing	overgrazing free from burning too dry for trees	channels of available moisture aquiferous substrate protected pockets favorable (moist) slopes logged/burned	(same as above)	aquiferous substrate seepage zone or spring stream valley (galleria) forest plantation
Arctic and Alpine (N. Canada, Alaska)	rock surface active slopes semipermanent ice or snow cover ponded water during growing season	above tree line semipermanent ice or snow cover active slopes periglacial processes active	above tree line ice, snow, and wind pruning mildly active slopes wet depressions	wind/ice pruning avalanche, landslide scars, fire recent logging near tree line permafrost near surface	(same as above)	protection pockets

SUMMARY

Knowledge of the composition and distribution of vegetation is an important part of the information set necessary for modern land use and environmental planning. In addition to its aesthetic, economic, and ecological roles in the landscape, it is also a critical indicator of the conditions of other components of the landscape such as soils, drainage, and land use. Indeed, vegetation is an excellent measure of the relative effectiveness of our attempts to successfully manage the landscape.

Most of the information on vegetation which is required for planning purposes can be generated from aerial photographs. Augmented by field observations and information from special sources such as infrared aerial photographs, forestry maps, and botanical reports, the planner can prepare reliable information packages which can be useful in environmental inventories, impact-statement preparation, site designs, land use plans, and even cost analysis considerations.

Though not treated in strict economic terms in the traditional context of land use planning, recent evidence shows that vegetation is an important cost factor in development. This is illustrated by the following excerpt from the U.S. Housing and Urban Development publication *The Costs of Sprawl,* which provides an appropriate closing for this chapter.

> For a 500 acre development (assuming uniform ground cover) clearing and grubbing [of vegetation and earth debris] could cost anywhere from $145,000 to $800,000. The decision to retain and work around natural site amenities such as trees or rock formations makes clearing of adjacent areas more difficult and possibly more costly per acre, although the total acreage cleared would decrease. Where large-scale planned development is the predominant development pattern, it is much easier to retain natural ground cover elements through improved site design and landscaping. This is also true of high density residential construction where care is exercised in retaining large portions of natural open space resulting in less acreage disturbed than in low density subdivisions.

Bibliography

Avery, G.: "Measuring Land-Use Changes on U.S. Department of Agriculture Photographs," *Photogrammetric Engineering,* vol. 31, 1965, pp. 620–624.

Cooper, C. F., and F. M. Smith: "Color Aerial Photography Toy or Tool," *Journal of Forestry,* vol 64, 1966, pp. 373–378. Discussion of attributes and liabilities of color aerial photography in soils and vegetation analysis.

Dill, H. W.: "Air Analysis in Outdoor Recreation: Site Inventory and Planning," *Photogrammetric Engineering,* vol. 29, 1963, pp. 67–70.

Fritz, N. L.: "Optimum Methods for Using Infrared-Sensitive Color Films," *Photogrammetric Engineering,* vol. 33, 1967, pp. 1128–1138. A thorough discussion of Kodak Ektachrome Infrared film including information on exposure characteristics and processing.

Heller, R. C., E. G. Doverspike, and R. C. Aldrich: *Identification of Tree Species on Large-Scale Color and Panchromatic Photographs,* U.S. Department of Agriculture Handbook 261, 1964, p. 17. Photo interpretation of tree species were found more accurate on large-scale color transparencies than on panchromatic prints at the same scale.

Knipling, E. B.: "Leaf Reflectance and Image Formation on Color Infrared Film," in P. L. Johnson (ed.), *Remote Sensing in Ecology,* University of Georgia Press, Athens, 1969, pp. 17–29. Straightforward discussion about color formation on

Ektachrome infrared film and the influence of differences in leaf reflectance in color imagery.

Nunnally, N. R.: "Interpreting Land Use from Remote Sensing Imagery," in J. E. Estes and L. W. Senger (eds.), *Remote Sensing: Techniques for Environmental Analysis,* Hamilton Publishing Company, Santa Barbara, Calif. 1974, Ch. 7. An overview of remote-sensing research on land use with some discussion of problems encountered in extracting information from imagery.

Smith, J. T. (ed.): *Manual of Color Aerial Photography,* American Society of Photogrammetry, Falls Church, Va., 1968, p. 550. A beautiful and useful book discussing and depicting color films and aerial photography.

Tarkington, R. G., and A. L. Sorem: "Color and False Color Films for Aerial Photography," *Photogrammetric Engineering,* vol. 29, 1963, pp. 88–95.

Tomlinson, R. F., and W. G. Brown: "The Use of Vegetation Analysis in the Photo Intrepretation of Surface Material," *Photogrammetric Engineering,* vol. 28, 1962, pp. 584–592.

CHAPTER **5**

FLOODS AND FLOODPLAINS

*Peter Van Dusen,
Jeff Dozier, and
William M. Marsh*

INTRODUCTION

THE WATER'S EDGE has been the main habitat of the human race since its African origins more than a million years ago. The riverbank, the floodplain, the lakeshore, and the seashore continue to be the most densely settled environments on the planet. The reasons for this are many, and we need not review them here. In any case, the urban explosion has placed great land use pressure on floodplains and coastal zones, resulting in not only natural disasters but also serious environmental alteration of these settings.

The early growth of most cities tended to be controlled by site and distance factors. As cities grew and accessibility factors produced wide differentiation in land values, sites with inherent physical shortcomings nevertheless became settled because of their favorable locations with respect to allied commercial land uses. Swamps were drained and filled, shorelines were filled and fortified, and these sites became occupied by intensive high-rent uses. Moreover, for similar reasons, residential development in recent decades has spread into these environments, though typically without appropriate site improvements.

Too frequently, the results of such land use in sites susceptible to flooding have been deleterious to both the land use and the environment. In spite of the tremendous amount of money invested in floodplain protection, losses from floods in the United States have continued to increase in the last hundred years.

In some cases it can be justly argued that the land use on the floodplain produces high enough income to offset the "natural tax"—the occasional destruction of buildings and other equipment. But more often destructive floods cause severe economic and social disruption, because major economic losses as well as loss of life may befall a large portion of a community, rather than just a few individuals.

Though many factors are important in our continued occupance of flood-prone areas, one of them is the lack of reliable planning information on processes, composition, and spatial extent of such unstable settings. In response to this information void, programs for mapping flood-prone areas have recently been initiated by various agencies. In particular, the U.S. Geological Survey has implemented an extensive project aimed at delimitation of areas where the probability of flooding in any one year equals or exceeds

1 percent. The following statement of purpose appears on their Maps of Flood-prone Areas.

> The purpose of the flood-prone area maps is to show administrators, planners, and engineers concerned with future land developments those areas that are subject to flooding. The U.S. Geological Survey was requested by the 89th Congress to prepare these maps as expressed in House Document 465. The flood-prone areas have been delineated by the Geological Survey on the basis of readily available information.
>
> Flood-prone area maps were delineated for those areas that meet the following criteria: (1) urban areas where the upstream drainage area exceeds 25 square miles, (2) rural areas in humid regions where the upstream drainage area exceeds 100 square miles, and (3) rural areas in semiarid regions where the upstream drainage area exceeds 250 square miles.
>
> The flood-prone areas shown on this map have a 1 in 100 chance on the average of being inundated during any year. Flood areas have been delineated without consideration of present or future flood-control storage that may reduce flood levels.
>
> Flood-hazard reports provide the information that is needed for economic studies, for formulating zoning regulations, and for setting design criteria to minimize future flood losses. When detailed information, such as that contained in the flood-hazard reports, is required, contact the U.S. Army Corps of Engineers; the U.S. Geological Survey; or the Tennessee Valley Authority in the areas of their jurisdiction.

Unfortunately the Survey's mapping program in many areas is not progressing nearly as fast as urbanization itself, and it is apparent that land use plans will need to be developed in areas where the flood-prone zones have not yet been delimited. Hence this chapter identifies and describes a variety of methods to assist in generating information on river flooding and local drainage problems. Much of the information required already exists in one form or another, and the interpretation of such information to provide rough estimates of flood-prone areas, even if only approximate, can provide a basis for choosing among land use alternatives. In addition, development itself creates a drainage problem which is defined in Chapter 3 and further treated in this chapter. It is the problem of the high rates of runoff and increased flooding in urbanized drainage basins.

THE DRAINAGE BASIN

In the latter part of the eighteenth century, earth scientists began to recognize that running water is the dominant landscape-forming agent in most areas. Water supplied by rain or snow flows over the ground or through the soil and coalesces to form streams, which in turn coalesce to form rivers. The total flow network is called a drainage net. Streams of various orders are defined by their position within the hierarchy. First-order streams are channeled flows that do not have tributaries; second-order streams are flow segments where *two* first-order segments combine; third-order segments are formed by the convergence of *two* second-order segments, and so on (Figure 5.1). The schematic diagram in Figure 5.1 illustrates this technique. Rivers erode and deposit sediment in their valleys, and concomitant processes on their valley sides such as runoff and slope failure bring new materials to the rivers. Geologic forces within the earth elevate the landscape and thereby

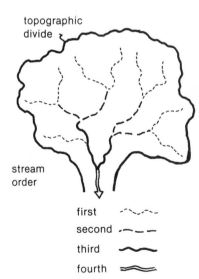

Figure 5.1. Classification of a drainage network according to stream order is often the first step in the analysis of a drainage basin.

prevent river drainage basins from "running down" to a final, extremely low slope state in which no further erosion or deposition takes place.

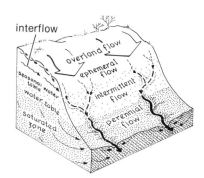

Figure 5.2. A schematic illustration of a hillslope showing ephemeral, intermittent, and perennial streams.

PRECIPITATION-RUNOFF RELATIONS

Water is supplied to river systems by precipitation which arrives at the river channels in the form of overland flow or groundwater. As is mentioned in Chapter 3, soil has an important characteristic called infiltration capacity. If the rate at which water is supplied to the surface exceeds the infiltration capacity, runoff occurs over the surface of the ground. Given sufficiently strong overland flow, water drains into local stream channels. Much of the water that infiltrates into the soil eventually reaches stream channels either by flowing downhill beneath the soil surface as through-flow and interflow or by percolating to groundwater and then to streams at lower elevations as shown in Figure 5.2.

Because water which flows to streams through the soil is very slow in getting to the channel, it provides an important source of streamflow during dry periods. Streams which receive this flow all year are called perennial. During periods without overland flow, they continue to carry a certain amount of water, called base flow, the level of which is approximately equal to that of the water table along the channel banks. Streams that do not flow throughout the year are called intermittent (Figure 5.2). A special kind of intermittent flow is the ephemeral stream which usually flows less than a month and flows primarily in response to individual rainstorms. These types of streams are shown in the illustration in Figure 5.2. The discharge of the trunk stream in a drainage basin depends on the rate of precipitation and upon the surface and subsurface characteristics of the drainage basin. The coefficient of runoff is a critical factor, and this is demonstrated in Chapter 3. The drainage area of a particular basin usually determines the total amount of water available from a given rainstorm. The shape, the number of channels, the slope, and the orientation of the basin with respect to the direction of storm movement are also important factors, as they influence the lag time, the time lapse between the peak rainfall intensity and the peak stream runoff. A graph showing the relationship between precipitation and resultant stream discharge is called a hydrograph (Figure 5.3).

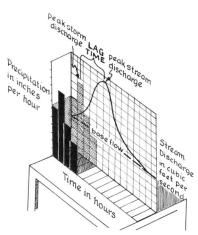

Figure 5.3. The hydrograph, shown on the gridded surface, represents the flow response of a stream to a given rainstorm. (Illustration by Peter Van Dusen)

FLOODPLAINS AND FLOODPLAIN PROCESSES

As a river erodes and deposits material, it may shift its course and over a period of time build up a deposit of material in its valley bottom. This deposited material takes the shape of a plain, called a floodplain, which forms at an elevation near that of the river surface. The floodplain is often separated from the river itself by natural levees, which in residential areas may be reinforced by walls or sandbags.

Because a river's flow is variable through time, it cannot be adequately expressed by just one number representing either a single instant in time or an average compounded over a long period of time. The atmospheric processes that supply water to a river, rainfall, snowfall, and snowmelt, for example, vary both seasonally and annually. In some years the rainy seasons are markedly wetter than in other years. As a result, the surface of the river rises and falls, overflows its banks, and shifts its course. In this manner the floodplain becomes considerably broader than the river itself, as is illustrated in Figure 5.4. Sometimes a river erodes down into its floodplain and forms a new floodplain, leaving the older one at a higher level. The portions of the older floodplain that remain are called terraces.

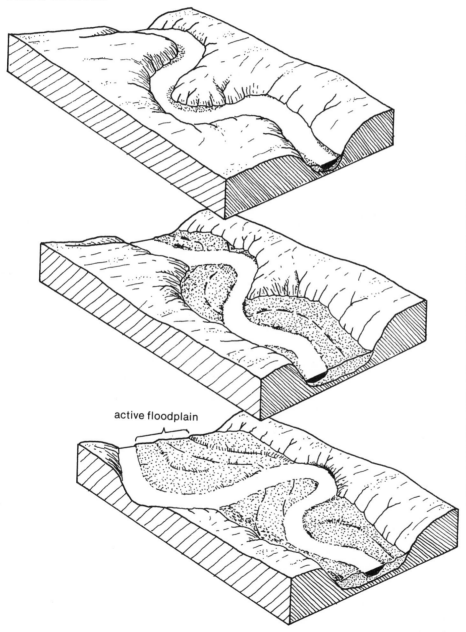

active floodplain

Figure 5.4. Despite what may be implied by the term, flood plains are not formed by floods. Rather, they are formed by lateral erosion and deposition of the river in its channel. (Illustration by Peter Van Dusen)

THE MAGNITUDE-FREQUENCY CONCEPT

The formal description of how often a flow of a given intensity can be expected to occur is called the magnitude-frequency concept. In a river, the basic variable that we can measure is the discharge. The magnitude of the discharge is the volume of water flowing past a point on the river, such as a bridge, per unit of time. The frequency, of course, is how often a given magnitude of flow occurs. The graph in Figure 5.5 schematically illustrates the principle of magnitude and frequency.

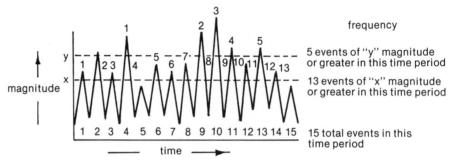

Figure 5.5. A schematic graph illustrating the magnitude and frequency of a river's flow.

In the United States the most commonly used unit of measurement for stream discharge is cubic feet per second, abbreviated "cfs" and sometimes called "second-feet." Other designations in use are acre-feet per month or year, millions of gallons per day, and cubic meters per second. Any unit can be used to describe discharge, as long as it expresses a *volume* per *time unit.* For determination of flood-prone areas, we are usually interested in the peak annual flow. This is the highest single discharge that occurs during the year. In order to evaluate analytically the importance of various magnitudes of events, we must express precisely their frequency of occurrence. In other words, we must determine the number of years which, on the average, separate events of a specific minimum magnitude. This is called the recurrence interval and is also known as the return period. For example, a practical person might wish to know that if the recurrence interval (t_r) of a given magnitude flood is fifty years, the probability (p) of occurrence is 0.02 in any given year:

$$p = \frac{1}{t_r} = \frac{1}{50} = 0.02$$

This flood is called the fifty-year flood and could ideally be expected to occur in 2 percent of the years over any period, for instance, a century. Given the opportunity to watch for the fifty-year flood over a period of, say, a thousand years, we might be surprised to find that few centuries would match the probability and produce exactly two 50-year floods. Some would produce four, others one or three, and some none. However, over many centuries, the probability of two per century would be met. It is important to realize that the term *recurrence* implies nothing cyclical about river flow and flooding.

Cyclic events are those which return to a given magnitude with a regular periodicity and are best exemplified in nature by biological processes such as the seasonal variations of plant growth in the midlatitudes. Since river flow is noncyclical, the fifty-year flood can occur in any year. The fact that it occurred last year does not mean that it will not occur again this year, or the fact that a large number of dry years have passed does not mean that a big flood is more likely this year. Again, the recurrence interval is simply the mean (statistical average) waiting time between events of a given magnitude. It can be used to determine the probability of occurrence of an event but cannot be used for prediction. By definition, a prediction implies identification of the time and place of occurrence.

Recurrence intervals can be determined from records which give the magnitude and time of peak flows over a sizable time period. Without a data record of past events, there is no basis for determining the recurrence interval. Moreover, the longer the record, the better the basis for determining probabilities, especially for infrequent events. The graph in Figure 5.6 shows the distribution of peak annual flows on the Eel River at Scotia, California, over the period from 1911 through 1969. Recall that the peak annual flow is the highest discharge recorded at a point on a river over the course of a year.

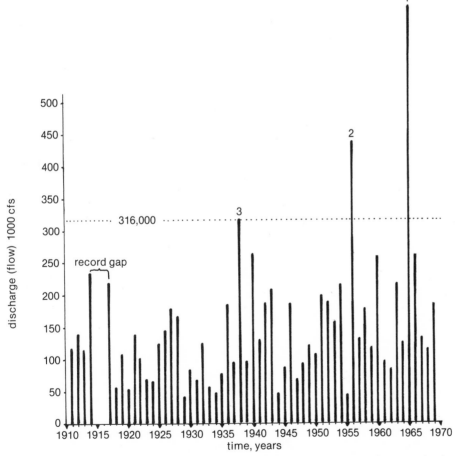

Figure 5.6. The distribution of peak annual flows on the Eel River at Scotia, California, for the period 1911–1969.

It is evident from this graph that only three flows were equal to or larger than 316,000 cubic feet per second (8949 or m³s). The recurrence interval of a flow equal to or greater than a given discharge is calculated with this formula:

$$t_r = \frac{n + 1}{m}$$

where

t_r is the recurrence interval in years
n is the total number of years, or events, i.e., 57
m is the rank of the peak annual flow (year) in question, e.g., the third largest flow is ranked 3

$$t_r = \frac{57 + 1}{3} = \frac{58}{3} = 19.3 \text{ years}$$

Thus, a flood flow of 315,000 cfs *or larger* magnitude has a recurrence interval of 19.3 years based on 57 years of peak annual discharge records. The probability for this event happening in any given year is

$$p = \frac{1}{19.3} = 0.05$$

This can also be read as 5 percent, a more meaningful expression to most of us.

With this three-step procedure, the probability of recurrence of *any* previously recorded peak annual flow of a river can be computed. For most planning purposes, this may be sufficient for general land use recommendations in and around river valleys. However, in some cases it may be necessary to analyze the data in

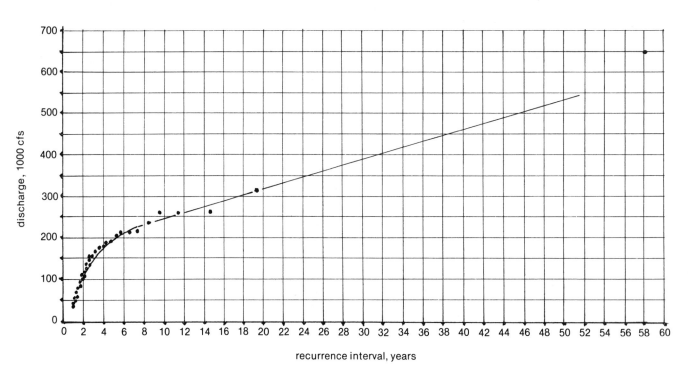

Figure 5.7. Peak annual flow plotted according to recurrence interval.

TABLE 5.1 THE YEAR, PEAK ANNUAL FLOW, AND RANK FOR THE EEL RIVER AT SCOTIA, CALIFORNIA

Year	Discharge (cfs)	Rank	Year	Discharge (cfs)	Rank
1911	116,000	32	1941	124,000	27
1912	137,000	24	1942	184,000	16
1913	111,000	35	1943	208,000	11
1914	231,000	7	1944	43,400	55
1915			1945	86,400	43
1916			1946	186,000	15
1917	218,000	8	1947	62,500	49
1918	53,600	52	1948	91,600	42
1919	108,000	36	1949	115,000	33
1920	52,000	53	1950	105,000	37
1921	138,000	23	1951	199,000	12
1922	100,000	38	1952	188,000	14
1923	69,200	47	1953	158,000	21
1924	62,000	50	1954	213,000	9
1925	121,000	30	1955	40,000	56
1926	141,000	22	1956	433,000	2
1927	179,000	18	1957	130,000	26
1928	166,000	20	1958	174,000	19
1929	37,100	57	1959	117,000	31
1930	81,800	45	1960	261,000	5
1931	64,600	48	1961	94,800	41
1932	123,000	28	1962	81,900	44
1933	53,600	51	1963	212,000	10
1934	44,500	54	1964	122,000	29
1935	77,300	46	1965	648,000	1
1936	182,000	17	1966	261,000	6
1937	95,300	40	1967	130,000	25
1938	316,000	3	1968	113,000	34
1939	96,500	39	1969	190,000	13
1940	261,000	4			

SOURCE: U.S. Geological Survey

greater detail and to make or evaluate projections of future flows. To accomplish this, the recurrence interval of *each* peak flow (Table 5.1) must be computed and plotted in a graph. Each recurrence interval is plotted against its respective discharge as illustrated in Figure 5.7.

A generalized line can be drawn through these points which provides a means to estimate the flow magnitudes for various recurrence intervals, or conversely, the recurrence intervals for various flow magnitudes. This can be especially useful for questions involving recurrence intervals and discharges which fall in the gaps in the data record, as in the gap between fifteen and nineteen years in Figure 5.7. The peak annual discharge with a thirteen-year recurrence interval (0.076 probability) is about 270,000 cfs (7645 m³s); the discharge with a ten-year recurrence interval (0.10 probability) is about 247,000 cfs (6995 m³s); and the recurrence interval for a discharge of 350,000 cfs (9912 m³s) is twenty-five years, or a probability of 0.04 of occurring in any year.

In order to use the graph in Figure 5.7 to make projections to estimate future flows and their probabilities, as well as to evaluate the meaning of the very largest flows, it is necessary to straighten the curve. This is imperative owing to the fact that any number of lines can be projected from the curved line. As tangents to the curve, the projections could all point in different directions and no one could be used with confidence. If, for example, the projection is made based on the lower part of the curve, then the estimates of very large flows (beyond the largest recorded flows) would be erroneously large. However, if the curve has been straightened, it can then be projected simply by ruling in a line beyond the largest flows.

The curve can be straightened by mathematical operations or by changing the scale on one or both axes of the graph. Recurrence-

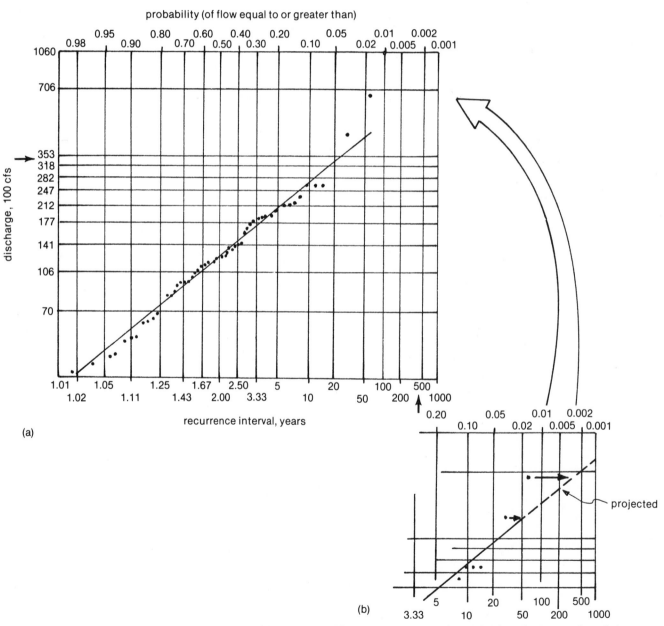

Figure 5.8(a). Peak annual flows and recurrence intervals plotted on a graph scaled to straighten the curve. (b). With a straightened curve, it is not only possible to project larger flows but also to evaluate the meaning of the very largest flows. For instance, the flow that is plotted as the fifty-eight-year flood really has a much larger recurrence interval when it is adjusted to the straightened curve.

interval data will usually plot in a straight graph line if a logarithmic scale is used on the discharge axis. That is, the logarithms of the discharge data rather than the data themselves assume a straight-line plot.

The graph in Figure 5.8(a) is the same as that in Figure 5.7 in which flow magnitude (discharge) is plotted against recurrence interval, except that the scales of the axes are different. In this particular case, the vertical axis is scaled logarithmically and the horizontal axis is scaled for probability in which the values are stretched out at the ends and compressed in the middle. (Such graph paper can be purchased from most drafting supply outlets.) These two scales combine in such a way that the data plot as a straight line and the necessary mathematical operations were performed by a simple alteration of the scales on the axes of the graph.

We are now in a position to consider the points originally posed; namely, the estimation of future flows and their probabilities and the meaning of the very largest flows. In the case of the latter, note that the highest discharges, at the right side of the graph, deviate considerably from the straight line at recurrence intervals greater than twenty years. The last point, which represents the highest flood (648,000 cfs) recorded on the Eel River with a recurrence interval of fifty-eight years, appears to have recorded a flood of even lower frequency (much higher magnitude of flow) than the true fifty-eight-year flow. To place the 648,000-cfs flood in more accurate perspective, we may adjust its point by moving it directly to the right until it falls on the straightened graph line [see Figure 5.8(b)]. Based on this adjustment, it appears that the probability of this flood is actually about 0.0025 and the recurrence interval is about four hundred years, rather than fifty-eight.

To check the accuracy of this interpretation, we can often look for botanical evidence in the river floodplain to indicate the date of the last flow of a comparable size. Tree trunks damaged by floodwater and its debris and the sprouts from flood-toppled trees are datable, and along the Eel River, they indicate that a similarly large flood occurred about three hundred to four hundred years ago. Floodplain vegetation is discussed in greater detail later in this chapter.

Projection of the curve beyond the magnitude and recurrence interval values of the largest recorded floods affords a limited basis for estimating unrecorded, infrequent flows. Since a projection is based on existing data representing a very short flow record compared to the total time that the river has been flowing, estimates must be interpreted with caution. Projected estimates are *not* predictions, but only probabilities and usually general ones at that. For the five hundred-year flood on the Eel River, for example, the discharge would be about 700,000 cfs (19824 m³s). This can be read from the graph as is shown by the arrows in Figure 5.8(a).

RELATIONS BETWEEN DISCHARGE, THE WATER SURFACE, AND THE TERRAIN

The discharge of a river is controlled by the processes that supply water to the river such as rainfall, snowfall, and snowmelt and by the characteristics of the drainage basin such as size, shape, orientation, network, and infiltration capacity. But the drainage basin itself is a creation of the river and presumably is related to a long history of erosion and deposition as well as to subsurface geologic structure. For planning purposes, it is necessary to translate discharge data and data on the elevation of the adjacent floodplain into information about the area flooded during high flows (Figure 5.9). The critical questions are how high will the water surface be and what will be the areal extent of the flooded zone for a given flood frequency? If the answers to these questions can be supplied for a range of flood frequencies, they would provide a rational basis for assigning land uses to river valleys as well as estimating flood impact on existing land use. Even if estimates are only approximate, the information can be helpful in defining land use alternatives and providing guidelines for environmental management.

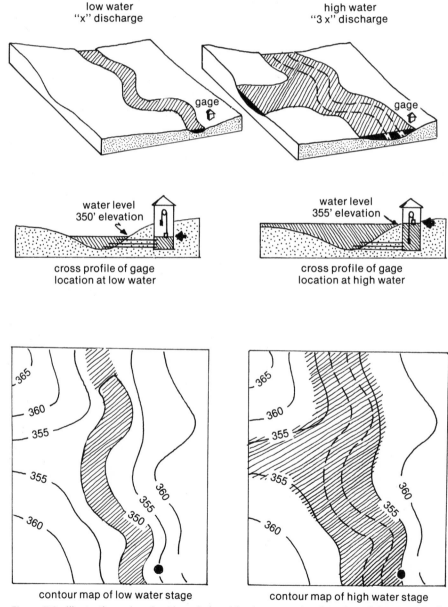

Figure 5.9. Illustrations showing the relationships between the elevation of the water surface and the elevation of the terrain in the river valley. (Illustration by Peter Van Dusen)

Much of the problem in assigning land use to presently undeveloped terrain lies in identifying areas of present-day floodplains and in relating these to flow magnitude and frequency. All floodplains are formed by similar processes, and thus they exhibit similar characteristics: (1) a relatively low, gently sloping surface, usually bounded by valley walls or terraces; (2) relatively high water table, consequently drainage may be poor; (3) vegetation consisting of species adapted to wet and flooded soil conditions; and (4) occasional inundation by river water.

As mentioned in the introduction to this chapter, the U.S. Geological Survey is presently mapping certain areas in the United States that would be flooded by the 100-year flood. This frequency was chosen arbitrarily as a measure of a severe flood. However, for several reasons a local or regional planning agency may wish to make its own estimates of flood-prone areas. The Survey may not yet have mapped the area in question, or the drainage basin may be too small to meet the Survey's criteria. An agency might also wish to examine flood-prone areas more critically; for example, there is often a need to identify flooded areas associated with the more frequent floods, so that the persistent annual problems are identified and anticipated, as well as the disastrous, infrequent events.

A number of methods of floodplain definition have been suggested by the geomorphologist M. G. Wolman (1971), and these are suitable for our purposes:

1. *Physiographic*—identification and mapping of the flat, low-lying areas near rivers.

2. *Soils*—identification of materials deposited by channel flows and flood flows.

3. *Vegetation*—delineation of plant assemblages which are associated with high soil moisture and flood conditions.

4. *Local and regional flood history*—determination of the extent of inundated areas based on river discharge records.

These methods are discussed in detail below beginning with Figure 5.10, which schematically summarizes the patterns of topography, vegetation, and soils typically found in river valleys.

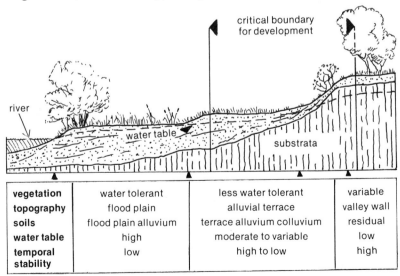

vegetation	water tolerant	less water tolerant	variable
topography	flood plain	alluvial terrace	valley wall
soils	flood plain alluvium	terrace alluvium colluvium	residual
water table	high	moderate to variable	low
temporal stability	low	high to low	high

Figure 5.10. The relationships of drainage, topography, soils, and vegetative conditions in a typical stream valley.

Physiography

The lowest part of a river valley is the floodplain, and studies carried out in the United States, Canada, England, and Australia have shown that this land is flooded on the average of once every one or two years. A floodplain can usually be identified from contour maps on the basis of several distinctive topographic features. First, its outer edges are often marked by the relatively steep slopes of the valley walls. Second, traces of former positions of the river channel can usually be found in the floodplain. These appear on topographic maps in the form of oxbow lakes, for example, which are water-filled segments of old channels now separated from the active channel. Terraces are a third topographic feature of floodplains, and they often appear as benches situated against the valley walls. Because they are higher than the floodplain floor, they are less susceptible to flooding. The contour map in Figure 5.11 depicts these topographical features in a typical floodplain.

Once the floodplain of a river is delimited, a relative indication of flood susceptibility can be assigned to various parts of it. For example, the lowest area (usually the floodplain floor) would be designated "highest susceptibility," and the highest area "lowest susceptibility." Terraces would be intermediate. The principal drawback

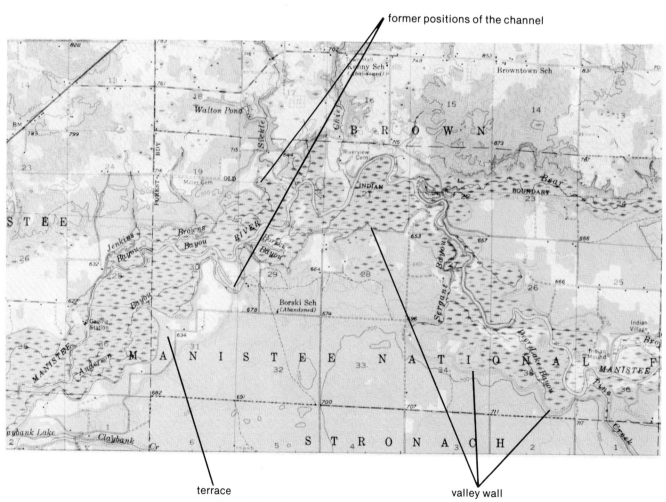

Figure 5.11. A topographic contour map showing various floodplain features.

of this method of mapping flood-prone areas lies in the difficulty of establishing reliable correlations between topographic form and flood frequency. In other words, the question of what area of the floodplain would be inundated by the ten-year flood, for instance, cannot be answered.

Mapping flood-prone areas by soils may be even more difficult

Soils

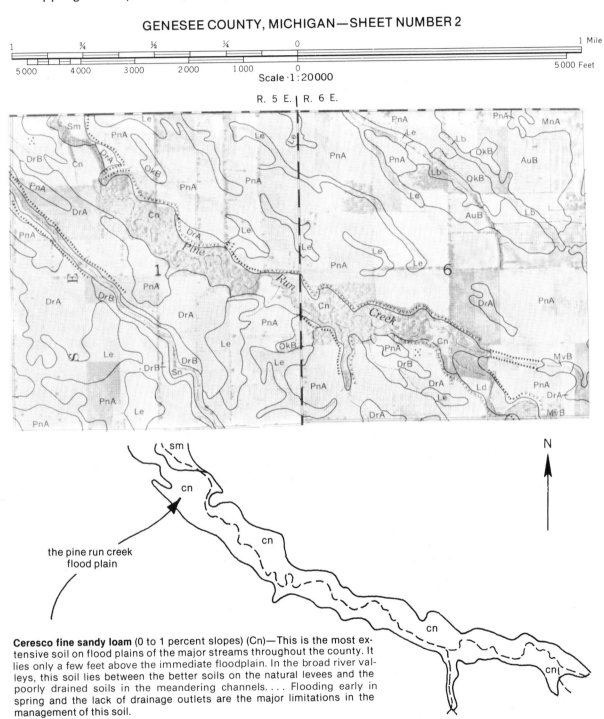

GENESEE COUNTY, MICHIGAN—SHEET NUMBER 2

Scale ·1 : 20 000

Ceresco fine sandy loam (0 to 1 percent slopes) (Cn)—This is the most extensive soil on flood plains of the major streams throughout the county. It lies only a few feet above the immediate floodplain. In the broad river valleys, this soil lies between the better soils on the natural levees and the poorly drained soils in the meandering channels. . . . Flooding early in spring and the lack of drainage outlets are the major limitations in the management of this soil.

Figure 5.12. Soils maps can provide information on the extent of floodplains. Shown here is an excerpt from an SCS county soil study for a valley that contains a stream for which there is no flow data.

the pine run creek flood plain

than by topography, because the required correlations are usually more difficult to establish. However, soil maps can often be utilized to strengthen estimates based on topographic features. The preparation of soil maps is costly and is not proposed here as a method of delimiting flood areas, but where soil maps already exist they may be used. Alluvial (river-deposited) soils must be distinguished from nonalluvial soils, and this information is often given in the Soil Conservation Service descriptions of local soils. At the very least, this would indicate areas that have been flooded in the past, although the specific relationship of flood frequency and soil type is difficult to establish. If, in selected areas, however, a certain type correlates strongly with the physiographic floodplain, then mapping can be extended by delineating this key soil on the Soil Conservation Service maps. The map and soil description in Figure 5.12 are taken from a SCS county soils report. Note that the soil designated "Cn" appears to provide a fairly accurate indication of the floodplain of this creek, for which, incidentally, no discharge records exist.

Vegetation

In many areas of the United States and Canada specific assemblages of plants grow on areas subject to flooding. Such plants usually have identifiable evolutionary adaptations to cope with the environmental stresses on the floodplain. For example, they must be able to withstand erosion and deposition around the roots as well as prolonged saturated soil conditions. They may be supple, to resist being uprooted by flowing water, or they may be able to continue growing even after being toppled, by sending out adventitious roots, with former limbs assuming the roles of trunks. The major drawback of mapping floodplains by vegetation assemblages is that individual species are usually found over a wide range, and while spatial differences exist, the ranges of the species are usually not sufficiently marked to accurately determine flood-prone areas. Nevertheless, in almost all regions some species, tolerant of wet, poorly drained sites, are identified as "riparian," and these can serve as rough indicators of areas subject to inundation.

The damage that vegetation suffers from floodwaters can sometimes be used to define the extent of recent floods and to date past floods. As the upper illustration in Figure 5.13 shows, the floating debris snagged from floodwaters by limbs and trunks can be used as an indicator of the level of a recent flood. In addition, the growth rings of stems which have sprouted from toppled trees can be counted to date the toppling of trees (Figure 5.13). If many of these can be found on a suspect floodplain, their dates may corroborate one another. The principal drawback of this technique is that the actual height of a flood cannot be determined. On the other hand, in some areas this method is often the only reliable indicator of high-magnitude floods, owing to the absence or brevity of discharge records.

According to the discussion in Chapter 4, the general structure of the vegetative cover can also be used to help delimit floodplains. In dry areas such as the Great Plains and the Southwest, floodplains are often the only sites which support tree-sized vegetation. In areas of intensive agriculture throughout the East, Midwest, and South, floodplains have traditionally been among the least desira-

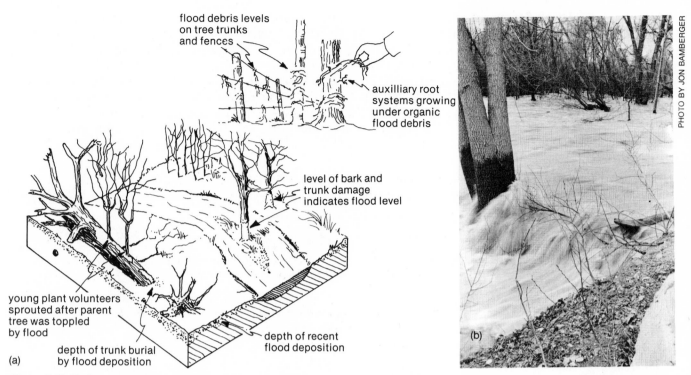

flood debris levels on tree trunks and fences

auxilliary root systems growing under organic flood debris

level of bark and trunk damage indicates flood level

young plant volunteers sprouted after parent tree was toppled by flood

depth of trunk burial by flood deposition

depth of recent flood deposition

(a)

(b)

Figure 5.13. Various vegetative indicators of past floods. (Illustration by Peter Van Dusen)

ble farmland. Consequently, they remain uncleared and appear as sinuous belts of forest winding through the farm fields. Although the lack of intensive agricultural use of floodplains frequently reflect the cumulative results of observations by several generations of farmers—a valuable source of information in itself—it may also reflect the absence of land use pressure in a particular area. In other words, the use of river valleys in some areas does not necessarily indicate the lack of a floodplain or infrequent flooding.

Flood History

In river valleys where large floods have occurred during the period of recorded discharge, their frequencies can be evaluated by the techniques described earlier in this chapter, and their heights and areal extents determined by a variety of methods. The most accurate of these methods is to actually map, by field survey and photogrammetry, the flood level associated with a given discharge. This level can usually be determined from deposits of sediment and bits of vegetative matter after a recent flood. Once the depth and water-surface slope are evaluated for a high discharge, the rough-

Flood Lines and Backwater Curves

ness of the channel can be estimated, and backwater effects can be considered. Using this information, the water-surface profile for other high discharges can be calculated, assuming: (1) no signifi-cant channel changes take place in the interim and (2) ice or other floating debris in the river does not significantly change the surface elevation–discharge relationship. The computations involved are standard engineering practice, but the cost is enormous in compari-son to other methods. Because of the detailed topographic informa-tion needed, it often exceeds $1000 per mile of channel.

Rough estimates of surface elevation and areal extent of recent floods can be determined by cheaper, more rapid methods, how-

Remote Sensing

ever. Remote-sensing imagery taken during or soon after a large flood might be used to map areas inundated, although poor weather associated with the flood might inhibit such efforts. Recent technological advances, such as radar, might be used to map flood extent over large areas during major floods. The use of Landsat imagery offers intriguing possibilities because of the frequency of coverage and the comparatively low cost. Rango and Salomonson (1974) utilized the near-infrared band (0.8–1.1 micrometers) to

TABLE 5.2   PEAK ANNUAL STAGE AND DISCHARGE FOR GAGING STATIONS ON THE CASS RIVER AND THE SOUTH BRANCH OF THE CASS RIVER, MICHIGAN

Streams Tributary to Lake Huron

1505. Cass River at Cass City, Mich.

Location.—Lat 43°35'10", long 83°10'35", in NE¼ sec. 4, T.13 N., R.11 E., on left bank 500 ft downstream from highway bridge, half a mile downstream from confluence of North Branch and East Branch, and 1 mile south of Cass City.

Drainage area.—370 sq mi, approximately.

Gage.—Nonrecording prior to Nov. 14, 1952; recording thereafter. At site 500 ft upstream prior to Nov. 14, 1952. Datum of gage is 697.92 ft above mean sea level, datum of 1929.

Stage-discharge relation.—Defined by current-meter measurements below 6,500 cfs.

Bankfull stage.—12 ft.

Remarks.—Only annual peaks are shown prior to 1953. Base for partial-duration series, 1,400 cfs.

Peak stages and discharges

Water year	Date	Gage height (feet)	Discharge (cfs)	Water year	Date	Gage height (feet)	Discharge (cfs)
1948	Mar. 20, 1948	15.80	8,460	1956	Apr. 3, 1956	8.32	1,500
1949	Feb 15, 1949	10.58	2,740		Apr. 30, 1956	10.13	2,830
1950	Mar. 28, 1950	14.31	7,250		May 6, 1956	10.71	3,310
					May 10, 1956	10.47	3,150
1951	Feb. 27, 1951	12.05	4,150		May 13, 1956	10.28	2,990
1952	Mar. 11, 1952	11.21	3,300				
				1957	Feb 26, 1957	a9.87	1,400
1953	Mar. 4, 1953	a10.42	2,200		Apr. 7, 1957	8.60	1,710
	Mar. 16, 1953	9.62	2,430		Apr. 28, 1957	8.30	1,500
	May 3, 1953	9.71	2,510				
				1958	Mar. 5, 1958	b9.02	1,280
1954	Feb. 16, 1954	10.54	3,150				
	Feb. 21, 1954	11.23	3,710	1959	Mar. 26, 1959	a10.94	2,800
	Mar. 1, 1954	8.19	1,430		Apr. 4, 1959	11.58	3,900
	Mar. 20, 1954	9.08	2,060				
	Mar. 26, 1954	11.85	4,240	1960	Dec. 13, 1959	8.43	1,430
	Apr. 27, 1954	9.00	2,060		Dec. 29, 1959	9.60	2,260
					Mar. 31, 1960	14.41	6,810
1955	Dec. 29, 1954	8.59	1,710		May 31, 1960	8.34	1,420
	Jan. 6, 1955	8.95	1,990				
	Feb. 23, 1955	a8.70	1,500	1961	Sept. 27, 1961	c9.00	1,400
	Mar. 4, 1955	8.46	1,600				
	Mar. 11, 1955	10.29	2,990	1962	Mar. 18, 1962	11.67	3,980
	Mar. 22, 1955	8.21	1,430		May 3, 1962	9.22	1,990
1956	Mar. 7, 1956	11.19	3,710				

a Backwater from ice.
b Occurred Mar. 3, 1958 (backwater from ice).
c Occurred Feb 24, 1961 (backwater from ice).

SOURCE: U.S. Geological Survey, *Magnitude and Frequency of Floods in the United States,* part 4, Water Supply Paper 1817.

detect standing surface water, excessive soil moisture, and stressed vegetation, which persist in a flooded area for two to three weeks after the occurrence of a flood. During this time such areas have very low reflectance in this band and are dark-colored on positive images. The imagery enabled them to map flooded areas from four floods in the United States in 1972.

A technique which offers reasonable accuracy and low analysis costs is one which compares floodwater elevation (stage) with the topographic elevation of the floodplain. This requires that discharge data and their respective stages are employed. For a discharge of a given frequency, one needs to extract from the USGS record the stage of this flow (i.e., the recorded height of the water surface) and then compare it to the elevation of the surrounding floodplain as is schematically illustrated in Figures 5.14 and 5.9. The method is illustrated below to estimate the area inundated by the

Interpolation from Gage Heights

1500. South Branch Cass River near Cass City, Mich.

Location.—Lat 43°34'10", long 83°06'30", in NW¼ sec. 7, T.13 N., R. 12 E., on left bank 1¾ miles downstream from bridge on State Highway 53, 3 miles upstream from confluence with North Branch, and 4 miles southeast of Cass City.

Drainage area.—251 sq mi.

Gage.—Nonrecording at site 1¾ miles upstream at different datum prior to Nov. 8, 1952; recording thereafter. Datum of gage is 719.5 ft above mean sea level, datum of 1929.

Stage-discharge relation.—Defined by current-meter measurements.

Bankfull stage.—10 ft.

Remarks.—Only annual peaks are shown prior to 1953. Base for partial-duration series, 1,100 cfs.

Peak stages and discharges

Water year	Date	Gage height (feet)	Discharge (cfs)	Water year	Date	Gage height (feet)	Discharge (cfs)
1949	Feb. 15, 1949	20.50	2,600	1956	Mar. 7, 1956	a10.25	2,650
1950	Mar. 28, 1950	23.07	4,940		Apr. 30, 1956	—	b2,100
					May 6, 1956	—	b2,500
1951	Feb. 26, 1951	20.93	2,920		May 10, 1956	9.24	2,610
1952	Mar. 12, 1952	20.5	2,600		May 13, 1956	9.83	2,370
1953	Mar. 4, 1953	a7.54	1,500	1957	Apr. 7, 1957	6.75	1,330
	Mar. 16, 1953	7.73	1,750				
	May 3, 1953	7.66	1,750	1958	Mar. 4, 1958	c6.74	d800
1954	Feb. 16, 1954	(a)	2,300	1959	Mar. 25, 1959	a10.17	2,200
	Feb. 21, 1954	9.60	2,850		Apr. 2, 1959	9.72	2,920
	Mar. 1, 1954	6.11	1,100				
	Mar. 20, 1954	7.27	1,550	1960	Dec. 12, 1959	6.57	1,180
	Mar. 26, 1954	0.77	2,970		Dec. 29, 1959	—	b1,780
	Apr. 27, 1954	6.97	1,430		Mar. 31, 1960	13.00	4,890
1955	Dec. 29, 1954	6.07	1,100	1961	Sept. 26, 1961	e7.61	1,190
	Jan. 6, 1955	6.88	1,390				
	Mar. 4, 1955	(a)	1,200	1962	Mar. 19, 1962	f10.94	2,690
	Mar. 11, 1955	8.45	2,130		May 3, 1962	7.86	1,830
	Mar. 22, 1955	6.24	1,110		June 15, 1962	6.80	1,160

a   Backwater from ice.
b   Occurred during period of no gage-height record.
c   Occurred Mar. 2, 1953 (backwater from ice).
d   Maximum daily.
e   Occurred Feb. 24, 1961 (backwater from ice).
f   Occurred Mar. 18, 1962 (backwater from ice).

SOURCE: U.S. Geological Survey, *Magnitude and Frequency of Floods in the United States,* part 4, Water-Supply Paper 1677.

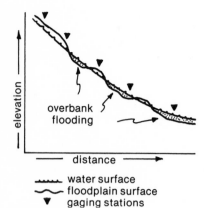

Figure 5.14. A schematic graph illustrating the relationship between the surface of floodwaters and the elevation of the adjacent terrain.

water surface
floodplain surface
gaging stations

flood of March 31, 1960, on the Cass River in Cass County, Michigan. The two gaging stations used are on the South Branch and one 4.4 miles downstream on the Cass River itself. The pertinent data are given in Table 5.2. These data are taken from U.S. Geological Survey *Water Supply Paper* no. 1677.

Where several gaging stations exist along a river, as is not uncommon in populous areas, a water-surface profile (or gradient) can be constructed for any given flood by constructing a straight line representing the elevation decrease between successive stations. If the elevations between gaging stations are not too great, the method is reasonably accurate. If this is not the case, the method should not be used, because most river gradients are concave, and a straight line between two points may not actually represent the true water-surface profile.

We may, however, make the assumption that for the Cass River the water-surface profile between the gaging stations is straight. The slope of this profile is 4.6 feet per mile. To facilitate translation of flood-stage data into information on the area inundated, the distance between the two stations may be divided into any number of segments. In this example, six equal area segments and the

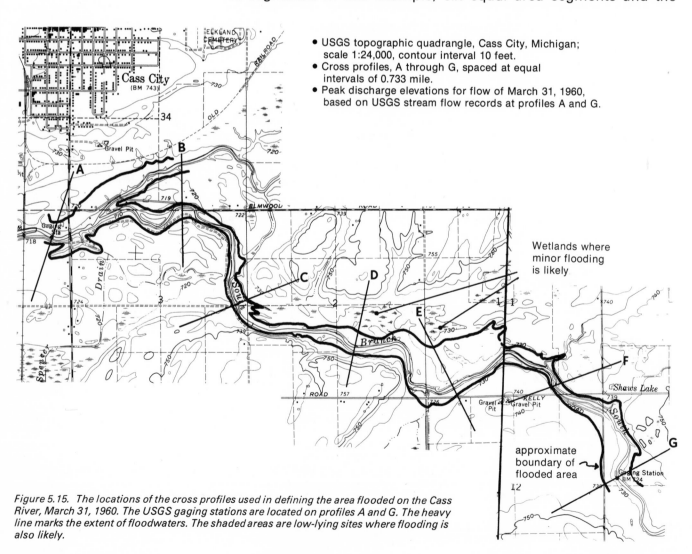

- USGS topographic quadrangle, Cass City, Michigan; scale 1:24,000, contour interval 10 feet.
- Cross profiles, A through G, spaced at equal intervals of 0.733 mile.
- Peak discharge elevations for flow of March 31, 1960, based on USGS stream flow records at profiles A and G.

Wetlands where minor flooding is likely

approximate boundary of flooded area

Figure 5.15. The locations of the cross profiles used in defining the area flooded on the Cass River, March 31, 1960. The USGS gaging stations are located on profiles A and G. The heavy line marks the extent of floodwaters. The shaded areas are low-lying sites where flooding is also likely.

seven profiles which bound them were constructed from the USGS topographic map of the area. The locations of these are shown in Figure 5.15 and the elevations of each are recorded in the graph in Figure 5.16(a). Bear in mind that only the elevations at the ends of the graph are actually known; therefore, each intervening elevation represents an interpolation from these two points.

With an estimate of the elevation of the March 31, 1960, flood at each segment [represented by the upper line in the graph in Figure 5.16(a)], we can now approximate the area of the valley that was

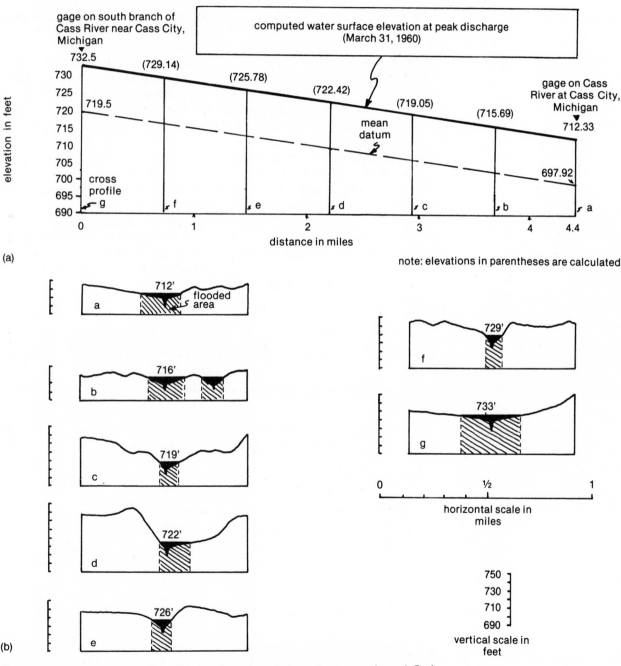

Figure 5.16(a). The elevation of the flood surface plotted along the stream channel. Each vertical line represents a cross profile. (b) The elevation of the flood in the river valley at each cross profile.

flooded. This requires merely plotting the flood elevation of each profile at the equivalent elevation on both sides of the river valley. These are shown in the form of the cross-sectional profiles in Figure 5.16b. Linked together, they delimit in Figure 5.15 the extent of the floodwater on the valley floor.

The potential for error in delimiting the areal extent of a flood of given frequency depends mainly on the shape of the river valley. Consider the four schematic cross sections shown below in Figure 5.17. In section A, there is only a small difference in the flooded area at stage "x" compared to that of the much larger flow represented by stage "y." The increased volume of flow is contained within steep valley walls. In section B, however, the same flows produce differences in the breadth of the flooded area, owing of course, to the gentle slope of the valley walls. In section C, once the flow overtops the channel banks, it spreads out over the entire flood-plain. If the flow is even higher, it will inundate portions of the valley walls, but the additional area flooded will not be substantial. In section D, a flood height just short of the elevation of the terrace will flood a much smaller area than a flood height just over the terrace elevation.

Depending on the shape of a river valley's cross section, it is possible to evaluate whether a precise estimate of the flood height associated with a given flow frequency is needed. Where small differences in stage would encompass large areas on the ground, the estimation of flood heights must be accurate and therefore carefully undertaken. On the other hand, where a large range in flow magnitudes would all flood about the same area, land use planning within that area need not depend on precise and expensive flood-height estimates.

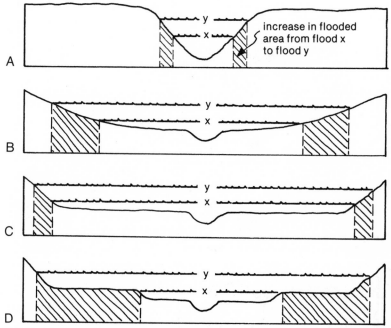

Figure 5.17. Diagrams showing the relationship of valley shape to the area inundated by floods of x and y elevations. The shaded areas represent the increase in flooded area with a rise in water level from x to y.

INFLOODING

Not all flood problems result from a stream overflowing its bank and spilling into nearby lowlands. Flooding also occurs in upstream areas when surface water collects in low spots before reaching a stream channel. This is called inflooding and is especially prevalent in areas of flat ground with low infiltration capacities or where drainage is closed in hilly terrain (Figure 5.18). Inflooding usually begins with the formation of "mud puddles" and reaches its maximum during or shortly after the rainstorm with the formation of shallow but extensive ponds, as depicted in Figure 5.19.

In small drainage basins, drainage caused by inflooding is often more serious than that caused by the overbank flooding described earlier. Crop damage, late planting, stunted crops, septic-field malfunction, cellar flooding, and lawn damage are some of the land

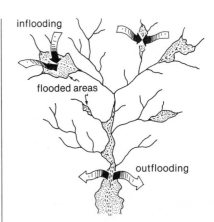

Figure 5.18. A schematic diagram of inflooding and outflooding in a drainage basin.

PHOTO BY PETER VAN DUSEN

Figure 5.19. Ponded water resulting from inflooding is shown in the foreground. The main body of water in the center of the picture is a result of outflooding from a stream channel.

use problems resulting from this process. Because small basins usually do not have USGS gaging stations, it is necessary to consult topographic maps and soil maps for indicators of inflooding. If relatively modern, large-scale contour maps and SCS soil maps are available, most areas susceptible to inflooding can be identified.

The hydrographic information (e.g., swamps and streams) which appears on USGS topographic contour maps should be viewed with a certain amount of suspicion, however, in small and marginal areas. Contemporary topographic maps are produced from aerial photographs, most of which are taken in the summer and fall when

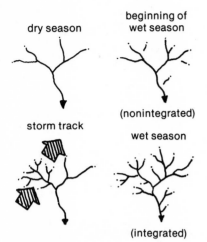

Figure 5.20. Changes in the extent of a drainage net in response to storm movement and seasons.

dry season

beginning of wet season

(nonintegrated)

storm track

wet season

(integrated)

many of the more subtle water features are relatively obscure. Moreover, the USGS maps attempt to show only perennial and intermittent streams. Ephemeral streams, which carry only storm runoff or which carry flows for less than a month during the year, are not shown. In relation to land use and land use decisions, however, the overall ephemeral flow network is important (see Figure 3.16, Chapter 3). Therefore, the drainage network should be viewed as a "pulsing" phenomenon, decreasing in the total extent during dry periods and increasing in extent as channels take on water in response to wet conditions as the illustration in Figure 5.20 attempts to portray. For planning purposes, ephemeral stream channels can often be identified from topographic maps, but we strongly urge an aerial photograph and field examination of areas in question (Figure 5.21). To fully appreciate the hydrologic changes that occur during such events, one should actually attempt to observe problem areas during a rainstorm.

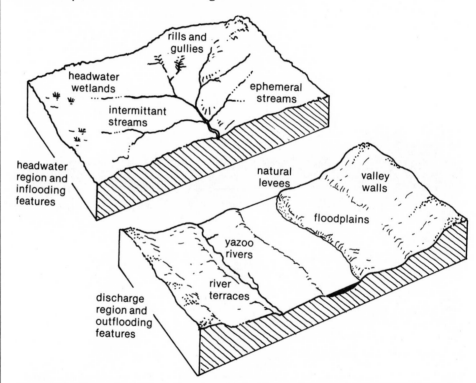

Figure 5.21. River valley features in areas of inflooding and areas of outflooding. (Illustration by Peter Van Dusen)

URBANIZATION AND FLOODPLAIN PROCESSES

While the drainage basin is a creation of the river itself, other processes can change the drainage basin's hydrologic characteristics. Land use changes, in particular, can dramatically alter the manner in which runoff from the drainage basin eventually makes its way to a river. Therefore, identification of relations between flood frequency and the areal extent of flooding may not be valid after a change in land use has occurred. This is particularly true if the land use changes from rural to urban.

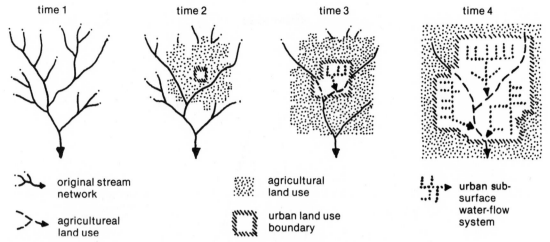

time 1　　　　　time 2　　　　　time 3　　　　　time 4

.⋅⟩⟨ original stream
network

⟩→ agricultureal
land use

⋰⋅⋅ agricultural
land use

⟩⟨ urban land use
boundary

⌐⌐⌐¬ urban sub-
surface
water-flow
system

Figure 5.22. Changes in a drainage network with agricultural and urban development (after Van Dusen, 1971).

The major hydrologic changes accompanying urbanization are changes in the surface characteristics, changes in the stream network, suppression of natural surface flow into subsurface conduits, and the addition of new, artificial flow systems.

Surface Cover and Runoff

The major change in surface characteristics is the increase in impervious area. As described earlier, much of the rain that falls on nonurbanized surfaces infiltrates into the soil, and only a small portion of it usually runs off over the surface of the ground. Many urban surfaces, however, are impervious. Streets, parking lots, and roofs all represent surfaces whose infiltration capacity is virtually zero, and therefore all the rain which falls on them will run off. The percentage of an area which becomes impervious due to urbanization will vary, of course. For small areas, it can be accurately measured from aerial photographs, but for large areas, this process may be too time-consuming. The hydrologist Luna B. Leopold points out that in large developed areas, rough estimates of the coefficient of runoff can be made, using either population density or average lot size (see Chapter 3 for a discussion of the coefficient of runoff).

Urbanization also alters the lower-order parts of the drainage network. As a region undergoes urbanization, a "pruning" of the stream network takes place, and the surface flow is routed into a submerged network of storm sewers. In addition, sanitary sewers and water supply lines provide new flow systems as indicated in the following schematic diagram (Figure 5.22).

Changes in the Rainfall-Runoff Relation

The principal effect of changing the surface characteristics and drainage network of a region is to alter the rainfall-runoff relation. Surface infiltration capacity is lowered, and very little water percolates into the soil. To prevent ponding in streets and parking lots and other inflooding problems, this water is transferred as quickly as possible into a storm-sewer system; thence it flows to a local stream.

The net effect is that *more* water runs off relatively soon after a storm, and it reaches the stream channel *faster* than it would under preurban conditions. The flood peak is thus higher and sooner

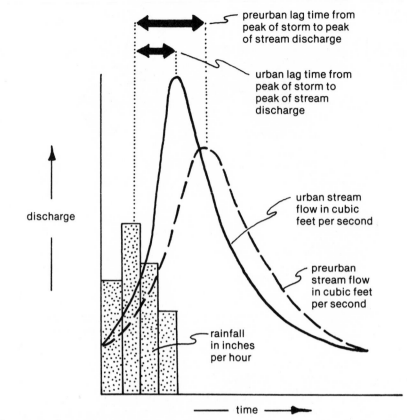

preurban lag time from peak of storm to peak of stream discharge

urban lag time from peak of storm to peak of stream discharge

urban stream flow in cubic feet per second

preurban stream flow in cubic feet per second

discharge

rainfall in inches per hour

time

Figure 5.23. Stream hydrograph changes resulting from urbanization of the drainage basin (after Leopold, 1968).

(Figure 5.23). The amount of increase is related to the percentage of impervious area and to the percentage of the area served by the storm sewers. With less infiltration, the amount of water reaching the groundwater will, of course, be smaller.

The increase in the magnitude of a flood of given frequency due to urbanization can bedevil careful land use planning. If a significant portion of a drainage basin is likely to become urbanized, estimates of post urban flood magnitude-frequency relations should allow for such an increase. However, enlightened planning can reduce the deleterious effects of urbanization. Even in areas of relatively high population densities, permeable areas such as greenbelts can be established to ensure some infiltration of surface water. Storm-sewer runoff need not be carried as quickly as possible into a major stream but can be routed to infiltration areas, temporarily stored underground, or held in surface retention ponds.

SUMMARY

Using a variety of information which is readily available throughout the United States, the land use planner can delineate areas where flood problems would be likely or can critically evaluate delineations made by consultants or other agencies. Combined with an understanding of the flood magnitude-frequency concept, this allows one to assign land uses to these zones according to flood hazard. In addition, land use plans can be adjusted to reduce somewhat the deleterious effects of urbanization on hydrologic processes.

Discharge records for approximately 8000 streams in the United States are kept by the U.S. Geological Survey and published annually for each state in the *Surface Water Records* (see the following chapter for a description of USGS publications). Occasionally these are updated, and many years of data for a large area are combined in a *Water Supply Paper*. Occasionally a summary of the entire data record for a single state is published as a special report. For example, the Eel River data in this chapter were found in a publication called *California Streamflow Characteristics* (1970). The entire flow records for every gaging station are stored on magnetic tape, and such tapes, or punched cards, are available at low cost from regional offices of the U.S. Geological Survey.

Bibliography

Chorley, Richard J., (ed.): *Water, Earth and Man,* Methuen, London, 1969. A collection of chapters dealing with both human and physical aspects of the hydrologic cycle.

Hjelmfelt, Allen T., Jr., and John J. Cassidy: *Hydrology for Engineers and Planners,* Iowa State University Press, Ames, Iowa, 1975. A recent hydrology text with emphasis on urban problems.

Leopold, Luna B.: *Hydrology for Urban Land Planning—a Guidebook on the Hydrologic Effects of Urban Land Use,* U.S. Geological Survey Circular 454, 1968. A summary of changes in stream regimen due to urbanization.

Leopold, Luna B.: *Water: a Primer,* Freeman, San Francisco, 1974. An elementary text on the hydrologic cycle and associated environmental problems.

Leopold, Luna B., M. Gordon Wolman, and John P. Miller: *Fluvial Processes in Geomorphology,* Freeman, San Francisco, 1964.

Meyer, William, and Robin I. Welch: "Water Resources Assessment," in L. W. Bowden and E. L. Pruitt (eds.), *Manual of Remote Sensing,* vol. II, American Society of Photogrammetry, Falls Church, 1975, pp. 1479–1551. Review of the use of remote sensing in water resources assessment and problems, including flood-area mapping.

Rango, Albert, and Vincent V. Salomonson: "Regional Flood Mapping from Space," *Water Resources Research,* vol. 10, 1974, pp.473–484. A description of the use of ERTS (now called Landsat) imagery to map flooded areas.

Schaake, John C., Jr.: "Water and the City," in T. R. Detwyler, and M. G. Marcus (eds.), *Urbanization and Environment: The Physical Geography of the City,* Duxbury Press, Belmont, 1972, pp. 97–133. Summary of water supply and flood hazards in urban areas.

Van Dusen, Peter: *Spatial Organizations of Watershed Systems,* Ph.D Dissertation, The University of Michigan, Ann Arbor, 1971.

Wisler, Chester O., and Ernest F. Brater,: *Hydrology,* 2d ed., Wiley, New York, 1959. Standard, well-written hydrology text with good discussion of determination of flood frequencies.

Wolman, M. Gordon: "Evaluating Alternative Techniques of Floodplain Mapping," *Water Resources Research,* vol. 7, 1971, pp. 1383–1392. An evaluation of the costs and drawbacks of various methods of mapping flood-prone areas.

CHAPTER **6**

PUBLIC SOURCES AND ACQUISITION OF ENVIRONMENTAL INFORMATION

M. Leonard Bryan

INTRODUCTION

THE PREVIOUS CHAPTERS focused on techniques for the generation of environmental information from conventional sources such as topographic maps, aerial photographs, and soil maps. Although often overshadowed by the emergence of new data and information technologies, these sources of environmental information remain fundamental to the planning process. Therefore, it is appropriate to examine the nature and origins of those sources' utility in the planning community.

Within the federal government of the United States, numerous agencies are continually involved in the production of maps, aerial photographs, and tabular data on the environment. Many of these sources are of little importance to land use planning because of continental or regional scales of coverage or the esoteric nature of the phenomena portrayed. Others, however, are of vital importance to the planning community. Primary among these are the various topographic maps and hydrologic data published by the U.S. Geological Survey, the soil maps published by the Soil Conservation Service, and the aerial photographs produced by the Agricultural Stabilization and Conservation Service (ASCS).

U.S. GEOLOGICAL SURVEY SOURCES

The entire coterminous United States has coverage in the form of state base maps at scales of 1:1,000,000 (1 inch to 16 miles) (1 centimeter to 10 kilometers) and 1:500,000 (1 inch to 8 miles) (1 centimeter to 5 kilometers) (Table 6.1). The 1:1,000,000 series is published in black and white and shows rivers, railroads, and settlements. Those settlements with populations in excess of 10,000 are indicated by an outline of the political boundaries, whereas a more precise indication of the population is given by the letter size used for the settlement's name. Major airports with scheduled service are indicated by an airplane symbol. County boundaries and the township and range lines are also shown; however, only the counties are named. Several spot elevations are indicated for each state. The utility of this series is primarily as base maps for regional planning. The black-and-white format facilitates sketching boundaries of selected broad regional phenomena. The absence of topographic contours and the age of some sheets (ten to twenty years),

	Compila-tion date	Scale 1:1,000,000			Scale 1:5,000,000				
		Base	Shaded relief	Overall size, in inches	Base	Base with highways	Topo-graphic	Shaded relief	Overall size, in inches
Alabama	1964	$0.50	——	16 × 24	$1.00	——	$2.00	$2.00	32 × 46
Arizona	1955	0.50	——	24 × 29	1.00	——	2.00	2.00	47 × 56
Arkansas	1965	0.50	——	18 × 21	1.00	——	2.00	2.00	35 × 39
California	1963	0.50	$1.00	42 × 48	——	——	——	——	——
North half	1963	——	——	——	1.00	——	2.00	——	46 × 64
South half	1963	——	——	——	1.00	——	2.00	——	46 × 64
Colorado	1954	0.50	——	22 × 23	1.00	——	2.00	2.00	42 × 53
Florida	1966	0.50	——	23 × 32	1.00	——	2.00	——	44 × 62
Georgia	1963	0.50	——	21 × 23	1.00	——	2.00	2.00	39 × 45
Idaho	1964	0.50	——	——	1.00	——	2.00	2.00	44 × 66
Illinois	1948	0.50	——	17 × 27	1.00	——	2.00	——	32 × 53
Indiana	1950	0.50	——	14 × 21	1.00	$2.00	——	——	27 × 42
Iowa	1965	0.50	——	17 × 23	1.00	——	2.00	——	33 × 46
Kansas	1961	0.50	——	17 × 29	1.00	——	2.00	——	32 × 56
Kentucky	1956	0.50	——	15 × 30	1.00	——	2.00	2.00	27 × 57
Louisiana	1966	0.50	——	20 × 22	1.00	——	2.00	——	40 × 44
Maine	1958	0.50	——	16 × 22	1.00	——	2.00	2.00	30 × 44
Maryland, Delaware and District of Columbia	1948	0.50	——	12 × 19	.75	——	1.50	1.50	23 × 36
Massachusetts, Rhode Island, and Connecticut	1943	0.50	——	13 × 18	.75	——	1.50	1.50	24 × 30
Michigan	1970	0.75	——	28 × 34	1.00[1]	——	2.00[1]	——	58 × 84
Minnesota	1963	0.50	——	25 × 29	1.00	——	2.00	——	49 × 56
Mississippi	1948	0.50	——	16 × 25	1.00	2.00	——	——	31 × 52
Missouri	1950	0.50	——	24 × 26	1.00	——	2.00	2.00	47 × 54
Montana	1965	0.50	1.00	24 × 40	2.00[1]	——	4.00[1]	——	47 × 79
Nebraska	1962	0.50	——	17 × 31	1.00	——	2.00	——	32 × 82
Nevada	1962	0.50	——	23 × 34	1.00	——	2.00	2.00	45 × 65
New Hampshire and Vermont	1950	0.50	——	12 × 15	.75	——	1.50	1.50	22 × 28
New Jersey	1948	0.50	——	12 × 15	.75	——	1.50	1.50	23 × 28
New Mexico	1967	0.50	——	25 × 29	1.00	——	2.00	2.00	49 × 56
New York	1953	0.50	——	23 × 29	1.00	——	2.00	2.00	44 × 58
North Carolina	1957	0.50	——	14 × 33	1.00	——	2.00	2.00	29 × 66
North Dakota	1961	0.50	——	18 × 25	1.00	——	2.00	2.00	33 × 50
Ohio	1951	0.50	——	18 × 20	1.00	——	2.00	2.00	34 × 37
Oklahoma	1948	0.50	——	18 × 29	1.00	2.00	——	——	35 × 54
Oregon	1965	0.50	——	22 × 28	1.00	——	2.00	2.00	44 × 56
Pennsylvania	1953	0.50	——	15 × 23	1.00	——	2.00	2.00	29 × 44
South Carolina	1970	0.50	——	17 × 21	1.00	——	2.00	——	32 × 40
South Dakota	1961	0.50	——	20 × 27	1.00	——	2.00	2.00	39 × 53
Tennessee	1957	0.50	——	11 × 35	1.00	——	2.00	2.00	19 × 66
Texas	1962	0.50	1.50	42 × 53	2.50[2]	——	5.00[2]	——	82 × 102
Utah	1953	0.50	——	20 × 25	1.00	——	2.00	2.00	39 × 48
Virginia	1955	0.50	——	18 × 32	1.00	——	2.00	2.00	30 × 64
Washington	1961	0.50	——	19 × 27	1.00	——	2.00	2.00	37 × 52
West Virginia	1963	0.50	——	18 × 20	1.00	——	2.00	2.00	36 × 40
Wisconsin	1966	0.50	——	23 × 24	1.00	——	2.00	——	42 × 46
Wyoming	1964	0.50	——	21 × 26	1.00	——	2.00	2.00	41 × 52

[1]Set of two maps.   [2]Set of four maps.

NOTES:
    All prices subject to change.
    Alaska maps.—Four as follows:
      Map A: base; scale 1:5,000,000; 15 × 25 inches, 50¢.
      Map B: scale 1:1,534,000; two sheets each 36 × 51 inches. Base $1.50; contour, contour interval 1000 feet, $3.
      Map C: highways: scale 1:12,000,000; 10 × 15 inches. Base, 10¢.
      Map E: scale 1:2,500,000; 34 × 48 inches. Base, $1; shaded relief, $2.
    Connecticut maps—Scale 1:125,000; 45 × 56 inches. Base, $1; topographic available with or without woodland, $2 for each; shaded relief, $2.

however, may prove to be a detriment to some users.

The 1:500,000 state base maps series is generally available in two formats. The first, identified as the "State Base Map," shows state and county boundaries, railroads, water features, and all but the smallest settlements. Printing is in black on white paper with a blue tint for water features. The base map does not include highway or topographic information. The second map, termed the "State Topographic Map," is an overprinting of the state base map with contours (in brown) and highways (in purple) plus national parks, wildlife refuges, Indian reservations, and national forests (in green). Contour interval varies from state to state; for example, Michigan's is 200 feet (61 meters), Colorado's is 500 feet (152.5 meters), and California's is 500 feet, with 100-foot (30.5-meter) supplementals. Every state is included in this series of maps and is covered by one or two sheets. For some states shaded relief sheets are also available. The State Topographic series is excellent for regional differentiation of drainage basins and topographic relief. Figure 6.1 is an excerpt from a state topographic map.

Topographic Maps: 1:250,000 and 1:125,000 Series

The 1:250,000- and 1:125,000-scale topographic series are composed of medium-scale maps which have utility at the county and multicounty level of planning. The complete 1:250,000 series con-

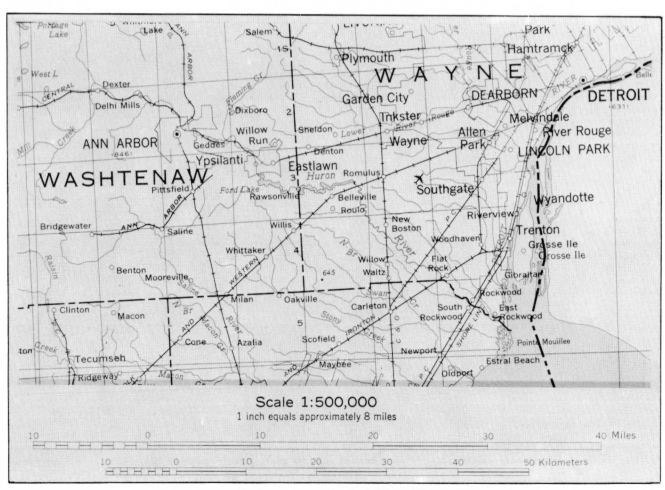

Figure 6.1. A sample portion of a USGS 1:500,000 state base map.

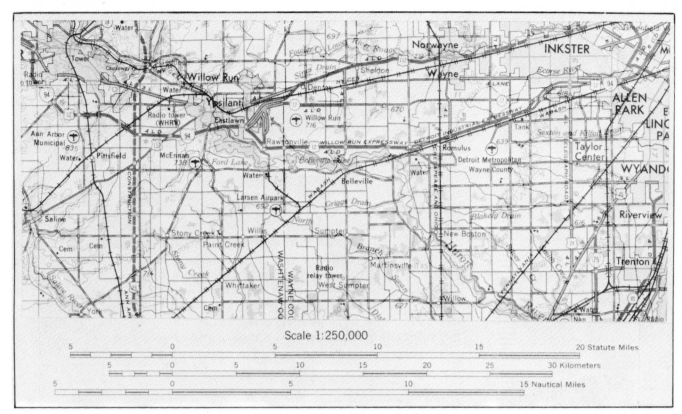

Figure 6.2. A small excerpt from a USGS 1:250,000 topographic map. This map is printed in a five-color format.

sists of 468 sheets covering the coterminous United States, 153 sheets for Alaska, plus several sheets for territories. Topography is represented by brown contour lines and, in some editions, by shading. Contour intervals range from 20 feet (6 meters) to as great as 500 feet (152.5 meters). Most of these maps, except for Alaska, are published in 1-degree-latitude by 2-degrees-longitude units on 22-inch (56-centimeter) by 34-inch (86-centimeter) sheets. All maps are named after some prominent city or natural feature located on the sheet. Figure 6.2 illustrates a small portion of one such sheet.

The companion set, at the next larger scale of 1:125,000 (1 inch represents 1.97 miles), covers 30 minutes of both latitude and longitude and is thus referred to as the 30-minute series. This series is being replaced by the next larger map series (1:62,500) because at this smaller scale, detail is not sufficient for either detailed work or broad regional planning. However, due to the extreme extent of the United States and the considerable time needed to cover the entire country at a scale of 1:62,500, the 30-minute series is often the most detailed map set available for many areas. The legend and format of this series (in fact, for all maps in the USGS topographic series) are comparable and follow the same scheme of symbolization.

This series is one of the standard topographic map series prepared by the USGS. Printed in quadrangles of 15 minutes latitude and longitude (and hence popularly termed the 15-minute series), these are generally at the scale of 1:62,500. Some maps in this series are also printed at a scale of 1:63,360, that is, where 1 inch

Topographic Maps: 15-Minute Series (1:62,500)

represents 1 mile. Both scales are on 17-inch (43-centimeter) by 21-inch (53-centimeter) sheets, and each covers an area of approximately 235 square miles.

Standard notation for legend and marginal information are used in these maps. Due to the scale, the 15-minute series is suitable for planning problems which are not in the regional context but approach a detailed analysis of a particular set of sites or areas. Township and range location notations with the sections overprinted in red appear for the first time and greatly facilitate the identification of specific sites. Individual buildings, especially in small villages or towns, are indicated, although in larger towns often only "index" buildings are specifically indicated. Transportation networks for all systems, from dirt roads through the continuum to interstate highways are noted, as are utility lines, pipelines, and railroads. One of the problems in using this series of maps is the date of the data portrayed. In many areas of the United States where this series is duplicated by sheets of the 7.5-minute series (see Figure 6.3), the 15-minute maps are quite antiquated. Consequently, when this series may be used for detailed topographic analysis and site planning, one should be especially cognizant of the publishing and revision dates of the sheets.

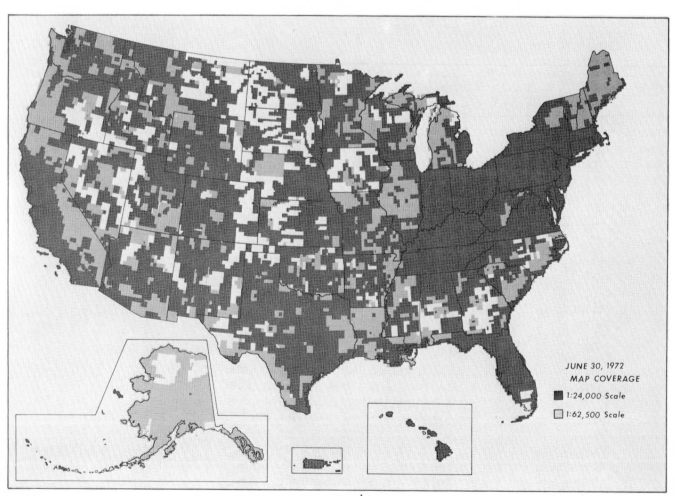

JUNE 30, 1972
MAP COVERAGE
■ 1:24,000 Scale
□ 1:62,500 Scale

Figure 6.3. Coverage of the United States in 1972 by 7.5-minute (1:24,000) and 15-minute (1:62,500) USGS topographic map series.

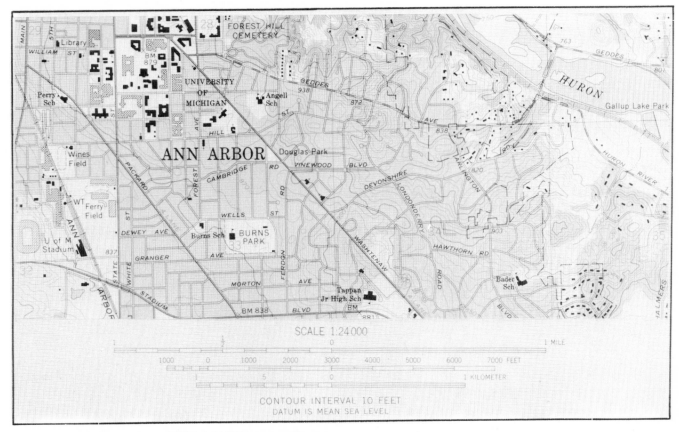

Figure 6.4. An example from a USGS 1:24,000 topographic map.

This series of topographic maps, originally published at 1:31,680 (1 inch to 0.5 mile) (1 centimeter to 0.8 kilometer) is being enlarged to 1:24,000 (1 inch to 0.4 mile) (1 centimeter to 0.25 kilometer), thus becoming the largest-scale series generally published by the U.S. Geological Survey. These maps show sufficient detail to be of value as data sources in the final stages of preparation for planning decisions where the need for topographic resolution is not in excess of 5- to 10-foot (1.5- to 3-meter) elevations. One problem with the 1:24,000 series (also referred to as the 7.5-minute series) is its incomplete coverage. The development and publication of the series is an ongoing task of the USGS, and it is a very ambitious, laborious, and time-consuming task. Consequently, total United States coverage is not expected for a considerable time. However, for most built-up areas—for instance, Detroit, Chicago, Los Angeles, northeastern United States, etc., and for some other areas where special needs have required maps at this scale, such as the Tennessee Valley area where the Tennessee Valley Authority is involved in regional planning and development—this series is quite complete (Figure 6.2).

The symbols, colors, notations, and other representations used in this series follow the basic format described for the 1:62,500 series. In addition, for heavily built-up areas, a pink overlay is provided and only "index" buildings are shown. More recent (photo) revisions of these maps are identified with a purple overprint. Figure 6.4 is an example of the 1:24,000 sheets in the National Topographic series.

Primary highway, hard surface		Boundaries: National	
Secondary highway, hard surface		State	
Light-duty road, hard or improved surface		County, parish, municipio	
Unimproved road		Civil township, precinct, town, barrio	
Road under construction, alinement known		Incorporated city, village, town, hamlet	
Proposed road		Reservation, National or State	
Dual highway, dividing strip 25 feet or less		Small park, cemetery, airport, etc.	
Dual highway, dividing strip exceeding 25 feet		Land grant	
Trail		Township or range line, United States land survey	
		Township or range line, approximate location	
Railroad: single track and multiple track		Section line, United States land survey	
Railroads in juxtaposition		Section line, approximate location	
Narrow gage: single track and multiple track		Township line, not United States land survey	
Railroad in street and carline		Section line, not United States land survey	
Bridge: road and railroad		Found corner: section and closing	
Drawbridge: road and railroad		Boundary monument: land grant and other	
Footbridge		Fence or field line	
Tunnel: road and railroad			
Overpass and underpass		Index contour	Intermediate contour
Small masonry or concrete dam		Supplementary contour	Depression contours
Dam with lock		Fill	Cut
Dam with road		Levee	Levee with road
Canal with lock		Mine dump	Wash
		Tailings	Tailings pond
Buildings (dwelling, place of employment, etc.)		Shifting sand or dunes	Intricate surface
School, church, and cemetery	Cem	Sand area	Gravel beach
Buildings (barn, warehouse, etc.)			
Power transmission line with located metal tower		Perennial streams	Intermittent streams
Telephone line, pipeline, etc. (labeled as to type)		Elevated aqueduct	Aqueduct tunnel
Wells other than water (labeled as to type)	o Oil o Gas	Water well and spring	Glacier
Tanks: oil, water, etc. (labeled only if water)	• • ● ⊘ Water	Small rapids	Small falls
Located or landmark object; windmill	o	Large rapids	Large falls
Open pit, mine, or quarry; prospect	x	Intermittent lake	Dry lake bed
Shaft and tunnel entrance		Foreshore flat	Rock or coral reef
		Sounding, depth curve	Piling or dolphin
Horizontal and vertical control station:		Exposed wreck	Sunken wreck
Tablet, spirit level elevation	BM △ 5653	Rock, bare or awash; dangerous to navigation	
Other recoverable mark, spirit level elevation	△ 5455		
Horizontal control station: tablet, vertical angle elevation	VABM △ 95/9	Marsh (swamp)	Submerged marsh
Any recoverable mark, vertical angle or checked elevation	△ 3775	Wooded marsh	Mangrove
Vertical control station: tablet, spirit level elevation	BM X 957	Woods or brushwood	Orchard
Other recoverable mark, spirit level elevation	X 954	Vineyard	Scrub
Spot elevation	x 7369	Land subject to controlled inundation	Urban area
Water elevation	670 670		

Figure 6.5. Standard map symbols on the USGS topographic maps.

This series is especially useful for very detailed topographic measurements similar to those described in Chapter 2. The level of detail and the large range of both natural and cultural features shown at this scale render this set of maps one of the most useful of the entire National Topographic series for local planning, site-evaluation base maps, and similar detailed studies in land evaluation and planning. Figure 6.5 shows the types of features and the manner of presentation used in all the USGS maps discussed thus far.

ADDITIONAL USGS MAP PROGRAMS

Although the topographic map series is the major USGS product with utility in environmental and land use planning, other maps of this agency can also be extremely useful. Table 6.2 gives a listing of these maps.

TABLE 6.2 NONTOPOGRAPHIC MAPS OF THE U.S. GEOLOGICAL SURVEY

Geologic Map of North America*
Geologic Map of the United States*
Indexes to Geologic Mapping in the United States*
Geologic Quadrangle Maps (GQ)*
Geophysical Investigation Maps (GP)
Miscellaneous Geologic Investigations Maps*
Coal Investigations Maps
Oil and Gas Investigations Maps
Mineral Investigations
Special Geologic Maps
Hydrologic Investigations Atlas*
National Atlas

*Discussed in this chapter.

Indexes to Topographic Maps of the United States

All maps which are part of the USGS Topographic series follow a progression in terms of both scale and location. All topographic maps are indexed on United States base maps for maps at scales of 1:250,000 and smaller, and on state base maps for larger scales. All indexes are available free from the U.S. Geological Survey, Map Information Office (MIO).[1] Each state index includes two map sizes (1:24,000 and 1:62,500) and, in addition, describes the special maps and sheets which are available for the state in question, including smaller-scale topographic maps, national parks, and shaded relief maps. Also included on the index sheet is a list of the reference libraries and local dealers for the topographic maps of the USGS for the particular state. Topographic map prices vary with the size and the number of sheets purchased, but generally the cost is between $0.75 and $1.00, with a discount of 30 percent for orders in excess of $300.00. All pertinent ordering information is printed on the map indexes. The indexes are updated approximately biannually and provide a ready source of map information for any planning agency and office. Figure 6.6 is a portion of one map index for the 1:24,000 series.

The Geologic Maps of North America and the United States are large-size maps which give a view of the geologic regions of the

[1]The office address for MIO is
  Map Information Office—Mail
    Stop 507
  U.S. Geological Survey
  National Center
  Sunrise Valley Drive
  Reston, VA 22092

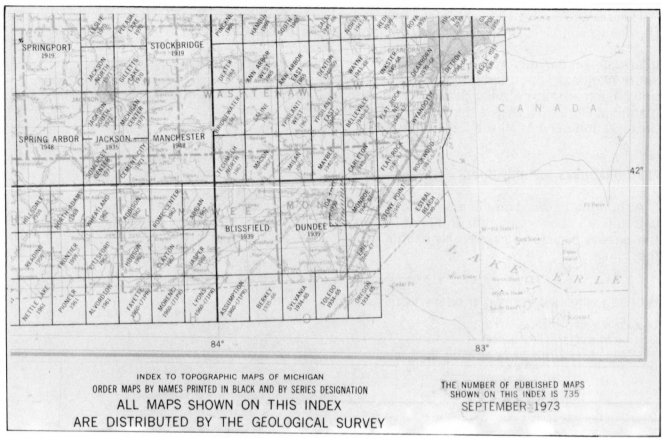

Figure 6.6. A small part of a USGS index to 1:24,000 topographic maps.

Geologic Maps of America and the United States

continent. Other than their tutorial value, they are of little use for any but the broadest scale (over large regional, e.g., several states) planning problems. The level of detail is small, for the scales are similarly small (North America is at 1:500,000, the United States is at 1:2,500,000). This series includes both basement maps (dealing with the crust of the earth below sedimentary deposits and on downward to the Mohorovičić discontinuity) and tectonic maps (dealing with regional assemblages of the geological structures of the crust) of the areas concerned. For North America a general surface geology map is also available. This set of maps, depending on the particular map needed, ranges in price from $1 to $5 and in size from 39 inches (99 centimeters) by 56 inches (142 centimeters) to 50 inches (127 centimeters) by 60 inches (152 centimeters). In several cases, one area is covered by multiple sheets.

State Geologic Maps

The U.S. Geological Survey does a considerable amount of detailed geological mapping in selected small, isolated areas and often for very specific tasks. Because the geologic mapping program has been conducted in cooperation with different federal and state agencies, and because the immediacy of the mapping is often pronounced, there are no easily defined sets of boundaries for the maps. Consequently, the easiest way to determine which maps are presently available for each state is to acquire an index. Geologic maps prepared by governments, commercial organizations, professional societies, and universities are included on these indexes. In addition to the maps which are available for sale from the USGS, the indexes also list the USGS open-file reports. Indexes are available from the Survey, but unlike their topographic counterparts, these are not free—rather a small charge (generally less than $1 per state index map) is levied. Once this index is acquired, one can easily determine if the area of particular interest is mapped and, if so, if the subject is of importance to the planning being considered. It should be noted, however, that these index maps are generally

TABLE 6.3   INDEXES TO GEOLOGIC MAPS OF THE UNITED STATES

State and year of compilation	Year of publication	Scale	Price
Alabama, 1950	1951	1:1,000,000	$0.40
Alaska, 1965	1967	1:2,500,000	0.50
●Arizona, 1957	1963	1:1,000,000	
Arkansas, 1952	1952	1:500,000	0.65
●California, 1951 (two sheets)	1952	1:750,000	
Colorado, 1954	1954	1:750,000	0.50
Florida, 1952	1953	1:1,000,000	0.60
Georgia, 1949	1949	1:750,000	0.35
Idaho, 1957	1959	1:750,000	0.60
Illinois, 1953	1954	1:750,000	0.60
Indiana, 1950	1950	1:750,000	0.45
Iowa, 1948	1948	1:750,000	0.35
●Kansas, 1954	1954	1:750,000	
Kentucky, 1952	1952	1:750,000	0.50
●Louisiana, 1950	1950	1:1,000,000	
Maine, 1958	1959	1:750,000	0.60
Maryland and Delaware, 1951	1951	1:500,000	0.40
Massachusetts, Rhode Island, and Connecticut, 1952	1952	2:500,000	0.60
Michigan, 1953	1953	1:750,000	0.60
Minnesota, 1953	1955	1:750,000	0.60
Mississippi, 1950	1950	1:1,000,000	0.25
Missouri, 1948	1949	1:75,000	0.30
Montana, 1955	1955	1:750,000	
Supplement, 1955–67	1969	1:750,000	0.75 per set
●Nebraska, 1947	1947	1:1,000,000	
Nevada, 1955	1955	1:750,000	0.60
New Hampshire and Vermont, 1952	1952	1:500,000	0.50
New Jersey, 1951	1951	1:500,000	0.40
New Mexico, ●Part A, 1956	1958	1:750,000	
Part B, 1958–68	1970	1:1,000,000	0.50
New York, 1952	1952	1:750,000	0.60
North Carolina, 1950	1950	1:750,000	0.50
North Dakota, 1954	1954	1:750,000	0.60
Ohio, 1970	1970	1:1,000,000	0.50
●Oklahoma, 1953	1953	1:500,000	
Oregon, 1949	1949	1:750,000	0.25
●Pennsylvania, 1952	1952	1:500,000	
South Carolina, 1950	1950	1:1,000,000	0.25
South Dakota, 1957	1958	1:750,000	0.60
Tennessee, 1949	1949	1:750,000	0.40
Texas, 1951	1951	1:1,000,000	0.60
Utah, 1954	1954	1:750,000	0.60
Virginia, 1959	1959	1:750,000	0.60
Washington, 1949	1949	1:750,000	0.35
West Virginia, 1949	1949	1:750,000	0.25
Wisconsin, 1953	1953	1:750,000	0.60
Wyoming, 1955	1955	1:750,000	0.60

several years old, and although they are periodically updated, it would be wise to check other sources, such as the listing shown in Table 6.3 for the most recent information on geologic maps.

Geologic Quadrangle Maps

The Geologic Quadrangle series is a set of maps constructed at the scales of the 1:24,000 and 1:62,500 topographic maps. Currently, approximately 900 sheets of these maps are available. Various sheet sizes are used in this series, but most measure 25 inches (64 centimeters) by 26 inches (66 centimeters) to 30 inches (76 centimeters) by 50 inches (127 centimeters). All maps in the series are designated by the letters *GQ* (for geologic quadrangle) followed by a number. In most instances, the numbers have been assigned sequentially. Because the maps are not prepared in a definite geographic order, however, the numbers are not indicative of the locations of the maps. This situation has tended to cause some confusion for persons seeking the various maps. Hence, for this series, the geologic map indexes mentioned previously are especially germane.

The data displayed on maps of the Geologic Quadrangle series cover a range of geologic topics, including surface geology, pre-Quaternary geology, and bedrock geology. However, most maps are simply entitled "Geology," indicating in this context that the uppermost rock units are shown without the soil cover. These multicolor maps indicate the several geologic features of the subject quadrangle, including rock units, rock ages, surface, and often subsurface contours. Where these data are of importance to the planning process, the detail is sufficient to allow a good determination of the bedrock and other subsurface conditions which may be encountered. The limited coverage of this series, however, dictates that planners in many areas who may have need for such information may be forced to rely upon other sources of geologic information, such as state geological surveys. This series is continually being expanded, and one would be well advised to check for the latest publications.

Miscellaneous Geologic Investigations Maps

The Miscellaneous Geologic Investigations Maps series is one of the most diverse in terms of subject matter and sheet size. At the same time, it is one of the most instructive series which will be encountered by the general planning community. The series, designated by the letter *I* prefixing a number, includes as diverse geographic areas as Saudi Arabia, Alaska, the Indian Ocean, the moon, and Mars, although these are relatively few in number. Of interest to planners in the United States are the numerous geologic maps which, like the geologic quadrangles noted above, are generally at the scales of 1:62,500 and 1:24,000. (Other scales from 1:12,000 to 1:25,000 are also included in the series.) A small listing of the types of maps in this series of possible interest to planners is given in Table 6.4.

Coverage is sporadic in terms of both geography and subject. Nonetheless, on the whole, this series of maps, and particularly those several sets discussed below, are of special importance to land use planners due to the guidance they can provide in identifying pertinent subjects of study. Maps are powerful tools for collating and presenting areal and point data over both space and time and, if properly used, can be one of the most efficient and effective

TABLE 6.4   EXAMPLES FROM THE U.S. GEOLOGICAL SURVEY MISCELLANEOUS GEOLOGIC INVESTIGATIONS MAPS SERIES

Sugar House Quadrangle, Salt Lake County, Utah (1:24,000)

I-766-A Surficial Geologic
      B Map showing relative ages of faults
      C Slope Map
      D Landslide and Associated Deposits
      E Relative Slope Stability
      F Construction Materials
      G Urban Growth

Knox County, Tennessee (1:125,000)

I-767-A Land Slopes and Urbanization
      B Geologic Map
      C Distribution of Sedimentary Rocks
      D Structure Map
      E Groundwater Yield Potential
      F Areas with Abundant Sinkholes
      G Basins Drained by Sinkholes
      H Soil Association Map
      I Physical Characteristics of Soils
      J Overburdens Related to Type of Bedrock and Engineering
         Characteristics of the Bedrock
      K Engineering Characteristics of Overburden
      L Categories of Relative Feasibility for Septic-Tank Filter
         Fields
      M Areas of Possible Flooding

conveyors of information. Thus, in much the same way that maps are conventionally used as representations of the three-dimensional nature of the earth's surface, they may be used for a myriad of other subjects. The USGS has entered into several detailed studies of specific quadrangles. Their coverage, although for only small areas, is especially timely. One set of this series covers the Sugar House Quadrangle of Salt Lake County, Utah, and is published under the common number I-766, followed by a capital letter (see Table 6.4). On map I-766-G, for example, the expansion of Salt Lake City, Utah, is dramatically portrayed for several time periods (before 1890, to 1936, to 1952, to 1969) using areas with more than 5 percent of the land surface covered with structures as the definition of urban. The sporadic dates of the maps on this special edition are a result of having employed USGS topographic maps as the source for base data. (The topographic sheets for the Sugar House Quadrangle were updated in 1936, 1952, and 1969.) Map I-766-C, which deals with slopes, illustrates in considerable detail both how the map was constructed and the basic knowledge needed for reading topographic maps of any scale (with special emphasis on the 1:24,000-scale series). It is an excellent example of a type of slope mapping discussed in the latter part of Chapter 2.

The I-767 series, covering Knox County, Tennessee, provides some additional examples of the diversity of this effort by the USGS. On sheet I-767-M ("Areas of Possible Flooding") several categories of water level are indicated; the normal river stage, the flood stage, and areas that are flood prone because they contain abundant sinkholes. For comparison, map I-784-M, based on the Hartford North Quadrangle, Connecticut, shows an area which has a 1 percent chance of being flooded for any given year but has no indication of either depth or duration of the expected flood. For these maps, and others in the series, the analysis categories employed are specifically and precisely defined and, in many cases, have been determined on the basis of local development ordinances that influence the manner in which environmental information must be assessed. Additional comments and bibliographic references are often included in the margins to aid in the map interpretation and understanding.

The general comment included on the maps in the I-767 (Knox County, Tennessee) set is indicative of the philosophy which underlies these recent USGS efforts:

LAND RESOURCE ANALYSIS MAPS OF KNOX COUNTY

Knox County has a 1972 population in excess of 270,000. The Metropolitan Planning Commission (1968) projects an increase in population to approximately 360,000 by 1990. As the population grows and favorable areas like west Knox County approach their limit of development, more and more marginal land will be utilized. In order to utilize the existing land resources safely and efficiently, and in order to maintain a suitable environmental quality, knowledge concerning the physical environment and its limitations should be readily available to planners and decisionmakers. To provide some of these data, a series of maps, I-767, summarizing current knowledge about critical aspects of the physical environment has been prepared.

While this special series covers only a limited area of the United States, the maps provide excellent illustrations of the types of data that may be collected and displayed for later analysis. Supplemented with techniques discussed in earlier chapters of this volume, this map series can offer considerable guidance to persons wishing to provide new insight into local problems. Finally, it should be noted that new sets of these maps are continually being prepared.

Hydrologic Atlas   The Hydrologic Atlas series deals specifically with problems relating to both surface and subsurface water as well as other water-related subjects. Prefixed by the designation *HA,* followed by sequential numbers, this series is published at numerous scales, including 1:12,000; 1:24,000; 1:26,720; 1:62,500; 1:125,000; 1:250,000; and 1:316,800. The 1:24,000 scale is the most common. Many of the maps in this atlas are published with the same area coverage as the topographic quadrangles of the same scale.

Two subjects compose the majority of the series: (1) floods, their extent and periodicity and (2) the availability and reconnaissance of groundwater supplies. Other subjects have included saline groundwater resources, sediment yields of rivers and streams, lake water budgets, geohydrology of aquifers, and annual precipitation and runoff. In 1969, a short set (HA-395 to HA-408) of this series was devoted to the Hurricane Camille tidal floods of August 1969 along the Gulf Coast. These maps, and a similar set being prepared by the U.S. Department of Commerce, are especially helpful in identifying high-risk areas along the coast. Maps of this HA series generally cost $1 or less per sheet and may be ordered in the same manner as USGS topographic sheets.

OTHER USGS PUBLICATIONS

Several sets of USGS publications in addition to those mentioned above are of special interest to urban and regional planners. A new series entitled Techniques of Water Resources Investigations of the United States Geological Survey (prefixed *TWI*) has been published since 1967. As stated in the preface: "The series of manuals on techniques describes procedures for planning and executing specialized work in water resources subject headings called books and further subdivided into sections and chapters. . . . The unit of publication, the chapter, is limited to a narrow field of publication as the need arises." Although this series is directed toward the professional and practicing hydrologist, urban and regional planners will also find it useful. The series is clearly written and provides a strong tutorial background for understanding the problems and principles involved in water-resources investigations.

The various publication units, or chapters, are prepared and published in a random manner, thus requiring the interested individual to check the monthly publication lists for the most recent offerings. A complete listing of the published chapters (through August 1974) is presented in Table 6.5. Prices are modest, generally less than $1 per chapter.

TABLE 6.5 LISTING OF PUBLICATIONS OF U.S. GEOLOGICAL SURVEY TECHNIQUES FOR WATER-RESOURCE INVESTIGATIONS SERIES. COMPLETE TO AUGUST 1974.

BOOK 2 COLLECTION OF ENVIRONMENTAL DATA
  Chap. D 1 Application of surface geophysics to groundwater investigations. 1974. $1.90.
  Chap. E 1 Application of borehole geophysics to water-resources investigations. 1971. $1.75.
BOOK 3 APPLICATIONS OF HYDRAULICS
  Chap. A 1 General field and office procedures for indirect discharge measurements. 1967.
  Chap. A 2 Measurement of peak discharge by slope-area method. 1967.
  Chap. A 3 Measurement of peak discharge at culverts by indirect methods. 1968. 40¢.
  Chap. A 4 Measurement of peak discharge width contractions by indirect methods. 1967. 35¢.
  Chap. A 5 Measurement of peak discharge at dams by indirect methods. 1967. 30¢.
  Chap. A 6 General procedure for gaging streams. 1968. 20¢.
  Chap. A 7 Stage measurements at gaging stations. 1968. 45¢.
  Chap. A 8 Discharge measurements at gaging stations. 1973. 70¢.
  Chap. A11 Measurement of discharge by the moving-boat method. 1969. 40¢.
  Chap. A12 Fluorometric procedures for dye tracing. 1968. 35¢.
  Chap. B 1 Aquifer-test design, observation, and data analysis. 1971. 40¢.
  Chap. C 1 Fluvial sediment concepts. 1970. 65¢.
  Chap. C 2 Field methods for measurement of fluvial sediment. 1970. 70¢.
  Chap. C 3 Computation of fluvial-sediment discharge. 1972. 75¢.

BOOK 4 HYDRAULIC ANALYSIS AND INTERPRETATION
  Chap. A 1 Some statistical tools in hydrology. 1968. 30¢.
  Chap. A 2 Frequency curves. 1968. 20¢.
  Chap. B 1 Low-flow investigations. 1972. 55¢.
  Chap. B 2 Storage analysis for water supply. 1973. 50¢.
  Chap. B 3 Regional analysis of stream-flow characteristics. 1973. 45¢.
  Chap. D 1 Computation of rate and volume of stream depletion by wells. 1970. 30¢.
BOOK 5 LABORATORY ANALYSIS
  Chap. A 1 Methods for collection and analysis of water samples for dissolved minerals and gases. 1974. $2.00.
  Chap. A 2 Determination of minor elements in water by emission spectroscopy. 1971. 50¢.
  Chap. A 3 Methods for analysis of organic substances in water. 1972. 50¢.
  Chap. A 4 Methods for collection and analysis of aquatic biological and microbiological samples. 1973. $2.85.
  Chap. C 1 Laboratory theory and methods for sediment analysis. 1969. 65¢.
BOOK 7 AUTOMATED DATA PROCESSING AND COMPUTATIONS
  Chap. C 1 A digital model aquifer evaluation. 1970. 35¢.
BOOK 8 INSTRUMENTATION
  Chap. A 1 Methods of measuring water levels in deep wells. 1968. 25¢.
  Chap. B 2 Calibration and maintenance of vertical-axis type current meters. 1968. 40¢.

SOURCE: U.S. Geological Survey Publication Lists.

Circulars

The USGS Circular series has the singular distinction of being free (upon application) from the director of USGS. The first of this series was published in 1933, and it has continued without interruption since 1946. The total series now exceeds 700 titles, and the publications generally have been numbered sequentially in order of issuance. Many of the earlier offerings are now out of print, although occasionally they are reprinted. Table 6.6 lists some of the circulars which are of special interest to the urban and regional planning community. It can be seen from the listing that the circulars may be divided into two major groups. The first category deals primarily with water, either the identification of water supplies, water uses, the computation of flood runoff and/or peak discharges, or problems of groundwater. Many of the papers included in this portion of the circular series are area specific, describing and analyzing a specific event or condition in a particular and well-defined geographic area. These water-oriented circulars make up the majority of the publications included in the earlier titles of the series that pertain to the tasks of land use planning.

TABLE 6.6   SOME CIRCULARS OF SPECIAL INTEREST TO PLANNERS

Circular number	Title of circular	Circular number	Title of circular
368*	Features shown on topographic maps. 1955. 23 pp.		1970. Pp. B1–B11.
414B	The challenge of water management. 1960. Pp. 7–13.	601C	Flood-hazard mapping in metropolitan Chicago. 1970. Pp. C1–C14.
414D	Ecological systems and the water resources. 1960. Pp. 21–26.	601D	Water as an urban resource and nuisance. 1970. 9 pp.
415	Water management, agriculture, and groundwater supplies. 1960. 12 pp.	601E	Sediment problems in urban areas. 1970. Pp. E1–E8.
455	Annotated bibliography of water-use data, 1960. 1961. 14 pp.	601G	Real-estate lakes. 1971. 19 pp.
487	Growing importance of urban geology, by J. T. McGill. 1964. 4 pp.	601H	Role of water in urban planning and management. 1973. 10 pp.
539	Flood information for flood-plain planning. 1967. 10 pp.	601I	Water facts and figures for planners and managers. 1973. 30 pp.
548	Reports and maps of the Geological Survey released only in the open files, 1967. 1968. 21 pp.	601K	An introduction to the processes, problems, and management at inland lakes. 1975. 22pp.
554	Hydrology for urban land planning—a guidebook on the hydrologic effects of urban land use. 1968. 18 pp.	629	Water laws and concepts. 1970. 18 pp.
		645	A procedure for evaluation of environmental impact. 1971. 13 pp.
601A	Water for the cities—the outlook. 1969. Pp. A1–A6.	671	A land use classification system for use with remote sensor data. 1972. 16 pp.
601B	Urban sprawl and flooding in Southern California.	676	Estimated use of water in the United States in 1970. 1972.

Open-File Reports

More recently, however, additional titles oriented more toward the application of the data to urban and regional problems have been presented. Included in this are the 601 series of circulars (issued under the general title Water in the Urban Environment and numbered 601A through 601K) as well as circulars numbered 608, 554, 539, and 487 and others. In general, the circulars have been nontechnical in format, and most include brief bibliographies, thus making them useful points of departure in problem investigation.

An additional set of circulars, not identified in Table 6.6, are those which are necessary for searching the open-file reports of the USGS. Open-file reports include: (1) preliminary results of research, (2) the presentation of data which have not been thoroughly analyzed, (3) the initial concepts and new ideas which are being explored by the USGS staff, together with (4) some maps and results of remote-sensing surveys. These open-file reports are not available for general distribution. They can be viewed, however, and studied at several sites around the country, and copies are available upon request and at the requestor's expense. Hence, a quick scan of the proper USGS circular will usually lead to quick identification of the papers of interest. Table 6.7 lists the numbers and the years of circulars pertaining to the open-file reports. Beginning in May 1974, open-file reports from the USGS have been included in the regular monthly publications listings.

A final set of circulars which provide flow data for streams and rivers is given in Table 6.8. This set of circulars, under the general title of Index to Surface-Water Records, has been published since 1949. Each new publication supercedes all previous publications in the series; Table 6.8 lists only the most recent of the set. The records are organized by major drainage basins in the United States, and this organization has remained constant throughout the duration of the series. Figure 6.7 shows the boundaries of these drainage areas.

TABLE 6.7 U.S. GEOLOGICAL SURVEY CIRCULARS WHICH LIST THE OPEN-FILE REPORTS (BY YEAR) THAT ARE AVAILABLE FROM SELECTED USGS OFFICES

Year(s)	Circular	Year	Circular
1946–47	*56	1961	463
1948	*64	1962	473
1949–50	*149	1963	488
1951	*227	1964	498
1952	*263	1965	518
1953	*337	1966	528
1954	*364	1967	548
1955	*379	1968	568
1956	*401	1969	618
1957	*403	1970	638
1958	*412	1971	648
1959	*428	1972	668
1960	448	1973	696

SOURCE: U.S. Geological Survey Circular 696.

NOTE: Beginning in 1974, such lists of open-file reports have been included in the regular monthly publications lists of the USGS.

*Report is out of print.

TABLE 6.8 INDEXES TO SURFACE-WATER RECORDS OF THE UNITED STATES. CURRENT TO OCTOBER 1973

Part	Geographical area	Circular number
1	North Atlantic Slope Basins	651
2	South Atlantic Slope Basins	652
3	Ohio River Basin	653
4	St. Lawrence River Basin	654
5	Hudson Bay and Upper Mississippi River	655
6	Missouri River Basin	656
7	Lower Mississippi River Basin	657
8	Western Gulf of Mexico Basins	658
9	Colorado River Basin	659
10	The Great Basin	660
11	Pacific Slope Basins of California	661
12	Pacific Slope Basins of Washington, Upper Columbia River Basin	662
13	Snake River Basin	663
14	Pacific Slope Basins of Oregon and Lower Columbia River Basin	664
15	Hawaii and Other Pacific	666
16	Alaska	665

SOURCE: U.S. Geological Survey publication lists.

NOTE: Termination data of records indexed is 30SEP70 (except for Circular 657 published in 1971).

As the title notes, this set is only an *index* to the surface-water records, not the records or data themselves. The information listed includes the gage (i.e., flow measurement) station name (in downstream order), its number, the upstream drainage area (in square miles), and the period of records and type of records available. These circulars are extremely valuable for analysis of problems such as flood frequency, which necessitate use of surface-water

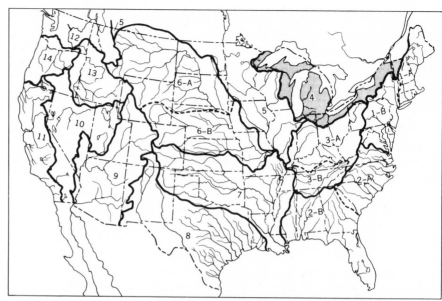

Figure 6.7. This map shows the major drainage basins used by the USGS for the organization and publication of flow data from its nationwide network of stream and river gages. The names of the basins and the corresponding circular numbers are given in Table 6.8.

records. Chapter 5 demonstrates the utility of these records in defining flood-prone areas.

The series of publications from the USGS known as Professional Papers is directed primarily toward the professional geologist, geomorphologist, hydrologist, and other earth scientists. Nonetheless, some of the recent publications have been oriented toward the application of geological and hydrological principles to problems in the planning fields. Table 6.9 presents a brief listing of USGS Professional Papers from recent years.

TABLE 6.9   SOME RECENT U.S. GEOLOGICAL SURVEY PROFESSIONAL PAPERS OF INTEREST TO PLANNERS

Number	Professional paper
434-F	A flood-frequency relation based on regional record maxima. 1971. 22 pp. 40¢.
506-B	A rainfall-runoff simulation model for estimation of flood peaks for small drainage basins. 1972. 28 pp. 40¢.
627-F	Summary of the hydrologic situation on Long Island, N.Y., as a guide to water-management alternatives. 1972. 59 pp. 65¢.
655-G	Channel changes of the Gila River in Safford Valley, Arizona 1846–1970. 24 pp.
701-A	Hydrology of two small river basins in Pennsylvania before urbanization. 1971. 57 pp. 75¢.
708	Groundwater hydraulics. 1972. $2.00
732-A	Channel movement of meandering Indiana streams. 1971. 18 pp. 35¢.
733	The San Fernando, California earthquake of February 9, 1971. 254 pp. $2.25
742	Characteristics of estuarine sediments of the United States, 1972. 99 pp. $1.25
751-B	Design and operation of the artificial-recharge plant at Nay Park, N.Y.

SOURCE: U.S. Geological Survey monthly publication lists.

One set of publications which was of major importance until 1973 was the Geological Survey Research series. Published annually in four chapters or books, these documents describe the significant results of USGS research programs. Chapter A includes recent scientific and economic results, lists the geologic and hydrologic investigations, and notes the progress on the status of various mapping programs. Chapters B, C, and D are composed of scientific notes and summaries of investigations in geology, hydrology, and related fields.

In 1973, Chapters B, C, and D were discontinued and replaced by a journal entitled *Journal of Research, U.S. Geological Survey,*[2] published six times per year. This change allows for a more timely publication of the research reports and, equally important, facilitates an automatic distribution of the reports through subscriptions. The contents of Chapter A continue to be published (in 1973, this was Professional Paper 850). Included in this publication is information gathered under the headings of: (1) research investigations of minerals, geologic and geophysical, and water resources, (2) geologic and hydrologic principles, processes and techniques (including sedimentology, soil moisture, limnology, plant ecology, and relationship between surface and ground water), (3) geology and hydrology applied to engineering and the public welfare (e.g., earthquake studies, engineering geology, urban studies, floods, land subsidence, environmental geochemistry, (4) remote sensing and advanced techniques, and (5) topographic surveys and mapping. Also included is a complete annual listing of USGS publications, a listing of selected regional offices in the United States and Puerto Rico, and a listing of all investigations in progress. This valuable source of information, when coupled with the monthly publications lists discussed earlier, provides the complete directory to all of the USGS activities.

Over 1400 USGS bulletins are available today. These papers present very detailed descriptions and analyses of specific geologic formations, geochemical studies, mineral deposits, nomenclature revisions, and lexicons of U.S. geologic formations, and topical bibliographies. In some instances the bulletins provide the major or single source of geologic information available for an area.

The Water Supply Papers, numbering over 2000 at present, can provide an enormous amount of data relative to both supplies and quality of surface and ground water. Most papers deal with very specific areas, identified both geographically and by a stream name. This set also includes all the records of stream flow in a series of volumes entitled *Magnitude and Frequency of Floods in the United States* as well as stream water-quality records which were indexed in the Index of Surface Water circulars mentioned earlier. The flood data are published in a separate volume for each of the drainage basins shown in Figure 6.7. An example of the data and page format are shown in Chapter 5, Table 5.7.

Prices for papers in the Water Supply set vary, but on the whole they cost less than $5 per paper. Other agencies, in addition to the USGS, collect similar hydrologic data for selected areas and water features in the country. Table 6.10 indicates the types of data collected by eighteen federal agencies. Inquiries concerning these data should be directed to the respective agency offices.

Professional Papers

[2] Subscriptions are available from the Superintendent of Documents at $18.90 for domestic subscription plus $2.75 for foreign mailing. Single copies at $3.15 each.

Bulletins and Water Supply Papers

TABLE 6.10 BASIC HYDROLOGIC DATA COLLECTED BY U.S. FEDERAL AGENCIES

Item	Agricultural Research Service	Bureau of the Census	Coast and Geodetic Survey	Department of Commerce	Corps of Engineers	Fish and Wildlife Service	Forest Service	Geological Survey	Department of the Interior	International Boundary and Water Commission	Mississippi River Commission	Naval Observatory	Public Health Service	Bureau of Reclamation	Smithsonian Institution	Soil Conservation Service	Tennessee Valley Authority	Weather Bureau
Consumptive use	•						•	•						•		•	•	
Density currents					•			•						•		•	•	
Drought								•										
Evaporation	•				•			•		•				•		•		•
Floods					•		•	•		•				•			•	
Groundwater	•				•			•						•		•	•	•
Humidity							•			•								•
Ice					•			•										
Infiltration	•						•							•		•	•	
Interception							•										•	
Lysimeters	•						•									•	•	
Precipitation	•				•		•			•				•		•	•	•
Chemical quality of water					•			•					•	•		•		•
River, lake, reservoir stages					•			•		•				•			•	
Runoff	•				•			•									•	
Sedimentation:																		
Suspended load	•				•			•						•		•	•	
Reservoir sedimentation	•				•		•	•						•			•	
Snow					•		•	•						•		•	•	•
Soil moisture	•															•	•	•
Solar radiation	•											•			•		•	•
Storms					•			•								•	•	•
Streamflow	•				•		•	•			•			•		•	•	•
Air temperature							•	•						•		•	•	•
Soil temperature	•				•		•									•	•	•
Water temperature				•		•		•						•		•	•	•
Tides			•		•			•										
Water use and waste disposal:																		
Drainage		•																
Industrial use		•		•					•				•				•	
Municipal use				•									•					
Sewage and waste disposal													•					
Wind	•				•		•			•						•	•	•
Experimental watersheds	•				•		•	•									•	

SOURCE: Langbein and Hoyt, 1959.

Conclusions on USGS Information Sources

This brief discription of the USGS publications programs, which are producing both data and information, is but a small portion of the extensive services which the Survey offers. As a means of identifying all existing USGS material, two books are indispensable—*Publications of the Geological Survey 1879–1961* (USGS, 1965) and *Publications of the Geological Survey 1962–1970* (USGS, 1972). Both are permanent catalogs and are free, upon request, from the USGS, Washington, D.C. 20242.[3] In addition, the Survey has monthly catalogs (USGS, 1973) which are also free upon request. A single request for a monthly catalog puts one's name on

[3] New address is the MIO and is given in footnote 1.

the list, and distribution for ensuing months is thereby automatic. Monthly catalogs are collated into an annual catalog which is distributed to recipients of the monthly lists approximately one year after the close of the calendar year it catalogs. Due to the continuing expansion of the programs, the introduction of new mapping programs, and the generally dynamic nature of the subject matter covered by the USGS, these catalogs are an absolute necessity in order to keep abreast of the available material. Occasionally, a map series which has outlived its usefulness is abandoned, and its obituary is dutifully announced in the catalog.

Finally, we should note that numerous problems are continually being encountered when trying to locate an elusive map. The Survey maintains the Map Information Office (see address in footnote 1) (p. 171) to answer such inquiries. This office is also most helpful in guiding requestors to other governmental agencies which may have the answer to the question concerning sources of environmental data information.

Map Information Office

MAPS FROM OTHER FEDERAL AGENCIES

Other federal agencies are involved in mapping programs similar to the Miscellaneous Geologic Investigations Maps prepared by the USGS. On the whole, however, these programs are not as widespread in either interest, geographic coverage, or map subjects as those of the USGS. A short pamphlet prepared and distributed by the USGS entitled "Types of Topographic Maps Published by Government Agencies" will guide the interested reader to the entire array of available maps. Consequently, only a few of the numerous maps and environmental data will be discussed in this section, including both standard ongoing projects and some of the more experimental and exploratory series.

Within the U.S. Department of Agriculture, the Soil Conservation Service (SCS) has been, and continues to be, the major provider of soil information to the agricultural and planning community. This function, conducted by the SCS and several forerunners, began in 1899 when the first soil surveys were prepared and published. Generally published in a book format, the surveys "furnish soil maps and interpretations needed in planning research and disseminating the results of the research. . . . They are used in educational programs, in giving technical assistance to farmers and ranchers, and in guiding other decisions about soil selection, use and management. [USDA, 1973]"

Soil surveys are generally done in cooperation with state agricultural experiment stations, land-grant colleges, state extension agencies, and other federal and state agencies. Consequently, the available soil information and data are generally procurable from local sources. According to a USDA booklet:

United States Department of Agriculture (USDA)

> Soil classification has improved as our knowledge about soils and their potential uses has increased. As agriculture has become more technical, a proper fit between the kind of soil and the combination of practices used has become more critical. Because of this, soils bearing the same names are more narrowly defined in recent surveys than in the older ones. . . . When soil survey work began in 1899 little was known about the soils of the United States. Since then

a great deal has been learned, methods have been improved, and the results of the surveys are more accurate and detailed. For planning farms, engineering structures, parks, urban developments, and other uses of land, the recent published soils surveys are more useful. The older surveys can be of considerable assistance for many uses, but their maps are more general than those in recent surveys and some of the interpretations need to be updated [USDA, 1973].

It is important to be especially cognizant of both the date of the publication which contains the data and the dates of data collection.

Most soil surveys are conducted and published on a county basis. Each publication, regardless of the reporting unit employed, contains a variety of information, including some or all of the following: (1) general statement of the nature, location, agriculture, and the climate of the county being discussed, (2) a description of the way the soil survey was conducted, and a description of the soils of the county together with their relationship to the topography, (3) data concerning the average yield of each soil for a variety of agricultural crops and pursuits, (4) uses and management of soils, including soil capability, suggestions for the management and use of the soil, soil engineering properties, with respect to highway planning, range management, sewage disposal, and (5) the grouping of soils into management units and capability classes and subunits. These discussions are followed by a set of maps, including a general soil map of the county and an index map which further guides the reader to a set of large-scale (generally 1:20,000 or 1:15,840) photomaps on which the various soils are identified. Thus, practically all information concerning the soils of a subject county is collated and made available in one complete package.

A soil survey published by the U.S. Department of Agriculture that is still in print may be obtained in one of the following ways:

> Land users in the area, surveyors and professional workers who have use for the survey can obtain a free copy from the local office of the Soil Conservation Service, from their county agent, or from their congressman.
>
> For a time after publication, copies may be purchased from the Superintendent of Documents, U.S. Government Printing Office, Washington, D.C. 20402.
>
> Many libraries keep published soil surveys on file for reference. Also soil conservation district offices and county agricultural extension offices have copies of local surveys that may be used for reference.

Most published soil surveys cover one or more counties and are so named. Where the survey covers only a part of one or more counties, the word "area" is a part of the name. (This is commonly used only in some Western states.)

Tennessee Valley Authority (TVA)

The Tennessee Valley Authority (TVA) has been actively involved in mapping areas of Kentucky and Tennessee through their Maps and Survey branch. Generally, their work is congruent, both in style, format, and scale, with the USGS 1:24,000 series and is included as a part of that series. However, Anderson et al. (1972) indicate that the TVA has been preparing a set of experimental maps designed to determine what land cover, identified according to a USGS classification scheme, could be derived from high-altitude color photography and presented in an understandable information format. An article by Stevens (1973) discusses the project and concludes that the data available at the more general level of the classification scheme can be obtained through elementary photo-interpretation techniques. The costs to the TVA for preparation of the maps at the 1:24,000 scale varied from several hundred dollars to as high as $3000 per map sheet. The area of the pilot study, Clinton, Tennessee, was mapped using both aerial-photograph base maps and the more expensive color-separation maps similar to the standard USGS color products. This was an experimental set and used an experimental land-cover classification scheme; consequently, it should not be considered as the final product. However, persons in planning agencies who are considering this type of mapping project should find a considerable amount of informative data in the paper by Stevens (1973) and in the maps he has prepared.

National Oceanic and Atmospheric Administration (NOAA)

The U.S. Department of Commerce (USDC), through the National Oceanic and Atmospheric Administration (NOAA), has recently been preparing a set of Storm Evaluation Maps.[4] As stated in the marginal data on the sheets of this map series: "This is a special purpose map designed for use by the National Weather Service and other agencies responsible for evaluation. Only selected map detail is shown." This detail is primarily in the form of major routes which could be used for population evacuation, urban areas, marshes and swamps, and flooding areas. The flood-prone areas are shown by altitude tints (shades of pink) in 5- or 10-feet (1.5- or 3-meter) increments from 0 to 30 feet (9 meters) above sea level. Because the maps presently available in the set deal with high tide elevations resulting from storms (primarily hurricanes), they are only available for selected portions of the Gulf of Mexico and Atlantic Ocean coasts of the United States. All maps are at a scale of 1:62,500, but unlike their counterparts of the USGS Topographic Map series, they are printed on much larger sheets (37 inch (94 centimeter) by 28 inch (71 centimeter) compared to the USGS 22 inch (56 centimeter) by 17 inch (43 centimeter).[5]

[4] These maps are available, for $2 per sheet, from
  National Ocean Survey
  Distribution Section
  6001 Executive Blvd.
  Rockville, MD 20852

One possible problem with this set is that the elevation above sea level is equated with flooding at a given tide height. In fact some areas of equal elevation may experience different probabilities of flooding for a given storm tide height due to the proximity and connection via lowlands and streams to the surrounding terrain. Still, the set does effectively emphasize the major danger areas which should be considered when planning development and urban expansion. As with the problems of river flood magnitude and frequency discussed in Chapter 5, hurricane- and storm-related tides tend to be periodic when averaged over many years. This is adequately illustrated by a presentation of tide heights related to twentieth-century storms at selected locations on each map sheet. Thus the planner has some idea of the average expected recurrence period of storms of hazardous intensities.

[5] Listings of new additions to this series are announced in *The Mariners Weather Log,* a monthly publication of the U.S. Department of Commerce, NOAA, Environmental Data Service.

National Aeronautics and Space Administration (NASA)

An interesting set of experimental maps has been prepared by the National Aeronautics and Space Administration (NASA), and is offered for sale by the USGS. As announced in the USGS monthly publication list (no. 775, February 1973), these are

Land use, Houston, Tex., Area Test Site (HATS). 1970. Prepared by the Earth Observations Division, Manned Spacecraft Center, Houston, Tex., in cooperation with the State of Texas, the Houston Chamber of Commerce. Includes counties of Austin, Brazoria, Brazos, Burleson, Chambers, Colorado, Fort Bend, Galveston, Grimes, Harris, Liberty, Matagorda, Montgomery, San

Jacinto, Walker, Waller, Washington and Wharton. Multicolored Experimental.

Scale 1:125,000 (1 inch = about 2 miles) 21 sheets (each sheet approx. 21 by 29 inches); 20 land use categories. $25 per set.

Scale 1:250,000 (1 inch = about 4 miles) 4 sheets (each sheet approx. 21 by 29 inches); 20 land use categories. $5 per set.

Scale 1:500,000 (1 inch = about 8 miles); 1 sheet (approx. 21 by 24 inches); 9 land use categories. $1. Available only from the Distribution Section, Denver, Colorado.

These maps are experimental in several ways. First, the maps were to assist in a study of the application of remote-sensor technology to resource management and environmental problems. The data used for the maps were derived from color Ektachrome aerial film, printed at a scale of 1:120,000. Because the maps are considered research tools rather than operational tools, little field checking was undertaken to assist in interpretation. Second, the land use categories are quite similar to those suggested in Anderson et al. (1972), a classification scheme which is also experimental. Third, and only a minor point, is that the presentation of the scales is reversed, with the metric scale being presented before (i.e., above) the more standard statute-mile scale, one of the first indications of the proposed forthcoming switch to the metric system in the United States.

All land use categories on the NASA experimental maps of the Houston Test Area are shown in color, which presents some minor interpretation problems. Patterns (lines, dots, etc.) are not used for identification of land use, presumably because of the visual confusion of these patterns or because the many small areas on the map would not present enough of the pattern to allow accurate recognition. As is expected, the maps with the smaller scales show considerably less detail and have fewer categories, that is, more generalization. Thus, the 1:500,000 map has only nine categories of land use, whereas the other two sets (1:250,000 and 1:125,000) have twenty categories each.

The value of these maps of the Houston Area Test Site set is twofold. First, it demonstrates the use (but not necessarily the utility) of color aerial photographs in the generation of land use data for large areas. Second, the cartographers are working on methods of categorizing these data into meaningful land use classes for easy and accurate cartographic presentation. Although only the HATS area has been studied at this level of detail, NASA is effectively pointing the way for other regionally oriented land use organizations to consider similar programs. That they desire comments is noted by the request printed on each map sheet.

EXPERIMENTAL MAP

Users are invited to submit their comments to
Earth Observations Division/TF2
Manned Spacecraft Center*
National Aeronautics and Space Administration
Houston, Texas 77058

*Now the L. B. Johnson Space Center.

Conclusion on Mapping

For years many nations have been preparing national atlases of their lands, waters, and territories. Surprisingly, the United States has been without a cohesive and relatively comprehensive map set assembled in a single volume and available to the general public. Consequently, there has often been a need for presentation on map sources such as the one in this chapter. However, there is now a U.S. national atlas available, both as a unit and as separate sheets. One section, entitled "Mapping and Charting," presents the same type of material as we have been discussing in this chapter. However, other types of maps are discussed (e.g., hydrographic charts, jet navigation charts, operational navigation charts) in addition to those presented here. Because the atlas is oriented to all users, no special attempts are made to identify those maps of special interest to planners. Indeed, we have included some types of publicly available information which have been left out of the National Atlas—for example, the data on maps which are not part of an ongoing series. Also, because the National Atlas is several years old, some of the experimental maps mentioned here have, by necessity, not been included. The Atlas does, however, include on page 295 a listing of the different types of data available and the agency from which these data are obtained. This listing is essentially the same as that included in the brochure entitled "Types of Maps Published by Government Agencies" (see Bibliography, p. 193).

Maps are important communication vehicles for many fields of study, and it is virtually axiomatic that each field presents its maps with a certain stylistic uniqueness. The eclectic nature of planning problems necessitates the drawing together of the maps of apparently disjunct fields, extracting from them pertinent information and integrating it in the context of a planning task.

Of the many fields and public agencies producing maps today, it is the USGS which produces those of greatest relevance to land use planning. The large-scale topographic contour map series (1:24,000) are among the most accurate and detailed records of the landscape produced in the world today. To the adroit interpreter, these maps provide a wealth of quantitative and qualitative information of utility in planning and environmental problems.

AERIAL PHOTOGRAPHY

Aerial photographs are a familiar source of data and information for planners. Despite the variety of aerial photographs available today through new technologies, standard panchromatic (black-and-white) aerial photography perhaps remains the most-used source of areal information on the environment. Aerial photographs are readily available for nearly all parts of the United States, but their acquisition is often more tedious than that of the topographic maps. This is because many agencies, within both the public and private sectors, are involved in ongoing projects and programs which produce aerial photography. As with the USGS topographic maps, the Map Information Office functions as a clearinghouse for information concerning aerial photography, although this office does not handle the photographs themselves. Table 6.11 lists the several federal agencies which offer aerial photographs for sale to the public.

Aerial photographs are generally recorded on 10-inch-wide film

TABLE 6.11 NAMES AND ADDRESSES OF FEDERAL AGENCIES WHICH SELL AERIAL PHOTOGRAPHS

	Agency	Address
U.S. Department of Agriculture	Agricultural Stabilization and Conservation Service (ASCS)	Coordinator of Aerial Photographic Work Washington, D.C. 20250 Western Laboratory[1] 2505 Parleys Way Salt Lake City, UT 84109 Eastern Laboratory[2] 45 South French Broad Ave. Asheville, NC 28801
	Forest Service (USFS)	Department of Agriculture Washington, D.C. 20250
	Soil Conservation Service (SCS)	Department of Agriculture Federal Center Building East-West Highway and Belcrest Road Hyattsville, MD 20781
U.S. Department of Commerce	National Ocean Survey (NOAA)	Washington Science Center Rockville, MD 20852
U.S. Department of Interior	Bureau of Land Management Map Information Office	Washington, D.C. 20240 USGS Washington, D.C. 20242
Tennessee Valley Authority	Maps and Surveys Branch	311 Broad Street Chattanooga, TN 37401
General Services Administration	National Archives and Records Service	Washington, D.C. 20408

[1]For ND, NE, KS, AR, LA, and states to the west.
[2]For all other states.

which yields a 9-inch (23-centimeter) by 9-inch (23-centimeter) negative for each frame. These can be prepared as contact prints (i.e., at the same dimensions as the negative) or, if necessary, they may be enlarged up to fifteen to twenty times. Print quality, of course, markedly decreases with each enlargement. Many organizations produce similar-sized, but less expensive, ozalid enlargements of aerial photographs. However, the quality of ozalids is usually poorer than that of photographic prints. All these formats may then be used in the field or office for direct interpretation and annotation.

Black-and-white (panchromatic and infrared), color (panchromatic or true color), and color infrared (or false color) film can be used to obtain environmental information. Color films, however, are more expensive than the black and white for both the original, reproduction, and/or enlargements because they require more stringent controls in the exposure and processing of the film. Therefore, they are not used on a regular basis by most governmental agencies. Although it is beyond the scope of this chapter to discuss the manifold applications of color aerial photography, we would like to note in passing that journals such as *Photogrammetric Engineering, Remote Sensing of the Environment,* and *Photogrammetria* are devoting more and more attention to applications of these films to problems of concern to planners and environmental specialists.

Several government publications on aerial photography are of special interest to planners and other environmental-oriented professionals. Krause (1969) described the customers who purchase aerial photography from the Agricultural Stabilization and Conservation Service. It is interesting to note that of a total of 471,000 photos sold in 1966, approximately 40 percent went to individuals, agencies, and businesses not affiliated with the federal government. These data and the customer data indicate that many diverse groups are purchasing government supplies of aerial photography. The federal government is organized to deal with purchases by nonfederal government agencies or private business as is evidenced by the promptness of responses to requests for photography. Experience indicates that purchases of aerial photographs normally will elicit a response within about two weeks, and the delivery of the products can be expected within about six weeks of the original order.

A second publication, or more properly a series of publications, is the *Air Photo Atlas of Rural United States* (USDA, 1970). The general format of this series facilitates a ready acquaintance with aerial photography. For each area covered, two facing pages are used; the first gives the aerial photograph mosaic, usually at the scale of 1:63,360, and the other the area covered on the index sheet. Numerous photographs are given to illustrate the major landforms found in the United States. In addition, each set of stereopairs is accompanied by a description of the land use, elevation and topography, climate, water, and soil of the area. Several USDA sources are used for the aerial photos, including the Soil Conservation Service (SCS) and the U.S. Forest Service (USFS).

The first step in ordering aerial photography is to contact the Map Information Office and request a copy of the latest editions of two maps: (1) "Status of Aerial Photography" and (2) "Status of Aerial Mosaics".[6] These maps, at a scale of 1:5,000,000, cover the entire United States. (Alaska is at a scale of 1:10,000,000.) The former map notes the coverage of the United States as reported by U.S. government agencies and also by some commercial firms and local governmental agencies. The federal government agencies include ASCS, SCS, USFS, USGS, U.S. Bureau of Land Management, TVA, and the U.S. Coast and Geodetic Survey. Address for all holders of aerial photographs are included on the back of the index.

Occasionally a mosaic (an assembly of aerial photographs which have been matched and mounted to form a large, continuous photograph) may be needed. The "Status of Aerial Mosaics" map will indicate the availability of these products. Because mosaics are used for a variety of purposes, and because their construction is fairly expensive, mosaic coverage of the entire United States is incomplete. Therefore, one may not be available for an area being studied; or if available, it may be at the wrong scale or format for a particular purpose. Figure 6.8 is an example of a portion of the uncontrolled aerial photography mosaic for the western suburbs of Detroit in Wayne County, Michigan.

In making requests for a photograph status map through the MIO in Washington, D.C., it would be advisable to describe briefly the

Aerial Photography Information Sources

[6]Also available from the USGS, Denver, Colorado 80225.

Acquisition of Black-and-White Aerial Photography

U.S. DEPARTMENT OF AGRICULTURE
AGRICULTURAL STABILIZATION AND CONSERVATION SERVICE
INVITATION NO ASCS-3-71 DC ITEM 5
FLOWN BY PARK AERIAL SURVEYS, INC., LOUISVILLE, KY.
YEAR FLOWN 1972 AERIAL NEGATIVE SCALE 1:40,000
SYMBOL XU 6" CAMERA

GRAPHIC SCALE OF INDEX

WAYNE COUNTY, MICHIGAN

Figure 6.8. An example of an uncontrolled aerial photograph mosaic for part of the Detroit metropolitan area. The Status of Aerial Mosaics map shows the mosaic coverage of the United States and is available through MIO.

area and the type project for which you are requesting aerial photography. This could include latitude and longitude, township and range, the dimensions of the project area, or an excerpt from a topographic map showing the study area. MIO will then be able to better advise you concerning the available photography.

Upon receipt of the status map, identify the agency which holds the photograph of the area. Several agencies (e.g., ASCS, USFC, SCS) maintain up-to-date brochures, available upon request, which show the status of the aerial photograph coverage held by that particular agency.

These materials normally show the coverage for each state by county and include the following information: area covered, areas presently under contract for aerial photography, scale of photos, type of film used, year of coverage, number of photo indexes per county, and lens length of camera used. The brochures show the coverage of the most recent aerial photography. Earlier films, especially those taken prior to the mid-1940s, will normally be held by the U.S. Archives Office.

Table 6.11 lists the several addresses for the agencies involved in the aerial photography of the United States. If, for example, you are dealing with a county, the most prudent move would be to acquire the aerial photo index of that county. An index is prepared by simply stapling all the photos of a county onto a board and then rephotographing the entire board. A print (about 20 inches (51 centimeters) by 24 inches (61 centimeters) and including up to 100 photos for $5 a sheet) is then sold as the index. Although the index has a "mosaiclike" appearance, it is "uncontrolled" and is therefore not suitable for purposes other than quick identification of the geographic area covered by each of the individual 9- by 9-inch (23- by 23-centimeter) photographs. Although the complete set of index sheets may run as high as $20 to $25 for an entire county, it is considerably cheaper than ordering all 110 photos of the county at a cost about ten times greater. Using the index, the photos may then be ordered in the desired format.

Black-and-white (panchromatic) aerial photography is available in a variety of formats, although 9- by 9-inch (23- by 23-centimeter) contact prints are generally the most useful and economical for planning purposes. Table 6.12 lists the formats available from several government agencies which sell aerial photographs to the public. It must be emphasized, however, that this information is based on 1973 data for panchromatic photography and may be subject to change as agencies alter their programs.

Standard Formats for Black-and-White Aerial Photographs

TABLE 6.12   THE FORMATS, PAPER TYPES, AND COSTS OF AERIAL PHOTOGRAPHY SOLD BY FEDERAL AGENCIES

Agency	Item	Size of print (in inches)	Paper Type	Cost/Photo 1–25	Cost/Photo More than 25
USDA-ASCS	Contact	9.5 × 9.5 (or 9 × 9)		$1.75	$1.25
	Enlargements	13 × 13	N.A.	2.50	2.00
		17 × 17	N.A.	3.00	2.50
		24 × 24	N.A.	4.50	3.50
		38 × 38	N.A.	9.00	8.00
	Index	20 × 24	N.A.	3.00	3.00
USDA-USFS	Contact	10 × 10	N.A.	1.75	1.25
			Plastic Coated	2.00	1.50
			Opaque White Polyester	2.50	2.00
			Stable Film Positive	3.00	3.00
			Glass Diapositives		
			0.060 in	6.50	6.00
			0.130 in	6.75	6.25
			0.250 in	7.50	7.00
	Enlargements				
	(1.5×)	14 × 14	N.A.	3.00	2.50
	(1.5–x.0×)	18 × 18	N.A.	3.50	3.00
	(2.0–3.0×)	26 × 26	N.A.	4.50	3.50
	(3.0–4.5×)	40 × 40	N.A.	9.00	9.00
	Index	Positive DSWM		3.00	3.00
		Negative		6.00	6.00
National Archives	Contact	10 × 10	Not Stated	1.75	1.75
	Index	24 × 24	Not Stated	3.00	3.00
USGS	(For contacts and enlargements, see prices for USDA-USFS above.)				
	Index of 7.5 × 15 ft quadrangle on 10 × 12 in sheet			2.50	2.50

SUMMARY

The planning, implementation, and maintenance of governmental projects for the generation of data and information on the environment is an exceptionally dynamic enterprise. The programs which have been discussed in this chapter represent, on the whole, the major commitments of only several agencies of the federal government. In addition, we have mentioned several of the smaller, ad hoc projects which have been initiated primarily as exploratory and feasibility studies for new products. In this latter group would fall the HATS mapping program (a product of NASA) and the Storm Evacuation Maps prepared by the U.S. Department of Commerce.

Due to the very diverse nature of the data programs maintained by the several states, we have refrained from discussing these even in a general way. Most states have departments of natural resources, state geological surveys, forest services, water management programs, and agricultural departments, which, in many respects, extend to the state and county level much of the work which is being done at the federal level. Consequently, many of the 1:24,000 USGS maps are, for example, prepared on a cooperative basis between individual states and the USGS; and similar cooperative mapping and data collection efforts are often common in water resources and remote sensing. One should contact the state agencies for specific and detailed information which they may have with respect to a particular local problem. Often it is discovered that state departments may have conducted some research on a particular set of watersheds or lakes, for example, and these data, although often limited, can be valuable for providing a base point for time-comparison studies of the environment. Likewise, county-level government organizations (drainage commissioners, planning commissions, highway boards) in addition to local citizen organizations, such as nature clubs, often prove to be valuable sources of the more exotic and locally important data.

Bibliography

American Society of Photogrammetry: *Manual of Photogrammetry,* Falls Church, Va., 1966. Vol. 1, 536 pp.; vol. 2, pp. 537–1199.

American Society of Photogrammetry: *Manual of Color Aerial Photography,* vol. 15, Falls Church, Va., 1968. 550 pp.

American Society of Photogrammetry: *Manual of Photographic Interpretation,* vol. 15, Falls Church, Va., 1960. 868 pp.

Anderson, J. R. et al.: *A Land Use Classification System for Use with Remote Sensor Data,* U.S. Department of the Interior, USGS Circular 671, 1972. 16 pp.

Avery, T. E.: *Interpretations of Aerial Photographs,* vol. 7, Burgess, Minneapolis, Minn., 1968. 324 pp.

Baker, S.: "Soil Surveys and Topographic Maps to be Used with Sample Areas Depicted in *The Look of Our Land*—An Airphoto Atlas of the Rural United States," *The Professional Geographer,* vol. 26, no. 2, 1974, pp. 201–207.

Branch, M. C.: *City Planning and Aerial Information,* vol. 15, Harvard, Cambridge, Mass., 1971. 283 pp.

Denny, C. S. et al.: *A Description Catalog of Selected Aerial Photographs of Geologic Features in the United States,* Washington, D.C., USGS Prof, Paper 590, 1968. 79 pp.

Eitel, D. F.: "Remote Sensing Education in the U.S.A.," *Photogrammetric Engineering,* vol. 38, no. 8, 1972, pp. 900–906.

Estes, J. E., and L. W. Senger: *Remote Sensing: Techniques for Environmental Analysis,* Hamilton Publishing Co., Santa Barbara, Calif., 1974. 340 pp.

Holz, R. K.: *The Surveillant Science: Remote Sensing of the Environment,* Houghton Mifflin, Boston, Mass., 1973. 240 pp.

Krause, O. E.: *Airphoto Use in Resource Management: A Survey of Non-Federal Purchases of Agricultural Stabilization and Conservation Service Photographs,* USDA Economic Research Service, Agriculture Information Bulletin no. 336, Washington, D.C., 1969. 26 pp.

Ray, R. G.: *Aerial Photographs in Geologic Interpretation and Mapping,* USGS Professional Paper 373, vol. 6, 1960. 229 pp.

Rudd, R. D.: *Remote Sensing: A Better View,* Wadsworth, Belmont, Calif., 1974. 135 pp.

Smith, H. T. U.: *Aerial Photographs and Their Applications,* vol. 14, Appleton-Century-Crofts, New York, 1943. 372 pp.

Stanton, B. T.: "Education in Photogrammetry," *Photogrammetric Engineering,* vol. 37, no. 3, 1971, pp. 293–303.

Stevens, A. R.: "Land Cover Delineation Methods and Presentation Alternatives Applicable to the Tennessee River Watershed," in Shahrokhi (ed.), *Remote Sensing of Earth Resources,* vol. 2, Space Institute, University of Tennessee, Tullahoma, Tenn., 1973, pp. 1269–1285.

Todd, D. K. (ed.): *The Water Encyclopedia,* Water Information Center, Port Washington, N.Y., 1970. 599 pp.

U.S. Department of Agriculture: *List of Published Soil Surveys,* USDA–SCS, 1973. 28 pp.

USDA: *The Look of Our Land: An Airphoto Atlas of the Rural United States,* USDA Economic Research Service, Washington, D.C., 1970. (This series of publications was published as follows:)

    The Far West, Agriculture Handbook no. 372, 1970. 48 pp.

    The Mountains and Deserts, Agriculture Handbook no. 409, 1971. 68 pp.

    The Plains and Prairies, Agriculture Handbook no. 419, 1971. 84 pp.

    North Central and Lake States, Agriculture Handbook no. 384, 1970. 64 pp.

    The East and South, Agriculture Handbook no. 406, 1971. 99 pp.

USDA: *Aerial-Photo Interpretation in Classifying and Mapping Soils.* USDA–SCS Agriculture Handbook 294, Washington, D.C. 1966.

USGS: *Publications of the Geological Survey,* vol. 6, Washington, D.C., 1965. 457 pp.

USGS: *Index of Surface-Water Records to September 30, 1970,* Part 1, "North Atlantic Slope Basins," USGS Circular 651, Washington, D.C., 1971. 89 pp.

USGS: *Publications of the Geological Survey,* vol. 4, Washington, D.C., 1972. 586 pp.

USGS: "Geological Survey Research, 1972," USGS Professional Paper 800A, Washington, D.C., 1972, Ch. A.

USGS: Monthly Catalogs (nonlisted), 1973.

    In addition, the USGS publishes a series of small pamphlets which describe the products and services of the survey.

    Following is a representative listing of this material.

      General Information on Maps.

      Information Sources and Services (1 sheet) GPO: 873-909.

      Selected Bibliography on Maps and Mappings (1 sheet) GPO: 919-021.

      Types of Maps Published by Government Agencies (1 sheet) USGS: INF-72-33.

      Topographic Maps Tools for Planning. 15 pp. GPO: 1971 0-446-049, Stock no. 2401-2047.

      Topographic Maps. 21 pp. GPO: 1972 476-697.

      Shaded Relief Maps (1 sheet) MIO-4, 1971.

      Geologic Maps Portraits of the Earth. 19 pp. GPO: 1972 0-472-522.

CHAPTER **7**

APPLICATIONS OF ENVIRONMENTAL ANALYSIS

Richard N. L. Andrews

INTRODUCTION

Available Data

WHEN AND WHY should one conduct an environmental analysis such as those described above, and how much time, money, and effort is it worth to gather and interpret various kinds of information? The costs depend upon the kind of information sought, upon the availability of it from existing sources, and upon the level of detail and the degrees of accuracy and reliability that are necessary. This chapter will suggest some of the principal uses and applications of environmental information and some of the essential considerations that must be addressed in deciding what kinds of analyses to undertake.

For perspective, it is useful to begin with two observations concerning the history of environmental analysis, especially in the United States. First, the data that are available for use in environmental analyses have been collected piecemeal and for diverse rather than coordinated purposes. Examples include U.S. Geological Survey base maps, Soil Conservation Service soil maps, Corps of Engineers floodplain maps, NASA satellite observations, and data files of hydrologic, water quality, and atmospheric monitoring stations. Virtually all these data have been generated by public agencies, at different times, for reasons associated with what were perceived as major problems at those times, and generally without any systematic efforts to integrate their data collection activities with the efforts or needs of other potential users.

Second, therefore, these data sets generally tend to be not only incomplete in coverage but also variable in their currency, and frequently incommensurable in their scales and classification systems. Even soil maps have only been completed for approximately 55 percent of the land area of the United States, at scales of 1:15,840 and 1:20,000. Topographic base maps are more complete than this, but many other categories of information generally are far less so.

Anyone who intends to conduct or utilize environmental analyses must begin by consciously understanding the sorts of decisions that must be made in the course of a project. If not, these decisions will be made by others or by accident if they are not made deliberately, and in many cases they will fundamentally structure both the content and the usefulness of the results. In the case of data already "available," such decisions already *have* influenced the structure, whether or not this structure is apparent. Nevertheless, it is advisable to entertain the following questions in structuring the analyses (Figure 7.1). First, what is the purpose of the analysis: what decisions are to be made on the basis of this analysis? Different decisions require different mixtures of information, and the construction of a road or a housing development may require a different mixture than the development of a land use or wildlife management plan. Second, what approach must one take in order to develop the desired mixture of information? Several of the principal approaches will be discussed below. Third, what specific analytical techniques should be used to ensure the accuracy, reliability, and adequacy of the data and information that are to be collected? This question has already been addressed in Chapters 1 through 5 and will not be further discussed here. The decisions that are made on

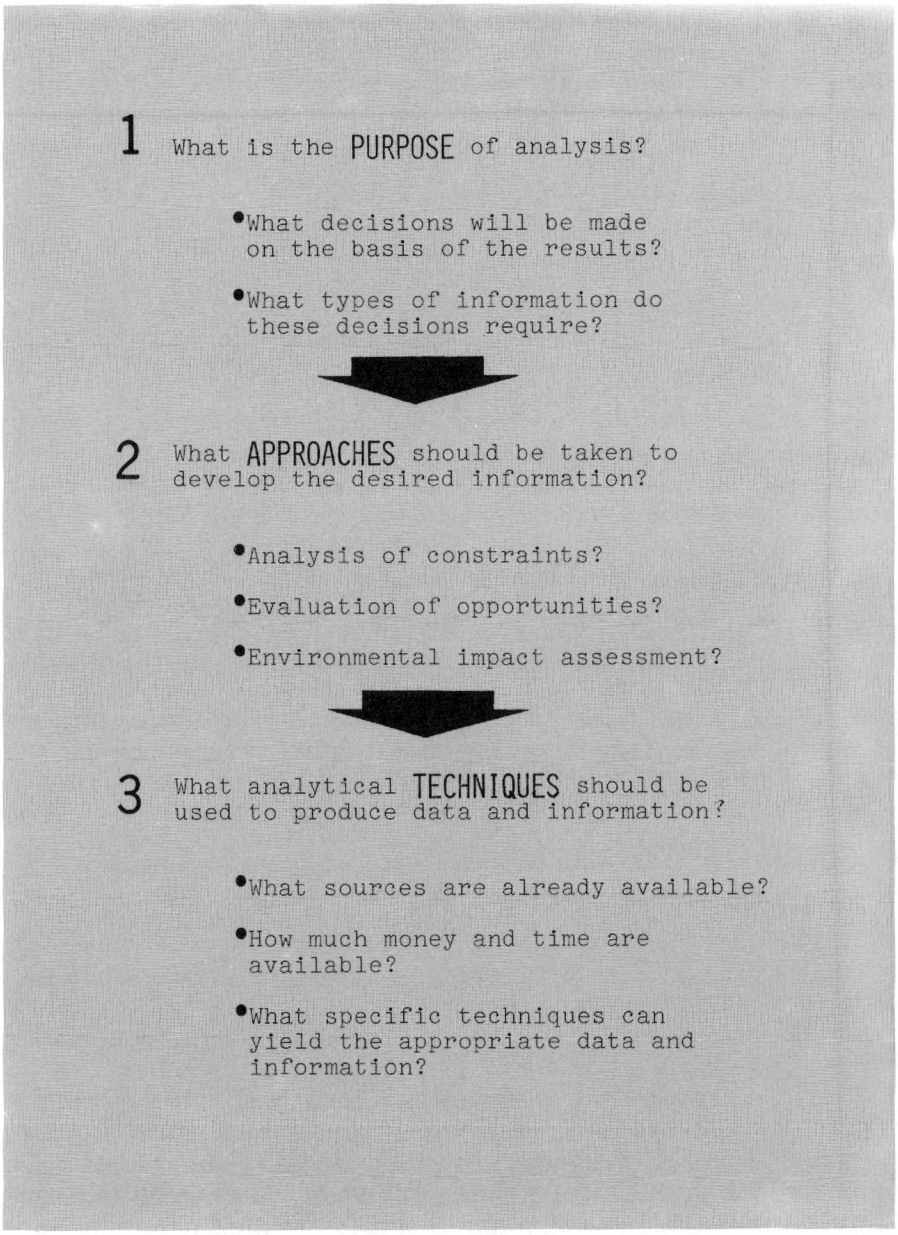

1 What is the PURPOSE of analysis?

> •What decisions will be made
> on the basis of the results?

> •What types of information do
> these decisions require?

2 What APPROACHES should be taken to
develop the desired information?

> •Analysis of constraints?

> •Evaluation of opportunities?

> •Environmental impact assessment?

3 What analytical TECHNIQUES should be
used to produce data and information?

> •What sources are already available?

> •How much money and time are
> available?

> •What specific techniques can
> yield the appropriate data and
> information?

Figure 7.1. The key questions of environmental analysis.

all these questions, however, for each kind of information, may shape the outcome of the eventual decisions just as profoundly as the final choice among major alternative actions.

PURPOSE OF ANALYSIS

A cardinal principle in using any kind of environmental information is that *data are collected for particular purposes.* This principle applies equally to data which one collects oneself and to "available data" already collected by others. Information collected for one purpose *may* be appropriate for others as well, but it cannot be assumed so without careful scrutiny. It may have been gathered at too small a scale; for example, U.S. Geological Survey topographic maps at 1:24,000 scale are adequate for planning rural land uses but are far too gross to serve the same purpose in an urbanized area. Or information may appear in the form of a classification scheme that is inappropriate to other purposes. Soil suitability for agricultural uses may in some cases be appropriate for general recreation planning but poorly suited to urban or residential development. In any case, one cannot intelligently gather or utilize environmental information without first knowing the purpose for which the information is needed, in what form the information must be in order to fulfill that purpose, and whether that purpose and form are compatible with the characteristics of the information that is to be gathered or utilized.

APPROACHES IN THE APPLICATION OF ENVIRONMENTAL INFORMATION

There are many specific applications for environmental information, but most may be grouped within three primary approaches: (1) the identification of environmental *constraints,* which might limit or endanger particular kinds of development, (2) the discovery of environmental *opportunities,* where conditions are unusually appropriate for particular kinds of activities, and (3) the predictions of environmental *impacts,* or changes in environmental conditions that would be likely consequences of proposed actions.

Identification of Environmental Constraints

The purpose of this approach is to identify environmental conditions that pose a constraint to proposed actions. The following examples will serve to illustrate some of the most important applications of this approach.

Feasibility Studies

A builder is looking for sites for new housing construction; a state highway agency is studying possible alignments for a new road; a city needs to develop a new landfill. Each has not only certain engineering and economic requirements that must be met, but also certain environmental constraints that must be recognized. Houses must not subside or be flooded; highways may not be federally funded if they destroy endangered species or their habitats; landfills must be properly drained. Without evidence of proper environmental conditions as well as satisfaction of engineering and economic constraints, actions may turn out to be infeasible. The later this is discovered in a project, the more costly it may prove to be.

Even after feasible sites have been identified, more detailed investigation of environmental conditions may be necessary to ensure that environmental constraints are not violated. In many localities, detailed site plans must be prepared and approved by the government before action can be taken, and many governments are now looking more closely than ever before at the relationships between proposed actions and environmental constraints. Even if they are not required by law, site plans which recognize and honor environmental constraints may provide significant benefits in the long run because they can help establish criteria for selection of the most appropriate use for a site. An area of organic soils and a floodplain may be poor places to locate houses, though perfectly appropriate and even attractive for open space among them. A steep slope may limit the location of buildings, and it may require preservation of its vegetative cover in order to prevent severe soil erosion and sedimentation of water features. Of course, environmental conditions are not the only factors to be considered in site planning, but they are important and in some cases are among the most critical constraints.

Site Planning

Many public agencies and governments recognize the importance to society of the functions performed by natural systems, the fragility of those systems in the face of development, and the irreversibility of the damage that may thereby be done to them. For these reasons they have sought to incorporate environmental constraints into public controls over land use. The most widespread of these controls is zoning, which prohibits certain kinds of development in designated zones. Though based mainly on socioeconomic factors, modern zoning may also be based on environmental factors. Specialized applications of environmental constraint zoning include agriculture zoning, intended to protect prime agricultural zones against competing urban uses; floodplain zoning, intended to prevent construction in areas subject to periodic flood inundation; and conservation zoning, which may include the two types mentioned above as well as areas subject to other sorts of environmental constraints. Two other recent variants of this instrument are (1) "performance zoning" or "impact zoning," which permits a wide range of development types so long as they satisfy numerous standards intended to prevent violation of environmental (and other) constraints, and (2) the designation of "areas of critical environmental concern," which are subject to unusual environmental constraints and must be regulated more closely than other areas. Examples of the latter include floodplains, wetlands, steep slopes, shorelands, aquifer recharge areas, and wildlife habitats. All these land use controls and others must be founded upon solid analyses of the appropriate environmental constraints. For a more detailed example of this approach, see the case study of slope-hazard mapping in "Special Topics," Chapter 9.

Land Use Controls

It is important to recognize that constraint mapping need not be limited to "environmental" constraints, and particularly not to the rather limited range even of environmental conditions, such as geophysical and hydrological hazards, and soil conditions, that

Types of Constraints

have dominated many applications of this approach in the past. Among the constraints related to the natural environment, however, three general types should be distinguished (Table 7.1).

TABLE 7.1   EXAMPLES OF NATURAL AND ARTIFICIAL
CONSTRAINTS CLASSED INTO THREE GROUPS

	Hazard constraints	Legal constraints	Social or professional values
Natural	Unstable slopes Earthquake zones Hurricane coasts Tornado belts Floodplains	Endangered species Special ecological communities Wildlife refuges	Urban open space Wooded areas Water features Pleasing designs Prime agricultural lands
Artificial	Aircraft landing paths Forest fire zones Air pollution areas	Use-zoned lands Historic sites Archaeological sites Parks Public lands	Stable neighborhoods Ethnic communities

NOTE: This table is illustrative only.

Natural Hazards

First, there are constraints based upon hazard. Active geological faults and areas of unstable soils are demonstrable geophysical hazards to development; floodplains are demonstrable hydrological hazards; areas having certain characteristics of climate and vegetation may present unusual fire hazards; and so forth. Note that this analysis can be extended to nongeophysical hazards as well: aircraft landing patterns are identifiable hazards, and thus constraints, to certain kinds of development; sonic conditions in the vicinity of airports, highways, and other noise sources may also be important hazards to the users of schools, hospitals, recreation facilities, and other forms of development.

Legal Constraints

Second, one may identify constraints based upon *law or regulatory prohibition.* Publicly owned lands normally are not available for development, and certain existing land uses such as historic and archaeological sites and parklands may be legally protected against changes in use at least by public agencies if not by all parties. The habitats of all species identified as endangered, either plant or animal, are partially protected by federal law. State laws, too, often prohibit one or more forms of development on lands that are poorly drained (by soil percolation test), on soils that are highly erodible, on marshes and other wetlands, and in designated "conservation zones," "critical zones," "critical environmental areas," and other resource lands. In some of these cases the nature and boundaries of the constraint are well identified on official maps, and need only be consulted prior to taking action. In others, however, the burden may well be upon the environmental analyst to determine whether or not a proposed site satisfies all criteria that have been established as constraints by law.

Social and Professional Values as Constraints

Finally, one may identify other constraints that are neither hazards nor legal obstacles, but which are important social or professional values that would be violated if a proposed action were taken. This is the most difficult area for the application of environmental analysis, for it forces the professionals to rely upon their own judgments and convictions in ways that may well be in conflict with the political or economic values of others, including employers and clients. It may not be hazardous or illegal to build a highway through a neighborhood, or to destroy a wooded area to build a shopping area, or to build a sewer through prime agricultural land, but it may not be good professional practice either. These issues are the essential and most difficult test of any professionals' willingness to expose their own values and their rationale to challenge. These are not the sorts of constraints which they can support by clear outside authority, such as legal requirements or hazard; but they may well require reasoned advocacy by the professionals who can give reasons why such factors *should* be treated as constraints, even though others may disagree. The professionals may not ultimately prevail in such cases, but they should not neglect their responsibility to express their judgment on them.

The identification of environmental constraints is the first of the three major families of approaches that is frequently adopted in applications of environmental analysis, and it can easily be linked to the identification of economic, engineering, and other constraints in a decision analysis. If well done, it should provide at least rudimentary understanding of conditions important to society that could be damaged by proposed actions (such as wetlands or wildlife habitats), conditions under which the proposed action might cause damage to others (such as building on erodible or unstable slopes), and conditions which might make the action itself hazardous, technically or economically infeasible, or illegal.

Discovery of Environmental Opportunities

In this second approach, the purpose of environmental analysis is to discover the natural potentials of an area that might provide appropriate opportunities for various kinds of activities. In the analysis of environmental constraints, the starting point was an action, and the analysis sought only to identify any environmental conditions that would conflict with that action. In the search for environmental opportunities, on the other hand, the starting point is the area itself and the many different ways in which it could be used. The analysis must therefore be more comprehensive in order to protect the natural values and functions of the area and to seek the wisest and most appropriate uses of them. The following examples will serve to illustrate some of the most important applications of this approach.

The preparation of site plans was already mentioned as a setting for environmental-constraint identification, but there is no reason why such analyses need be limited to the identification of constraints. Environmental conditions do impose constraints, but they also provide opportunities. A steep slope may be a poor site for apartments but an excellent location for a ski run, an aesthetic resource, or a buffer. A floodplain which is too hazardous for housing may be an excellent site for a recreation facility. The identification of environmental opportunities is not normally required by law or by development plan reviews, but it is consistent with the best interests of everyone concerned, including the professionals who can put their own imagination to work more creatively

Site Planning

than is often possible in the identification of constraints (Figure 7.2).

In site-planning applications, the analyst normally begins with a particular site, say a piece of land owned by a client, and endeavors to identify the various potentials or opportunities of that site. A similar application, but at a broader scale, may be undertaken as an element of regional planning, such as for the future development of a township, county, multicountry area, or watershed. Here the client would normally be a public agency rather than a private owner or developer, but the principles of the analysis are similar. The analysis of both the constraints and the opportunities that are present by environmental conditions may provide better knowledge upon which to base decisions concerning future use of natural resources.

A somewhat different application of environmental analysis is aimed at the fulfillment of particular missions or goals. Here the search for environmental opportunities starts not from a single site, but from a goal or purpose such as to identify private development

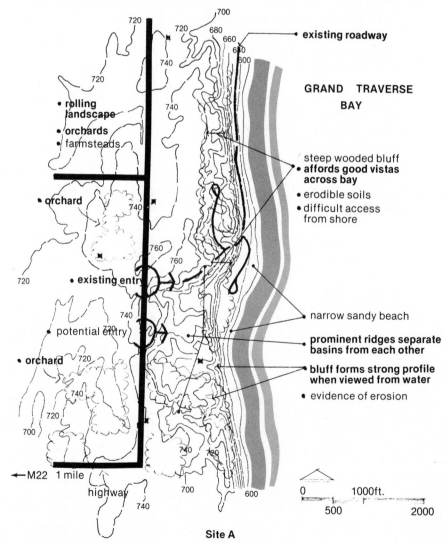

Figure 7.2. An example of a diversified segment of shoreland where consideration was given not only to constraints, but also to selected opportunities (in bold lettering). (Courtesy of Johnson, Johnson and Roy, Inc.)

opportunities (industries, ski areas, residential developments); to locate sites for public functions (such as to protect wildlife, to generate hydroelectric power, or to build a highway); or to provide opportunities to harvest timber or raise crops, to extract minerals, or to provide recreation facilities. Consequently, the search is a selective one, perhaps comparing many sites according to the particular characteristics that relate to the chosen purpose rather than inventorying a single site for diverse kinds of opportunities. This type of environmental analysis should incorporate the identification of environmental constraints and then extend further to include the identification of opportunity characteristics as well. In practice, however, the latter frequently is conducted as an independent activity. This application of environmental analysis has been widely used by both public agencies and private resource utilization industries, especially in the field of economic geology and in U.S. public land management agencies.

A distinguishing characteristic of the opportunities approach is to discover the present and potential values of environmental conditions in one or more uses. In the past, most of the uses so considered have been those that provided direct economic benefits, since the opportunity for economic gain has provided one of the most persistent motives historically for natural resource identification and exploitation. However, it is now widely recognized that resources also have many other potential values to society and even to individual owners. Some of these values may have major indirect effects on economic values—for instance, the view from a residence, the purity of the air, the access to recreational water bodies, and other environmental amenities. Others may simply be socially valued for their own sakes, such as open space, quietness, songbirds, mature vegetation, and roadside scenery.

Most important, it is now recognized that many environmental conditions provide important benefits to people only when they are not actively "used." Woodlands, for instance, provide not only wildlife habitat and recreation areas, but also important benefits of erosion control and climate moderation. Marshes and other wetlands provide not only waterfowl habitat, but also a means of water treatment which may avoid the need for additional capital investment in special facilities. In this recognition, the logical relationship between environmental constraints and environmental opportunities becomes most obvious: namely, opportunities requiring change in environmental conditions must always be evaluated against the opportunities to retain the values already provided by these conditions, which might be lost if the action were taken. The discovery of environmental opportunities is an exciting challenge for the environmental analyst who has a creative but well-informed imagination. It demands an inventory of the possibilities of the biological and geophysical environment, with and without various modifications, to provide economic, aesthetic, and other values to human society in the future.

One important relationship between these two approaches, therefore, which should not be overlooked, is the possibility of converting constraints into opportunities. Frequently, environmental conditions that constrain some types of action may provide unusual opportunities for others if one stops to think about them.

One must avoid the common error of mapping areas categorically as constraints to development and instead try to suggest both compatible and incompatible uses of them.

Prediction of Environmental Impacts

In this third approach, the purpose of environmental analysis is to predict important changes in environmental conditions that would be likely consequences of proposed actions. In the analysis of environmental constraints, the starting point was an action proposal. Here the starting point is the same, but the purpose of the analysis is to identify consequences of the action upon environmental conditions rather than constraints which those conditions impose upon the action. This approach thus completes the triangle of approaches to environmental analysis, sharing with the first approach its starting point (a particular proposal for action) and with the second its orientation toward future consequences and potentials. The following examples will serve to illustrate some of the most important applications of this approach.

Environmental Impact Statements

The National Environmental Policy Act of 1969 (Public Law 91-190) requires that for every "major federal action" which may "significantly affect the quality of the human environment," the responsible official must prepare a "detailed statement." This statement must discuss the environmental impacts of the proposed action, any "adverse effects" that cannot be avoided, alternatives to the proposal, trade-offs between long-term and short-term consequences, and any "irreversible and irretrievable commitments of resources" that would be involved.

In practice, this law applies not only to federal construction projects, but also to *any* action in which there is a "major" federal involvement, including technical or financial assistance, issuance of a license or permit, or other participation. There are very few exceptions, though a notable one is water pollution discharge permits. The law applies to highways or hospitals built with federal matching funds, licenses for electrical transmission lines, research carried out with federal grants, sales of federal timber, leases for coal and oil extraction on federal lands, and many other actions. It applies even if the action is taken primarily by private parties or other levels of government, so long as there is a federal action involved.

In addition to the federal requirement, similar requirements have been established either by law or by executive order in twenty-two states, many local municipalities, and several foreign nations. At least some of these equivalent laws, such as the one in California, apply not only to the actions of state agencies but to those of *subdivisions* of state government as well, including local governments issuing building permits, and to private developers.

These laws have resulted in the preparation of thousands of "environmental impact statement" documents, and the preparation of these statements has accordingly become one of the most widespread applications of environmental analysis currently in existence.

Many actions which do not require preparation of a formal environmental impact statement to meet legal requirements may still require the preparation of a preliminary "environmental report" or "environmental assessment," or the equivalent information by any other name. In some cases, this will be required by a public agency in order to determine the need for a fully developed environmental impact statement. In other cases, it may be adopted by a private firm or other client simply for its own use as a forewarning of possible controversy, as a public information document, or even as a new kind of information source for management decisions such as the location of a new industrial plant. The use of environmental analysis to identify consequences of action proposals has increasingly broad significance as an input to intelligent decision making of many kinds, both in the public and the private sectors.

Environmental Reports, Environmental Assessments

The impact assessment approach to environmental analysis differs from the previous two in several important respects. First, its focus is on predicting the consequences of a proposed action, including both the consequences that are desired and others that may be unintended. In a sense it incorporates the previous two approaches, since some of the consequences will be the fulfillment of environmental opportunities and others may be the violation of environmental constraints. But impact assessment must go beyond both these approaches, in order to identify *all* the important environmental consequences that are *likely* to result from the action, whether or not they are identified as opportunities, constraints, or just changes.

Special Characteristics of Impact Analysis

Second, since its focus is on predicting impacts, it requires information about environmental processes over time, not merely descriptive inventories of existing conditions, constraints, or opportunities. For environmental conditions that are highly stable and that have directly identifiable relationships with a proposed action, information of a more or less static nature (e.g., related toward composition rather than processes) on features such as soils and geology may provide an adequate basis for prediction. However, impacts on more dynamic conditions and on more complex relationships, such as hydrological or ecological systems, may require different kinds of information, analysis, and interpretation. At the very least, analysis of such conditions usually necessitates identification and documentation of seasonal variations in the intensities of processes such as stream flow and water-table fluctuation. Generally speaking, relatively good time-series data exist in most areas concerning climate and hydrology (see Chapter 5), but relatively limited data exist on ecological systems or even land use change over time, except at a highly aggregated scale or on individual sites that have been monitored for academic purposes.

The essential point is that the goals of analysis must be stated clearly from the start, before any money or effort is expended even on gathering available data, because the goal of predicting consequences requires a significantly different approach from the goal of inventorying constraints or opportunities even in the collection of information. Comprehensive inventories are expensive and static and may reveal very little about the future state of an environmental system. In the absence of the available data or the time necessary to make field measurements, it may be necessary to compare the process or condition in question with that in a similar site in order to understand what would likely result from the proposed action.

Third, impact assessments frequently are intended to illuminate alternative action proposals, which would achieve certain common goals in ways that would have greater, less, or simply different impacts upon environmental conditions. If this is the case, the collection and analysis of environmental information must be done *selectively,* focusing on the significant differences among the alternatives rather than upon the exhaustive description of one of them. The information must also be comparable for each alternative, both in its form and in its accuracy and reliability, if it is to play a valid role in the choice of one action over another. Finally, it must be *phased* over time to parallel the choice process, saving enough resources to invest in resolving vital uncertainties in the middle and late stages of planning rather than spending them all at the beginning on a comprehensive inventory or at the end on an after-the-fact justification study.

Some Problems with Impact Assessment

Finally, impact assessment in practice has frequently suffered from a serious conflict between its logical purpose of predicting consequences and its actual purpose of satisfying legal or administrative requirements. As a logical approach to the application of environmental analysis, impact assessment offers a new and appropriate response, though one whose concepts and techniques are only slowly being worked out and agreed upon. As a practical matter, however, this approach has been created far more rapidly than either of the previous two, principally due to legal and administrative documentation requirements enforced by the threat of lawsuits. Under these conditions, impact assessments have frequently been viewed as a necessary evil or political nuisance, rather than as a positive approach to environmental analysis and decision making. Accordingly, many impact assessments have failed in varying degrees to incorporate the considerations discussed above in that they have often made excessive use of descriptive inventories, given little attention to predictive methods, dismissed alternatives without careful scrutiny, and in many cases, even been carried out after a decision on a proposed action had already been made. For these reasons impact assessment is still the weakest and least clearly developed of the three approaches, but its value has begun to be widely recognized and its quality has gradually improved, though not uniformly or universally. Some of the conceptual models and methodologies that have been developed for impact assessment are discussed at greater length in Chapter 9, "Special Topics."

STRUCTURING ENVIRONMENTAL ANALYSES

The paragraphs above have outlined three principal approaches to the application of environmental analysis and a representative range of applications within each approach. Each of the applications requires the collection and analysis of environmental information, and each in turn has a purpose that shapes the kinds of information that are collected and the interpretations that are undertaken.

Management of Environmental Information

Since no analysis can serve all purposes at once, how should environmental information be gathered and interpreted in order to best serve the wide range of applications for which it is needed? Obviously no one user can gather all the information that might be needed to serve the needs of all, let alone keep it up to date, for he would have neither the money, the interest, nor even the foresight to anticipate them all. Yet it is conceivable that some combination of forethought and imagination could provide a closer approximation of what is needed than now exists in many public agencies. The need is to discern some means by which these various applications could better complement and reinforce each other over time, both in completeness and in accuracy and reliability, rather than continuing to operate piecemeal and in isolation from one another.

At present there are only a few types of environmental data that are even widely available, let alone in commensurable scale, and some of these would require extensive reinterpretation in order to serve different purposes. More complete information and at larger scales generally has been developed only on an ad hoc basis to serve particular missions or purposes, such as the siting of a nuclear power plant, or the preparation of an environmental impact statement for a major governmental action, or in a few cases an unusually well-developed site or regional plan. Such studies have been more intensive because they have had to be, but even they frequently suffer from a lack of monitoring and updating over time.

At the other extreme there occasionally have been proposals for comprehensive, computerized "environmental data banks" which would help store, monitor, and update all the various sorts of environmental information that any of the potential users might need. This system is ideal in theory, but it too has important drawbacks. First, even a large data bank could not conceivably encompass all the environmental information or interpretations of that information that potential users would need. Second, the cost of gathering and updating so much information would be far out of proportion both to people's willingness to pay for it and to its potential value, since data collection is costly and is of little value unless it is kept up to date. The idea of a comprehensive bank of environmental data, therefore, must be considered an "ideal type" to define the theoretical end of the spectrum, rather than a feasible solution to the problem at hand.

Between these two extremes, the present and the ideal, however, there is considerable room for innovation and incremental progress. There are *some* kinds of data that would be of sufficiently wide utility to merit common collection and updating. Topographic maps and soil surveys have already been placed in this category by government investment, as have the various forms of data collected by remote sensors. There are also some kinds of data that presently are gathered redundantly by different agencies and developers, but which could be collected both more cheaply and more accurately by some pooling of resources. A solution might be some change in procedures for financing the collection and interpretation of environmental information, which would place this activity on a common rather than a piecemeal basis. At the state and regional

Environmental Data Bank

Coordination of Environmental Information

scale, some legislatures have proposed greater state responsibility for planning of land use in environmentally sensitive areas. These efforts might encourage greater coordination in the collection and monitoring of particular kinds of environmental information. At the local level, one could envision significant benefits if environmental analyses were kept current by a single county or regional agency, rather than requiring piecemeal preparation of hundreds of environmental impact statements by individual developers and their consultants. A principal barrier to this latter idea is the lack of financing for it; but if the gains were sufficient, it could perhaps be financed in part or in total by development permit fees as is already done in some areas.

Whatever the approach taken in a particular application of environmental analyses, it is important to recognize and consider potential relationships to other applications, not only among the results of the analyses, as different uses are planned for environmental resources, but also among the kinds and forms of information that are needed as inputs. While these applications are not always commensurable, the possibilities and benefits of greater coordination among them have barely begun to be considered.

Key Questions in Environmental Analysis

Purpose of Analysis

Within an individual application framework, environmental analysis must be approached systematically and with a clear purpose in mind, literally as a "decision process *within* a decision process." What is the purpose of analysis, one must ask; and if so, what do you need to know in order to achieve that purpose, in what form, at what scale and level of detail, and with what degree of certainty? These are the initial questions to ask in structuring any environmental analysis.

Initial Scan of Information

Once these initial questions have been posed and answered at least with workable assumptions, the next task is to scan the possible sources of the necessary information that are cheap and easily available, such as previous reports and the opinions of knowledgeable professionals. This is a "rough cut" search process, not a comprehensive one. Its purpose is to assist in setting priorities for more intensive analysis, not to gather *all* available data to be sorted later. At this stage, the analyst seeks only those sources of information that have been identified as necessary, not all information about a particular area.

The third stage of the analysis is the evaluation of the results of the initial scan. How accurate, how reliable, how current, how applicable is this information relative to the task or study objectives? Most important, how closely does it "fit" with the information needs defined in the first step, and which of it is significant for your purposes and which is not? It is a great temptation and a most common error to gloss over these questions and to unwittingly redefine the initial problem in order to fit the available information (or the available technologies for gathering information, such as remote sensors) rather than candidly identifying limitations of available data. This is a most important task if the analysis is to be useful in solving real decision problems rather than becoming merely an end in itself.

Fourth, and most important, one must use the evaluation of the initial scan results to *define priorities for more intensive search and analysis.* This includes specifying not only the types of information but also the level of detail, the methods to be used, and the costs to be incurred for each piece of the investigation. One output of this process should be a work plan for the completion of the environmental analysis process. Another should be a set of contract specifications in cases where subcontractors or consultants will be used to assist in the generation and analysis of new data. It is at this fourth stage, too, that explicit attention should be given to other considerations in more detailed analyses, such as the usability of outputs for other purposes or applications, and consistency of format and assumptions with other available data in order to permit some cumulative learning and time-series comparisons.

Finally, the detailed collection and analysis of new environmental information should be carried out, and its results evaluated as in step three. Note that while the principal commitment of budget and staff effort should normally occur at this stage, one should always expect that in at least some areas of analysis the evaluation will reveal a need to reiterate steps four and five; and some time and budget accordingly should always be reserved for this purpose.

SUMMARY

This chapter has only touched the surface of the issues and approaches that arise in the application of environmental analysis to everyday problems and decisions. The generality is deliberate, in part, since our purpose is to suggest that the range of possibilities *is* much broader than any one chapter could treat in detail. At the next level of detail, each approach and application area would require more exact treatment of more complex technical issues, including variables to be examined and interpretations to be made, techniques of data collection, constraints imposed upon information processes by political decision processes, and budget limitations, to suggest a few of the most important. The final chapter, "Special Topics," provides more detailed illumination of several representative application areas and suggests some possible answers to more specific application issues.

At the very least, this chapter has sought to make three points. First, that environmental information does have important and tangible applications in many fields, both in public and in private sector decisions; second, that the purpose of any such application has a major shaping influence not only upon the outcome of the decision but also upon the "decisions within the decisions," concerning what environmental information will be collected and in what way; and third, that careful thought and innovation is needed in developing better ways to relate these bodies of information to one another, for the sake of efficiency and more comprehensive understanding about environmental conditions and processes over time. Environmental constraints, opportunities, and impacts are fundamental dimensions of human activities, and we neglect them at our peril, yet the information and expertise necessary to incorporate them explicitly into those activities have so far developed piecemeal, fragmented, and grossly incomplete. It is our hope that the ideas in this chapter and indeed in this book may help to reduce this incongruity.

Bibliography

Andrews, Richard N. L.: "A Philosophy of Environmental Impact Assessment," *Journal of Soil and Water Conservation,* vol. XXVIII (September–October), 1973, pp. 197–203.

Andrews, Richard N. L.: "Impact Statements and Impact Assessment," *Management and Control of Growth,* vol. III, The Urban Land Institute, Washington, 1975.

Andrews, Richard N. L.: "Impact Analysis and Land Use Planning," *Proceedings of the Conference on Integrating Land Use Planning and Environmental Impact Analysis,* Michigan State University, East Lansing, Mich., 1976.

Corwin, Ruth Ann, and Patrick H. Heffernan: *Environmental Impact Assessment,* Freeman, Cooper, and Company, San Francisco, 1975.

Detwyler, Thomas R.: *Man's Impact on Environment,* McGraw-Hill, New York, 1971.

Detwyler, Thomas R., and Melvin G. Marcus et al.: *Urbanization and Environment,* Duxbury Press of Wadsworth Publishing Company, Belmont, Calif., 1972.

Dickert, Thomas G., and Katherine R. Domeny (eds.): *Environmental Impact Assessment: Guidelines and Commentary,* University of California Extension, Berkeley, Calif., 1974.

Gosselink, James G., Eugene P. Odum, and R. M. Pope: *The Value of the Tidal Marsh,* Working Paper no. 3, Urban and Regional Development Center, The University of Florida, Gainesville, Fla., 1973.

Johnson, Johnson, and Roy, Inc.: "Identification of Social, Economic, and Environmental Effects," *Planning and Design Methodology Relating to Environmental Impact Considerations in the Highway Planning and Route Location Process,* Michigan Department of State Highways, Lansing, Mich., 1972.

Meshenberg, Michael J.: *Environmental Planning: 1,* Planning Advisory Service Bulletin 263, American Society of Planning Officials, Washington, D.C., 1970.

Shelton, Ronald L.: "Supporting Document for Information/Data Handling Guidebook," Technical Report C, *State Resource Management Programs: A Primer: Critical Areas and Information/Data Handling,* Office of Land Use and Water Planning and U.S. Geological Survey Resource and Land Inventory Program, U.S. Department of the Interior, Washington, D.C., 1976.

Shelton, Ronald L., and Ernest E. Hardy: "Design Concepts for Land Use and Natural Resource Inventories and Information Systems," *Proceedings of the Ninth International Symposium on Remote Sensing of Environment,* The University of Michigan, Ann Arbor, Mich., 1974.

Sorenson, Jens C., and James E. Pepper: *Procedures for Regional Clearinghouse Review of Environment Impact Statements—Phase II,* Association of Bay Area Governments, Berkeley, Calif., 1973.

CHAPTER **8**

COMMUNICATION OF ENVIRONMENTAL INFORMATION

Katharine P. Warner

COURTESY OF
APPLIED ENVIRONMENTAL RESEARCH,
ANN ARBOR

INTRODUCTION

THE PLANNER'S ROLE in environmental and land use studies does not begin and end with the generation of a package of information and a set of recommendations. The very important task of establishing an effective communication system to facilitate information flow at every level of the study is an integral part of the planning process. Why is communication so important?

First, there are generally many people involved in the planning process whose perspectives and objectives are different from those of the planner. At a minimum, these people include planning commissioners, local politicians, citizens, other local and state agency staff. The planner needs to recognize the roles and perspectives of these people and they, in turn, need to understand their own roles in the planning process and how and why various action recommendations are developed.

Second, the preferences, priorities and opinions of many different groups and individuals can be important inputs to the process of establishing land use alternatives and determining procedures for implementation.

The communication component of an environmental planning study usually is neither as well funded, as carefully conceived, nor as well managed as the technical parts of the study. But without effective communications, the results and recommendations from analysis activities generally lead to little or no change in the political, social, and land use arenas. Indeed, the dusty reports which abound in the files of most professional planning offices are silent testimony to this fact.

On the other hand, one can sympathize with this state of affairs owing to the fact that building an effective communications program is a difficult and often frustrating task. To begin this effort, one needs a conceptual framework within which to structure his/her activities and organize the array of program alternatives from which he/she must choose. This must be followed by definition of (1) audiences and information sources; (2) formats for presenting environmental information; and (3) mechanisms through which this information can be considered and integrated within an action mode. This chapter is devoted to a discussion of each of these, the elements of an information communications program for land use and environmental planning.

THE COMMUNICATIONS FRAMEWORK FOR PLANNING

Background

The communications activities accompanying land use planning studies have often been labeled "public relations" or the modern equivalent, "public information." The emphasis in both cases has been on disseminating information about the planning agency's activities in order to increase people's awareness of the importance of both the study and the agency. It is then generally expected that well-informed audiences will lend support and assistance in getting the planning recommendations acted on. A one-way flow of information from the agency outward is characteristic of this system.

In the 1960s, the public relations model was strongly questioned both for ideological reasons (e.g., the technicians should not make all the important choices) and for practical ones, in that planning recommendations were increasingly being set aside as unworkable, or restudied because of vehement controversies. In addition, federal and state legislation and administrative regulations, most notably the National Environmental Policy Act in 1969, mandated new procedures and study considerations that increased the access of other agencies and publics to the environmental planning process. This, in turn, reemphasized the need for the planning agency not only to disseminate information about the progress of its efforts, but also to obtain information and opinions *from* the other people affected by and/or interested in study results.

But the key question then arose: Communications how and with whom? Traditionally the communications task of an agency was handled by a public relations officer or a separate staff group that relied heavily on press releases, pamphlets, and brochures for information dissemination. Though sometimes well written and graphically pleasing, the messages were styled in the format of the mass media. Moreover, communication specialists were often compartmentalized within the planning agency and had little interaction with technical planners about program content and communication needs. On the other hand, the technical staff members individually often had established excellent informal contacts with people in other agencies or various civic and private organizations, but these did not get plugged into the communications program.

Current Communications Needs in Planning

Given the new demands on the planning community for more effective communications as well as greater public involvement, agencies have begun to adopt a more systematic framework for these activities. The following is a list of key guidelines that we see as critical to the improvement of planning communications. Many of them are reflected in new or revised agency approaches, some of which are cited in the bibliography.

1. Planning communications is viewed as a *two-way process.* That is, information is not only disseminated from the agency to those outside, but those outside are also viewed as sources of valuable information, both of a factual and value-preference nature (see Note 1).

Communications as Public Relations

Two-Way Communication

> **NOTE 1—PUBLICS AS SOURCES OF PLANNING INFORMATION**
>
> Often planners forget that publics can be important sources of information for environmental planning studies. Some examples of information provided by publics include:
> 1. Longtime residents in a watershed can often provide information on past flood levels which can be useful in estimating flood risk.
> 2. As resource users, residents can often describe details about particular problems with services and resources—for example, water supply shortages, septic field backups, river and stream sediment loadings, increased traffic congestion, crowding at recreation areas—that would not otherwise be readily available to the planners.
> 3. People for whom the plan is prepared must contribute to the establishment of plan objectives and priorities. Their preferences are important in establishing weights and performance criteria for choosing among potential projects and program activities.

Role of Communications in Technical Planning

2. Communications activities are not considered a separate specialty but rather an *interdependent* part of the technical planning program. That is, if communications activities are to be meaningful, their results should have an effect on the technical deliberations of the study staff throughout the planning process (see Note 2).

> **NOTE 2—INTERDEPENDENCE OF COMMUNICATION AND TECHNICAL WORK THROUGHOUT THE STUDY PROCESS**
>
> By identifying the major concerns and questions of people within the area, planners can establish and revise work programs more effectively, that is, decide which studies are most important to do, which alternatives should be thoroughly investigated, so that big information gaps are less likely near the conclusion of the planning study, and expensive restudies are not necessary.
>
> *For example,* a regional park authority recently unveiled its proposal for creating a large day-use park by damming and impounding a creek which flows through a rolling, pastoral agricultural area. Key questions about water-quality impacts of the impoundment have delayed a final administrative decision on creation of the park. Such questions might have been anticipated earlier during the initial planning efforts if more "early warning" communication channels had been established between the recreation planners and park proponents and opponents. In this case, scientific studies now underway might have been started then.
>
> The initially defined study objectives and alternatives need to be periodically reassessed and revised in light of changes in technological and social conditions. The latter category includes people's perceptions and preferences as an important element.
>
> *For example,* when detailed plans for the development of a specific site and facility at a national lakeshore were revealed recently, a storm of controversy erupted at the final and only public hearing. The planners then went back and reexamined their interpretation of what the "intensive" development objective meant in the original approved park master plan. The second set of development plan specifications were considerably modified.

Continuous Communications

3. As an interdependent part of the technical work program and as an extension of technical planning efforts, communications activities should occur *throughout* the study process, not just at milestone completion points. If reaction to a completed study phase is the primary purpose of planning communications, a major portion of the potential information benefit has been lost. In addition, since it is difficult to change what has tentatively been concluded, the planning agency is endangering its credibility and thence the

willingness of people to contribute further information and feedback.

4. In order to establish meaningful and effective communications, the planning agency must have established an image of *credibility* among those with whom information is exchanged. This means the audience must see the agency as providing valid and useful information and, equally important, those contacted must feel the agency is legitimately seeking feedback and will carefully consider their opinions (see Note 3).

5. The implications of social and environmental *issues* which have already aroused public concern in the study area should be considered carefully by the planning agency while designing its technical work program and communications process. Among the types of questions which might be raised are:

　　a. Was there a strong division of opinions among local interest groups? (This may carry over into the planning study itself.)

　　b. Was there a major conflict between a government agency and local interest groups? (This may signal credibility problems for the public planning agency.)

　　c. Are local organizations interested in and have they developed positions on the types of environmental conditions to be studied? (They may serve as sources of valuable assistance in terms of information exchange if this is the case.)

6. Since a planning agency will need to communicate with a number of diverse audiences and information sources, throughout the course of a study, the communications process should include a variety of different information formats and mechanisms. Choosing the appropriate ones will depend on the types of people to be contacted, the resources of the planning agency, and the length and phasing of the study process. The implications of who is contacted and what formats and mechanisms might be used are discussed in the next three sections.

AUDIENCES AND INFORMATION SOURCES

Once the purpose of a study or project has been defined and an approach to analysis has been identified, the planner needs to consider who might be provided with information, how it should be presented, and what additional types of information or opinions are needed. The first step in developing this strategy involves identifying and characterizing the individuals and organizations that should

Credibility of the Planner

Context for Communication

Formats and Mechanisms

be contacted. These persons or groups can be broken down into the following categories:

1. Elected and administrative officials
2. Administrative commissions and boards
3. Public agency staff members at various governmental levels
4. Those likely to be directly affected by the potential actions taken, e.g., riparian landowners
5. Members of special interest groups not included in category 4—for example, environmentalists, business people, and civic groups such as the League of Women Voters
6. Unaffiliated individuals

All these categories of people may have an important role in developing and implementing recommendations for future action. However, the first three categories assume the major governmental decision-making and enforcement roles, while the latter three types affect the political context by seeking to influence and monitor the decisions and subsequent program activity.

Elected and Administrative Officials

Elected and administrative officials are usually at the top of the audience list. However, it is not uncommon to find that elected officials are too busy to become directly involved in the consideration and interpretation of environmental information. They usually prefer to take a "wait and see" posture until the technical implications of the study and their constituents' preferences and positions are crystallized. But such officials should be kept abreast of the study's status and time schedule.

Administrative officials, on the other hand, frequently have a more specialized interest in the findings of the study. Thus, they should be apprised of study findings and consulted about data interpretations, particularly where these results affect their specialized authorities or jurisdictions. This not only gives these officials the opportunity to contribute the expertise of their own staff, but increases the likelihood of their support of the final recommendations owing to the fact that they participated in the study. Note 4 contains a list of some types of elected and appointed officials who could have been involved in an example project involving wastewater planning. The exact position titles and agency groupings may vary from state to state. The key point to remember is that on any given environmental issue of importance locally or regionally, there will be diverse sets of public agencies and officials with both legal responsibility and/or a professional interest in resolving the situation.

Administrative Commissions

In communicating with public agencies and officials, planners will find themselves frequently working within two particular types of organizational contexts. One is that of the public organization which is headed by an appointed, and usually volunteer, board or commission which has legal responsibility and administrative authority over the paid agency staff. The other is the intergovernmental complex or hierarchy within which planning activities are carried out.

Local planning commissions, boards of public works, boards of supervisors, as well as road, drain, highway, and natural resources commissions are common examples of bodies that have responsibility for environmental planning studies. Members of these groups tend to be the public opinion leaders in the community. Such organizational bodies usually meet at regularly scheduled intervals, for instance, once per month. They frequently have lengthy agendas and, therefore, do not often spend long periods of time or multiple meetings deliberating one particular issue. Because most of the members also hold full-time jobs, they tend to rely heavily on their professional staffs for advice and recommendations. As one of these staff members, planners need to ascertain for themselves the type, format, and detail of information which is appropriate for their board or commission on various issues. Usually board members are provided with certain printed materials at least one week prior to the meetings. Frequently the body's chairperson, or individual members with a particular interest in one or several agenda items, will arrange to have the staff personally brief them prior to the meeting. However, the printed materials and the staff and public presentations at the meetings are clearly the predominant communication channels.

NOTE 4—PUBLIC OFFICIALS AS AUDIENCES FOR AND SOURCES OF ENVIRONMENTAL INFORMATION

CASE EXAMPLE: Waste-water planning. The issue involves choosing between a regional interceptor sewer or expansion of local treatment plants.

Federal level
  Congressman
  U.S. Environmental Protection Agency
State level
  State Legislators
  State Department of Natural Resources
  State Water Resources Council—this organization is charged with final decision-making authority at the state level and includes representatives from the departments of:
      Transportation
      Agriculture
      Public Health
      Natural Resources
Regional level
  Regional Council of Governments
Local level
  County Government
    Board of Commissioners
    Department of Public Works
    Drain Commissioner
    Planning Commission
    Department of Public Health
  City Government
    Mayor and City Administrator
    Common Council
    Department of Public Works
    Planning Department

Governmental Agency Context

The second organizational context to which planners must adapt their communications efforts is the complex intra- and intergovernmental lattices within which many of the planning activities related to the environment are carried out. No matter where the planner fits into the hierarchy of government, there will always be appreciable communication with various federal, state, regional, and local public agencies. Note, for example, the variety of public organizations which might be involved in the environmental issue represented in Note 4.

Federal regulations which have grown from the National Environmental Policy Act and similar legislation, such as the 1972 amendments to the federal Water Pollution Control Act (Public Law 92-500), form the basis for various environmental standards and procedures as well as for grant programs established by federal agencies. Planners need to be knowledgeable about these federal guidelines and regulations, in order to write and process grant applications and to implement funded programs. This holds for not only federal programs, but state and regional programs as well. Note 5 provides an indication of some of the many planning-related functions carried out in the area of environmental land use management by one major state agency in Michigan.

All communities or local agencies have a designated regional and/or state clearinghouse through which applications for federal funds must be routed for review and comment. Because of the regional overlap of many planning projects—for instance, highways, flood control, and pipeline extensions—it is extremely impor-

---

NOTE 5—ENVIRONMENTAL PERMIT PROGRAMS OF ONE STATE AGENCY: An example of intragovernmental complexity as of January 1976

The following list of environmental protection activities carried out by one state agency, Michigan's Department of Natural Resources, illustrates the range and complexity of functions which affect environmental and land use planning. It also indicates the variety of different organizational units with which a land use planner needs to be familiar and periodically in contact.

Air Pollution Permits, Air Pollution Control Division

Construction Permits for Municipal Wastewater, Municipal Wastewater Division

Contruction Grants for Municipal Wastewater, Water Development Services Division

County Drain Preliminary Plan Approval, Hydrological Survey Division

Permits for Construction of Dams, Hydrological Survey Division

Permits for Dredging and Filling of Inland Waters, Hydrological Survey Division

Adoption of a Local River Management District, Water Development Services Division

Approval of Local River Management Plans, Water Development Services Division

Inland Lake Level Control, Hydrological Survey Division

Review of Local Soil Erosion and Sediment Control Procedures, Water Quality Control Division

Order Permitting Occupation or Alteration of a Floodway, Hydrological Survey Division

Permits for Development in High-Risk Erosion Areas on Great Lakes Shoreline, Water Development Services Division

---

tant that agency staff effectively exchange various kinds of environmental information with each other. But this is not always easy, given time and staff limitations. Carefully structured communication ties with other agencies can help to facilitate the process.

An important first step is to develop an accurate institutional map of the area indicating which agencies are responsible for various land use and environmental planning functions in different parts of the region. Given this map, contact persons in various key agencies can be identified, and a system can be worked out for exchange of information. The agency that serves as the regional clearinghouse for federal A-95 reviews can supply information which may be helpful in establishing communication channels with other agencies.

Laymen as Audiences for and Sources of Environmental Information

The term *publics* is used to refer to those persons or groups who are likely to be affected by a proposed action, represent special interests, or are members of civic organizations. There is no single public that represents all these parties; rather, there are many, and the awareness and involvement of each in various planning issues tends to be defined by their perception of what is at stake in the issue's resolution. While it is difficult to predict the kinds of publics that will get involved, experience shows that if people believe their efforts could influence important decisions, their willingness to become involved increases. In addition, active public participants also tend to be people who are already active in various organized community groups and who are from higher income levels. Note 6 discusses some methods for identifying publics as well as three key concepts to remember in developing public involvement programs.

NOTE 6—IDENTIFICATION OF PUBLICS

Identifying those publics that are expected to be important audiences for and/or sources of environmental and planning information is a two-step procedure: (1) determining which *types* of publics are especially important to involve as sources of information feedback and/or as representatives of various interest groups or organizations, e.g., environmentalists, affected industries, and so forth, and (2) discovering what *specific* individuals and groups compose these categories in the local area.

The three primary approaches to identifying publics include (Willeke, 1974):

A. *Self-identification*—where organizations or individuals through their own efforts make their interest known to you. Ways of doing this include:
   1. Petition
   2. Testimony at public hearings
   3. Letters
   4. Suits
   5. Protests and complaints
   6. Publicity

B. *Staff identification*
   1. *Analysis of organizations* in terms of officers' and members' names.
   2. *Geographic analysis*—review of elected officials, opinion leaders, and other interested persons within a defined spatial area.
   3. *Demographic analysis* of population groupings in terms of major char-

acteristics, that is, sex, age, race, income, so that opinions can be sought from each.
4. Use of general lists, such as city directories.
C. *Third-party identification*—asking others to name key individuals and opinion leaders.
Key Concepts to Remember about Identifying Publics:
    1. This process is just a beginning point for public involvement.
    2. Not all publics will participate, nor can you ensure that they all will.
    3. But everyone should have a meaningful *opportunity* to participate and be *aware* of that opportunity.

The active publics concerned with certain planning issues will include persons who are termed "opinion leaders" by social scientists. These people are especially interested in specific issues and they are particularly attentive to communications regarding them. Because they have a following or represent a formal group, opinion leaders usually play a key role in transmitting and interpreting the environmental information disseminated by the media and official sources. Thus, they are quite influential in shaping public reaction to programs and proposals made by "technical experts." Their assessments will also affect the importance and credibility ascribed by broader publics to additional media coverage. Note 7 describes one methodology for identifying opinion leaders.

NOTE 7—A METHOD FOR IDENTIFYING OPINION LEADERS

Opinion leaders may be defined using a combination of three approaches.
A. *Positional approach*—people holding formal leadership positions in public and/or private organizations are identified.
B. *Decisional approach*—people who have been active and assumed advocacy positions on important planning and environmental issues are identified. Area newspaper files are usually an excellent source for such names.
C. *Reputational approach*—people are nominated by those interviewed from the first two lists (positional and decisional) in response to the following type of question: If a decision on a land use planning issue had to be made, which people's opinions from this area do you feel would carry the most weight?
The three lists will frequently overlap, particularly as they become more the strength of opinion leadership. For a more detailed description of the application of an opinion leader identification method, see T. E. Borton et al. (1970).

FORMATS FOR COMMUNICATION

What is the most effective format for presenting environmental information to this or that public? The range of possibilities is extraordinary. The modes of communication can be verbal, written, graphic, or some combination of these. Speeches, workshops, and interviews are among the more common verbal formats. Brochures, newspaper articles, and study reports are frequently used written forms. Graphical formats include photographs, maps, site plans, and process diagrams. The particular formats that are used in a program depend on many factors, some of the most important of which include:

The balance between conceptual and situational (site specific) information

The amount of technical detail
The technical level of vocabulary
The type and number of visual and graphic aids

In choosing a format, a conscious effort should be made to take into consideration what each format assumes of both audiences and planner. In addition, the complexity of the subject matter, the program objectives, as well as the resources and the time available for contact, are important considerations.

conceptual

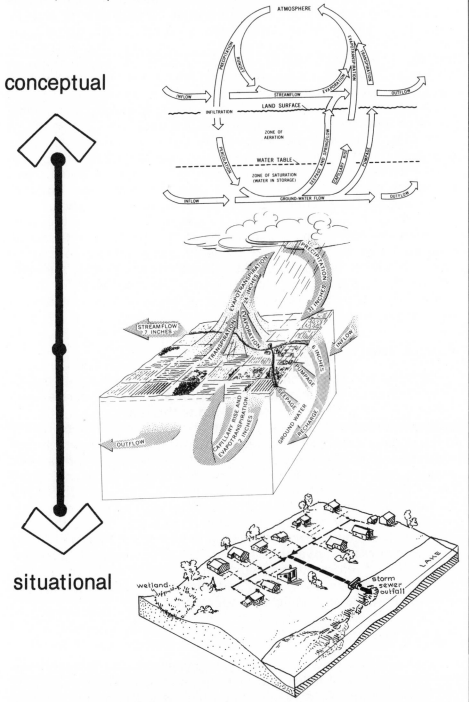

situational

Figure 8.1. The proper combination of situational and conceptional information is an important aspect of format. This diagram shows an example of the range of possibilities related to a water-quality problem.

Conceptual and Situational Considerations

In issues concerning complex environmental problems, one is often confronted with the question of how much background material of an abstract or conceptual nature should be presented. In considering, for instance, the issue of pollution of one large section of a lake or reservoir, is an explanation of the watershed model necessary, or should one present only situation information, that is, information specific to that locale only (Figure 8.1)? Usually it is necessary to include both, but the proper balance can be surprisingly difficult to achieve. While there is no rule of thumb to apply here, a brief survey of the audience can help determine the level of interest in the larger issues of water quality, the expectations of further involvement in the project, and the time individuals have set aside for the presentation.

Where a long-term audience commitment is sought, it is advisable to educate participants about essential ecological and land use processes. However, this needs to be done skillfully so as not to deaden interest in further participation. One way of retaining people's interest is to demonstrate how certain natural and human processes affect the quality of their own land and water environment. Graphics are usually essential to such demonstrations. Schematic diagrams of the processes integrated with photographs showing examples and consequences of the processes in the study area are often highly effective in tieing a principle or concept to reality. In cases where experiential knowledge is already substantial, relatively more time can be devoted to consideration of the causes of problems, to concepts such as rates and feedback as well as to action strategies.

Technical Detail

Planning documents and study results are often weighty collections of charts and statistics. The level of audience understanding which this presumes, immediately limits the readership to technicians and those with special interest or occupational responsibility in the subject area. To relate technical information to nontechnical audiences, it is often advisable to adopt a graphical format and language style that are familiar to them. In a case involving runoff from a developed area, for instance, it may be necessary to convey the concept of the coefficient of runoff using schematic diagrams rather than tabular data and formulas (Figure 8.2). In addition, the standard hydrologic terminology should be translated into ordinary word and phrase equivalents. To gain added ensurance of successful transfer of information to such audiences, it is also helpful to provide summaries, overviews, and abstracts of technical material with key phrases and statistics underscored.

Technical Vocabulary

Language has grown increasingly specialized with the proliferation of professional fields and planning and associated disciplines are no exception. As a result, that which is clear to one group is often confusing and imprecise to another. Gauging the level of

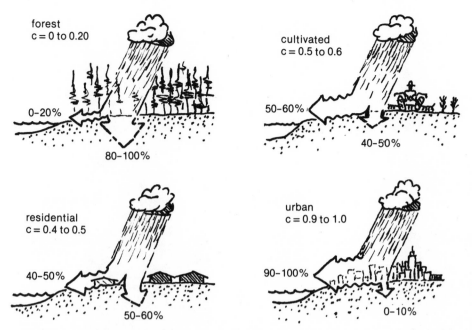

forest
c = 0 to 0.20

0–20%

80–100%

cultivated
c = 0.5 to 0.6

50–60%

40–50%

residential
c = 0.4 to 0.5

40–50%

50–60%

urban
c = 0.9 to 1.0

90–100%

0–10%

Figure 8.2. The use of graphics is one means of avoiding bulky tables and data. The principle behind the coefficient of runoff is illustrated here.

technical expertise of an audience can prove to be a delicate task. On the one hand, people can be insulted if they are "talked down to," while on the other they can be equally offended by overuse of what they consider technical jargon.

Where printed material is distributed to diverse audiences, inclusion of a glossary of technical terms can be helpful. Graphic aids such as photographs, maps, and diagrams can also lend assistance in translating technical information, but they must be clear, fully labeled, and integrated into the textual material or else they may have the opposite effect. One means of guarding against overly technical presentations is to pretest a portion of the prepared information on nontechnical acquaintances. Modifying the vocabulary in a report or presentation does not necessarily mean unrealistic simplification of complex relationships or issues. Rather, it usually necessitates the use of a wider assortment of physical formats and more carefully chosen verbiage.

Graphics

As we have already indicated in this chapter and suggested by example throughout this book, graphics are essential in the communication of environmental information. In fact it is not uncommon in planning to find that graphics provide the *primary* means of communication, far outweighing the written or spoken word. Creating meaningful graphics is one of the more challenging aspects of environment communications. We can do little more, however, than touch on it here. The section entitled "Synthesis and Display of Spatial Information" in Chapter 1 provides some additional comments on graphical formats.

Graphical formats range from highly realistic representations

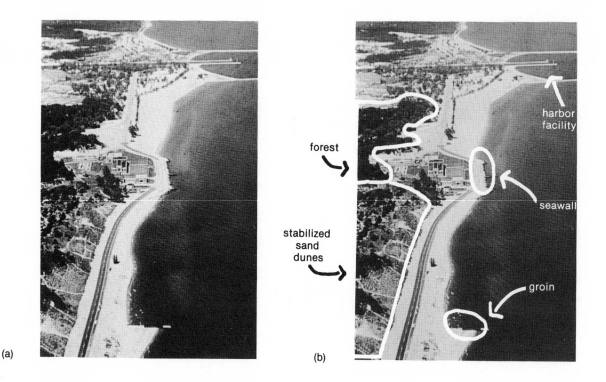

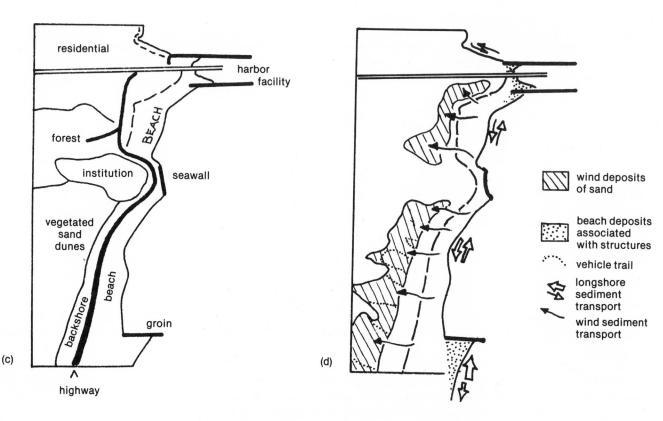

Figure 8.3. For complex environments such as the one shown in (a), it is sometimes advisable to enhance the photograph (b) or to transform the photograph into illustrations which provide interpretation for the viewer (c) and (d).

such as color slides to abstract renderings such as Venn diagrams from mathematics. The most appropriate graphics for a given situation depend not only on the communication objectives, but also on the audience and the nature of the subject matter. Simply put, certain graphical formats just do not lend themselves to certain information and audiences. While the photograph of the coastal environment in Figure 8.3 would be appropriate in a presentation to professionals, it may prove to be too detailed and complex to be effective as the prime display in a presentation to the amateur. This problem can be resolved by enhancing key features either by delineating them on the photograph or by converting the photograph to a sketch that eliminates unnecessary detail [Figures 8.3(b) and (c)]. If further specificity is desired, schematic diagrams can be developed which help provide the audience with insight into the scene. For instance, processes, interrelationships, and spatial trends can be identified, and if such diagrams are cross-referenced with the original photograph, an air of authenticity can be added to the whole presentation [Figure 8.3(d)].

Graphics are also a useful means of conveying concepts that would otherwise be extraordinarily difficult to explain. Such renderings are usually abstract, but not so much so that they require special knowledge to interpret. Figure 8.4 shows a concept diagram that accompanied a printed discussion on how information from diverse sources can promote a crisis atmosphere among inland lake property owners. The material went on to point out the necessity for accurate and systematic environmental records as a basis for sound planning and management of lake environments.

Another important use of graphics is in the demonstration of how to do something. Where laymen are involved in the planning pro-

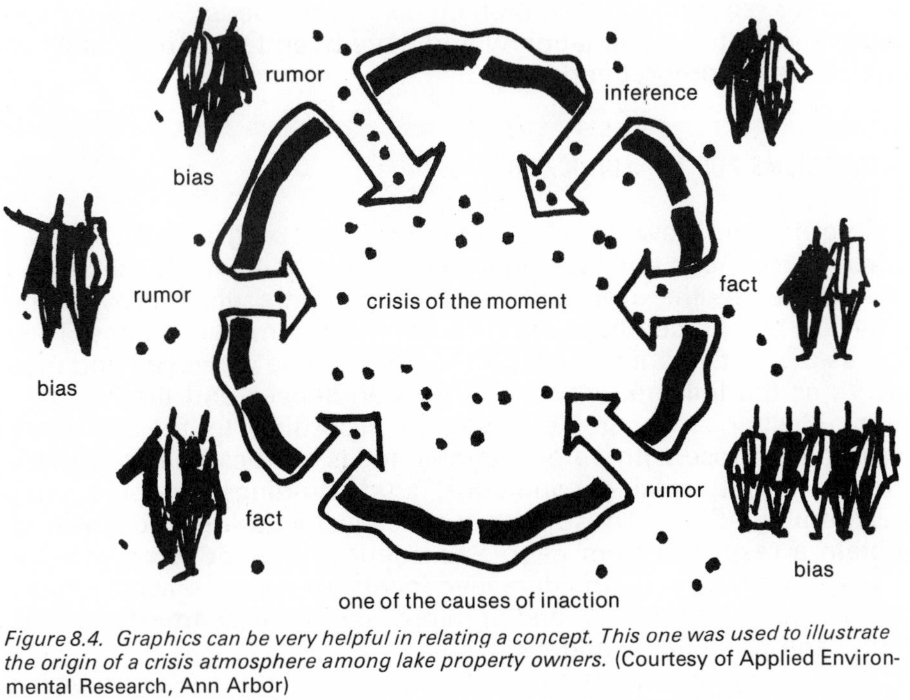

Concept Diagrams

Figure 8.4. Graphics can be very helpful in relating a concept. This one was used to illustrate the origin of a crisis atmosphere among lake property owners. (Courtesy of Applied Environmental Research, Ann Arbor)

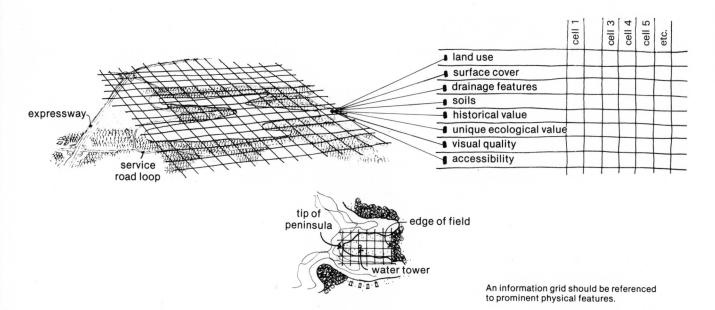

land use
surface cover
drainage features
soils
historical value
unique ecological value
visual quality
accessibility

	cell 1		cell 3	cell 4	cell 5	etc.

expressway

service road loop

tip of peninsula
edge of field
water tower

An information grid should be referenced to prominent physical features.

Figure 8.5. *Instructions on how to do something are often enhanced by graphics. In this case, illustrations were the primary means of relating instructions to laymen on the use of a grid for recording watershed information.* (Courtesy of Applied Environmental Research, Ann Arbor)

"How to" Graphics

cess, there is usually the need to describe how, for example, information can be recorded and presented, proposals for change can be made, and organizations can be established and sustained. In many cases of "how to," it is necessary to describe a sequence of steps many of which are most effectively conveyed through graphics. The illustrations in Figure 8.5, for example, were the key vehicle in explaining to property owners' associations how a grid system is set up for recording information on lake watersheds. Without these illustrations, the explanation would have been far more difficult to present and comprehend.

MECHANISMS FOR COMMUNICATION

Information flow in a communications program is affected through methods and techniques called mechanisms. Mechanisms are defined as the organizational arrangements which provide the physical and procedural setting for planning communications. They act as contexts within which information can be conveyed and they serve as the linkage between various audiences and the information. Mechanisms can be classified according to their primary objective. Those with an educational focus are designed to inform people about existing conditions, study findings and/or agency recommendations. Those with a reactive focus are structured to obtain a response from people to agency ideas or recommendations, and those with an interactive focus are aimed at achieving an exchange of information and opinions about environmental conditions and potential changes.

The educational mechanism emphasizes the one-way provision of information. It is important in building an awareness and even an understanding about the environment, project, and issues. It is also an important means of updating an audience with current information, and is probably the most widely used mechanism in planning communications.

The reactive mechanism is also one-way, but it is designed to elicit feedback for planners and officials. This input is important in establishing study and administrative objectives, in gauging the acceptability of various courses of action, and in monitoring implementation efforts in terms of achievements, costs, and related impacts. Without such evaluative responses from outside sources, alternatives tend to be compartmentalized within somewhat narrow areas of interest or technical competence. The democratic pluralism which characterizes our form of government requires that a wide diversity of demands and judgments be taken into account in environmental planning.

The interactive mechanism utilizes two-way interaction. This provides people with an opportunity to ask questions about problems and implications of projects as well as to raise value issues. Such interaction also permits planners to test and refine assumptions and analyses in conjunction with the information users themselves. Table 8.1 lists a number of communications and public involvement mechanisms according to their primary objective. Notice that many of these mechanisms also qualify as formats.

TABLE 8.1

	Objective		
	Inform/Educate	Review/React	Interact/Exchange
Mechanism	Newspaper articles Radio and TV programs Speeches and presentations Field trips Exhibits Films and slides Brochures Newsletters Letters Reports Conferences School programs Public meetings	Public meetings Public inquiries Public hearings Survey questionnaires	Workshops Special task forces Interviews Advisory boards Informal contacts Study group discussions Seminars Charettes

To achieve effective information flow, it is usually necessary to use a combination of mechanisms. Selecting those which are most appropriate can be guided by questions such as these:

What am I trying to achieve: awareness, feedback, and/or new information?

At what *times* in the study process will the results of each be needed?

Who am I trying to communicate with? What is their level of interest, information, and time available? Are their opinions representative of a larger organized or unorganized group? Can they provide data, ideas, suggestions, and opinions which would otherwise not be as adequately considered?

What kinds of organizational arrangements and procedures will provide people with adequate *access* to study information and with *opportunities* to contribute data, ideas, and support to ongoing planning activities?

What kinds of *agency resources,* that is, staff time and money, do I have available to develop this communications process?

In order to answer these questions, one needs to be familiar with the operational characteristics of each type of mechanism. Four such characteristics that should be taken into account: (1) focus, both scope and specificity, (2) degree of emphasis on two-way communication, (3) level of participant activity required, and (4) total demands on staff time (Table 8.2).

TABLE 8.2

Type of mechanism	Operational characteristics				
	Scope of focus	Specificity of focus	Degree of two-way communication	Level of participant activity	Demands on staff time
Workshops	L	H	H	H	H
Public hearings	M	L	L	H	M
Mass media (including use of newspapers, radio, and television)	H	L	L	L	L
Task forces	L	H	H	H	H
Agency publications	H	M	L	L	M
Speeches and presentations	M	M	M	L	M
Survey questionnaire	M	H	L	M	M
Advisory board	L	H	H	H	H
Informal contacts	L	H	H	M	M
Public meetings	M	L	M	M	H

H—high degree; M—medium degree; L—low degree

Scope of focus refers to the number of people who can be contacted and provided with information. Generally, the more interactive the mechanism, the fewer the number of people that can effectively participate. Specificity of focus refers to the capacity of a mechanism to channel information both to and from particular publics. Those mechanisms with a broad scope also tend to have a low level of specificity. The mass media are the most extreme case of low specificity of focus.

Participant Activity Levels

The level of participant activity refers to the amount of personal time and energy that must be committed by publics in order to take part in the program. Interactive mechanisms tend to require a substantial commitment by participants to become informed about the issues under discussion because it is a prerequisite to effective participation. Interactive mechanisms also tend to require involvement in an ongoing series of meetings and discussions. In contrast to interactive mechanisms are those mechanisms with an informational emphasis, such as publications and radio. These mechanisms imply a more passive reader or listener role, and the participant investment tends to be less. As a result, they are especially useful in the earlier stages of a program which is designed to evolve into reactive or interactive mechanisms.

TABLE 8.3

Audience	Objective		
	Provide information	Receive feedback	Exchange information
Elected officials	*Map* of study area *Newsletters* containing periodic *summaries* of study progress *Official letter notices* of public meeting	*Memoranda* requesting comment and opinion	*Official briefing* to release conclusions and recommendations *Memoranda* or *meetings* discussing public works needs and funding implications identified in the study
Administrative staffs of other agencies	*Map* of affected area *Prospectus describing work elements* *Project work schedule* *Memoranda* identifying implications of study for agency's programs and activities	*Summaries* of data and preliminary results *Briefing* on conclusions reached at each stage, with provision for formal questions	*Official letters* requesting related information and staff input *Memoranda* suggesting processes for maintaining communication ties *Working papers* and *meetings* to negotiate responsibilities of the action program
Appointed planning commission	*Orientation packet* including *maps, concept diagrams, background materials* *Status reports* and staff time and facility costs *Work schedules* including dates of completion for project stages; timetable of public meetings and various reports	*Oral and written review* of initial plan of work elements and timetable *Review* of maps, diagrams, data, tables, photographs, written and oral summaries	*Question and answer sessions* on study alternatives *Delphi-type* exercises to explore future program implications *Working charts* and *diagrams* depicting program philosophy, future lines of work, and overall meaning of such work
Special interest groups, e.g., League of Women Voters	*Flier* or *brochure* specifying the project objectives, timetable, meeting dates and places, key individuals to contact for information *Newsletters* to group leaders	*Discussion* with group leaders of project objectives, organization, and results *Review* of *factual scenarios* on alternative solutions *Questionnaire response forms* or other means of generating formal feedback	Establish an *information access system,* identifying the procedure for obtaining and inputing information Institute *study committees* to review particular uses and to provide linkage with broader publics
General citizenry	Initial *press release* giving the purpose, location, and cost of the study *News articles* highlighting the "human side" to the project, e.g., the experiences of floodplain victim Periodic *news updates* on study programs *Public notices* of meetings	*Call-in radio programs* with agency officials and staff *Public hearings* *Tear-out newspaper questionnaires*	Personal *meetings with media heads,* e.g., editors, TV and radio commentators, and educators *News articles* indicating agency contact phone numbers and addresses to gather further information or to get questions answered

The demand placed on staff time is an important constraint in the design of communications programs. Those mechanisms with potentially the greatest payoff in terms of useful information

Agency Resource Requirements

obtained, that is, interactive ones, also tend to require the greatest commitment of agency resources. This is because staff time is required not only for the interaction itself, but also to prepare appropriate support materials and to respond to the concerns raised during the discussions. The latter activity is essential in order to maintain participant motivation in the program.

Although we have treated mechanisms and formats as separate entities of a communications program, in actuality, they are more conveniently handled together. Table 8.3 is an attempt to identify a number of sets of mechanisms and formats that would be appropriate in a floodplain management study. Notice that only a modest level of technical sophistication and resource commitment would be required by each set.

SUMMARY

The primary objective of communications activities in environmental planning is to exchange information with different sectors of society and government in an effort to maximize the effectiveness of planning projects. In the early phases of a study, communications activities can help call attention to important concerns and controversial issues at a time when such input can be useful in designing the analysis. Later in the study, communications and involvement activities can be helpful in generating pertinent information, structuring project results, and disseminating these results to various audiences.

Effective communication of environmental information begins with the identification of the audiences or publics with which information is to be exchanged. This is followed by the formulation of an audience profile which includes information on how problems and issues are perceived by public officials, opinion leaders, agency staff members and interest groups. Mutual misconceptions about the content, purpose, and importance of environmental planning studies can lead to distrust, poor communication, and unrealistic expectations. On the other hand, common or at least consistent perceptions of the problems and issues is a prerequisite for cogent evaluation of objectives, impacts, and alternative solutions.

Information on audiences is fundamental to the selection and development of formats and mechanisms for a communications program. Scores of combinations of formats and mechanisms are available, and the innovative communications program utilizes those which complement and reinforce each other at the various stages in a project. For major projects involving new and complex issues, this may warrant considerable planning as well as experimentation and development.

As a general rule in the development of any communications program, whether aimed at lay public or governmental officials, it is extremely important to make clear to your audience what you are doing, what the objectives and implications of the activity are, what you are expecting from the audience, and what procedures and time schedules will be followed. At the very least this allows everyone to start with the same frame of reference. If these points can be repeated during the study, it affords everyone the opportunity to keep abreast of the study as well.

Altshuler, A.: *The City Planning Process,* Cornell University Press, Ithaca, N.Y., 1965.

Borton, Thomas E., and Katharine P. Warner: "Involving Citizens in Water Resources Planning: The Communication Participation Experiment in the Susquehanna River Basin," in *Environment and Behavior,* 1975, pp. 284–306.

Borton, Thomas E., Katharine P. Warner, and J. William Wenrich: *The Susquehanna Communication—Participation Study,* U.S. Army Corps of Engineers, Institute for Water Resources, Report No. 70-6 (available from NTIS), Washington, D.C., 1970.

Controller of the United States: *Public Involvement in Planning Public Works Projects Should Be Increased,* Report to the Congress B-153449, Washington, D.C., 1974.

Delbecqu, Andre L., Andrew H. Van de Ven, and David H. Gustafson: *Group Techniques for Program Planning,* Scott Foresman, Glenview, Ill., 1975.

Fairfax, Sally K.: "Public Involvement and the Forest Service," *Journal of Forestry,* vol. 73, no. 10, 1975.

Havelock, R. G.: *Planning for Innovation through Dissemination and Utilization of Knowledge,* Center for Research on Utilization of Scientific Knowledge, Institute of Social Research, The University of Michigan, Ann Arbor, 1971.

League of Women Voters Education Fund: *The Big Water Fight,* Stephen Greene Press, Battleboro, Vt., 1966.

Ragan, James, David A. Aggerholm, Jerry J. Swift, and Ann Widditsch: *Assessment of Public Participation in the Implementation of the Federal Water Polution Control Act Amendments of 1972,* Final Report to the National Commission on Water Quality, 1975.

Rogers, Everett, and Floyd Shoemaker: *Communication of Innovations,* 2d ed., The Free Press, Glencoe, Ill., 1971.

Shore, William S. (ed.): *Listening to the Metropolis,* Regional Plan Association, New York, 1974.

Strong, Ann L.: *Private Property and the Public Interest: The Brandywine Experience,* Johns Hopkins University Press, Baltimore, Md., 1975.

U.S. Forest Service: *A Guide to Public Involvement in Decision Making,* U.S. Department of Agriculture, Washington, D.C., 1971.

Wagner, T. P., and L. Ortolano: "Analysis of New Techniques for Public Involvement in Water Planning, *Water Resources Bulletin,* 1975, pp. 329–344.

Warner, Katharine P.: *Public Participation in Water Resources Planning,* National Water Commission, NTIS Publication PB 204 245, Washington, D.C., 1971.

Webb, Kenneth et al.: *Obtaining Citizen Feedback: The Application of Citizen Surveys to Local Government,* URI 18000, Urban Institute, Washington, D.C., 1973.

Willeke, Gene E.: *Identification of Publics in Water Resources Planning,* Environmental Resources Center, Georgia Institute of Technology, Atlanta, 1974.

Bibliography

CHAPTER **9**

SPECIAL TOPICS

CHAPTER **9.1**

LANDSLIDE HAZARD MAPPING FOR LOCAL LAND USE PLANNING

John D. Vitek and
William M. Marsh

A stretch of old Route 1 along the Pacific Coast south of San Francisco in 1936 and in 1974 after abandonment. (Photograph courtesy of Raymond Sullivan)

INTRODUCTION

ALTHOUGH IT IS conventional for developers to consider factors such as property value, availability of services, and open space in suburban residential development, it is less conventional for them to consider potential physical limitations of the site, especially those which are not the readily apparent. Often overlooked in each phase of development planning is the susceptibility of a particular site to natural hazards such as landslides, earthquakes, and floods. The social and monetary costs of such oversights have been tremendous in the United States. And the evidence conclusively shows increasingly higher rates of loss from natural hazards with each decade. The roots of the problem are complex, and the details are not well documented. Certainly the trend could be reversed in many areas given public policy sufficiently strong to curb development in settings known to be hazard prone. The development of floodplain zoning ordinances in some states suggests a movement in this direction. More frequently, however, the problem is related to insufficient information on the behavior and distribution of hazardous processes. In addition, the inherently attractive nature of waterside and hilly settings, for example, has drawn residential development into close proximity with potentially hazardous processes. In the face of the strong social value placed on these settings, the information on which recommendations against development are based must, perforce, be reliable and convincing.

LANDSLIDE HAZARDS

Many natural forces interact at the earth's surface to produce changes in landscape. Geologic, geomorphic, and climate forces operate at irregular intensities over time, sometimes in an interdependent fashion and sometimes in mutually independent fashion. Climatic processes, for example, usually operate independent of geologic processes. In contrast, geomorphic processes such as landslides are often directly tied to both climatic and geologic events. This is particularly so in the case of massive slope failures in mountainous and hilly regions which are geologically active, that is, still building from within the earth's crust. Heavy rainfall or snowmelt may produce a condition of soil saturation which weakens soil resistance to downslope movement. If an earthquake should occur, tremors may break the internal binding strength of the soil. These processes, operating separately or in combination, can set the entire soil mass, and all the structures on it, into motion. Usually the movement is small, perhaps several feet, but in residential areas this is sufficient to break waterlines, gas lines, power lines, and to damage streets, sidewalks, foundations, and other hard-surface materials. Less frequently, the movement is over a distance of hundreds or thousands of feet and is very sudden. Such failures have produced some of the most frightening natural disasters of this century. The objective of this paper is to review environmental conditions that are associated with landslides and related earth movements and to identify the sources of information and the analytical techniques which may be employed by planners to locate slide-prone areas.

THE PORTUGUESE BEND, CALIFORNIA, LANDSLIDE

Numerous reports on landslides have been filed by scientists and engineers in the past several decades. The Portuguese Bend landslide of 1956 is outlined here as an example of a movement which, although not massive, caused severe property damage. The Palos Verdes Hills is a residential area located approximately 25 miles from the heart of Los Angeles, along the southwestern edge of the Los Angeles basin (Figure 9.1.1). The hills are composed of elevated marine sediments underlaid by metamorphic bedrock. The area is bounded by faults on the northeast and southwest. From the axis of the hills, at an elevation of 600 to 700 feet, the area slopes gently eastward (Merriam, 1960). In 1956 landslide movement in the vicinity of Portuguese Bend began in a 6 to 7 degree slope. The rates of movement varied from 0.03 to 0.1 foot per day. After the first six months, displacement on the surface was nearly 17 feet. Had the

Figure 9.1.1. A view of a portion of the Palos Verdes Hills. The area outlined represents the Portuguese Bend landslide, and the arrows show the direction of movement. (Photograph by Department of Building and Safety, Los Angeles)

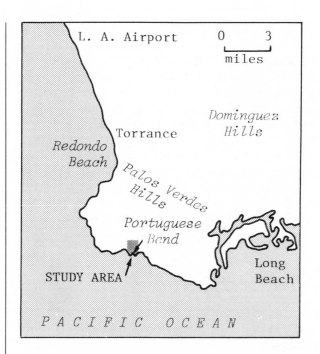

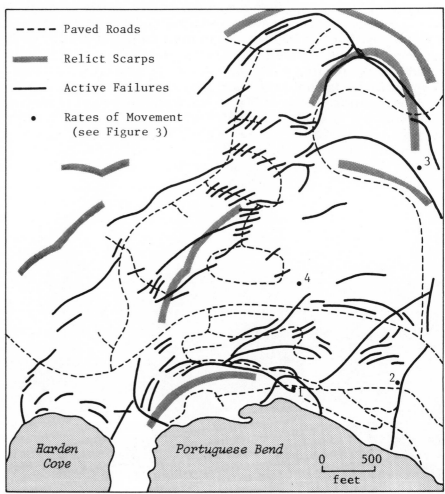

Figure 9.1.2. The pattern of ancient slide features in the Portuguese Bend area (after Merriam, 1960).

area been uninhabited, the slide would surely have occurred without immediate notice. In this seemingly peaceful residential area, however, property damage in the millions of dollars was incurred. A review of the factors that contributed to this disaster serves to highlight a methodology for identifying slide-prone areas.

The question of why the slide occurred in this area is easy to answer. First, topographic evidence indicates that the area experienced sliding prior to settlement. Aerial photographs and topographic maps indicate that the entire area was a complex of ancient landslides, a fact not known at the time of residential development (Figure 9.1.2). Second, the structure and composition of the underlying material was susceptible to failure. For example, the beds of two shale formations tended to reach a plastic state relatively quickly with the addition of water. Since many factors can initiate slope failure, the question of why movement was reactivated was somewhat more difficult to answer.

In several dry years preceding 1956, deep desiccation cracks formed in the soil which provided routes of entry to the subsurface for surface water. And in less than one week in 1956, 5 inches of rain fell on the area, much of which entered the subsurface via the cracks. In addition, it was estimated that the 150 houses situated on the slide sector contributed 32,000 gallons of water per day to the underlying strata through septic tanks, cesspools, and lawn irrigation. In sum, these human activities may have contributed enough water to effectively double the annual amount of precipitation. It was not surprising, then, that the soil and rock material sampled along the rupture lines after movement was nearly or completely saturated. As noted in Chapter 3, saturated soils tend to be more susceptible to slope failure than dry soils. This is related not only to the consistency change but also to pore water pressure associated with groundwater flow and the weight added to the soil by the water. Additionally, the weight of a road fill near the head of the slide also may have contributed to the failure. Hence, we may conclude that it was people coupled with nature which was responsible for the reactivation of landslides in the Palos Verdes Hills.

The disaster was not a sudden event but a gradual movement of the surface over several years. As Figure 9.1.3 illustrates, the rate of movement in the slide fluctuated in response to the amount of water added from the surface. In an effort to secure the slope, caissons or shear pins, 4 feet in diameter and 20 feet long, were embedded in the slide. Proposals were advanced to either stabilize the toe or remove subsurface water by pumping, but they were rejected. Finally, the proposed use of storm sewers and sanitary sewers to remove water was rejected because of the potential disruption related to the construction of each system and the excess costs involved. While some houses were successfully moved from the area, many were destroyed, along with roads and utilities, resulting in total losses estimated at $10 million (Merriam, 1960). Investigations prior to development may have prevented the Portuguese Bend disaster. Careful examination of the topography would almost certainly have revealed the evidence of previous landslides. Given this knowledge, proper steps could have been taken to provide geologic data on subsurface materials and ultimately limit development of the area.

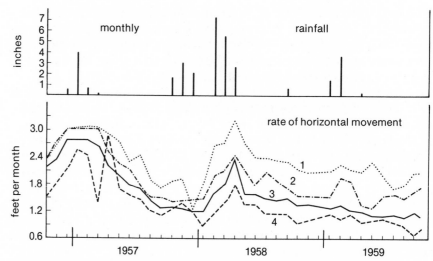

Figure 9.1.3. The rate of movement of the Portuguese Bend landslide based on measurements made at four locations compared to the monthly pattern of precipitation (above) over the same time period (after Merriam, 1960).

MECHANISMS OF SLOPE FAILURE

Seldom is just one mechanism responsible for slope failure; generally, many factors combine to produce a movement. Although the mechanics of soil behavior are very complex, it is necessary here that we outline at least the fundamental concepts of slope failure and stability. Two sets of forces operate in all inclined materials; one set, called shear stress, tends to produce movement or failure, whereas the other set, called shear strength, tends to resist movement or failure. Whether a slope is stable or unstable depends on the balance of these forces; for example, if shear strength exceeds shear stress, then the slope is stable; and conversely, if shear stress exceeds strength, then the slope is unstable. The point of balance between these forces is the critical threshold, which, of course, varies greatly in different earth materials.

For any slope, failure can be triggered by reducing shear strength or increasing shear stress (or both) until the critical threshold is exceeded. As most experienced mud-pie cooks know, clayey soils tend to lose shear strength with the addition of water; and so it is in nature. Water tends to change the soil consistency such that it is less able to maintain a given slope angle (see "Slope Failure Related to Groundwater," Chapter 3). In addition, in areas of hilly or mountainous terrain, groundwater is usually inclined downslope and is, therefore, pressurized under its own weight. This can create strong water pressure between particles which tends to drive them apart, thereby reducing the shear strength otherwise gained from interparticle contact. In areas where groundwater has been markedly increased, as appears to have been the case at Portuguese Bend, the evidence indicates that these mechanisms are important causes of slope failure.

One of the most common causes of slope failure in developed areas is undercutting. As the foot of a slope is excavated, for

TABLE 9.1.1   FACTORS CONTRIBUTING TO SLOPE FAILURE

Factors that contribute to *high* shear stress	Factors that contribute to *low* shear strength

1. Removal of lateral or underlying support
   a. Bank cutting by streams and rivers
   b. Human agencies—cuts,
     excavations, mining. etc.
   c. Weathering of the weaker strata
     at toe of slope
   d. Removal of granular material by
     seepage erosion, piping, etc.
 	
2. Slope loading
   a. Natural agencies—weight of snow,
     ice, rainwater, and talus (rock
     debris)
   b. Human agencies—fills, buildings,
     stockpiles of ore, rubbish, etc.
 	
3. Seismic tremors
   a. Earthquake
   b. Heavy traffic, mining activity
 	
4. Regional tilting
	1. Initial state of the material
	   a. Composition—inherently weak
	     materials such as poorly consoli-
	     dated clay
	   b. Texture—low friction between the
	     particles—loose soils with
	     unstable grain structures
	   c. Internal structure—many faults,
	     joints, bedding planes, varves,
	     etc.
	
	2. Disturbed soil such as landfill
	
	3. Weathering of soil and bedrock resulting
	   in the removal of cementing materials
	
	4. Increase in intergranular pressure due to
	   ground water increase
	   a. Buoyancy in saturated state
	   b. Loss in capillary tension upon
	     saturation
	   c. Seepage pressure of percolating
	     groundwater
	
	5. Disruption of natural vegetation
	   a. Deforestation—land clearing
	
	6. Seismic tremors
	   a. Earthquakes

example, and the slope angle is increased, shear stress is also increased. For any material, there is a maximum level of stress associated with specific slope inclination which can be tolerated before failure. This inclination is called the "angle of repose", and a number of examples are given in Chapter 2. Shear stress may also be increased in several other ways; for instance, the weight of the slope can be increased with addition of water, rock, fill material or structures, and the angle of the slope can be increased by geologic activity which results in wholesale tilting of the terrain. Table 9.1.1 lists a number of important contributors to slope failure.

Finally, to return to the original remark that most slope failures are produced by a combination of mechanisms, it is important to add that the most disasterous failures occur when seasonal and longer-term events simultaneously combine to lower shear strength and increase shear stress. The probability of such combinations is usually not great, but it nonetheless is ever present. Table 9.1.2 identifies some of the combinations which are known to produce severe failure.

TABLE 9.1.2   EVENT COMBINATIONS KNOWN TO PRODUCE FAILURE

Heavy rains/soil saturation + earthquaking
Heavy rains/soil saturation + excavation
Heavy rains/soil saturation + deforestation
Deforestation + excavation
Raising of reservoir + slope undercutting

BUILDING A SLOPE INFORMATION BASE FOR LAND-USE PLANNING

The susceptibility of hilly and mountainous areas to slope failure varies considerably from region to region. The coastal mountains of California have shown a propensity for failure, and since development has been intensive here, slope problems have gained some attention in land use planning (Figure 9.1.4). The U.S. Geological Survey initiated an experimental study on landslide susceptibility in the San Francisco Bay Area (e.g., see Brabb et al., 1972). Outlined in this study is a methodology for mapping failure-prone areas. The following discussion is based in part on that outline.

Figure 9.1.4. An example of the misfortune that can beset residential development in a slide hazard area. (Photograph by Department of Building and Safety, Los Angeles)

Figure 9.1.5. Location map of San Mateo County, California, where the U.S. Geological Survey conducted an experimental study on mapping areas susceptible to landslides.

San Mateo County stretches from the southern part of San Francisco Bay to the Pacific Ocean and encompasses sprawling suburban areas amongst the coastal hills (Figure 9.1.5). Given the current trend of sprawl from the Bay area, further development of these sparsely populated hills seems inevitable. The rate at which this development proceeds depends on the improvement of access routes and subsequent reduction of commuting time to cities in the Bay area. It also depends, however, on the pressure exerted by the

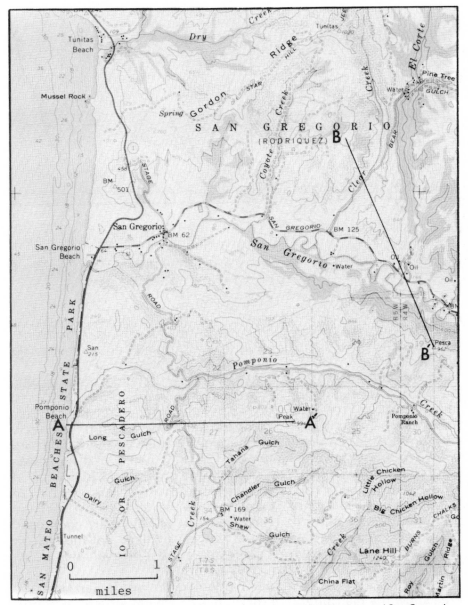

Figure 9.1.6. An excerpt from the USGS topographic map for the area around San Gregorio, San Mateo County. Slope, vegetation, drainage patterns, roads, and houses are shown on this map. The lines AA' and BB' mark the locations of the example transects cited in the following discussion.

people for the "good life" in the rural fringes of metropolitan areas. As development of rural areas progresses, hillslopes will inevitably be consumed by residential land uses.

Should development proceed in these areas without the benefit of information on slope stability? Certainly not, of course, but to make allowances for this constraint, certain information must be compiled on the slopes of the area. To generate information for a large diversified area through the use of field survey techniques could take many years and hundreds of thousands of dollars. What can be done short of this? Actually, conventional maps, aerial photographs, and geological maps can yield information suitable

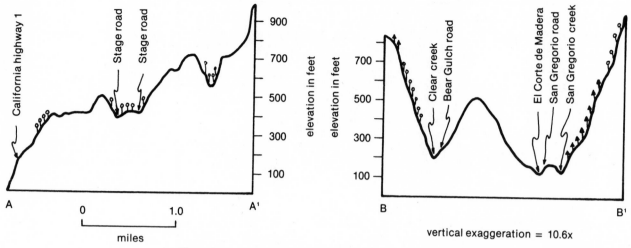

Figure 9.1.7. Topographic profiles of transects AA' and BB'. Roads, creeks, and tree cover are also shown.

for most land use planning purposes. Armed with this information, planners and developers can guide development into relatively safe areas.

The topography of the area, including drainage patterns and major zones of vegetation, is shown on the USGS topographic map in Figure 9.1.6. From this map we can determine the slope angles for a valley or along a particular transect. Two example transects (AA' and BB') are marked on the map in Figure 9.1.6 and both are shown in profile form in Figure 9.1.7. If the stability of a slope was controlled solely by its inclination, then a preliminary indication of failure susceptibility could be ascertained from an examination of the slope profiles alone. This is in fact the case in parts of the Midwest, for example, where extensive areas of hills are composed of essentially one basic soil type. However, this is not the case in San Mateo County, and thus slope angle must be evaluated in the context of other factors, especially bedrock.

The bedrock maps developed by geologists for the San Gregorio area show the distribution of rock types as well as structural trends, weaknesses (faults), and the dip (or inclination) of the bedrock. The underlying material is predominantly marine sediments in the form of siltstones, mudstones, and sandstones, all of which, geologists indicate, are highly susceptible to failure. The types of bedrock intercepted along the slope profiles are illustrated on Figure 9.1.8. In both profiles, the rocks which make up the slopes are prone to low failure thresholds. That is, they are inclined to fail when exposed in low angles. Unconsolidated deposits (i.e., soil material) overlie the bedrock throughout most of the area. As a whole, they are not susceptible to failure, except where they are steepened to angles greater than 25 to 35 degrees.

With these two lines of information, namely, slope angle and material, an approximate delineation can be made of failure-prone slopes. However, to provide somewhat more specificity, the area can be examined for evidence of past failures. Aerial photographs are particularly helpful in this task. Careful stereoscopic surveys of

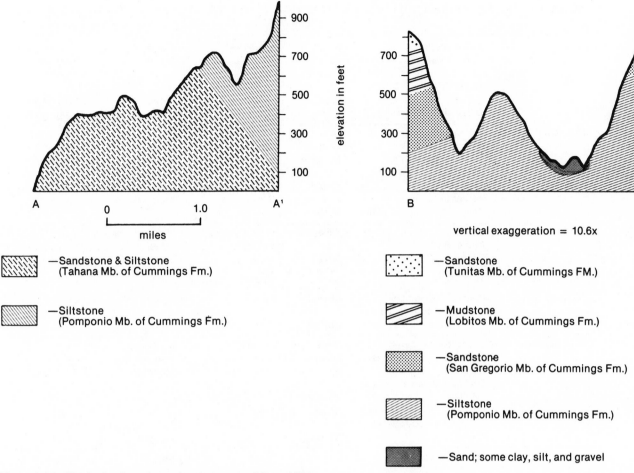

elevation in feet

A   0   1.0   A'
miles

vertical exaggeration = 10.6x

— Sandstone & Siltstone
(Tahana Mb. of Cummings Fm.)

— Siltstone
(Pomponio Mb. of Cummings Fm.)

— Sandstone
(Tunitas Mb. of Cummings FM.)

— Mudstone
(Lobitos Mb. of Cummings Fm.)

— Sandstone
(San Gregorio Mb. of Cummings Fm.)

— Siltstone
(Pomponio Mb. of Cummings Fm.)

— Sand; some clay, silt, and gravel

Figure 9.1.8. The bedrock geology along transects AA' and BB'.

the slopes will usually lead to the identification of most failure sites. (See Chapter 2 for illustrations of the physical features of a slope failure.) The locations of former failures along the two sample transects are shown on the profiles AA' and BB' in Figure 9.1.9.

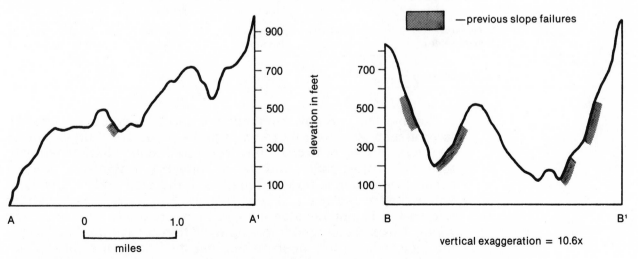

— previous slope failures

elevation in feet

A   0   1.0   A'
miles

vertical exaggeration = 10.6x

Figure 9.1.9. Zones of previous slope failure along transects AA' and BB'.

TABLE 9.1.3   CHECKLIST CRITERIA THAT CAN BE USED TO EVALUATE AN AREA FOR SUSCEPTIBILITY TO SLOPE FAILURE

		Low	————————→		High
Relief:	Valley depth	Small	Moderate	Large	Very large
	Slope steepness	Low	Moderate	Steep	Very steep
	Cliffs	Absent			Present
	Ht. Diff. Between Diff. Valley	Small	Moderate	Large	Very large
	Valley-side shape	Spur	Straight	Shallow cove	Deep cove
Drainage:	Drainage density	Low	Moderate	High	Very high
	River gradient	Gentle	Moderate	Steep	Very steep
	Slope undercutting	None	Moderate	Severe	Very severe
			Present at	Present	Present
	Standing water	Absent	local base level	Slowly draining	Rapidly draining
	Recent incision	Absent	Small	Moderate	Large
	Concentrated seepage flow	Absent			Flow
Soils:	Site	Valley floor	Gentle slopes	Moderate slopes	Steep slopes
	Angle of rest	Low	Moderate	Steep	Very steep
	Depth	Small	Moderate	Large	Very large
Earthquake tone:	Tremors felt	Never	Seldom	Some	Many
Slope history:	Previous landslides	Absent	Rare	Some	Many
	Remnant deposits, Lobes or sheets	Absent	Rare	Some	Many
Artificial features:	Excavations—depth	None	Small	Moderate	Large
	Excavations—positions	Valleybottom	Low valley	High valley	Hill Crest
	Reservoir	Absent	Small	Moderately deep	Very deep
	Drainage diversion across hillside	Absent			Present
	Lowering of reservoir level	None	Small	Moderate	Large
	Loading of upper valley-side	None	Some	Moderate	Large
Drainage:	Pore water pressure	Low	Moderate	High	Very high
Bedrock:	Exposures	Absent	Partial		Full
	Jointing density	Low	Moderate	High	Very high
	Direction of joints	Away		Normal	Towards
	Amount of dip	Horizontal	Small	Moderate	Large
	Strong beds over weak beds	Absent			Present
	Degree of weathering	None	Small	Moderate	Large
	Compressive strength	Very low	Low	Moderate	High
	Coherence (particularly of lower beds)	Very low	Low	Moderate	High
Soil:	Shear stress	Very low	Low	Moderate	High
	Liquidity index	Low	Moderate	High	Very high
Legacies from past:	Deep weathering	None	Slight	Moderate	Much

The analysis can now be supplemented with additional data on factors such as proximity to earthquake zones, local undercutting by rivers, mining or excavation, impaired drainage associated with reservoirs, forest cover, and so on (Table 9.1.3). Which factors are considered depends upon the nature of the area under consideration as well as the availability of the data. For example, in the upper Midwest it is not necessary to include proximity to earthquake zones. The particular method employed to record and synthesize all the factors is largely open to the investigator. In the case of the USGS study, maps on slope, bedrock geology, and previous landslides were overlaid, and from the correlations, a seven-class failure-susceptibility scheme was devised. The resultant map, shown in Figure 9.1.10, indicates that much of the San Gregorio area is very susceptible to slope failure. It is interesting to note that on

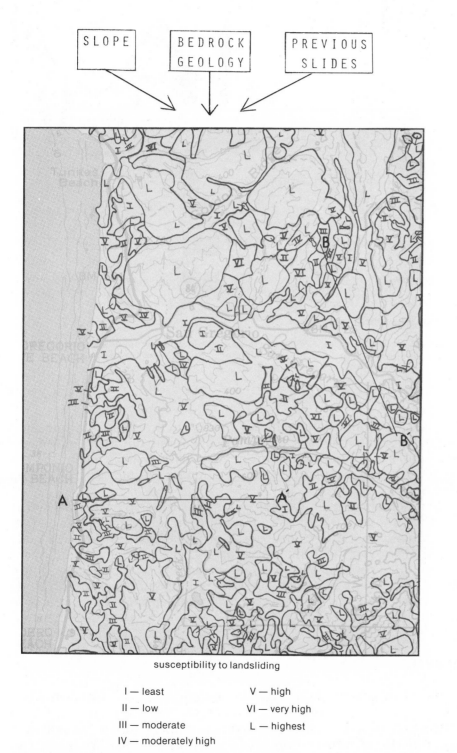

susceptibility to landsliding

I — least   V — high
II — low   VI — very high
III — moderate   L — highest
IV — moderately high

Figure 9.1.10. The U.S. Geological Survey classified slopes into seven categories according to landslide susceptibility (Brabb and Pampeyan, 1972a).

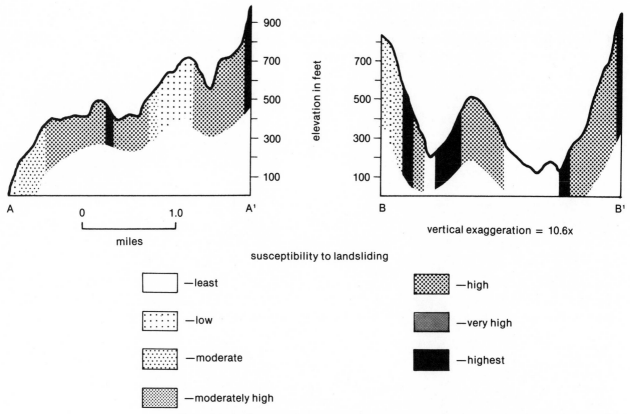

susceptibility to landsliding

☐ —least

▨ —low

▨ —moderate

▨ —moderately high

▨ —high

▨ —very high

■ —highest

vertical exaggeration = 10.6x

Figure 9.1.11. Transects AA' and BB' classified according to failure (landslide) susceptibility. Notice the steepest slopes do not necessarily pose the greatest failure threat.

profiles AA' and BB' in Figure 9.1.11 it is not the steepest slopes that are most prone to failure. Some are, of course, but many intermediate slopes are also highly prone to failure, which illustrates the importance of the bedrock and previous slide factors in building this map.

The procedure was carried one step further by the USGS. The data from Figure 9.1.10 were transformed into an isopleth map of the probability of the occurrence of slope failure (Wright et. al., 1974). However, this transformation appears to have little utility for planning purposes, especially at a county or local scale (Vitek, 1975). Since time and cost factors may be prohibitive for the study of a small area, the map overlay technique appears to be appropriate for generating slope stability information for land use planning.

SUMMARY

When uncontrolled development extends into areas of diversified terrain, geophysical problems can greatly add to societal costs. One of the keys to reduction of losses due to slope failure is the availability of accurate information on failure-prone areas. While we can perhaps never totally eliminate such losses, the chances of avoiding major setbacks are much greater where potentially unstable slopes have been identified and taken into consideration in land use planning.

Simple, yet reasonably accurate, techniques are available to planners for mapping slope hazard areas. These techniques rely on topographic maps, bedrock data, and aerial photographs for the necessary data and information. The map overlay method appears to be a satisfactory means of synthesizing slope, slide history, and bedrock data to produce a suitable information base on slide-prone areas.

Bibliography

Brabb, E. E., and E. H. Pampeyan, (compilers): *Preliminary Geologic Map of San Mateo County, California,* United States Geological Survey, Miscellaneous Field Studies Map MF-328 (scale 1:62,500), 1972a.

————. *Preliminary Map of Landslides in San Mateo County, California,* United States Geological Survey, Miscellaneous Field Studies Map MF-344 (scale 1:62,500), 1972b.

Brabb, E. E., E. H. Pampeyan, and M. G. Bonilla: *Landslide Susceptibility in San Mateo County, California,* United States Geological Survey, Miscellaneous Field Studies Map MF-360 (scale 1:62,500), 1972.

Brown, Robert D., Jr.: *Active Faults, Probable Active Faults and Associated Fracture Zones, San Mateo County, California,* United States Geological Survey, Miscellaneous Field Studies Map MF-355 (scale 1:62,500), 1972.

Cooke, R. U., and J. C. Doornkamp: *Geomorphology in Environmental Management,* Oxford University Press, London, 1974. 413 pp.

Karol, R. H.: *Soils and Soil Engineering,* Prentice-Hall, Englewood Cliffs, N.J., 1960. 194 pp.

Merriam, Richard: "Portuguese Bend Landslide, Palos Verdes Hills, California," *Journal of Geology,* vol. 68, no. 2, 1960, pp. 140–153.

Strahler, A. N.: *Dynamic Basis of Geomorphology,* Geological Society of America, Bulletin, vol. 63, 1962, pp. 923–938.

Tuan, Yi-Fu: *Topophilia: A Study of Environmental Perception, Attitudes, and Values,* Prentice-Hall, Englewood Cliffs, N.J., 1974. 260 pp.

Van Burkalow, Anastasia: *Angle of Repose and the Angle of Sliding Friction,* Geological Society of America, Bulletin, vol. 56, 1945, pp. 669–708.

Varnes, David J.: *Landslides, Types and Processes in Landslides and Engineering Processes,* Highway Research Board Special Publication 29, 1958, pp. 20–47.

Vitek, John D.: "Preparation and Use of Isopleth Maps of Landslide Deposits: Comment," *Geology,* vol. 3, no. 4, 1975, p. 217.

Wright, R. H., R. H. Campbell, and T. H. Nilsen: "Preparation and Use of Isopleth Maps of Landslide Deposits," *Geology,* vol. 2, no. 10, 1974, pp. 483–485.

Young, Anthony: *Slopes,* Oliver and Boyd, Edinburgh, 1972. 288 pp.

CHAPTER **9.2**

REMOTE-SENSING APPLICATIONS IN WATER QUALITY MANAGEMENT

C. T. Wezernak
and
William M. Marsh

NASA IMAGERY

INTRODUCTION

REMOTE-SENSING DATA from both satellites and aircraft are widely recognized sources of information on land use and environment. A large volume of remote-sensing data is in the public domain, including that produced by LANDSAT, manned spacecraft photography (Skylab, Apollo, Gemini), and NASA research aircraft photography. All of these are available from the EROS (Earth Resources Observation Systems) Data Center, an agency of the U.S. Geological Survey. The discussion which follows is centered on the emerging role of remote sensing as an information source for environmental planning and management. For information on sensor systems, data processing, and applications, the reader is referred to the technical literature (e.g., Wenderoth et. al., 1974; American Society of Photogrammetry, 1975; NASA, 1972).

In general, remote sensing offers the most effective means of generating data for large geographical areas. In the past several decades, the capacity of remote sensing has increased markedly owing to improved image resolution, increased sensor capacity, and satellite sensing programs. In studies dealing with large environmental systems, the combination of satellite and aircraft remote sensing has frequently proven to be an inexpensive means of building an information base. Accordingly, some of the imagery produced by these systems can make valuable contributions to land use planning and environmental management. Our concern here is with the utility of remote sensing in three major areas of water quality management: (1) nonpoint sources of pollution, (2) lake eutrophication, and (3) the coastal environment.

IDENTIFYING NONPOINT SOURCES OF POLLUTION

Until recently, the focus in pollution abatement has been largely centered on the control of specific point sources, such as municipal and industrial discharges. Abatement problems of this type still exist and presently require considerable attention from regulatory agencies. However, it is widely recognized that control of point sources of pollution is only one part of the problem of protecting and improving the quality of the nation's water resources. As control over these sources has been achieved in the past several years, the relative importance attributed to nonpoint sources has grown sharply, and nonpoint sources are now considered a major control issue.

Nonpoint sources are generally defined as geographically diffused sources of pollution such as residential areas and cropland. Owing to the heavy loading of natural waters from these sources, the water quality objectives mandated under federal law are generally not being realized. As a result, the relationship between water quality and land use activities, which for so long was largely unrecognized, is now at the focus of major water research and management efforts. In the United States, provisions of Public Law 92-500 (Federal Water Pollution Control Amendments, 1972), and in particular sections 201 and 208, require the establishment of areawide management plans for the control of nonpoint sources of pollution, including pollution from land use activities. In effect, Public Law 92-500 recognizes land use planning as an important mechanism in achieving the desired environmental goals.

Pollutants from nonpoint sources gain entry into the aquatic environment primarily through surface runoff and secondarily through precipitation and groundwater seepage. In general, control of the nonpoint sources associated with land use will require identification of the contributing activity followed by the institution of management practices to reduce or eliminate the pollution.

In the development of management plans to control nonpoint pollution, particular emphasis must be directed toward evaluating the environmental impact of "cultural" activities. This includes activities which directly alter some aspect of the aquatic environment, as well as land use activities which could, if not properly controlled, contribute to a degradation of the aquatic environment. Specific examples of important land use activities are:

1. *Land disposal of wastes,* including sanitary landfills, land disposal of liquid municipal and industrial wastes, wastewater spray irrigation, and wastewater ponds.

2. *Storage of raw materials* and on-site storage of waste products related to industrial operations.

3. *Construction activities,* including all large-scale public works, residential and commercial developments. The primary concern here is with practices which promote excessive erosion and sedimentation of surface waters.

4. *Mining activities* related to the large-scale removal, preparation, and storage of fossil fuels, minerals, ores, stone, sand, and gravel, including the disposal of "tailings" and overburden.

5. *Forestry activities,* including harvesting, log transport, and regeneration methods. The major concern here is also with practices which promote excessive erosion and sediment loading of surface waters.

6. *Agriculture,* including feedlot operations, field fertilization, and runoff.

7. *Urban development,* including street and yard runoff as well as discharges from commercial and public institutions. To weigh the importance of these activities, it is also necessary to inventory and assess undisturbed or "natural" environments as a part of the total ecosystem.

Numerous factors enter into the assessment of pollution from nonpoint sources and inventories and analyses must be

Figure 9.2.1. Water features, land use, and the coastal zone are clearly shown in this LANDSAT-1 image of Lake Okeechobee, Florida. MSS Band 7; scale approximately 1:1,000,000.

approached at several levels. While a discussion of the factors involved is outside the scope of this presentation, we should underscore the fact that the success of this effort will depend in part on our ability to identify problem areas and to provide adequate and timely land use information. Remote sensing can provide an important input to the total process. The potential contribution of satellite and high-altitude aircraft data can be illustrated by direct interpretation of imagery such as that shown in Figures 9.2.1, 9.2.2, and 9.2.3.

Shown in Figure 9.2.1 is a LANDSAT-1 image of a portion of the Florida peninsula. Lake Okeechobee is located in the lower center portion of the image and Palm Beach, Florida, in the lower right. The image shown represents a composite of data points from one of the four spectral bands recorded by the LANDSAT-1 (formerly ERTS-1) satellite from an altitude of approximately 570 miles (920 kilometers). The four multispectral scanner (MSS) bands recorded by both LANDSAT-1 and its newer twin, LANDSAT-2, are given in Table 9.2.1. Each of these bands is recorded on each satellite pass, which, for any spot in the United States, takes place about once

TABLE 9.2.1 LANDSAT MULTISPECTRAL SCANNER BANDS

Band	Wavelength (μ)	
4	0.5–0.6	visible
5	0.6–0.7	
6	0.7–0.8	infrared
7	0.8–1.1	

every eighteen days while the satellites are operating. Though clouds may obscure the earth's surface on some passes, virtually all locations in the United States can expect at least fifteen or twenty clear passes per year. The smallest parcel of surface discernible by the satellite scanners, referred to as *spatial resolution,* is approximately 1.1 acre (0.45 hectare). LANDSAT data are available from the EROS Data Center in photographic formats and in the form of computer-compatible tapes. The latter allow for computer processing to tabulate, classify, and display the data in terms of selected land uses and cover types.

An examination of Figure 9.2.1 serves to underscore the potential of LANDSAT as a data source for analysis of major geographic features at a regional scale. Lakes, canals, stream patterns, agricultural fields, wetlands, and urban centers are easily recognized in this single band display. Computer processing of the data from tapes (utilizing the four spectral bands) can be used to produce a 7- to 10-category land use map as well as some related statistics on the area.

Additional information is attainable if the scene is segregated into more than one spectral band, as is illustrated in Figure 9.2.2. Agricultural fields are easily recognized in this scene, and the spectral differences reflect crop type, density of growth, and soil moisture conditions. The low-reflectance areas (dark) in band 5 and the correspondingly high reflectance in band 7 indicate dense green crop areas. The dark fields in band 7 and light areas in band 5 are undoubtedly newly planted fields under irrigation. By combining data collected at two important time periods in the growing season, additional information is obtainable regarding vegetation type within the agricultural areas and the surrounding terrain.

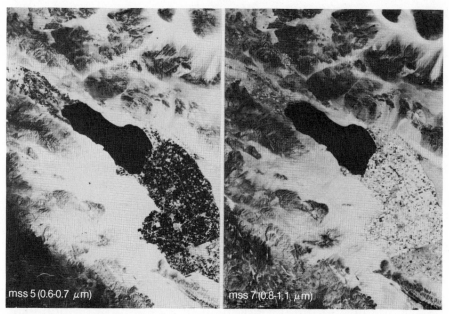

mss 5 (0.6-0.7 μm)   mss 7 (0.8-1.1 μm)

Figure 9.2.2. The Imperial Valley of California shown in LANDSAT MSS Bands 5 and 7. The dark areas in Band 5 and the corresponding light areas in Band 7 are fields of dense green plants. Scale approximately 1:1,000,000.

Figure 9.2.3. High-altitude infrared photograph of Riverside, California. The original rendition is in color. Scale approximately 1:130,000.

In summary we can say that LANDSAT is an important source of land use information that can be useful in evaluating nonpoint sources of pollution. For problems and programs of a regional scope, the spatial resolution of 1.1 acre (0.45 hectare) is well within the limits of acceptability. For some areas of the country, additional high-altitude photographic imagery are available from the EROS Data Center, Sioux Falls, South Dakota (Figure 9.2.3). For such areas, high-quality photography can greatly contribute to the information data base. This information can be used to supplement the low-altitude imagery available from government and commercial organizations which specialize in aerial photography. As a general rule, a combination of remote-sensing products derived from high-altitude and low-altitude sensor systems will provide the most cost-effective solution to the development of a data base on nonpoint sources of pollution over a large area. Computer processing of scanner data offers further options for mapping and data analysis.

EUTROPHICATION OF INLAND LAKES

Inland lakes (including reservoirs) are important water resources that have in the past several decades become major foci of residential and recreational activity. As a result, the shorelines and watersheds of thousands of inland water bodies are now intensively developed. This has led to increased nutrient loading of runoff and, in turn, to increased rates of eutrophication of lake water. Although lake eutrophication is a natural process, human activities can accelerate it dramatically. Poor development practices and land use activities contribute to the nutrient load entering a body of water, producing a heavier aquatic biomass and changes in plant and animal species.

Various methods are used to improve lake water quality, including lake restoration and watershed management. Lake restoration or reclamation, which may involve chemical treatment and dredging, is usually costly, and in many cases, it is simply not practical. Hence, the emphasis in eutrophication control must be on prevention, and this requires effective planning and management action in the watershed.

The contribution of remote sensing to the eutrophication problem is threefold: (1) assessment of land use and drainage conditions in the watershed, (2) evaluation of the trophic state of lakes, and (3) change detection over time. For most inland lakes and reservoirs, maximum image resolution is needed for these problems. Therefore, sensing from low-altitude aircraft is generally preferable to sensing from high-altitude systems.

Since the problem of eutrophication begins with runoff in the watershed, information on land use is usually needed for the entire lake watershed. The number of categories employed can vary somewhat depending on the problem. This information, together with information on soils, topography, and climate, is required for computing the nutrient loading function. Additionally, the physical dimensions of the water body are needed in order to compute the volume of water and loading per unit volume per year. Data on land use and surface cover are readily obtainable from aerial photographs [Figure 9.2.4(a)] and when combined with data on slope, drainage patterns, and soils (from USGS topographic maps and SCS soils maps) a suitably strong information base can be built for watershed analysis [Figures 9.2.4(b) and (c)].

The determination of the trophic state of an inland lake is normally based on many biochemical and physical parameters; however, a select number of these parameters can serve as fairly reliable indicators of the trophic state. Certain of these parameters are detectable through remote sensing, because eutrophication alters the optical properties of water. Through statistical analysis, the reliability of these parameters as indicators of eutrophication can be tested and those that test out significantly can be used to formulate a trophic index (Shannon, 1970; Wezernak, 1974). The use of a trophic index based on remote sensing can facilitate lake classification in regions where there are so many lakes that standard ground techniques are impractical. This includes, for example, large regions of Minnesota, Wisconsin, Michigan, Ontario, Maine, and New York. Given several overflights of a region in successive

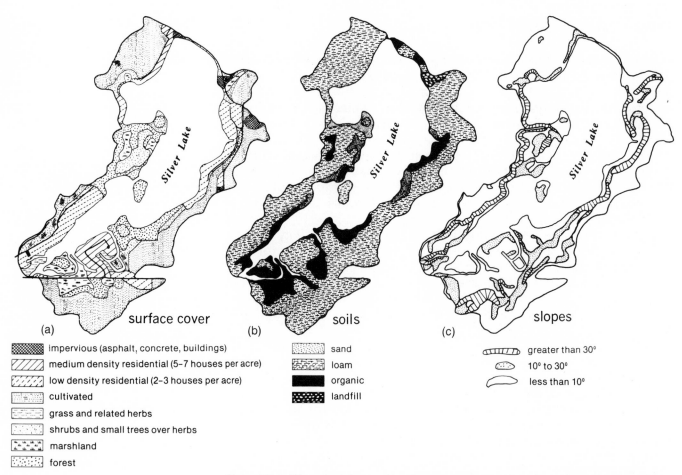

surface cover   (a)

soils   (b)

slopes   (c)

impervious (asphalt, concrete, buildings)
medium density residential (5–7 houses per acre)
low density residential (2–3 houses per acre)
cultivated
grass and related herbs
shrubs and small trees over herbs
marshland
forest

sand
loam
organic
landfill

greater than 30°
10° to 30°
less than 10°

Figure 9.2.4. Watershed data such as these are necessary in order to determine the nutrient loading function of an inland lake. The lake shown here is the southernmost lake in Figure 9.2.5 (from Marsh and Borton, 1976).

years, a basis can be established for detecting change in the trophic states of lakes. Such information can be an important factor in evaluating the effectiveness of regional and statewide water management programs.

An example of trophic state potential of remote sensing is illustrated in Figure 9.2.5, which shows two computer-processed images generated from multispectral scanner data taken at low altitudes. The particular spectral bands used to produce these images are sensitive to differences in water transparency and chlorophyll content, both of which are good indicators of eutrophication. Notice that differences are not only evident between the two lakes, but also within each lake. Tabular data on these parameters can usually be obtained using digital processing techniques.

In the case of large bodies of water, the potential of satellite remote sensing also deserves serious consideration. Shown in Figure 9.2.6 is a map of water transparency for the western basin of Lake Erie. This map was produced through computer processing of LANDSAT-1 data from an early June pass of the satellite. In addition to transparency, suspended solids at the surface and chlorophyll are also determinable from LANDSAT imagery when they occur in high concentrations.

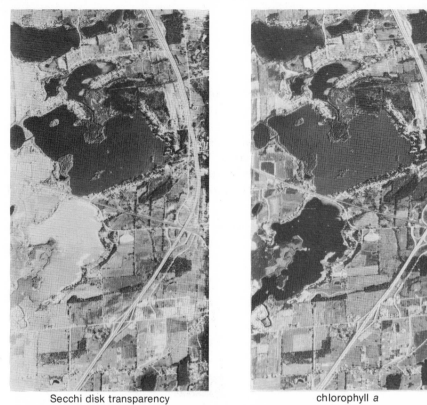

Secchi disk transparency   chlorophyll a

*Figure 9.2.5. Two computer processed images produced from multispectral scanner data.
The lighter tones indicate high transparency and high chlorophyll content. On the basis of
this, the large lake appears to be in a more advanced trophic state than the lake just south of it.
(Imagery by the Environmental Research Institute of Michigan.)*

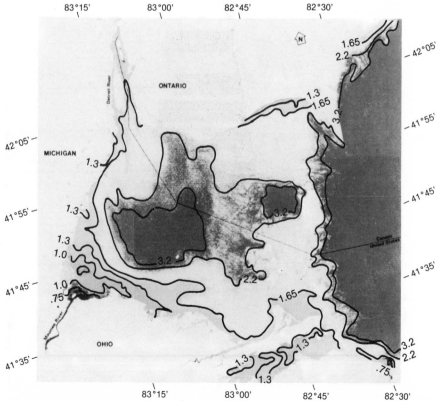

Water Transparency
Western Basin Lake Erie
2 June 1974
(E-1679-1513)
Secchi Disk Depth in Meters

*Figure 9.2.6. Water transparency in the western basin of Lake Erie produced from LANDSAT-
1 data (from Wezernak and Lyzenga, 1976).*

THE COASTAL ENVIRONMENT

   The coastal zones of the oceans and Great Lakes are among the most prized yet problematic environments in the United States. In addition to the traditional problems of shore erosion, flooding, and land use, we are now faced with serious management problems related to eradication of wetlands, offshore drilling and mineral extraction, and the disposal of wastewater from municipalities and industry. In response to such problems, legislation is being enacted

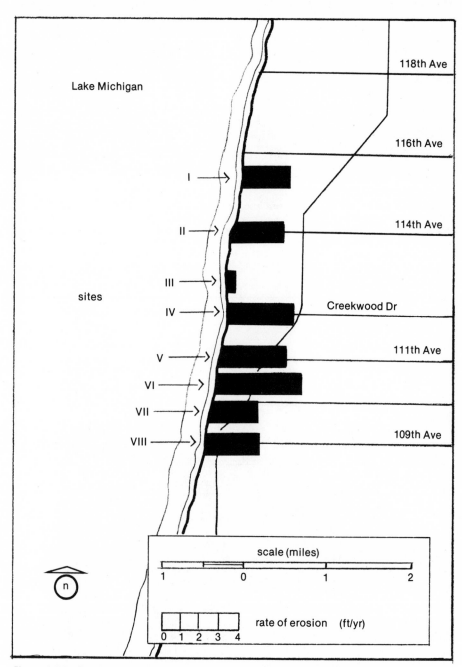

Figure 9.2.7. Erosion retreat rates for a section of the Lake Michigan shoreline. The rates were determined by comparing several sets of aerial photographs taken in different years (from Seibel, 1972).

Figure 9.2.8. A black-and-white infrared photograph showing the sharp difference between water and vegetated surfaces. Owing to this feature, such photographs can be very useful in mapping wetlands.

at many levels of government, including recent passage of the Coastal Zone Management Act (Public Law 92-583) by the federal government. With this action has come the need for more information on the coastal zone and remote sensing holds good promise as a means of fulfilling much of that need.

Standard aerial photographs are an excellent source of information in shore-erosion surveys. Areas of active erosion are easily identifiable on the basis of soil exposures, slide scars, and fallen trees on eroded slopes (see Figures 2.6 and 2.8 in Chapter 2). Erosion retreat rates of shorelines are determinable from several sets of aerial photographs taken at the standard seven- to ten-year intervals or at shorter intervals if specially contracted. Using photogrammetric techniques or machines designed for image superimposition, the location of the shorelines can be compared from one photo set to the next and a retreat rate computed from the resultant data. Figure 9.2.7 shows results of such an analysis for one segment of the Lake Michigan shoreline (Seibel, 1972).

Wetlands are a prevalent feature in the coastal environment and in recent years they have become the focus of conservation and management activity. Accurate inventory and monitoring programs are needed for such efforts, and remote sensing is particularly suitable for the task. At a localized scale, standard black-and-white aerial photographs are useful for wetland mapping, but infrared photographs (both black-and-white and color) are even better (see the sections on infrared photographs in Chapter 3). This is owing to the fact that on infrared film water-covered land is vividly differentiated from dry land. This is generally true where there is vegetation emerging from the water as well (Figure 9.2.8).

For larger areas, mapping and monitoring of wetlands can be accomplished with LANDSAT imagery. Although the resolution may be marginal in some cases, LANDSAT offers the capability of detecting seasonal and longer-term change because of the multiple passes over every area each year. Shown in Figure 9.2.9 is a portion of the Florida Gulf Coast as recorded by LANDSAT in MSS Band 4. The wetlands appear in gray tones, the water in white, and the land in black. Analysis of a series of such frames for this area would enable one not only to delimit wetland boundaries but to record boundary changes as well.

Multispectral remote sensing from aircraft also has utility as a source of information on the coastal environment. Pollution of estuaries, embayments, and offshore waters can be detected from multispectral data by analyzing the various MSS bands or channels in different ways. The images shown in Figures 9.2.10 and 9.2.11 were produced by expressing the signal recorded in one channel as a ratio to that recorded in another. Figure 9.2.10 shows the distribu-

Figure 9.2.9. A LANDSAT infrared image of the Florida Gulf Coast between Tarpon Springs and Keaton Beach. The photo negative of the image is printed here, so the water appears in white and the wetlands in grayish tones. MSS Band 4; Scale approximately 1:1,000,000.

Figure 9.2.10. *The distribution of a green algae* (Cladophora) *along a stretch of the southern shore of Lake Ontario. This image was processed from a ratio of two multispectral scanner channels. (Imagery by the Environmental Research Institute of Michigan.) Scale is 1:14,000.*

|← —————— 2.286 km (1.42 mi) —————— →|

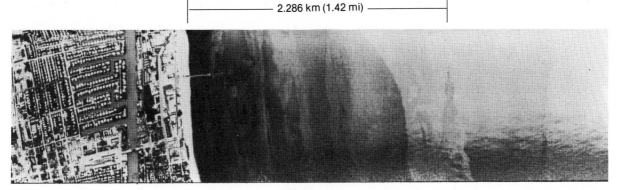

$$\frac{0.50\text{-}0.54\ \mu m}{0.41\text{-}0.48\ \mu m}$$

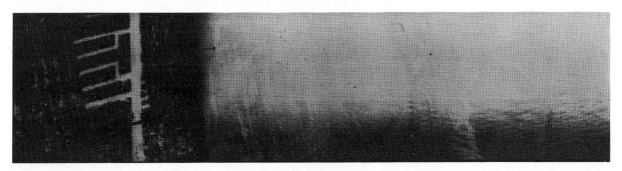

0.50-0.54 μm

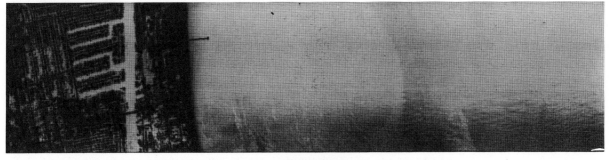

0.41-0.48 μm

Figure 9.2.11. *The southern coast of Florida at Pompano Beach from an altitude of 2000 feet. Images B and C each represent a single multispectral channel, whereas image A is a product of the ratio of B and C. A municipal sewage outfall is evident about a half mile off shore in image A.* (Imagery by the Environmental Research Institute of Michigan)

tion of a green algae *(Cladophora)* along a portion of the southern coast of Lake Ontario (Wezernak et al., 1974). Dense algal growths such as these are strong evidence of heavy nutrient loading of coastal waters.

The sources of these nutrients are point and nonpoint outfalls along the shore. Detection of these outfalls is usually difficult, because they are either very small and widely scattered or hidden underwater. Recorded in image A in Figure 9.2.11 is an example of an offshore outfall which was detected through multispectral scanning from an altitude of 2000 feet (610 meters). This image was produced from a ratio of the two channels represented by images B and C in Figure 9.2.11. Notice that image A provides considerably more information than either of the parent images, including not only the sewage outfall, but the major pattern of ocean currents as well.

SUMMARY

Remote sensing is a valuable source of information for a wide variety of problems and programs concerned with management of the environment. In some cases, remote sensing offers the only practical approach to data acquisition, mapping, and monitoring of the environment. This is especially so for extensive geographical areas and large environmental systems which are subject to rapid change.

A considerable body of remote-sensing data is in the public domain and available to the environmental planner, including that from the LANDSAT satellites, high-altitude photography, and standard low-altitude photography. In addition, special remote-sensing technologies, such as multispectral scanning from aircraft, are available on a contractual basis from private firms and governmental agencies.

For problems related to management of the aquatic environment, a combination of photographic and nonphotographic (e.g., scanner) imagery can yield critical information. Scanner data can be analyzed with the aid of computer techniques or through manual interpretation of images produced from one or some combination of bands or channels. Photographic imagery are usually analyzed through photointerpretation with the aid of various cartographic and photogrammetric techniques for measuring area, distance, and so on. Photographic and nonphotographic imagery together with the various techniques available for imagery analysis provide us with a singularly rich source of information on the aquatic environment.

Bibliography

American Society of Photogrammetry: *Proceedings, Symposium on Remote Sensing in Oceanography, October 2–5, 1973,* Falls Church, Va., 1973, pp. 595–1055.

American Society of Photogrammetry: *Manual of Remote Sensing,* vol. I, "Theory, Instruments, and Techniques," vol. II, "Interpretation and Applications," R. G. Reeves (ed.), Falls Church, Va., 1975. 2144 pp.

Anderson, R. R., V. Carter, and J. McGinness: "Applications of ERTS Data to Coastal Wetland Ecology with Special Reference to Plant Community Mapping and Typing and Impact of Man," *Proceedings, Third Earth Resources Technol-*

ogy Satellite Symposium, Washington, D.C., December 1973, NASA SP-351, 1973, pp. 1225–1242.

Johnson, P. L.: *Remote Sensing in Ecology,* University of Georgia Press, Athens, Ga., 1969. 244 pp.

Klemas, V., D. Bartlett, W. Philpot, R. Rogers, and L. Reed: "Coastal and Estuarine Studies with ERTS-1 and Skylab," *Remote Sensing of Environment,* vol. 3, no. 3, 1974, pp. 153–174.

Marsh, William M., and Borton, Thomas E.: *Inland Lake Watershed Analysis: A Planning and Management Approach,* U.S. Environmental Protection Agency, Washington, D.C., 1976.

National Academy of Sciences: *Remote Sensing with Special Reference to Agriculture and Forestry,* Washington, D.C., 1970. 424 pp.

National Aeronautics and Space Administration: *Data Users Handbook,* Goddard Space Flight Center, Greenbelt, Md., 1972.

National Aeronautics and Space Administration: *Proceedings of the NASA Earth Resources Survey Symposium,* Houston, Tex., June 1975, NASA TM X-58168 JSC-09930, NASA Lyndon B. Johnson Space Center, Houston, 1975. 2685 pp.

Shannon, E. E.: *Eutrophication-Trophic State Relationships in North and Central Florida Lakes,* Ph.D. Thesis, University of Florida, Gainesville, 1970.

Thomson, K. P. B., R. K. Lane, and S. C. Csallany: *Remote Sensing and Water Resources Management,* American Water Resources Association, Urbana, Ill., 1973. 435 pp.

Wenderoth, S., E. Yost, R. Kalia, and R. Anderson: *Multispectral Photography for Earth Resources,* Long Island University, Greenvale, N.Y., 1974.

Wezernak, C. T., and D. R. Lyzenga: *Satellite Remote Sensing Study of the Trans-Boundary Movement of Pollutants,* Report Grant No. R803671-01-0, U.S. Environmental Protection Agency, Washington, D.C., 1976.

Wezernak, C. T., F. J. Tanis, and C. A. Bajza: "Trophic State Analysis of Inland Lakes," *Remote Sensing of Environment,* vol. 5, no. 1, 1976.

Wezernak, C. T., D. R. Lyzenga, and R. A. Shuchman: "Application of Passive Multispectral Scanner Techniques for the Analysis of Coastal Bottom Features," *Technical Report,* 116700-1-X, Environmental Research Institute of Michigan, Ann Arbor, 1975. 31 pp.

Wezernak, C. T.: "The Use of Remote Sensing in Limnological Studies," *Proceedings, Ninth International Symposium on Remote Sensing of Environment,* Environmental Research Institute of Michigan, Ann Arbor, 1974, pp. 963–980.

Wezernak, C. T., D. R. Lyzenga, and F. C. Polcyn: *Cladophora Distribution in Lake Ontario (IFYGL),* EPA-660/3-74-028, U.S. Environmental Protection Agency, Corvallis, Ga., 1974. 84 pp.

CHAPTER **9.3**

ELEMENTS AND METHODS OF IMPACT ASSESSMENT

Richard N. L. Andrews

INTRODUCTION

THE NATIONAL ENVIRONMENTAL Policy Act (NEPA) of 1969 (Public Law 91-190) directed federal agencies to prepare a "detailed statement of environmental impacts" for every "major federal action significantly affecting the quality of the human environment." To comply with this requirement, the agencies as well as many applicants for federal grants and permits have had to develop new conceptual frameworks and procedures for analyzing impacts. Some of these procedures have been developed by the agencies themselves. Others have been developed by consultants hired by the agencies, and still others have been developed independently by academic researchers.

The purpose of this paper is to identify the principal tasks that must be performed in an impact assessment and to introduce and critically compare a series of procedures that have been developed or used for such assessment. It will be shown that these procedures vary considerably in their general usefulness and that most are appropriate for only some, rather than all, the tasks associated with impact assessment.

IMPACT ASSESSMENT TASKS

The process of planning major actions can be broken down into four principal activities: problem definition, formulation of alternatives, impact analysis, and evaluation of trade-offs. All these activities occur, in a tightly interrelated fashion, at *each* stage of planning. Over time, the data inputs to these activities become more detailed, and the primary emphasis among the activities shifts from problem definition to alternatives, then impact analysis, and finally evaluation. But the change is only in emphasis, since to an extent all four activities continue to take place simultaneously. Therefore, it can be argued that the impact assessment must take place as an integral element of the process of planning, not merely as a separate analysis after a course of action has been fully planned or chosen on the basis of other criteria.

In the context of the planning process, impact assessment involves six principal tasks. The first of these is the identification of those variables, hereafter referred to as evaluative factors, that are of particular importance in the planning task at hand. The second is to identify the relationship among the evaluative factors, including systems-type relationships as well as the relationships between dependent and independent factors, such as between flooding and runoff. Step three involves the formulation of alternatives, with special attention to what might be called "alternative scenarios of desired futures." The fourth step calls for forecasting the effects of the various alternatives. The fifth task of impact assessment is the display of the differences, or "trade-offs," among the alternatives, in terms of the evaluative factors and alternative scenarios. Finally, impact assessment must include someone's evaluation of the differences among alternative sets of actions, and among the alternative future scenarios, followed by a decision or recommendation of which to adopt.

IDENTIFICATION OF "EVALUATIVE FACTORS"

Checklists are by far the most common approach used to identify the factors that will be considered in the impact analysis. Two basic types of checklists have been developed. One is a simple listing of evaluative factors and the other is the matrix, exemplified by the procedure developed by Leopold et al. of the USGS (Figure 9.3.1).

The USGS procedure utilizes a matrix format to identify the existence, magnitudes, and significance of relationships between causative actions taken by the agency (100 examples of such actions are listed) and 88 "environmental components and characteristics," including historical, cultural, and social components as well as biological ones. The analyst is directed to check each column representing a causative action and then slash the appropriate box opposite each environmental characteristic likely to be impacted. Finally, a number between 1 and 10 is placed above and below each slash to indicate, respectively, the magnitude and the importance of the impact. A separate matrix is prepared for each alternative; the matrix is used to show only adverse impacts, on the assumption that beneficial impacts would be discussed in the engineering report. The basis for preparation of the matrix is assumed to be the professional judgment of one or more impact analysts.

Procedures such as checklists, and checklist-type matrices, are extremely simple to understand and use. In addition, checklist approaches serve two purposes. First, as elements of agency guidelines, they serve to identify categories of potential effects that are important as matters of policy, and second, they provide sources of ideas concerning potentially significant types of effects, which the impact analyst can use to help avoid omitting important factors from the analysis.

On the other hand, checklist procedures have some important limitations. Such lists by themselves are static, tending to suggest only the direct effects of various types of actions. At best, they suggest a large number of direct impacts of individual actions on individual environmental characteristics, but they provide little assistance in identifying the real interrelationships between them. Moreover, most lists make no attempt to show relationships among specific evaluative factors. Therefore, they usually afford little insight into the functional relations in the environment, which is an

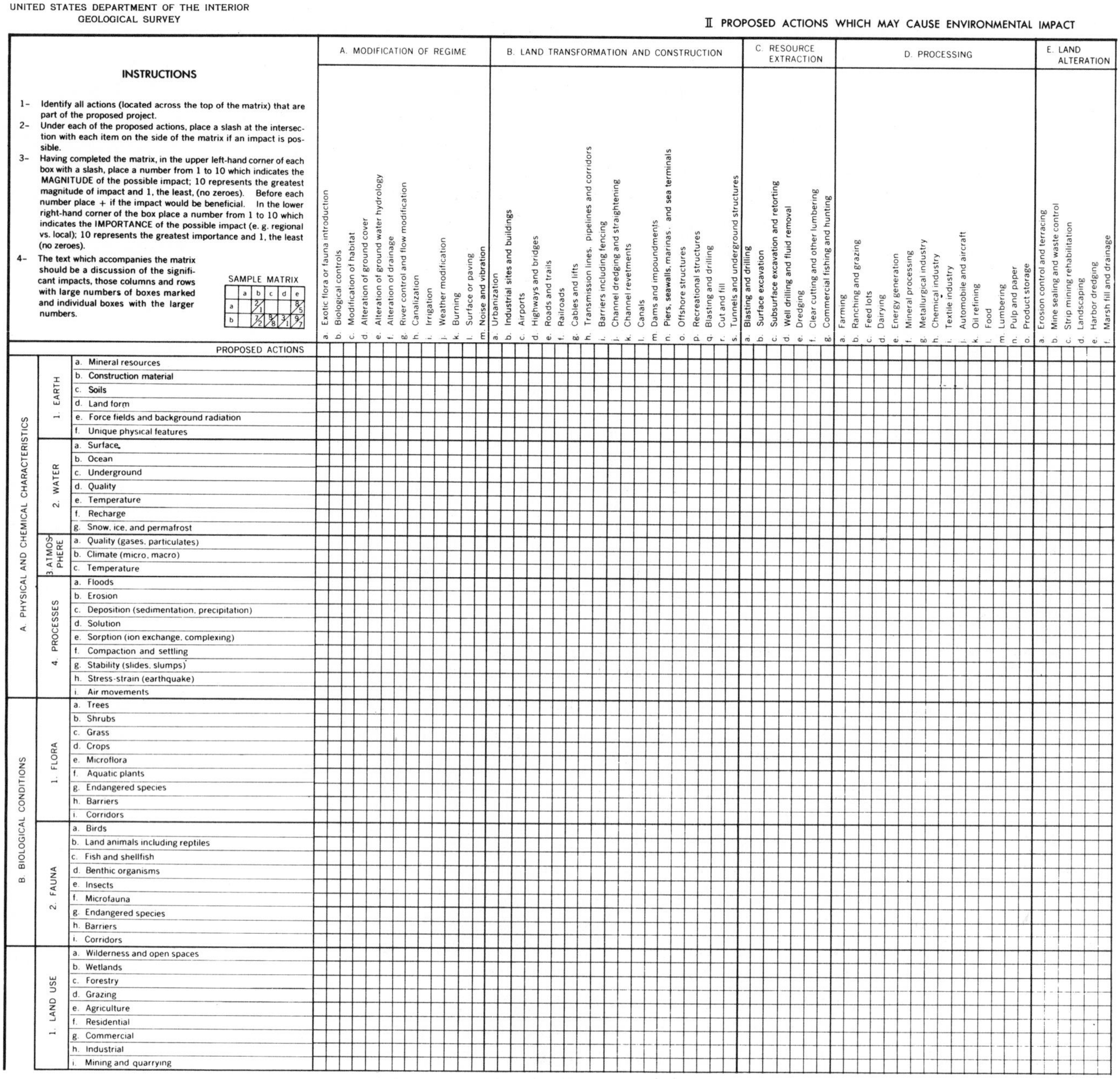
UNITED STATES DEPARTMENT OF THE INTERIOR
GEOLOGICAL SURVEY

II PROPOSED ACTIONS WHICH MAY CAUSE ENVIRONMENTAL IMPACT

INSTRUCTIONS

1- Identify all actions (located across the top of the matrix) that are part of the proposed project.
2- Under each of the proposed actions, place a slash at the intersection with each item on the side of the matrix if an impact is possible.
3- Having completed the matrix, in the upper left-hand corner of each box with a slash, place a number from 1 to 10 which indicates the MAGNITUDE of the possible impact; 10 represents the greatest magnitude of impact and 1, the least, (no zeroes). Before each number place + if the impact would be beneficial. In the lower right-hand corner of the box place a number from 1 to 10 which indicates the IMPORTANCE of the possible impact (e. g. regional vs. local); 10 represents the greatest importance and 1, the least (no zeroes).
4- The text which accompanies the matrix should be a discussion of the significant impacts, those columns and rows with large numbers of boxes marked and individual boxes with the larger numbers.

SAMPLE MATRIX

	a	b	c	d	e
a		2/1			8/5
b		7/2	8/8	3/1	9/7

A. MODIFICATION OF REGIME: a. Exotic flora or fauna introduction; b. Biological controls; c. Modification of habitat; d. Alteration of ground cover; e. Alteration of ground water hydrology; f. Alteration of drainage; g. River control and flow modification; h. Canalization; i. Irrigation; j. Weather modification; k. Burning; l. Surface or paving; m. Noise and vibration

B. LAND TRANSFORMATION AND CONSTRUCTION: a. Urbanization; b. Industrial sites and buildings; c. Airports; d. Highways and bridges; e. Roads and trails; f. Railroads; g. Cables and lifts; h. Transmission lines, pipelines and corridors; i. Barriers including fencing; j. Channel dredging and straightening; k. Channel revetments; l. Canals; m. Dams and impoundments; n. Piers, seawalls, marinas, and sea terminals; o. Offshore structures; p. Recreational structures; q. Blasting and drilling; r. Cut and fill; s. Tunnels and underground structures

C. RESOURCE EXTRACTION: a. Blasting and drilling; b. Surface excavation; c. Subsurface excavation and retorting; d. Well drilling and fluid removal; e. Dredging; f. Clear cutting and other lumbering; g. Commercial fishing and hunting

D. PROCESSING: a. Farming; b. Ranching and grazing; c. Feed lots; d. Dairying; e. Energy generation; f. Mineral processing; g. Metallurgical industry; h. Chemical industry; i. Textile industry; j. Automobile and aircraft; k. Oil refining; l. Food; m. Lumbering; n. Pulp and paper; o. Product storage

E. LAND ALTERATION: a. Erosion control and terracing; b. Mine sealing and waste control; c. Strip mining rehabilitation; d. Landscaping; e. Harbor dredging; f. Marsh fill and drainage

PROPOSED ACTIONS

I EXISTING CHARACTERISTICS AND CONDITIONS OF THE ENVIRONMENT

A. PHYSICAL AND CHEMICAL CHARACTERISTICS
1. EARTH: a. Mineral resources; b. Construction material; c. Soils; d. Land form; e. Force fields and background radiation; f. Unique physical features
2. WATER: a. Surface; b. Ocean; c. Underground; d. Quality; e. Temperature; f. Recharge; g. Snow, ice, and permafrost
3. ATMOSPHERE: a. Quality (gases, particulates); b. Climate (micro, macro); c. Temperature
4. PROCESSES: a. Floods; b. Erosion; c. Deposition (sedimentation, precipitation); d. Solution; e. Sorption (ion exchange, complexing); f. Compaction and settling; g. Stability (slides, slumps); h. Stress-strain (earthquake); i. Air movements

B. BIOLOGICAL CONDITIONS
1. FLORA: a. Trees; b. Shrubs; c. Grass; d. Crops; e. Microflora; f. Aquatic plants; g. Endangered species; h. Barriers; i. Corridors
2. FAUNA: a. Birds; b. Land animals including reptiles; c. Fish and shellfish; d. Benthic organisms; e. Insects; f. Microfauna; g. Endangered species; h. Barriers; i. Corridors

1. LAND USE: a. Wilderness and open spaces; b. Wetlands; c. Forestry; d. Grazing; e. Agriculture; f. Residential; g. Commercial; h. Industrial; i. Mining and quarrying

Figure 9.3.1. An excerpt from the USGS matrix (from Leopold et al., 1971).

important step in setting priorities for impact analysis. Lastly, standard checklists may not include all factors that are significant in a particular case. Therefore, they should serve as one source of ideas for impact assessment; but they should not be relied upon as an exclusive source of such ideas.

OTHER TECHNIQUES TO IDENTIFY EVALUATIVE FACTORS

Approaches other than checklists may be more useful in identifying some of the evaluative factors that various disciplines and public groups consider most important in a particular planning situation. Public meetings and personal contacts are frequently used for this purpose but often fall short of their purpose because of insufficient publicity, unrepresentative attendance, distrust of the agency, and other problems. Opinion surveys, listening sessions, and workshops may also be used to solicit such factors from interested publics as well as from a wide range of professional disciplines.

One other technique which deserves mention here is gaming, such as the IMPASSE procedure developed by Greenblat and Duke (1975). IMPASSE has been used as a device for eliciting key factors and conflicting assumptions about potential impacts. It is used in a workshop setting, in which participants who are supposed to represent a range of competences or views on the planning situation, may start with a blank board such as that shown in Figure 9.3.2, and place around its edge the items which each considers most important. A particular action is then assumed, and the participants attempt to identify which items might be significantly affected by it, first individually, and then, by discussion and argument over conflicting assumptions, collectively as a consensus. Gridded "scaling cards" can be used around the outside of the board to keep track of conflicting assumptions, magnitudes of impacts, or sequences of impacts.

Techniques such as IMPASSE have essentially the same advantages and limitations as other checklist procedures, except that they are explicitly designed to incorporate multiple and conflicting judgments into a particular situation rather than to provide a standard checklist to fit all situations. As a result, they involve greater risks of ignoring some types of impacts, since they are very sensitive to the views and abilities of the participants using it. For the same reason, however, they provide a better tool for sorting out the most significant impacts and thus for setting priorities for further research and analysis. They can also contribute to establishment of an open dialogue between agency personnel, nonagency professionals, and interested citizens, which could be educative for all of them.

Summary on Identification of Evaluative Factors

In summary, we can say that evaluative factors must be sought from many sources for each planning situation. No technique or prepared checklist can provide these factors to fit the priorities of every situation. Depending on the list's construction, they at best may provide: (1) a source of ideas concerning the range of impact types that should be considered, (2) a list of the impacts that one person or policy maker considers important enough to be considered, or (3) a list of the impacts most likely to follow particular causative actions, or like IMPASSE, a procedure for generating such lists in a particular planning situation by incorporating the judgments and values of diverse participants. Beyond these functions, no technique can replace the responsibility of the planner or impact analyst for setting priorities and allocating resources for information gathering.

IDENTIFICATION OF RELATIONSHIPS AND SYSTEMS

Cross-Impact Matrices

Two types of techniques are commonly used for systems descriptions: cross-impact matrices and networks. Cross-impact matrices

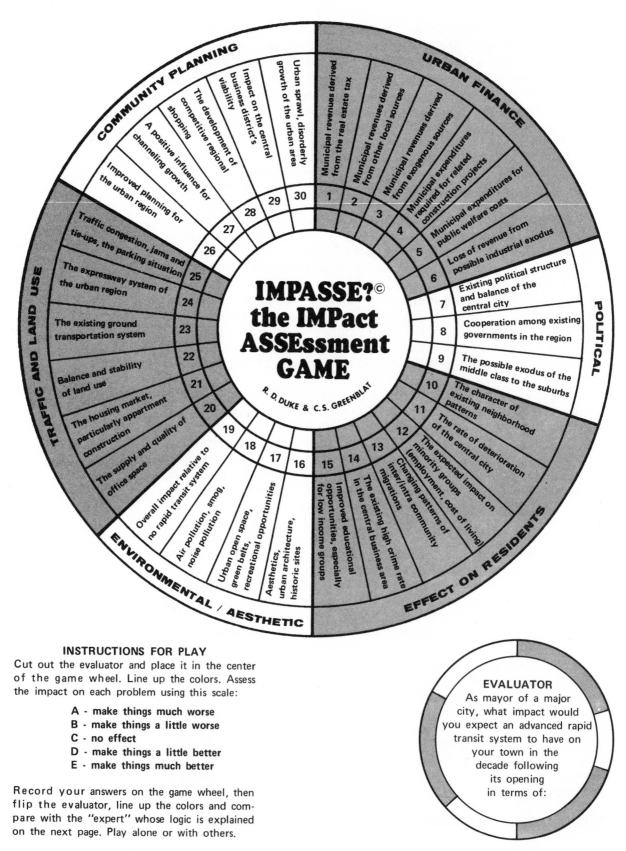

IMPASSE?©
the IMPact ASSEssment GAME

R. D. DUKE & C.S. GREENBLAT

COMMUNITY PLANNING

Urban sprawl, disorderly growth of the urban area

Impact on the central business district's viability

The development of competitive regional shopping

A positive influence for channeling growth

Improved planning for the urban region

URBAN FINANCE

Municipal revenues derived from the real estate tax

Municipal revenues derived from other local sources

Municipal revenues derived from exogenous sources

Municipal expenditures required for related construction projects

Municipal expenditures for public welfare costs

Loss of revenue from possible industrial exodus

POLITICAL

Existing political structure and balance of the central city

Cooperation among existing governments in the region

The possible exodus of the middle class to the suburbs

The character of existing neighborhood patterns

The rate of deterioration of the central city

EFFECT ON RESIDENTS

The expected impact on minority groups (employment, cost of living)

Changing patterns of inter/intra community migrations

The existing high crime rate in the central business area

Improved educational opportunities, especially for low income groups

ENVIRONMENTAL / AESTHETIC

Aesthetics, urban architecture, historic sites

Urban open space, green belts, recreational opportunities

Air pollution, smog, noise pollution

Overall impact relative to no rapid transit system

TRAFFIC AND LAND USE

The supply and quality of office space

The housing market, particularly appartment construction

Balance and stability of land use

The existing ground transportation system

The expressway system of the urban region

Traffic congestion, jams and tie-ups, the parking situation

1 2 3 4 5 6 7 8 9 10 11 12 13 14 15 16 17 18 19 20 21 22 23 24 25 26 27 28 29 30

INSTRUCTIONS FOR PLAY

Cut out the evaluator and place it in the center of the game wheel. Line up the colors. Assess the impact on each problem using this scale:

A - **make things much worse**
B - **make things a little worse**
C - **no effect**
D - **make things a little better**
E - **make things much better**

Record your answers on the game wheel, then flip the evaluator, line up the colors and compare with the "expert" whose logic is explained on the next page. Play alone or with others.

EVALUATOR

As mayor of a major city, what impact would you expect an advanced rapid transit system to have on your town in the decade following its opening in terms of:

Figure 9.3.2. An example of a gaming technique that can be used to identify evaluative factors. This particular game, called Impasse, was developed by R. D. Duke and C. S.

1-(E) Improved viability of the central business district would result in higher land values.

2-(D) More active business climate would result in higher tax derived from business.

3-(E) A successful, advanced rapid transit system will spawn other projects requiring federal aid.

4-(A) Basic changes in transportation capability will result inevitably in secondary costs for roads, sewers, etc.

5-(C) Some welfare recipients will be better off, but others will arrive to replace them.

6-(B) The existing tendancy of industry to decentralize will be encouraged.

7-(B) Populations will shift as land use patterns adjust to transit capability, affecting wards.

8-(E) The very magnitude of a rapid transit system requires discussions; perhaps agreement!

9-(B) The existing tendancy of the middle class to leave the city will be encouraged.

10-(B) Populations will inevitably shift; construction will intrude on existing neighborhoods.

11-(E) A viable rapid transit system inevitably makes a city a more viable "central place".

12-(D) Many actual improvements (low-cost transport, new jobs) will be offset by new indigents.

13-(B) Construction side effects as well as improved mobility will result in shifting populations.

14-(D) A more active, viable central area will discourage street crime.

15-(D) Better transit gives better access, more opportunity to reach a variety of facilities.

16-(B) Construction of this magnitude inevitably causes damage, some of which is permanent.

17-(E) Improved mobility brings a greater area of access to residents; more people moved in a given space.

18-(E) Existing pressures for change will have a better chance for success.

19-(E) No rapid transit system will inevitably lead to more sprawl and deterioration of the city.

20-(D) Entrepreneurial response to a new transport system is dramatic; perhaps too dramatic.

21-(E) The new transport mode will make large areas more accessible to the city.

22-(E) In the long run, more-dense land uses will locate near the terminals; A more European pattern will result.

23-(E) Assuming proper integration (!) more people will commit to public transport.

24-(C) Expressways are here to stay; rapid transport is a complimentary system.

25-(D) Some improvement is to be expected, however the auto is always with us.

26-(D) A rapid transport system is a major component in regional growth permitting improved planning.

27-(E) Growth can be expected to concentrate at the terminals of the rapid transit system.

28-(A) New shopping centers can be expected at the nodes or transit terminals.

29-(E) The central business district will be more readily accessible and therefore more viable.

30-(E) Growth will be channelled by the transit system, planning decisions will be more orderly.

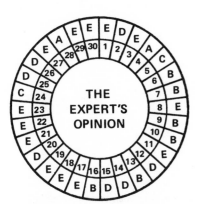

THE EXPERT'S OPINION

Our "expert" for this game is Dr. William Drake, Assoc. Dean for Research, School of Natural Resources, the University of Michigan. Dr. Drake is director of the Ann Arbor Transportation Authority, which has successfully pioneered in the use of "Dial-a-Ride" mini-buses.

Should your perceptions differ (either with regard to the problems in the impasse wheel, the "expert's" values as assessed, or the brief explanation of his choice) drop a note to the editor marked "Rapid Transit Impasse".

Greenblat, and appears in their book Gaming-Simulation: Rationale Design and Applications, Halsted Press, New York, 1975.

may be used either as a table of relationships or as input to the construction of networks. They differ from cause-effect matrices such as those of the USGS procedure discussed above in an important respect, namely, that they can show two-way linkages and feedbacks rather than simply first-order, one-way causal relationships. Where the USGS procedure has "causes" on the columns and "effects" on the rows, a cross-impact matrix has basically the *same* list of items on both columns and rows, so that all interrelationships may be considered.

Networks

A somewhat more sophisticated approach to systems description can be achieved with networks. An example is provided by the Deepwater Ports study prepared for the U.S. Army Engineer Institute for Water Resources. This study starts from a major, complex problem, namely, deep-water port alternatives for off-loading petroleum and other bulk cargoes. It immediately redefines this problem as a study of alternative delivery systems for these cargoes and disaggregates the alternative systems into lists of their components— for example, dredging, ship movements, loading and unloading, and processing. In other words, it identifies the specific system elements associated with each alternative system for bulk cargo delivery. Similarly, it next disaggregates the existing situation or "environment" into a list of those specific components or "evaluative factors" that are of interest to affected publics, professions, and policy makers. Once these lists are derived, net-

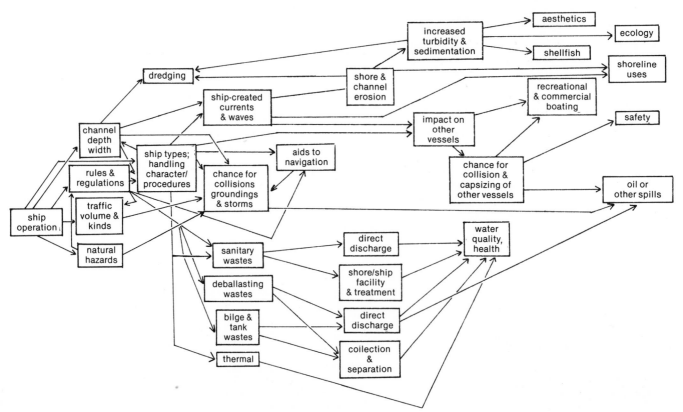

Figure 9.3.3. A graphical display of a network approach to the identification of the system of relationships formed by evaluative factors and actions (from U.S. Army Engineer Institute for Water Resources, Report 72-8, by Robert R. Nathans Associates).

work diagrams or webs are constructed showing relationships among the components and, in turn, insights into some of the chains of consequences that might be produced by alternative delivery systems. An example of one such network is shown in Figure 9.3.3.

Some of the problems in this particular example are evident: in particular, the arbitrariness and oversimplification of the networks in their present form, and the absence of any attempt to construct feedbacks and interrelationships among the system elements. On the other hand, it allows for disaggregation of a complex planning problem into its key constituents, without regard to jurisdictional limitations; it directs attention to indirect impacts; and it traces *sequences* of impacts, ultimately and logically leading to the factors of greatest interest for decision makers.

Several approaches have emerged which attempt to combine the advantages of matrices and networks with the analytical capabilities of computer systems. The first of these is a "stepped-matrix"

Combinations of Matrices and Networks

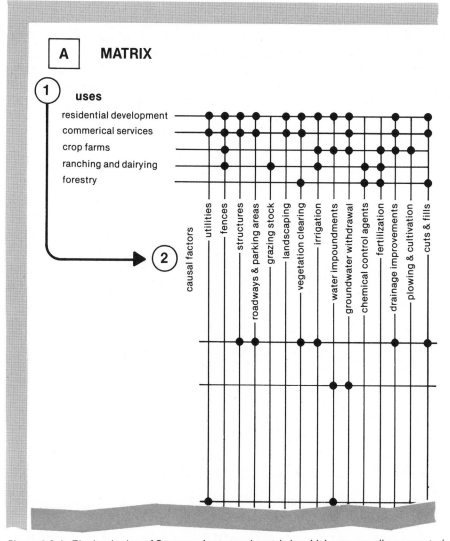

Figure 9.3.4. The beginning of Sorenson's stepped-matrix in which uses are disaggregated into actions or "causal factors" (from Sorenson, 1971).

procedure for analyzing conflicts among resource uses in the coastal zone, which builds directly on the USGS and network approaches and incorporates some of their problems as well as their strengths (Sorenson, 1971). A second is the computer simulation approach, exemplified by the K-SIM technique by Kane et al. (1973), which uses only a limited number of variables in order to focus on the implications of differing sets of assumptions and their relationships. The latter approach to systems description is without doubt the most sophisticated in concept, though oversimplified in application, of any of the approaches reviewed here.

The stepped-matrix approach begins with a matrix which disaggregates each significant use of the coastal zone into the various specific causative factors associated with it (Figure 9.3.4). Alternatively, a single use or proposed project could be taken as a starting point. In the second step of the matrix, shown at the bottom of Figure 9.3.4, dots are used to identify relationships between each causative factor and a list of initial environmental conditions. A forecast of consequent conditions is then made, based upon both known relationships among the initial conditions and the impacts of the causative factors that had been identified. Finally, from these expected consequent conditions a forecast of effects is made, in terms of what we are calling evaluative factors (see Figure 9.3.5).

In contrast to the stepped-matrix approach, and indeed all of the approaches discussed above, is the computer simulation approach exemplified by K-SIM. This is conceived explicitly as an attempt to

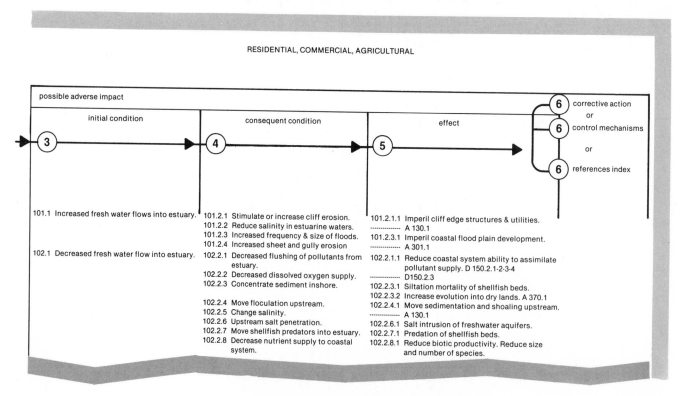

Figure 9.3.5. The latter part of Sorenson's stepped-matrix in which impacts are forecast from causal factors. This diagram is a continuation of the one shown in Figure 9.3.4. (from Sorenson, 1971).

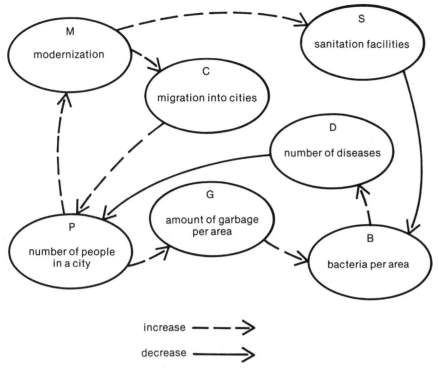

increase — — — →

decrease ————→

Figure 9.3.6. A network derived from the K-SIM computer simulation approach which shows the principal interactions that have been estimated by the participants (from Kane et al., 1973).

apply systems concepts to the assessment of impacts and cross-impacts. It was not developed in response to the demands of the National Environmental Policy Act; rather it emerged simply as a particularly useful illustration and tool for the task of systems description.

As in IMPASSE, K-SIM starts with a group of participants, identifying three to fifteen factors which they consider significant elements of the system in question. This list is then entered in both the rows and the columns of a blank grid, forming a cross-impact matrix. All cells of the matrix are then filled in, using the participants' estimates of the strength and direction of the relationship between each pair of factors. Single and double plusses and minuses can be used for this, or the magnitudes can be scaled as percentages between 0 and 100 in a range of possible values agreed to by the participants for each variable. This matrix can then be transformed, either directly by a computer or manually if desired, into a network representing the interactions that have been estimated (Figure 9.3.6). Finally, a tracing of their relationships over time is generated, using a nonlinear (sigmoid) growth curve in a "canned" computer program to represent the assumed form of each relationship. Figure 9.3.7 shows one example of this output.

The chief values of K-SIM are that it provides a simplified and understandable introduction to systems description and analysis and that, unlike any other approach discussed above, it provides feedback to the participants about relationships among their assumptions. In general, K-SIM illustrates well the basic thought

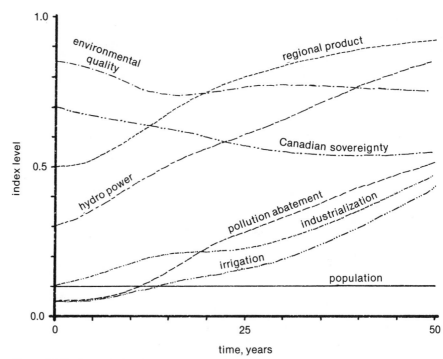

Figure 9.3.7. A graph showing projections of the behavior of a system based on the K-SIM computer simulation approach (Kane et al., 1973).

process that is necessary for describing social and natural systems at a level that permits understanding and active participation by persons who are not professional systems analysts or modelers.

The principal drawback of K-SIM is its severe oversimplification. Its input is limited to one or two dozen variables, in order to avoid overwhelming the workshop participants: far more complex system models exist, of course, and can be utilized if one desires a more complex systems description. In addition, it simplistically assumes that all relationships can be represented by a simple nonlinear growth equation. Not all functions follow this pattern, and for this reason, K-SIM should be used as a gaming device rather than as a predictive tool. Finally, the output of K-SIM is determined by the group judgments and the way they are handled by the computer program; therefore, it can be no more accurate than those judgments and assumptions on which they are based. For this reason as well, results should not be taken as predictions. The principal value of this sort of output, however, is that it provides quick and inexpensive feedback about the relationships among initial sets of assumptions.

Summary on Relationships and Systems

Systems description is an important task in impact assessment, primarily because of the multiple interrelationships among important factors in any planning situation that may alter the initial impact on any single factor. Despite this importance, systems description is rarely mentioned, and even more rarely performed in most impact assessment procedures that have emerged to date. Most checklists and checklist-type matrices suggest the use of increasingly comprehensive "environmental inventories"; but to the extent that these inventories seek only to increase comprehensiveness, rather than clarification of system relationships, their value for impact prediction is limited. Network approaches improve upon checklists by tracing sequences of impacts that might follow modification of one or more elements, but the failure of most of them to include two-way relationships and feedbacks limits their capacity to represent systems accurately. Of the approaches reviewed, only K-SIM provides an appropriate conceptual basis for systems description. It was designed, in fact, expressly to provide this for persons not professionally engaged in computer simulation and systems modeling. Nevertheless, it is only an oversimplified first step in an area in which further work is needed.

FORMULATION OF ALTERNATIVES

The task of formulating alternatives is aimed at developing sets of related actions, or "alternative intervention systems," that could be implemented. All alternatives should have in common certain expected effects, namely the purposes of the action. However, each would differ significantly from the others in its effects on other social values.

None of the approaches to impact assessment that are reviewed here provide guidance on the formulation of alternatives. Alternatives should be formulated to provide meaningful choices among the major alternative scenarios of a region's future, rather than just to reflect differences in structural means or economic costs. In addition, alternatives should be solicited from a wide variety of professional disciplines and interested publics, not simply formulated in-house by planners. Beyond these admonitions, the formulation of alternatives remains a responsibility of professional planners, for which the impact assessment techniques reviewed here provide no substitutes. Figure 9.3.8 is an attempt to illustrate schematically a suggested set of steps that could be employed in conceptualizing alternative actions.

The only further comment that might be made here, however, is that a good system description may be of great assistance in formulating alternatives, since it can be used to illuminate the multiple "leverage points" in the system that can be used to achieve project purposes. For instance, if a project purpose is to maintain shipping in a particular channel (presumably for economic reasons), one traditional leverage point for doing so is dredging. Dredging, however, may interfere with other purposes or values, such as shellfish. Other leverage points, therefore, which are visible in Figure 9.3.3, include: changes in shipping types to shallower draft; changes in ship operating procedures, and in shoreline protection measures, so as to reduce erosion and siltation of the channel; changes in shoreline use patterns for the same reasons; or moving shellfish farming elsewhere, where it will not be adversely affected by dredging. Conversely, a related and equally important use of the system description is to identify alternatives which, whatever their initial attractiveness, do *not* appear to affect the systems described in the initially expected and desired ways.

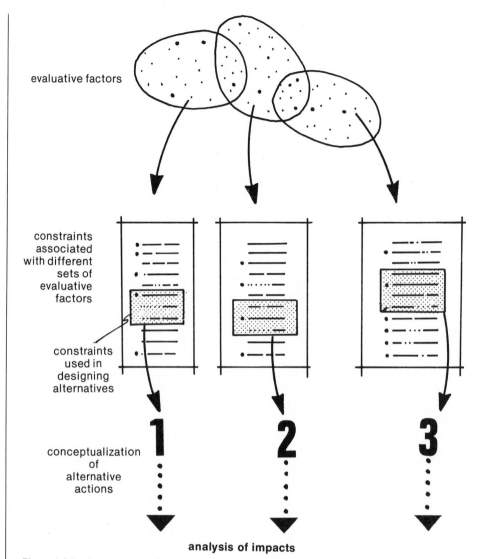

evaluative factors

constraints
associated
with different
sets of
evaluative
factors

constraints
used in
designing
alternatives

conceptualization
of
alternative
actions

1   **2**   **3**

analysis of impacts

Figure 9.3.8. A conceptual diagram which attempts to illustrate the major steps leading to the formulation of ideas for alternative actions.

FORECASTING OF EFFECTS

Forecasting effects, or predicting impacts, is of course the heart of the impact assessment process. The principal test of any impact assessment approach must be its reliability and effectiveness as a tool for predicting important impacts. It is rather surprising, therefore, to note how little attention is given to methods of prediction by most EIS procedures.

Most approaches produce intuitive predictions, relying either upon the professional judgment of the agency user, as in the case of the USGS, cross-impact and network approaches, or upon the collective consensus of the workshop participants, as in the cases of IMPASSE and K-SIM. More sophisticated approaches to prediction do exist: for example, Delphi techniques for assembling expert consensus, statistical correlation techniques, and quantitative modeling. The preoccupation of most of the approaches to impact assessment that have emerged in response to NEPA, however, seems to be with two issues: taxonomy of the environmental characteristics to be considered and the construction of procedural flow charts and display formats which give each approach a distinctive appearance but say little about the actual procedures and criteria to be employed in gathering data and developing predictions.

This general criticism may seem unduly harsh, and it admittedly glosses over important differences among the approaches. An approach like K-SIM, for instance, does rely wholly upon the judgments of its users and the assumptions built into its mathematics; but it also generates feedback to those assumptions, to stimulate further questioning and refinement of them. It also introduces the user to the more sophisticated predictive tools available through simulation modeling and can itself be transformed into such a tool by refinement of its assumptions and data inputs. In contrast, the USGS procedure provides no guidance as to what basis should be used for the slashes and ratings entered in its matrix, except initial professional judgments.

Of the approaches reviewed, the ones that have the most value for predicting impacts are those which attempt at least rudimentary description or simulation of systems, such as the ones described by Sorenson and by Kane et al., for the obvious reason that they make the most careful attempts to identify the linkages through which impacts are transmitted. The other approaches have value for preliminary brainstorming about general sorts of impacts that might occur, but they are not appropriate to later stages of planning when hard decisions must be made about gathering information and developing reliable forecasts.

In short, all the techniques discussed to this point are at best frameworks for research, not substitutes for it. A good checklist may provide many ideas about possible impacts that should be considered; a good assessment procedure may help to define a problem and organize data in such a way that the information needed for decision is clarified. But if all relevant sources are not consulted, all evaluative factors may not be considered; if seat-of-the-pants judgments form the data base, the results will have only seat-of-the-pants validity; and if existing inventory data are used rather than studies of systemic relationships, none of the techniques discussed here can provide any better forecasts of impacts and effects than intuitive judgments.

Summary on Forecasting Effects

DISPLAY OF TRADE-OFFS

Many of the techniques we have discussed above include useful display formats. Cross-impact matrices can show graphically the changes that might be expected from a particular action. With computer tracings, such as the output of the K-SIM procedure or of more advanced system models, it is possible to portray anticipated changes in a time framework. Other techniques may also be useful. For instance, overlay maps provide a spatial display of forecasts and can be used to highlight potential conflicts; and physical models of watersheds, terrain, and water bodies can provide even

COST DESCRIPTION—ALTERNATIVE COOLING INTAKE SYSTEMS

		ALTERNATIVES	A		B		D	
INCREMENTAL GENERATING COST		Present Worth						
		Annualized						
CAPACITY FACTOR								
ENVIRONMENTAL COSTS		UNITS	Magnitude	Page	M		Magnitude	Page
1. Natural Surface Water Body								
1.1 Impingement or entrapment by cooling water intake structure								
1.1.1 Fish								
1.2 Passage through or retention in cooling systems								
1.2.1 Phytoplankton and zooplankton								
1.2.2 Fish								
1.3 Discharge area and thermal plume								
1.3.1 Water quality, excess heat								
1.3.2 Water quality, oxygen availability								
1.3.3 Aquatic organisms								
1.3.4 Wildlife (including birds, aquatic and amphibious mammals, and reptiles)								
1.3.5 Fish, migratory								
1.4 Chemical effluents								
1.4.1 Water quality, chemical								
1.4.2 Aquatic organisms								
1.4.3 Wildlife (including birds, aquatic and amphibious mammals, and reptiles)								
1.4.4 People								
1.5 Not applicable								
1.6 Consumptive use (evaporative losses)								
1.6.1 People								
1.6.2 Property								
1.7 Plant construction (including site preparation								
1.7.1 Water quality, physical								

Figure 9.3.9. An example of the "account sheet" method for displaying alternatives (from the Nuclear Regulatory Commission).

more realistic displays of some impacts and alternatives.

Another display technique should also be mentioned here, since it was specially designed for showing the different impacts among alternatives which is the principal goal of this task. This involves the use of trade-off balance sheets or "accounts" to summarize the impacts of each alternative under consideration. A good example of this display technique is contained in guidelines of the Nuclear Regulatory Commission (formerly the Atomic Energy Commission).

The account format does not have the visual impact of the more graphic techniques such as computer traces or overlay maps, but it does present a great deal of information in a form that facilitates comparisons. A separate account is prepared for each subsystem for which alternatives may be considered. Figure 9.3.9 shows such an account for alternative cooling systems. The first column contains a list of "environment costs" which form the basis for measuring impacts. The second column identifies the units in which impacts on each factor are measured. The remainder of the columns show, for each alternative, the magnitude of expected impact on each factor and a page citation for supporting information.

The AEC accounting approach has several important advantages. First, it displays a great deal of technical information in a way that permits direct comparison of all alternatives on each point. Second, it disaggregates complex actions into their component causative actions, with alternatives for each subsystem as well as for the system as a whole. Third, it provides a terse and usable summary as well as page references for more detailed information if desired. But it has limitations also; for example, it does not show well the composite effects of each alternative system as a whole, and it does not show the interrelationships among impacts and subsystems.

EVALUATION

Evaluation procedures can be classified into three general types: direct display techniques, constraint setting, and weighting procedures. Direct display techniques include all the techniques that present comparisons directly to the user for choice, such as the AEC accounts discussed above. The purpose of this approach is to provide *disaggregated* information for users so that they may make their own decisions among alternatives, with as little prejudgment as possible on the relative importance of the evaluative factors.

The "factor profile" technique described by Bishop (1972) is an example of this approach. It provides a basis for direct comparison of profiles of all major alternatives while displaying their relative impacts on each of the principal evaluative factors. The most persuasive argument for this type of approach is that most important decisions are made and reviewed by many different users, who may have quite divergent values and wish to make up their own minds concerning the alternatives. In this respect, direct display techniques are far more useful than either of the other two types of approaches; however, they provide less opportunity to illuminate the reasoning that led one to choose one alternative over another.

Constraint setting, the second type of approach to evaluation, is useful if some set of standards and criteria can be agreed upon by all parties involved in the evaluation process. In contrast to direct display techniques, which present all comparisons in a disaggregated tabulation, constraint setting *simplifies* and reduces the number of trade-offs that must be balanced. The approach simply requires that *all* actions comply with specified thresholds or standards. Given that the standard can be met by each alternative, further decisions can be based upon trade-offs between other fac-

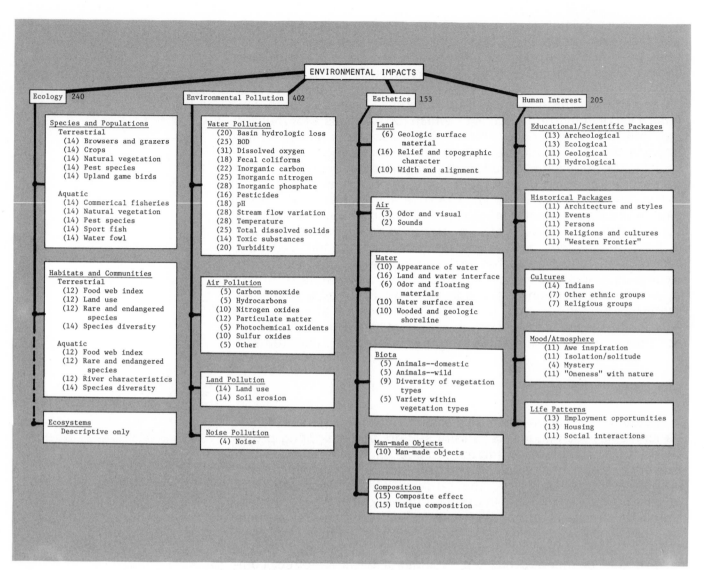

Figure 9.3.10. Listed here are the 78 evaluative factors used in the Environmental Evaluation System developed for the U.S. Bureau of Land Reclamation. The number next to each factor represents the weight assigned to it by the analyst. The actual numbers shown here are only exemplary (from BLR, "Environmental Evaluation System," Developed by Battelle-Columbus Laboratories).

tors that were not originally accepted as constraints.

To some extent the constraint approach is an inevitable part of any complex decision, because no one can rationally balance all factors at once. The hazard of it, however, is that a particular standard or constraint may not be universally acceptable, particularly if the standard is considered to be obsolete. In the case of air or water quality standards, for instance, some users may be satisfied that existing standards would not be violated by any proposed action, but others might consider existing standards insufficiently stringent in the light of emerging knowledge; still others might object to choosing an alternative on the grounds that while it satisfied the standard, it degraded water or air quality to the maximum level acceptable, thereby eliminating the possibility of further development without violating the standard. In short, constraint setting is a necessary element of complex decisions but frequently an inadequate one. In order to ensure its usefulness, great care must be taken in selecting and stating the assumed constraints, to make sure that they are generally acceptable and that they do not hide important differences among alternative proposals.

Finally, weighting procedures attempt to solve the evaluation problem by *aggregating* the various evaluative factors, quantifying each in some fashion and then assigning to each a multiplier which is intended to reflect the relative importance of the factor. The principal argument usually made for this approach is that weighting takes place intuitively anyway, and that quantification thus forces these value judgments to be made more openly in public view. Despite claims that this procedure makes professional value judgments more explicit, numerical weighting procedures may in fact tend to *bury* value judgments behind numbers whose meaning is neither clear nor widely accepted. The weights inserted into Leopold's USGS matrix discussed earlier, for instance, provide an example of this problem. Another, more ambitious example is the "Environmental Evaluation System" developed by Battelle-Columbus Laboratories for the U.S. Bureau of Land Reclamation (Dee et al., 1972).

This system begins with a checklist of seventy-eight study factors or variables which are classed into four main categories: ecology, pollution, aesthetics, and human interest (Figure 9.3.10). Each variable is assigned a percentage weight reflecting the analyst's estimate of its importance relative to all seventy-eight variables. The impact of each alternative on each variable is then forecast, and this

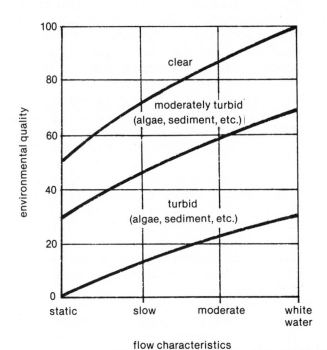

Figure 9.3.11. An example of a forecast of the impact of an alternative on an evaluative factor (or variable) based on the Bureau of Land Reclamation approach. The forecasts are translated into an "environmental quality" scale, shown on the left side of the graph (from BLR, "Environmental Evaluation System," developed by Battelle-Columbus Laboratories).

is translated by the analyst into a percentage scale of "environmental quality" (Figure 9.3.11). Finally, these scaled scores are multiplied by the initial "importance" weights assigned to each variable, and the products are summed to a single composite score for each alternative.

It is claimed that this approach has the advantage of making explicit value judgments which do in fact take place in planning. If the weights and scaling functions could be agreed upon by all concerned, this technique would reduce the arduous process of evaluation and decision to a simple, mechanical scoring process. It is hardly necessary to note, however, that in significant or controversial decisions such agreement is virtually never likely. Rather than revealing trade-offs and decision issues, numerical weighting tends to hide them beneath layers of value judgments such that objective review is difficult.

CONCLUSIONS

This chapter has outlined a series of techniques that have been proposed or implemented for impact assessment and has commented on the strengths and limitations of each for performing the various tasks associated with impact assessment. The list of EIS techniques reviewed here does not pretend to be comprehensive; rather, it is a representative sampling of various techniques for the assessment of environmental and other impacts of "major federal actions significantly affecting the quality of the human environment."

Several general conclusions may be drawn from this review. First, none of these techniques for impact assessment contains magic formulas to solve the problems and difficulties of that enterprise. Most deal well with only a few of the tasks of impact assessment and, at best, may serve three functions. They may provide ideas concerning types of impacts and relationships that might deserve study; they may structure and systematize a thought process that will provide better understanding of the consequences of alternative actions; and finally, some of them may provide clearer displays of trade-offs than are currently used, thus facilitating more rational choice.

Second, most of these approaches are appropriate only to the initial and most intuitive stages of impact assessment, including initial identification of potential factors for study, initial conceptualization of possible relationships among them, and initial brainstorming about possible consequences of alternative actions. In practice, these initial judgments must be supplemented by input from multiple professions and diverse publics, and tested and refined by information gathering.

Third, most of these techniques do not deal effectively with many important considerations in impact assessment, such as systems description; public involvement; uncertainty and risk and probabilistic impacts; differing time periods during which impacts occur; cumulative and jointly caused impacts; scale of action and analysis; and conflicts among evaluation criteria.

Fourth, the results of all the approaches discussed are dependent on the sets of impacts and alternative actions selected for study, upon the quality of the data used, upon the methods by which they are analyzed and converted into predictions, and upon the expertise of the analyst. None of them is a foolproof manual or "cookbook."

Despite the new term and the new mystique, impact assessment is not a new or separate process to be assigned to a new office, agency, or profession. It is a new conceptualization of the process of plan formulation and planning analysis. A broader range of consequences is involved, and impact assessment requires a conscious linkage between the identification of potentially significant impacts and the selection of alternatives for further consideration. The fundamental questions that the field manager or planner must ask, however, in impact assessment or in planning, are familiar ones. What future conditions do we want to achieve? What sorts of actions might help to achieve those actions? Which of those are so significant or uncertain that they should be studied in more detail? And whose preferences and ideas should be involved in answering these questions and in evaluating alternative proposals?

Impact assessment has not changed the fundamental questions, but it has added new sophistication and increased breadth to the ways in which we go about trying to answer them.

Bibliography

Andrews, Richard N.L.: 1973. "A Philosophy of Environmental Impact Assessment," *Journal of Soil and Water Conservation,* vol. xxviii (September–October), 1973, pp. 197–203.

Bishop, A. Bruce: "An Approach to Evaluating Environmental, Social, and Economic Factors in Water Resources Planning," *Water Resources Bulletin,* vol. 8, no. 4, 1972.

——: "Evaluation of Impacts and Alternatives," Paper presented at the Short Course on Impact Assessment in Water Resources Planning, Amherst, Mass.; Ann Arbor, Mich.; and Eastsound, Wash., 1973.

Dee, Norbert, Janet K. Baker, Neil L. Drobny, Kenneth M. Duke, and David C. Fahringer: *Final Report on Environmental Evaluation System for Water Resource Planning,* Prepared by Battelle-Columbus Laboratories for the U.S. Department of the Interior, Bureau of Land Reclamation, under Contract No. 14-06-D-7182, 1972.

Greenblat, Cathy S., and Richard D. Duke: *Gaming-Simulation: Rationale, Design and Applications,* Halsted Press, New York, 1975.

James, I. C., II, B. T. Bower, and N. C. Matalas: "Relative Importance of Variables in Water Resources Planning," *Water Resources Research,* vol. 5, no. 6, 1969.

Kane, Julius, Ilan Vertinsky, and William Thomson: "A Methodology for Interactive Resource Policy Simulation," *Water Resources Research,* vol. 9, no. 1, 1973.

Leopold, Luna B., Frank E. Clarke, Bruce B. Hanshaw, and James R. Balsley: *A Procedure for Evaluating Environmental Impact,* U.S. Geological Survey, Circular 645, 1971.

McHarg, Ian L.: *Design With Nature,* Natural History Press, Garden City, N.Y., 1969.

Nathans, Robert R., Associates: *U.S. Deepwater Port Study, The Environmental and Ecological Aspects of Deepwater Ports,* vol. IV, U.S. Army Engineer Institute for Water Resources, IWR Report 72-8, 1972.

Ortolano, Leonard: "Impact Assessment in Water Resources Planning," Paper presented at the Short Course on Impact Assessment in Water Resources Planning, Amherst, Mass.; Ann Arbor, Mich.; and Eastsound, Wash., 1973.

Sorenson, Jens C.: *A Framework for Identification and Control of Resource Degradation and Conflict in the Multiple Use of the Coastal Zone,* University of California at Berkeley, Department of Landscape Architecture, 1971.

U.S. Atomic Energy Commission, Directorate of Regulatory Standards: *Guide to the Preparation of Environmental Reports for Nuclear Power Plants,* issued for comment August 1972.

U.S. Department of the Army, Corps of Engineers: *Planning: Guidelines for Assessment of Economic, Social, and Environmental Effects of Civil Works Projects,* Engineer Regulation 1105-2-105, 1972.

U.S. Water Resources Council. "Proposed Principles and Standards for Planning Water and Related Land Resources," *Federal Register,* vol. 36, no. 245, 1971, pp. 24144–24194.

INDEX